ROMAN POWER: A THOUSAND YEARS OF EMPIRE

The Roman Empire was one of the largest and most enduring in world history. In his new book, distinguished historian William Harris sets out to explain, within an eclectic theoretical framework, the waxing and eventual waning of Roman imperial power, together with the Roman community's internal power structures (political power, social power, gender power, economic power). Effectively integrating analysis with a compelling narrative, he traces this linkage between the external and the internal through three very long periods, and part of the originality of the book is that it almost uniquely considers both the gradual rise of the Roman Empire and its demise as an empire in the fifth and seventh centuries AD. Professor Harris contends that comparing the Romans of these diverse periods sharply illuminates both the growth and the shrinkage of Roman power as well as the empire's extraordinary durability.

The pupil of extraordinary Oxford teachers, W. V. Harris counts himself fortunate to have escaped at the age of twenty-six to the hyper-stimulating environments of New York City and the Columbia University History Department. The author of *War and Imperialism in Republican Rome*, *Ancient Literacy*, *Restraining Rage: the Ideology of Anger Control in Classical Antiquity* (which won the Breasted Prize of the American Historical Association), *Dreams and Experience in Classical Antiquity*, and *Rome's Imperial Economy*, he has also edited books about ancient money, the ancient Mediterranean, and the spread of Christianity, among other subjects. Among other honours, he is a Fellow of the American Academy of Arts and Sciences and a Corresponding Fellow of the British Academy.

ROMAN POWER

A Thousand Years of Empire

W. V. HARRIS

CAMBRIDGE
UNIVERSITY PRESS

CAMBRIDGE
UNIVERSITY PRESS

University Printing House, Cambridge CB2 8BS, United Kingdom

Cambridge University Press is part of the University of Cambridge.

It furthers the University's mission by disseminating knowledge in the pursuit of education, learning, and research at the highest international levels of excellence.

www.cambridge.org
Information on this title: www.cambridge.org/9781107152717

First published 2016

Printed in the United Kingdom by TJ International Ltd. Padstow Cornwall

A catalogue record for this publication is available from the British Library.

Library of Congress Cataloging-in-Publication Data
Names: Harris, William V. (William Vernon), author.
Title: Roman power : a thousand years of empire / W. V. Harris.
Description: New York : Cambridge University Press, 2016. |
Includes bibliographical references and index.
Identifiers: LCCN 2016008143 | ISBN 9781107152717 (hardback)
Subjects: LCSH: Rome–History–Empire, 30 B.C.–476 A.D. |
Rome–History–Republic, 265–30 B.C.
Classification: LCC DG270.H27 2016 | DDC 937–dc23
LC record available at http://lccn.loc.gov/2016008143

ISBN 978-1-107-15271-7 Hardback

for W.E.S.H., with love

Contents

Illustrations

Maps

Preface

I especially want this book to be accessible and useful to people who, while they want to learn about the Romans and their empire, know little about Roman history as it is now understood. With such readers in mind, I have explained technical terms and identified historical actors more than I would have done in a narrowly academic book, and I have also provided a table of dates. At the same time, the book has some moments of originality (sketched out in Chapter 1) which may attract the attention of other scholars of ancient history.

'As it is now understood': with that phrase I intend to say that I have attempted to take very recent as well as older scholarship into account. But alas no one can possibly claim to have read and seen everything that pertains to a thousand years of Roman history. Roughly 130 ancient writers are mentioned in this book (not counting the authors of documentary texts), and there exist texts that I have not read. Meanwhile the modern bibliography of Roman history, literature, law, and archaeology is a tropical jungle. I have attempted to take account of as much of it as possible, down to the early months of 2015.

In the interests of transparency I have referred as often as possible to the primary sources and to the vastly variegated material evidence that a Roman historian has at his or her disposal. I have also provided in the notes a basic guide to modern scholarly writing about Roman power, tending to emphasize what is recent but not shying away from older works. I have emphatically *not* provided full bibliographies on every controversy. And I have – regretfully – privileged works in English: Roman history is an international subject, and a scholar must attend carefully to literature in at least five modern languages, but one has to recognize that many anglophone students are monolingual.

The book is short in relation to its gigantic subject-matter. I have elided two aspects of this subject-matter, and the reader deserves explanations. In the first place, I have not said a great deal about the biases, motives, interests, methods, presuppositions, or general background of the men (they are virtually all men) who provide us with our textual evidence. A full discussion would have required a separate volume of a quite different character. Readers on the alert will undoubtedly notice a number of implicit evaluations.

I have also elided almost all discussion of the natural environment of the Romans and their neighbours. That is my next big project. The reader of this book will notice some references to mineral and timber resources, access to which was quite crucial to Roman power on a number of occasions. The reason why there is not more here about the natural environment is fairly simple: too much is uncertain at this date. Two examples: deforestation is hard to define, let alone assess; there was a lot of it, but the inhabitants of the Roman Empire may have managed their woodlands well enough that no major ecological or economic harm was done. I have discussed this matter elsewhere (Harris 2011a). Then there is the related matter of climate change: it is generally agreed that there was a 'Roman Warm Period', but when exactly, and what difference did it make to the viability of the Roman Empire? (See Hin 2013 and Manning 2013 for overviews). In short, we are still some distance away from being able to relate the growth, survival, or decline of Roman power in a definite and convincing way to environmental factors.

Walter Scheidel, as I am happy to acknowledge, started me thinking systematically about this subject by inviting me to write an essay about power for the *Oxford Handbook of Roman Studies*. Many thanks to him for that stimulus.

This book would have taken even longer to write if it had not been for a generous award from the Andrew W. Mellon Foundation, for which I am profoundly grateful; I am especially grateful to the officer of the Foundation who was most responsible, the distinguished sociologist Harriet Zuckerman.

I am also deeply grateful to Emma Dench, Kyle Harper, Evan Jewell, Irene Sanpietro, and Caroline Wazer for critical reading of various chapters of this book. I owe another very large debt to Emily Cook, a rising young art-historian who spent many hours helping me put together the book's visual apparatus. A number of other generous friends and acquaintances have stimulated thought and provided pertinent information, in particular Jairus Banaji, Mary Beard, Anne Hunnell Chen, Holger Klein, Myles Lavan, David Leith, Jonathan Prag, and Walter Scheidel himself. I thank one of my most talented former students, Sara Phang, for providing the sketch map that became Map 5. The Cambridge University Press's anonymous readers were extremely constructive, and I thank its energetic and learned Michael Sharp for enlisting them.

Many thanks, finally, to the American Numismatic Society and its officers for their generous help with coin images. I am grateful to the Stanwood Cockey Lodge Fund for its help with the illustrations, and to Jose Solorio for his help with the index.

Timeline

c. 393 BC	Rome captures and destroys Etruscan Veii
c. 390	Rome temporarily occupied by marauding Senonian Gauls
390s–380s	M. Furius Camillus' political career at its height
367	Licinian-Sextian laws
356	First plebeian 'dictator'
351	First plebeian censor
340–338	Rome at war with the Latins
338	Foundation of the first citizen colony, at Antium
334	Foundation of the first 'Latin' colony, at Cales
327	Beginning of Rome's constant wars outside Latium
321	Battle of the Caudine Forks
313?	Abolition of debt-bondage
312	Via Appia
311	Doubling of number of legions
c. 305	Friendship with Rhodes
295	Battle of Sentinum
c. 287	Secession of the *plebs*; Lex Hortensia
273	Foundation of the Latin colonies of Cosa and Paestum
272	Tarentum succumbs to Rome
264–241	First Punic War
c. 244	Extra praetorship created
241	Battle of Aegates Islands
218–202	Second Punic War
218–206	Scipios in Spain
216	Battle of Cannae
215–205	First Macedonian War
202	Battle of Zama
200–197	Second Macedonian War
190	Battles of Myonnesus and Magnesia
188	Treaty of Apamea with Antiochus III

186 BC	Suppression of the cult of Bacchus
179	Lex Voconia
173	First year in which both consuls were plebeians
168	Battle of Pydna
167	Mass enslavement in Epirus
160s to 130s	Polybius' history of Roman expansion
146	Destruction of Carthage and Corinth
143–71	Era of major slave rebellions in Italy and Sicily
139–130	Ballot laws
133	Tribunate of Tiberius Gracchus
133–129	Establishment of direct Roman rule in Asia Minor
123–122	Tribunates of Gaius Gracchus
107	Marius opens legions to all citizens
91–89	Social or Marsic War
90	Lex Iulia enfranchises many peninsular Italians
82–80	Dictatorship of Sulla
73–71	Rebellion of Spartacus
67–62	Pompey's eastern wars
59–58	High water of popular power at Rome
58–50	Caesar's conquest of Gaul
48	Battle of Pharsalus
44	Caesar 'perpetual dictator'; assassinated
42	Battles of Philippi
31	Battle of Actium
30	Roman occupation of Egypt
27	Octavian becomes 'Augustus'
20	Settlement with Parthia
19	Death of Vergil
12	Beginning of Rome's attempt to conquer east of the Rhine
AD 14–37	Reign of Tiberius
16	Tiberius brings German war to a halt
27–37	Tiberius rules from Capri
41–54	Reign of Claudius
43	Invasion of Britain
54–68	Reign of Nero
67	Nero orders the suicide of his best general Domitius Corbulo
69	Year of the Four Emperors
69–79	Reign of Vespasian

AD 79	Vesuvius destroys Pompeii and Herculaneum
81–96	Reign of Domitian
92	First Roman consul from the Greek world
98–117	Reign of Trajan
101–2, 105–6	Conquest of Dacia
110s	Tacitus writing *Annals*
115–17	Roman Empire reaches its maximum extent
117–38	Reign of Hadrian
131–5	Bar-Kochva revolt in Judaea
138–61	Reign of Antoninus Pius
161–80	Reign of Marcus Aurelius
166–75, 178–80	German wars of Marcus Aurelius
167	Beginning of Great Pestilence
175	Revolt of Avidius Cassius
180–92	Reign of Commodus
193–211	Reign of Septimius Severus
211–17	Reign of Caracalla
212	Caracalla extends citizenship to almost all free inhabitants of the Roman Empire
217	Reign of Macrinus
218–22	Reign of Elagabalus
222–35	Reign of Alexander Severus
226–42	Ardashir ruler of Persia
244–9	Reign of Philip the Arab
248	1,000th birthday of Rome
249–51	Reign of Decius
251	Goths defeat Romans at Abrittus
253–68	Reign of Gallienus
260	Christians tolerated
270–5	Reign of Aurelian
293–305	Rule of the Tetrarchs
301	Diocletian's Price Edict
312	Battle of Saxa Rubra brings Constantine to power in Rome
312–37	Reign of Constantine
324	Constantine sole emperor, foundation of Constantinople
337–63	Rule of Constantine's dynasty
378	Battle of Hadrianople
378–95	Reign of Theodosius I

AD 385	First execution of 'heretics'
391	Closing of temples of the traditional gods, banning of animal sacrifices
394	Battle of the Frigidus
395–408	Reign of Arcadius
395–423	Reign of Honorius
401	Alaric invades Italy
406	Radagaisus invades Italy
410	Alaric and the Visigoths sack Rome
421–50	Galla Placidia 'Augusta'
438	*Theodosian Code*
439	Vandals capture Carthage
451	Council of Chalcedon
455	Gaiseric and Vandals sack Rome
474–91	Zeno emperor in the east
476	Romulus Augustulus deposed
527–65	Reign of Justinian
533, 543–9	Roman reconquest of north Africa
535–55	Roman reconquest of Italy
541	Beginning of 'Justinian's Plague'
559	Cotrigur Huns reach Constantinople
565–78	Reign of Justin II
568	Lombards invade Italy
582–602	Reign of Maurice
584	Avars in the outskirts of Constantinople
590–604	Pope Gregory rules in Rome
602–10	Reign of Phocas
610–41	Reign of Heraclius
614	Persians capture Jerusalem
621	Most of the Roman Middle East in Persian hands
627	Heraclius invades Persia
632	Death of the Prophet
636	Battle of the Yarmuk
638	Battle of Qadisiyya
639–41	Muslims conquer Egypt
641–68	Reign of Constans II
654	Muslims attack Constantinople
656–61	Muslim civil war
698	Muslims capture Carthage

Abbreviations

AÉ	*L'Année Épigraphique*
Barrington	R. Talbert (ed.), *Barrington Atlas of the Greek and Roman World* (Princeton, 2000)
CAH	*Cambridge Ancient History* (2nd edn)
CIL	*Corpus Inscriptionum Latinarum*
CJ	*Codex Iustinianus*
CQ	*Classical Quarterly*
CTh	*Codex Theodosianus*, ed. T. Mommsen (Berlin, 1901), English translation by C. Pharr (Princeton, 1952)
Digest	*Digesta*, ed. T. Mommsen and P. Krueger (11th edn, Berlin, 1908), English translation ed. A. Watson (Philadelphia, 1985)
DOP	*Dumbarton Oaks Papers*
EFH	*Entretiens [de la Fondation Hardt] sur l'antiquité classique*
ILLRP	A. Degrassi (ed.), *Inscriptiones Latinae Liberae Rei Publicae*
ILS	H. Dessau (ed.), *Inscriptiones Latinae Selectae*
IOSPE	V. Latyschev (ed.), *Inscriptiones Antiquae Orae Septentrionalis Ponti Euxini Graecae et Latinae*
JRS	*Journal of Roman Studies*
OED	*Oxford English Dictionary*
OGIS	W. Dittenberger (ed.), *Orientis Graeci Inscriptiones Selectae*
P.Abinnaeus	H.I. Bell *et al.* (eds.), *The Abinnaeus Archive: Papers of a Roman Officer in the Reign of Constantius II* (Oxford, 1962)
P.Cair.Isid.	A.E.R. Boak and H.C. Youtie (eds.), *The Archive of Aurelius Isidorus* (Ann Arbor, 1960)
PG	*Patrologia Graeca*, ed. J.-P. Migne
P.Horak	H. Harrauer and R. Pintaudi (eds.), *Gedenkschrift Ulrike Horak (P.Horak)* (Florence, 2004)
PIR	*Prosopographia Imperii Romani*
PL	*Patrologia Latina*, ed. J.-P. Migne
P.Lond.	F.G. Kenyon *et al.* (eds.), *Greek Papyri in the British Museum*

PLRE	A.H.M. Jones *et al.* (eds.), *Prosopography of the Later Roman Empire*
P.Oxy.	*The Oxyrhynchus Papyri*
PSI	*Papiri della Società Italiana per la ricerca dei papiri greci e latini in Egitto*
Riccobon 1941–1943	S. Riccobono, *Fontes Iuris Romani Anteiustiniani* (Florence, 1941–1943), 3 vols.
RRC	M.H. Crawford, *Roman Republican Coinage* (Cambridge, 1974)
SB	*Sammelbuch griechischer Urkunden aus Aegypten*
SEG	*Supplementum Epigraphicum Graecum*
Select Papyri	A.S. Hunt and C.C. Edgar (eds.), *Select Papyri*
SIG^3	W. Dittenberger (ed.), *Sylloge Inscriptionum Graecarum* (3rd edn)

CHAPTER 1

The long-term evolution of Roman power

The idea of Rome and the idea of power are inextricably linked. Rome's empire lasted longer than any other except China's and, though often surpassed in size by later empires it was rivalled in ancient times only by the Persian Achaemenids and the Han dynasty in China. We may wonder what human being ever exercised significantly greater power than the more effective kind of Roman emperor, Augustus, say, or Trajan.

But what is power, and what are the best ways of analysing its workings in a historical society? These questions were never easy, and since Foucault made such 'promiscuous' use of the term,[1] the complexities have increased still further. No concept, perhaps, is more pervasive or protean (not to say vague) in current intellectual discourse. Half of the non-fiction book titles now being published seem to contain the word. And the modern concept of 'power' commonly combines both raw physical power (German *Macht*) and institutionalized power (German *Herrschaft*).[2] Nonetheless power exists all right, the power of human beings to determine the actions and experience of other human beings, and its sources and characteristics in any given society can be analysed.

An added difficulty in studying Roman power is that its modern historians seem to be especially liable to power-worship. This is in fact the main obstacle, apart from sheer foolishness, that has made it difficult for people to write the history of how the Roman Empire was put together in the first place. One symptom of this subservience is the reluctance that scholars sometimes show to call Roman republican imperialism 'imperialism',[3] a bizarre evasion that need not detain us for long (I shall say a little more

[1] Green 1999, section 1. For Foucault's conception of power, see p. 69.

[2] Gotter 2008, 181.

[3] For Roman historians, the Republic means the period 509 to 31 BC (the middle Republic being, more debatably, the period 367 to 133), the Principate the period from 31 BC to AD 284. The subsequent period is now called late antiquity.

about it later: p. 36). And when we come to late antiquity, the related problem of 'vicarious identification' identified by Brent Shaw[4] seems if anything to intensify: contemporary historians commonly seem to consider the empire of Justinian to have been somehow 'our side', which leads to all sorts of distortions. Far from being an impersonal matter, the rise and fall of the Roman Empire engages strong feelings, even now.

The worship of power can maintain a certain level of respectability because it merges into the fascination with power that is very widespread if not universal: how it is gained and lost, how it is abused and resisted – these are the themes of a large part of our myths and histories. And since we are inevitably subjected to power, even if we are born to be the emperor of Rome or China, or the Sultan of Brunei, it is just as well that we should try to understand it.

The questions that this book sets out to answer are the following. Why in the first place did Roman power spread so widely and last so long? External factors such as the relative weakness of many neighbouring peoples had major effects, but no one will doubt that internal factors were also crucial. Some of these were geographical, demographic, or economic, but power relations within the Roman world probably made a great deal of difference too. So how should we characterize these relations? How much power of various kinds – political, legal, economic, psychological, discursive, or any other kind – did some inhabitants of the Roman world have over others? And I shall implicitly be asking whether we help ourselves as historians if we take the tempting analytic course and distinguish political power, legal power, economic power, and so on, even though we know that in pre-modern societies most kinds of power were often concentrated in the hands of a single elite and its agents.

What in the end went wrong, wrong that is from the Roman point of view? The Roman Empire still in the age of the reconqueror Justinian (AD 527–65) extended from one end of the Mediterranean to the other, finally ceasing to be an empire only under the rule of Heraclius (AD 610–41). Why did it fail to maintain its place in the world, and what were the internal power structures that accompanied that failure?

Any worthwhile analysis of power in the Roman world, however brief, has to be three-dimensional. It has to capture the dimension of national power, the domination by the gradually expanding group of those who called themselves Romans over the rest of the empire's inhabitants, together with their power along the empire's edges and beyond them. It

[4] Shaw 1999, 134.

must also capture the dimension of social differentiation or social class, without underestimating the importance of the political institutions and structures, or of slavery, or of gender power, or of power within the family.

Finally it must take full account of time and of the discontinuities as well as the continuities to be encountered in a thousand years or so of more or less accessible Roman history, from say Camillus (the shadowy military hero of the 390s and 380s BC) to Heraclius. There are strikingly few Roman histories – in fact, almost none – that attempt to cover the whole arc of Roman imperial history. Not only is it a unitary subject, but the earliest and the latest phases greatly illuminate each other, and we would have been spared a good deal of implausible story-telling about the sixth- and seventh-century AD Roman Empire if its historians had paid more attention to the Republic, and vice versa. And there were many continuities, most notably slavery: 'it is likely that more than 100 million people were enslaved in the millennium during which the Roman empire rose and was eclipsed'.[5]

Some readers will be startled to see Roman history divided into three such long periods.[6] This is programmatic. We normally end our Roman histories too early, in many cases much too early. When did the Roman Empire come to an end? Not in any case, as many historians continue to imply, with the reign of Constantine (AD 312–37), or when Rome was captured by the Visigoths (410). The latter event was a symptom but not by any means the end, for the centre of gravity had shifted from west to east between 324 (the foundation of a new capital at Constantinople) and the early fifth century. Montesquieu [Figure. 1.1] already knew very well not to make this error.[7] Just as Rome had gradually grown stronger in the fourth and third centuries BC until it was clearly an empire, so the Roman Empire gradually grew weaker from the late fourth century onwards. But the enterprise survived much longer as an empire. Some treat the fall of the emperor Maurice in AD 602 as the empire's end.[8] The only significant exception to premature endings in recent anglophone historiography is a text-book by David Potter.[9] But there *was* an end: after the Battle of the Yarmuk (636), when the Muslim Arabs deprived the Byzantine emperor

5 Webster 2010, 62.

6 In practice they will be subdivided.

7 Montesquieu 1734.

8 A.H.M. Jones 1964, 315, etc.; the *Cambridge Ancient History* ends inexplicably in 600. Ernest Stein, one of the most acute of all twentieth-century historians of late antiquity, intended to conclude with the death of Heraclius in 641 (Stein 1949, xxiv).

9 Potter 2009.

Figure 1.1. Charles de Secondat, Baron de Montesquieu, whose book *Considérations sur les causes de la grandeur des Romains et de leur décadence* (Amsterdam, 1734) was the first important historical analysis of the Roman Empire in modern times

of the vital Syrian provinces, it begins to make much more sense to see Byzantium not as an empire in any proper signification of the term but as one state among a number of others that covered western Eurasia and the Mediterranean. Antioch fell to the Muslims in 637, Jerusalem in the same year, Alexandria in 641 (but it was only in 698 that they destroyed Carthage), and before very long the Umayyad Caliphate was larger than the Roman Empire had ever been.

By 636 the Roman Empire had few Latin-speaking subjects, but that is a secondary issue: the sixth- and seventh-century Byzantines believed that they were Romans and that their territory was *Romanía* (hence John the Lydian naturally started his *On the Magistracies of the Roman People* – his people, even though he was born in western Asia Minor – with Romulus),[10] and their continuous history entitled them to that belief. After the disastrous events of 636–42, however, the question is whether the Byzantine Roman Empire was still powerful enough to be counted as an empire – and it did not fit that description again for more than 300 years, not in fact until the early eleventh century and the last years of the emperor Basil II. The years between 636 and the failures of the emperor Constans II (641–68) should be recognized as the real end of the Roman Empire.

As to why serious Roman historians virtually never cover the entirety of Roman history, there are more and less obvious reasons. The most obvious is that it is very difficult. Almost everything changes, not only the sources and the material culture, but the principal language and the dominant religion. But that is a challenge not an excuse.

Having determined the chronological limits, the historian should try to decide where the major discontinuities lie. The years AD 16 and 337 seem to me the best choices, all the more so because they are to some extent counter-intuitive. Neither date represents an obvious revolution. I choose 16 because it was in that year that the emperor Tiberius slowed down the expansion of the Roman Empire – how long-term a change he expected this to be we cannot tell –, and because he, more than anyone, finished off the old aristocracy and made the monarchy absolute (not that I would want to minimize the tyrannous nature of the regime of Augustus). I choose 337 because, although the house of Constantine continued to rule for another twenty-six years, internal political cohesion began to disintegrate at once, and it is in the next generations that we may reasonably look for the emergence of the factors that led to the collapse of the Roman Empire in the west.

[10] Chrysos 1996.

A great advantage of the long view taken here is that, as I suggested above, the distinctive aspects of the periods in question will stand out more clearly. Cross-cultural comparisons are, rightly, an important part of the current historical agenda, but we should not neglect cross-period comparisons when, as in the case of Roman history, the imperial, geographical, and environmental contexts remain the same or are broadly similar.

Nonetheless a history such as this will be notably more valuable if it takes at least some notice of other comparable empires. It can for instance be safely assumed that most empires maintain their power with the help of co-opted local elites – so what was specific or exceptional about the ways the Romans did that? A number of empires have structured power relations by means of complex systems of law, so why is it that we look upon the Roman Empire as the great historical example of this phenomenon? If we want to answer such questions, or questions about the rise and decline of the Roman Empire – questions about causation are the most important ones of all –, we need to consider other large and/or long-lasting empires, such as those of Britain and China. This is becoming a received doctrine. It is less commonly observed that if we are to understand the rise of Roman power we also need to study the Romans' less successful rivals (why no Spartan empire, why no Etruscan empire?), and other less successful ancient-Mediterranean empires whose affairs are relatively well known to us; that means above all the empire of the Athenians.

Yet this is not a comparatist account, in the sense of a full-blown attempt to delineate a set of actual or potential imperial systems. Others have recently attempted comparisons between Rome and China, and between Rome and the Mughals. The Byzantine and Ottoman empires offer ample scope here. But my intent is to make use of comparisons that throw bright light on the Romans, and in particular on the reasons for historical changes, rather than to list similarities and 'divergences' or formulate universal historical laws.[11]

And the most meaningful comparisons of all, so I maintain, juxtapose one Roman period against another; taking an unusually inclusive time-frame, more than ten centuries, is therefore a great advantage – and we can say at once that Rome's republican successes as an imperial power can teach us things about the late-antique Roman Empire's military failures, and vice versa. In particular, the contrast between the mid-republican

[11] Vasunia 2011 surveys recent work on the comparative study of empires. Comparative collections such as Scheidel 2009a have not so far thrown much light on the causes of historical change in the Roman world.

army on the one side and the armies that served the emperors Honorius, Maurice, Phocas, and Heraclius on the other is intense.

A system of law is an abstraction, and that will remind us that abstractions as well as people and groups of people exercise power: the Roman Empire itself is an abstraction, the Roman state is an abstraction, so is any given social class, so is religious belief. The ideas conveyed by images and buildings can have power, so that it has become natural to speak of the power of the images themselves. Traditions can have power, as *mos maiorum* ('ancestral custom') did at Rome. So can rhetoric. Emotions – anger, for instance – can have power, as historians have increasingly come to recognize. Stoicism, arguably the most powerful ideology of the high Roman Empire, is another abstraction. Slogans can exercise power too, especially perhaps if their meaning is highly unstable – *libertas* is the extreme Roman example.[12] It used to be widely held that ideas exercised relatively little power in the Roman world, but fewer now believe this. So part of our task is to decide which abstractions truly altered behaviour.

To ward off excessive abstraction, however, I intend to illustrate the big historical processes, as much as possible in this limited space, with the behaviour of individuals. Some of these will be the obvious men of power who could sway the power of the state, and might, according to circumstances, bestow or withhold a livelihood, social position, freedom or the right to go on living. But not all powerful individuals were emperors or senators, for it is a characteristic of power that even in the most centralized state it is extremely diffuse: the village policemen and the petty tax-gatherers of the Roman Empire exercised a sort of power, as well as the mighty dignitaries, and even within a system of brutal slavery, power of various kinds could in certain circumstances come into the hands of the unfree. One historian says that even Christian visionaries had power in the high Roman Empire,[13] and in a limited sense that is clearly true.

Here [Figure. 1.2] is an illustration of local power: a third-century AD mosaic floor from Smirat in coastal Tunisia commemorates a *venatio*, that is to say a massacre of wild animals, a favourite Roman sport. There is text as well as pictures, and the cries of the spectators are imagined: '...when was there ever such a show (*munus*)?... Magerius pays. That's what it is to be rich, that's what it is to have power (*hoc est posse*)...'.[14] This Magerius, who

[12] Cf. Mouritsen 2001, 9–13.
[13] Lane Fox 1994, 130.
[14] Beschaouch 1966; Bomgardner 2009; Fagan 2011, 128–32.

Figure I.2. This mosaic from Smirat (Tunisia) shows a *venatio* or slaughter of wild animals, in this case leopards, which was funded by the local magnate Magerius. It explicitly emphasizes his (local) power (see the text). Mid-third century AD. Museum of Sousse, Tunisia

is otherwise unknown, has wealth and local power (how much? in virtue of what exactly?). But others have power at Smirat too, not only the local fat cats like Magerius, but also the spectators to some extent, and also the 'hunters', the Telegenii, who provided the leopards and killed them in the arena.

Local power is indeed something of an additional challenge for this project. Dorotheos of Gaza (sixth-century AD, very late in this history) wrote rhetorically that a man who was number one at little Gaza would be rated below the great men at nearby Caesarea, and would count as a mere outsider [*paganos*] in Antioch and as a poor man in Constantinople (*Didaskaliai* [*Instructions*] 2.34)[15] – the difference, roughly, between village, town, city, and capital. This was an obvious if imprecise truth, but for much of Roman history the story was still more complicated, chiefly because the people who owned the land and other assets in the small places were very often the wealthy from the capital and the cities.

[15] 2.6 in some editions. I first learned of this text from Potter 2011, 258. For a concrete example of the difference between village magnates and town magnates, at Tralles in Asia Minor in the fourth century, see Thonemann 2007.

How then did the Romans themselves, at various periods, think of the workings of power? We shall see going forward. But two questions are worth posing immediately.

(1) Was Roman thinking about power exceptionally legalistic? The natural answer seems to be yes: the Republic expressed many of the major changes in its own evolution in the form of laws, and there was a strong strain of legal pedantry in its public life. Technically proficient and politically influential experts on law were a constant feature from the first century BC onwards. But it may be that the intense attention given to the delimitation of *potestas* (legally or constitutionally established power) and *imperium* (the right of certain high officials to get their orders obeyed)[16] was a result not simply of an especially legalistic mentality, but of the particular nature of the Roman social-political system itself. Under the Republic this system was aristocratic – the inner circle of power was indeed hard to enter – and even under the Principate it was socially exclusive; but at the same time the ordinary citizens had specific rights,[17] and for centuries these were jealously guarded. Legal status very often mattered, and this continued to be true in the later empire. Definitions were necessary.

(2) A considerable amount of what Romans said and wrote about power consisted of myth-making, and we ought to identify the prevailing myths. One – the myth that Rome was a citizen democracy – is illustrated by a passage of Cicero, *On Laws*: speaking of the relationship between the citizens and the magistrates, he wrote that 'he who obeys ought to hope that one day he will command (*imperaturum*)' – which for most Romans would have been the wildest delusion.[18] Two centuries later, Aelius Aristides (*To Rome* 90; cf. also sect. 60) could solemnly, though perhaps not without some private irony, tell the Romans that their political system was, under the rule of one man, a 'complete democracy'.[19] And this notion left traces even later, as we shall see. Modern ideas, it may be noted parenthetically, can be equally paradoxical: Trajan's rule was 'not a monarchy', a recent authority assures us.[20] Another Roman myth had it that Rome ruled the entire world: this idea was first articulated by Romans in the second century BC, and by the

[16] On the exact meaning of these terms, see Kunkel and Wittmann 1995, 21–8.

[17] See among others Wirszubski 1950, 24–30.

[18] *On Laws* 3.2.5. In Chapter 3 we shall consider what 'democracy' may mean in a Roman context.

[19] Plenty of Greeks knew how false this was: see, for instance, Philostratus, *Life of Apollonius of Tyana* 5.34.

[20] Griffin 2000, 130.

Figure 1.3. Denarius of the moneyer Cn. Lentulus (later consul), 76/5 BC. The globe on the reverse (b), together with the sceptre, wreath and rudder, indicates the Roman idea, much emphasized in these years, that Rome ruled the entire world. Crawford, *RRC* no. 393/1a

70s BC was widely accepted, being reflected for instance in coin-types representing the globe [Figure. 1.3].[21] It appears commonly in Cicero.[22] It echoes on as late as the fifth century AD (Orosius, *History against the Pagans* 6.20.2). All the while the Roman elite, not to mention the Roman army, knew perfectly well on some level that they did not rule the whole earth or anything like it (though there is evidence that they underestimated the size of the territories that remained outside their power).

Presumably such myths – fantasies or delusions, if you will – were functional; they may indeed offer us important clues. Rome's imaginary

[21] Harris 1985, 126, 129.
[22] Richardson 2003, 140.

democracy reflected some continuing belief in the rights of the citizen. As for the notion of world-power, we shall want to ask when steely self-confidence turned into merely self-deluding arrogance.

Existing definitions of power, which are numerous, are somewhat unsatisfactory. One thing that is usually missing is the element of durability: the emperor or the paterfamilias may of course disappear from the face of the earth from one moment to the next, but in any given situation he is most unlikely to do so; power, in short, is more or less *insistent.* When Max Weber described power as 'the probability that one actor *within a social relationship* will be in a position to carry out his own will despite resistance' [my italics],[23] he seemed to imply that power had this characteristic of insistence, but his description was quite unusual in that respect.

Readers are entitled to ask which, if any, theory of power is most consonant with what this book has to say. My approach, as far as theory is concerned, is selective and highly critical. I simply seek throughout this study to discover how much the character of the Roman state's constantly changing external relations was determined by its constantly changing internal power structures, and vice versa. This is how I want to consider the dynamics of imperial power and of its eventual demise. This is my principal objective.

To a quite startling degree modern studies of external and internal power in world history ignore each other. (Machiavelli, however, brought the two together in *The Prince*, chapters 19 and 21). Standard anthologies and general scholarly works tend to concern themselves either with 'empire' or with 'power', the latter being understood as a matter that concerns a given society's internal relationships.[24] Even those analysts of political power who recognize that it also belongs to strong states at work beyond their own borders[25] have little if anything useful to say about international power.

Theorists of empire have done rather better, and, since Stanislav Andreski and more recently Michael Mann, have made valiant efforts to relate imperial power to the internal dynamics of the imperial state. Keith Hopkins and I attempted more than thirty years ago to do just that, with regard to mid-republican Rome.[26] A brief but important paper by

[23] Weber 1968 [original ed. 1921–2], I, 53.

[24] E.g. Lukes 1986. Yet another example of this failing, on the part of an ancient historian: Mennen 2011, esp. 5–10.

[25] Such as Galbraith 1983, to take one example out of many.

[26] Hopkins 1978; Harris 1979.

Tim Cornell applied a similar approach to the early Principate.[27] But the later you go in Roman history, the less of this work you find – the venerable example of Gibbon notwithstanding.[28] Neither Andreski nor Mann possessed expert knowledge about Roman history. International relations theorists, meanwhile, – always under the suspicion of being driven by presentist concerns[29] – have normally paid scant if any attention to the dictates of domestic politics.[30]

Marxists of various stripes have notoriously paid ample attention to the nexus between economic and political formations and imperialism, and continue to do so down to this day.[31] But this work – so it seems to me – only illuminates the history of pre-modern states and empires in the most fitful way. As Moses Finley implied, the anti-Marxists are more dangerous than the Marxists,[32] but Marx's ideas, even in their most sophisticated modern re-formulations, do not help one much to understand the relationship between the specific history of Roman imperial power and its internal power relations.[33] I shall certainly pay attention to the economic imperatives that conditioned Roman behaviour, but not because of any theoretical dogma.

This failure to connect has in fact a very long tradition behind it: some of the most brilliant older analysts of imperial power, Thucydides for instance, have partly failed to explain the internal power structures of the states they have written about, while some of the most brilliant analysts of intra-state power, Rousseau for instance, have been feeble commentators on external power.[34] The historian of the Roman Republic, however, is fortunate to have two sources, Polybius and Sallust, who for all their shortcomings (especially serious in the case of Sallust) succeeded in linking the patterns of Rome's behaviour towards the outside world with its internal structures.

27 Cornell 1993.

28 Motyl's *Imperial Ends* (Motyl 2001) is to some extent a praiseworthy exception to this complaint, but it is too superficial and derivative to help much (see 57–8 for his attempt to explain the decline of Rome); the same comments apply to Parchami 2009.

29 To put it in no unkinder terms. Low remarks on the 'historical contingency of many modern theories of international politics' (2007, 15); I would say not 'many' but 'virtually all'.

30 For confirmation, see Handler 2013, an anthology, where the items excerpted in chapter 15 represent minor exceptions from the 1990s.

31 Anievas 2010 and Callinicos 2011 can lead one into the vast literature.

32 Harris 2013a, 119.

33 De Ste Croix 1981, chapter 6, for example, is disappointing in this respect.

34 Cf. Hassner 1997.

Various other thinkers about the workings of power, in particular Aristotle, Montesquieu, Marx, and Foucault, will be referred or alluded to in the pages that follow, but it will be obvious that the book as a whole is not Marxist, or Foucauldian, or within any other school.[35] Readers may infer from my recurrent stress on the interests of the large landowners that I want to understand the material basis of political power, but that does not mean that I consider this to be its only basis. Readers will also encounter the recurrent suggestion that Roman government was sometimes more oligarchical than it seems, but that does not make me a follower of Robert Michels (who invented the 'iron law of oligarchy'). When Arendt asserts that 'power is never the property of an individual',[36] she is scarcely right; but when she continues that 'it belongs to a group and remains in existence only as long as the group keeps together', she enunciates a general truth; exceptions will always need to be justified.

What is wrong with what contemporary political science has to offer on the subject of Roman power is not so much its proneness to serious factual errors, though that will always jar with a historian, or to sheer fantasy (such as the notion that the late Roman Empire overtaxed its subjects).[37] The problem is rather that the explanations do not measure up to the phenomena. Take Peter Turchin, for instance, who knows more about the Romans than many. His conclusion is that:

> two factors explain the rise of the Roman Empire: the high degree of the internal cohesiveness of the Roman people, or asabiya, which reached a peak *c.* 200 BC; and the remarkable openness to the incorporation of other peoples, often recent enemies.[38]

That is all right, *as far as it goes*; the second of these factors is a commonplace of the historiography, and we shall have much to say about it. Rome's 'internal cohesiveness' is more problematic. States that consistently win wars do indeed demonstrate this quality, and conversely we can certainly say that the diminished cohesiveness of the late Roman Empire was an important factor in its declining power, and that the main task of the historian of that phenomenon is to analyse why its cohesiveness

[35] There is no need to list here the theorists whose work I have found unhelpful. The falsest prophet, in my opinion, is Bourdieu.

[36] Arendt 1969, 44.

[37] For the latter idea, see Motyl 2001, 40. Historians of imperialism sometimes get things seriously wrong too: thus Maier (2006, 41) considers that republican Rome had no empire.

[38] Turchin 2005, 163. His errors about Roman history are not relevant here. *Asabiya* is Arabic for 'cooperation', a quality much stressed by Ibn Khaldun (Turchin, 91).

decreased. But this is merely a necessary condition of empire-building. A lot more is needed, in particular an aggressive willingness to make war, a political elite with the capacity to organize and mobilize the state for war, and the ability to find the organizational techniques that are needed to retain and make use of what has been won.[39]

Finally, people, collectivities, and states exercise power, so do abstractions and myths. So do images, as it first became fashionable to say about a generation ago. At its best, such work has raised vital questions about the ability of the powerful to control and influence diverse populations by means of architectural programmes, coin-types, public statuary and monuments, and more evanescent spectacles. Physical evidence of such kinds has already appeared several times in this short introduction. But there is still much work to be done on sociological and psychological as well as strictly archaeological aspects of this matter: to put it concisely, we know how the agents of Augustus shaped the Temple of Isis and Osiris at Dendur in upper Egypt, where he was depicted as a pharaoh (and we can remind ourselves by going to the Metropolitan Museum), but how the provincials who saw it reacted to it is, to say the least, uncertain. In recent times art-historians have begun to pay more attention to such questions.[40] A neglected key, in my view, is the elite audience. The Arch of Constantine, to take another example, no doubt evoked generalized awe in many of those who saw it, while its iconographic programme spoke only to a few – but those few were often men of influence.

39 Turchin has returned to the fray with different formulations (Turchin 2009, Turchin *et al.* 2013), but the theories of 'imperiogenesis' sketched in these papers have no explanatory power as far as the Roman Empire is concerned.

40 See Stewart 2008, chapter 4, for a good discussion.

CHAPTER 2

The Romans against outsiders, 400 BC to AD 16

> Generally the Romans use violent force for all purposes, and they think that they absolutely must carry their projects to conclusion, and that nothing is impossible once they have decided on it. This élan has given them many successes... (Polybius 1.37).

We can begin with a period that runs all the way down to the first years of the emperor Tiberius, down specifically to AD 16, because one of the most extraordinary aspects of Roman expansion is how long it went on as a more or less continuous process, from the late fourth century BC (which was not, however, the absolute beginning) until Augustus' successor decided on the first serious halt. That was an important turning point, even though it turned out to be a deceleration, and not by a long chalk the end of imperial expansion.

About 400 BC the Romans controlled some of their own hinterland but not even the whole of Latium and not even the mouth of the River Tiber. They had no navy and few if any political contacts beyond their immediate neighbours; they were locked in conflict with their Etruscan neighbour Veii a mere twelve miles away (they finally prevailed over Veii in about 393) (Map 1 shows the principal locations in republican Italy that are mentioned in this chapter). In the early 380s Senonian Gauls from just across the Appennines briefly occupied and plundered Rome itself.[1] 400 years later, however, as a result of almost uninterrupted expansion, the Romans controlled and taxed everything from the English Channel to the Euphrates and southern Egypt, and were working at conquering the Germans. How did this amazing expansion come about?

[1] Cornell 1995, 314–18. The details are much contested: Delfino 2009.

Map 1. Italy and Sicily under the Roman Republic, down to 90 BC

Armed force and enduring control under the middle Republic: an outline

When Scipio Africanus' forces stormed New Carthage (Cartagena, on Spain's Mediterranean coast) in 209 BC, 'he directed most of them, according to the Roman custom, against the people in the city, telling them to kill everyone they met and to spare no one, and not to start looting until they received the order (Map 2 shows the principal locations outside Italy that were crucial in the third and second centuries BC). 'The purpose of this custom, I suppose' – it is the cool rationalist historian Polybius speaking (10.15) – 'is to strike terror. Accordingly one can often see in cities captured by the Romans not only human beings who have been slaughtered but even dogs sliced in two and the limbs of other animals cut off. On this occasion the amount of such slaughter was very great' (though in fact nearly 10,000 people survived to be enslaved).

Rome's power over its neighbours came in the first place from the sharp end of its soldiers' spears and swords, but even in the first stages of Rome's historically known expansion, in the fourth century BC, matters were much more complex. What was most remarkable of all was not the Romans' extraordinary ability to win battles so often – though this was indeed most extraordinary –, but their propensity for establishing enduring power over the peoples they defeated, so that the territory under Roman control expanded by about 3,000 per cent between 400 BC and 280, until it stretched from the Arno valley to the Italian peninsula's heel and toe.

When the curtain rises (that is to say, when we first have good enough sources to write any non-speculative history), Rome was extending its power a short way up the Tiber valley, and the victory over Veii enabled the Romans to colonize Ostia and other sites. Between the 380s and 338 they imposed their power over the Latins to the east and south of the city. This was already a very remarkable degree of expansion. What came next – two generations of fighting (327 to 272) that led to domination over the whole Italian peninsula up to the Arno – was more remarkable still. The first war against Carthage (264–241) gave Rome control of Sicily, Sardinia, and Corsica. Victory in the second war against Carthage (218–202) made Rome the dominant power in the western Mediterranean. The defeat of the Seleucid regime (based in Syria) in 190 gave them naval domination across the rest of the Mediterranean, and the defeat of the king of Macedon at Pydna in 168 firmly established their power across the whole region. The Romans could now be said – and were said by Polybius – to rule the entire Mediterranean world. By that time they had already begun to add territory far from the Mediterranean littoral (in northern Spain from 179), yet it was still for the most part a Mediterranean empire, steadily consolidated down to 30 BC. It was Julius Caesar in the 50s who first led them decisively in a northern direction; Caesar led them to the Rhine, Augustus to the Danube.

Map 2. The Roman world in the second and first centuries BC

20°E
30°E
40°E
50°N
40°N
30°N
PANNONIA
Savus
ILLYRICUM
Danube
THRACIANS
Black Sea
Sinope
PONTUS
BITHYNIA
PAPHLAGONIA
Halys
Dyrrachium
MACEDONIA
Philippi
Brundisium
Pella
Tarentum
Apollonia
Pydna
Lampsacus
MYSIA
GALATIA
PHRYGIA
Callicinus
EPIRUS
THESSALY
Cynoscephalae
Corcyra
Pharsalus
Pergamum
ASIA
Magnesia
Apamea
CAPPADOCIA
Actium
Delphi
Smyrna
Chios
Myonnesus
Ephesus
Taurus M.
Tarsus
Carrhae
Athens
ACHAEA
Aphrodisias
CARIA
CILICIA
Antioch
Corinth
Delos
Side
Apamea
Olympia
Gyaros
Sparta
Rhodes
Salamis
Cyprus
Crete
Jerusalem
Cyrene
Alexandra
Pelusium
CYRENAICA
AEGYPTUS
Nile

Map 2 (*cont.*)

Rome was able to achieve its imperial expansion in the middle Republic (say 400 BC to 146) because of a combination of advantages, including its geographical position. There was no geographical inevitability involved, but Rome initially grew at a sort of crossroads, at the site of the easy Tiber crossing that was nearest to the sea, the Tiber itself being already an important trading route, and in an area that by Mediterranean standards was unusually fertile.[2] Fertility translated into demographic fertility, and in archaic Roman warfare numbers must have mattered greatly, there being – apparently – little technological difference between one central-Italian population and another. These Romans were well organized for war[3] – though once again the same may have been true of many neighbouring states. In the decades around 400 BC, Rome's revenues must have increased, especially after the crucial defeat and destruction of Veii; that in turn probably improved the supply of high-quality military equipment.

Rome's war-oriented and honour-oriented landowning elite, as its wealth increased in the fourth century BC, had more and more time to think about military expansion and carry it out, and furthermore it could rely on a disciplined citizen population which was evidently convinced that it benefited from this same expansion.

Let's look first at this elite.[4] I mentioned Camillus, Rome's leader in the decisive war against Veii, but he is a largely legendary figure,[5] and it is only two generations later, in the late fourth century, that the Roman aristocracy as a whole comes into focus. From then on we can see its members at work, largely consistent in their ideals and behaviour until the age of the Gracchi (133–121) or even of Sulla (dictator 82–80). Their personalities were formed, in every case, by military service, and their dominant non-material goal was a fairly specialized form of honour that was epitomized in the concepts *gloria* and *laus* (praise). Using the credit of this kind that each man gained for himself, they competed for public office, which meant more than anything else military leadership; they found the culmination of success in the triumph ceremony, when the *triumphator* was Jupiter and/or king for one special day.[6] This was the most important form of public spectacle in mid-republican Rome, occurring on average

[2] The ecological basis of power offers plenty of material for speculation: of the six Mediterranean cities that were the capitals of ancient empires, Rome was easily the rainiest.

[3] Cornell 1995, 183–90.

[4] For a much more detailed account of the military ethos of the mid-republican aristocracy, see Harris 1985, chapter 2, and for an account, necessarily speculative, of how it came into being Harris 1990.

[5] See Ungern-Sternberg 2001.

[6] Many have written recently about the triumph ceremony and its meanings: for a variety of views, see Beard 2007; La Rocca and Tortorella 2008; Östenberg 2011.

about once every eighteen months. The super-successful general, such as Scipio Africanus (consul in 205 and 194), could also take an extra name to commemorate his conquests. Physical memorials of outstanding generals, already known in the fourth century, later became more elaborate.[7] And the *triumphator* would want to perpetuate his fame with an inscription such as this one, which was set up on the front of a new temple in the Campus Martius:

> Sent out to finish a great war, to subdue kings ... Lucius Aemilius the son of Marcus [L. Aemilius Regillus, victorious commander in the decisive battle of Myonnesus in 190, for which see below] ... under his auspices, his command and his blessed leadership the fleet of King Antiochus [III of Syria], ever before invincible, was defeated, shattered and put to flight ... before the very eyes of Antiochus and his whole army, his cavalry and elephants... (Livy 40.52.5–6).

This competitive system worked well from a Roman point of view, in part because virtually annual warfare was a severe training ground, in part also because the system tended to eliminate the less competent (as well as the less fortunate) nobles, while permitting a limited infiltration by well-to-do non-nobles with the required talents.

The system sustained the opportunistic belligerence of the Roman Senate (which was made up in practice of the ex-office-holders, from the quaestors upwards, appointed for life). Except on the rarest of occasions, Rome made war every year throughout the middle Republic, which made it an extreme case of willingness to go to war.[8] There were at most four years of peace between 327 and 241, and most of those were consequent on bitter internal strife at Rome itself.[9] In every normal year the leaders of the community, self-confident (no doubt) and largely undeterred by personal risk, mobilized sufficient citizen and Italian allied manpower, and all other necessary resources, in order to carry war to the enemies of the moment.

They were able to do this thanks in large part to a peculiar kind of manpower momentum: successful warfare produced slaves who could work the land, and slave labour on the land freed farmers to go to war. When exactly this kind of momentum – which no doubt helped other ancient states to expand from time to time, Carthage for instance – began to have a noteworthy impact on Roman affairs it is difficult to say: at the very

[7] Tanner 2000, 28–9.
[8] Cf. Finley 1983, 129.
[9] Harris 1985, 256–7.

latest in 311, when Rome doubled the number of legions, but perhaps at least a generation earlier.

Much misunderstanding persists as to the economic motives that may have encouraged members of the senatorial elite to undertake aggressive wars and to organize territorial control. No one doubts that both they and the state over which they presided grew vastly richer, but there are still those who suppose that such gains were incidental.[10] A large part of the trouble is a widespread assumption that aristocrats are uninterested in all kinds of material gain – which, as we shall shortly see, was most definitely not the case at Rome. And some have even complained that the Roman sources do not make it clear that economic motives were important – as if bank robbers can only be found guilty if they confess their crimes. The reticence of the Roman sources on this subject is easy enough to understand,[11] though in fact they give us plenty of relevant information, as we shall see. Roman wars were a well-organized system of pillage, which did not cease when the battle was won and the survivors on the other side had been sold into slavery or ransomed. For then Rome appropriated land for its own citizens (in Italy and also later in some of the provinces), and in the territories outside Italy extracted regular revenues.

The practice of making war virtually every year, and in places that were steadily more remote from Rome, then remote from Latium and eventually from Italy, would not have worked if it had not also enjoyed widespread support among Rome's citizens and indeed among the Latins (in effect, second-class citizens) and Italian allies (in effect, subjects). Such evidence as there is shows that over a long period the Roman citizen body as a whole – for the most part hardy rustics and artisans – went along quite willingly, indeed eagerly, with policies that produced constant warfare, and it is fairly easy to understand why. There was undoubtedly a degree of social control, there was conscription, and within the army there was stern discipline. But the potential gains, both material and psychological, were considerable, and everyone was aware of them. Serving in the legions was in fact something of a privilege, from which the poorest citizens were normally excluded until the late Republic.

Sometimes of course Rome suffered serious defeats (at the Caudine Forks in 321, for example, in Sicily in 249, and at Callicinus in Thessaly in 171), and when Hannibal came to Italy (218–203) Rome went through

[10] A variant on this theme is the claim (Raaflaub 1996, 293) that while Romans as individuals went to war partly for material gain, such motives were secondary 'on a public or "governmental" level'.

[11] Harris 1985, 57.

a freedom-threatening crisis that inflicted terrible casualties. As it turned out, a citizen militia weathered even this storm, since its members evidently believed that the system worked for their benefit – and since Rome managed to keep a sufficient proportion of its Italian allies in line. In the whole military history of the middle Republic, we know of only one occasion, a minor one, when Roman soldiers effectively mutinied in the face of superior enemy force (Polybius 1.21, 260 BC).

By the mid-second century matters had become more complicated: the empire now provided multifarious economic opportunities for individuals, and in the same period (from 151) we begin to see signs that Roman citizens were becoming more selective, partly if not wholly on an economic basis, about the wars that they were keen to fight. Much later still, in the late Republic and under Augustus, it was no burden for the Roman people to support imperial expansion, and Augustus' boasts in the *Res Gestae* ('I extended the frontiers of all the provinces of the Roman people on whose boundaries were peoples not subject to our rule', *Res Gestae* 26) make it obvious that they still did so.

Techniques of domination under the middle Republic, to 241 BC

But back now to the first period of astonishingly rapid expansion, when Rome progressed from being a local power in central Italy, with independent neighbours such as Caere, Veii, and Praeneste close by, to effective control of all of Italy. The earliest known phase, say between the domination of Fidenae (426?), Veii (393?), and Tusculum to the south-east (381), is necessarily the most mysterious. The 'canonical' Roman account in Livy rests ultimately on weak foundations, and the frescoes in the aristocratic and elaborately decorated François Tomb at Etruscan Vulci [Figure 2.1] show that around 300 BC some stories circulated about the wars between the city-states of central Italy radically different from the ones we read in the Roman sources. But Rome effectively destroyed some places (Veii) and preserved others – there is nothing complicated about that; the abrupt end of Veii is plainly visible in the archaeology. Much if not all of the land of the Veians was distributed to Roman citizens (Livy 5.30). But what, for example, was involved in the colonization of Sutrium and Nepet – were these genuinely 'federal' initiatives of the Latins? And in the next generation there are many historical problems, exemplified by Rome's relations with Caere, which seems to have been friendly to the Romans in the 380s, with the result that Rome awarded the Caeritans

Figure 2.1. One of the cycles of wall paintings inside the François Tomb from Vulci in Etruria shows that stories about central-Italian wars were quite different from those told by Livy and other Roman sources circulated *c.* 300 BC. Here 'Marce Camitlnas' (Camillus??) kills one 'Cneve Tarchunies Rumach' (Cn. Tarquinius from Rome). Painting now in the Villa Albani, Rome

Roman citizenship without the vote, whatever that meant at the time.[12] In 353, however, Rome and Caere fought a brief war, possibly connected in some way with Rome's move at roughly that date to colonize Ostia.

All this took place in a very small area by the standard of Rome's operations of a generation later. Some of the later techniques of domination were already emerging, however, most notably particular forms of colonization (see below). Much is uncertain, whether for example Rome *already* went to war in some fashion every single year: we can only be sure about this after 340, but between the 380s and 340 there had been a series of armed conflicts with the more independent of the Latin cities, mainly Praeneste and Tibur, and a series of successful wars to the east and south against the Aequi and the Volsci, and later against the Hernici beyond the Alban Hills, later still with some of the Etruscan cities. The sheer boldness of some of these initiatives is striking: the Romans had a way of appearing with an army in the enemy's rear, in Sora for instance in 345 (beyond the Hernici and well up the valley of the Liri), among the Aurunci that same year (beyond the Volsci), and still further to the south-east in Campania in 343.

By this time it is likely that Rome's power had already benefited from a practice that later struck an intelligent observer, King Philip V of Macedon, as an important ingredient in Roman success – the immediate inclusion of freed slaves in the body of citizens, which greatly added to the supply of manpower.[13] Manumission was evidently a common practice by 357, since in that year it was decided to tax it (which admittedly hints at some ambivalence); Livy (7.16) claims that the tax produced 'considerable revenue'.

When the Latins rebelled against Rome en masse (340–338), with some allies from further south, they had left it too late to save their independence, as the relative brevity of the conflict shows. Having prevailed in this war, Rome's leaders had to devise suitable means for maintaining their power. In part, they extended existing mechanisms. Four of the main towns of Latium – Praeneste, Tibur, Velitrae, and Antium – suffered land confiscations, for the benefit of Rome's own citizens. Another method was to revive the practice of formal colonization, with different types of colonies, small citizen colonies on the coast that were effectively military garrisons (starting with Antium in 338), and larger 'Latin' colonies that served to reward non-citizens as well as citizens (starting with Cales in Campania in 334).

[12] Harris 1971, 45–7.

[13] *SIG*[3] 543 (translated in Lewis and Reinhold 1990, 1, 418).

Yet another method was to extend Roman citizenship, with or without voting rights, to some of the towns of Latium and Campania (Livy 8.14), which Rome now defined as *municipia*. This was the most important step of all, though not without risk, because it immediately brought about a very large increase in potential military manpower. These policies together brilliantly showed their worth during the wars of 337 to 264.

From this period, at the latest, dates the custom of fighting wars virtually every year. The first opponents were Campanians, then there followed a sequence of remorselessly successful conflicts with the Samnites (starting in 327), the Etruscans (starting in 311), and many others. There were occasional lost battles early on in the Samnite wars, always avenged. From about 314 onwards the ambition to control the entire peninsula evolved quite quickly.[14] The invention in 311 of new official positions to supervise naval construction (Livy 9.30) is sufficiently indicative. And Rome now negotiated with outside powers – Carthage in 306 (though this was not the first contact), and the fairly distant island naval power Rhodes shortly afterwards. (Polybius' evidence on the latter point has now been vindicated by a Rhodian inscription.)[15] If the Samnites and Etruscans had joined forces in time, they might conceivably have blocked Rome's advance, but that did not happen until the campaign of Sentinum in 295. The Romans' victory in that battle seems to have tipped the scales decisively, and by 290 they had defeated almost all significant enemies south of the rivers Arno and Aesis. Conflicts continued in the 280s, and in 281 the democratic leaders of the Greek city of Tarentum invited King Pyrrhus of Epirus to come to their aid, which caused Rome a temporary setback; but by the late 270s Tarentum was the only free city left, and it succumbed in 272. At some time in the previous generation Rome apparently imposed the name of 'Italia', which had previously been merely the name of the peninsula's toe, on the whole peninsula up to the Arno, aiming probably to weaken the identities of the conquered Italian peoples; ironically, the new identity took root, and two centuries later served as a rallying point for the peninsula's last major rebellion against Rome in 91–89 [Figure 2.2].[16]

By 273 Rome was demonstrably preparing for a war against Carthage, the great established power in the central and western Mediterranean.[17]

[14] Harris 2007, 312–14.
[15] Harris 2007, 315–18. The Polybius passage is in 30.5.
[16] Harris 2007. Cf. further Russo 2012, Harris forthcoming 2016a.
[17] Harris 1985, 183–4.

Figure 2.2. Denarius minted by 'Italia' during the rebellion against Rome (the 'Social War'), 90–89 BC. The reverse (b) shows the Italian bull goring the Roman wolf, legend (right to left, in Oscan): C. Paapi (C. Papius was a Samnite general). On the obverse (a), a head of Bacchus, whose cult the Romans had suppressed. Most Italia coin-types, it should be said, emphasize not hatred of Rome but the solidarity of the rebels. Campana 1987, no. 98

(Republican Rome, as Montesquieu observed,[18] tended to go after its more fearsome enemies). This war began in 264 as a contest for power in eastern Sicily, but once again Roman ambitions fed on success, notably after the defeat of the Carthaginians at Agrigentum in 262. Rome created a large fleet for the first time (260), and in the same year scored a major naval victory at Mylae, off the Sicilian coast; the victorious consul C. Duilius was honoured with a column in the forum decorated with the prows of enemy ships, and no doubt he did his best to publicize the fabulous booty he

[18] Montesquieu 1965 [1734], 68.

Figure 2.3. One of the most extraordinary results of underwater archaeology has been the excavation at Marsala in western Sicily of this Punic vessel, which according to some is a warship (possibly one of those that went down in the Battle of the Aegates Islands, Rome's decisive victory over Carthage in the First Punic War in 241 BC). See Frost 1981. But others do not see it as a warship: Averdung and Pedersen 2012. Marsala, Museo Archeologico Regionale 'Lilibeo'

brought home (though the surviving inscription which describes his successes was probably not composed till after his death[19]). Rome now carried the fight to Sardinia and North Africa, though with mixed results at first – Sicily remained the main battleground. After remarkable perseverance on both sides, naval victory in 241 [Figure 2.3] gave Rome Sicily to exploit, together with a large indemnity from Carthage, and shortly afterwards the power to blackmail the Carthaginians into surrendering Sardinia.

How to explain this dramatic century of military success? We are still in a period with almost no contemporary sources, and much is therefore conjectural. There was seldom if ever a technological advantage on the Roman side. Organizational advantages counted for something, and it must not be forgotten that almost all the campaigns in question were

[19] It can be read in Warmington, *Remains of Old Latin* IV, 128–31.

fought in hostile territory. So what happened on the battlefield itself[20] was much influenced by efficient logistics. Rome's relatively ample supply of manpower was clearly very important, in spite of the obscurities of Italian demography in the fourth and third centuries BC.[21] What counted most of all, however, was the single-minded devotion of the elite and much of the rest of the population to warfare, a devotion whose social and political components are clear (see below; its psychological components are necessarily more obscure).

When it came to holding on to power, as distinct from winning wars – the factor that distinguishes a nascent imperial state from a state that achieves relatively short-term military successes – what mattered was 'the invention of new organizational techniques that greatly enhanced the capacity to control peoples and territories'.[22] This flat phrase of Michael Mann's, 'organizational techniques', is a vital key to understanding the story I am telling in this chapter. The Greek equivalent was 'ruling with political intelligence' (*politikôs*) (Strabo 17.839: the Romans got control of the whole of Italy by fighting wars and ruling *politikôs*).

Which techniques were actually new in the first crucial period between 337 and 280 is clear only in part: oppressive bilateral treaties made in perpetuity – Rome's most frequent means of settling things with defeated Italian peoples and towns – may not have been new, though the scale certainly was. The treaties that Rome imposed normally involved the expropriation of land (which became Roman 'public land' and a source of strife among the victors) and a system of virtual conscription (not taxation, largely because most of Italy was only just beginning to use coinage at the dates in question). Rome also on occasion disrupted local religious life, completely destroying for example the cult centre of the Etruscans and later (in 186) carrying out a serious persecution of the worshippers of Bacchus/Dionysus. With slightly more subtlety, it appears that by officially considering 'prodigies' (extraordinary events that were believed to need expiation) that occurred in Italian-ally territory the Senate 'assert[ed] the religious unity of Italy and Rome's central place in that unity'.[23]

Rome also interfered in criminal justice in important cases: 'for all the crimes that are committed in Italy that require official investigation, such as cases of treason, conspiracy, poisoning and first-degree murder, they are

[20] For a summary of Roman battlefield organization in this period, see Rawlings 2007, 55–8.

[21] Even if we suppose that Roman citizens were relatively numerous in this period, the amount of military service they performed was very great: see Scheidel 2008, 40.

[22] Mann 1986, I, 3.

[23] MacBain 1982, 28.

in the Senate's jurisdiction' (Polybius 6.13.4).[24] Roman power furthermore tended to marginalize and later eliminate local languages (in 280 Latin was still of course a minority language in peninsular Italy – most of the inhabitants spoke only Etruscan or Greek or a form of Oscan).

Yet this system would not have worked in the long run if there had not been a persistent effort to accommodate those Italians who collaborated, above all the members of local ruling elites. Every Italian city had a specific Roman patron, it is said (Dionysius of Halicarnassus, *Roman Antiquities* 2.11, evidently alluding to mid-republican times, at least in part), who will have been of senatorial rank. The local bigwigs, the landowners, exercised a high degree of local autonomy, while the Romans, having no need or wish to administer local affairs, concentrated on their own military and material interests. The well-to-do anti-democrats at Tarentum would have liked to make an accommodation with Rome, and so it went all over the peninsula: Rome's leaders evidently made it known that they would protect property rights, while the most vigorous resistance tended to come from the masses (this seems to have been particularly true in Etruscan and Greek localities). There were of course many variations on this theme: the best-known case concerns Volsinii (modern Orvieto), where Rome intervened in 265–264 to restore the power of the old elite.[25] This preference for the few, the existing social elite, the landowners, was a constant in Roman policy over many centuries.

Other organizational techniques were perhaps more original: Roman-style colonization in this period served the strategic power of the Roman state, and Rome, unlike the colonizing Phoenician and Greek cities of the past, retained fairly tight control.[26] The systematic measuring out of land, 'centuriation' in the modern terminology, is likely to have started in 273 at the latest (Paestum), and it ensured precise – though not of course equitable – shares for all the colonists. Filippo Coarelli has in fact argued cogently that centuriation was already used along the line of the later Via Appia before the latter was laid out in 312.[27] Above all, the colonies were very numerous: between 338 and 263, at a more or less steady rate, five or

[24] It can hardly have concerned itself with every such murder. Mouritsen (1998, 46) had no substantive reason to reject Polybius' statement.

[25] Harris 1971, chapter 4.

[26] Bispham 2006 strains too hard to overthrow every orthodox opinion about republican colonization. On the immediate military functions of these colonies, see Patterson 2006, 191–4, who, however, rightly sees them as partly motivated by a wish to distribute land to Romans and Rome's supporters.

[27] Coarelli 2005, 186–8.

six citizen colonies and some nineteen 'Latin' colonies were established in Italy (these enabled Rome to satisfy and make use of its second-class citizens),[28] with about thirty-five more of one type or the other before the end of the second century.[29] The colonies had the predictable extra advantage of increasing Rome's military manpower. Yet another technique that was probably original was long distance road-building, rudimentary in this phase but still a very important means of control and also a potent physical symbol of Roman power: thus they initiated a road to Capua in 312 (the Via Appia) and another eastwards across the Appennines in 307.

Then there is the matter of Roman citizenship, particularly difficult to disentangle in this early period because its significance changed greatly later on. While it is clear that Rome gave certain rights to selected outsiders and sometimes effectively incorporated both individuals and even communities in this way, it is less clear what these rights meant in practice. In 268, the whole free population of Sabines – those who had survived the Roman invasion in 290 – was given full Roman citizenship, but this technique was not used again on anything like the same scale – the Italian allies were too different from Romans, for the most part, and too numerous. Much later (91–89, the 'Social War', that is to say the war against the *socii* or allies) many of them rebelled, and Rome reacted sensibly though tardily by extending Roman citizenship to a vast new population – all the Italians south of the River Po.

Rome made regular and heavy use of units of Italian allied troops against King Pyrrhus in 280–279 and in the First Punic War,[30] and it is convenient to trace at this point how this partnership developed over the succeeding 150 years. In the 190s the proportion of allied to citizen soldiers was nearly 2 to 1, and though it declined later, for reasons that are unclear, the proportion was normally more than 1 to 1 throughout the second century.[31] In this respect Rome was in appearance a normal imperial power, but it seems to have done exceptionally well in that it convinced the Italians fairly soon to recognize Rome in the role of leader. This was no doubt in part because of the alliance with local elites mentioned above, but also in part because of a more general Italian recognition of Rome's

[28] For a map, see Cornell 1995, 382. Asconius p. 3 Clark shows that Placentia (218 BC) was counted as the 53rd or 54th foundation, which is reasonably consistent with the other evidence.

[29] On what the ethnic mix was actually like in a young Latin colony, see Crawford 2006 (on Paestum).

[30] P. Kent, however, correctly points out (2012, 76–7) that the Samnites and Pyrrhus also made use of Italian allies.

[31] Harris 1984, 98–100. See further Erdkamp 2007a.

energy, resources, and determination (see Polybius 3.90 on the Italians' view of Rome after the terrible Roman defeat at the Battle of Cannae in 216). Roman power in Italy was now imposing enough, but also acceptable enough, to ensure – though by a quite narrow margin – that the many Italians who welcomed the invader were balanced by many others who stayed obedient.[32]

Many Italians remained unconvinced, however. Why some of them rebelled in 91–89 is disputed, but more perhaps than it needs to be. Plenty of evidence, including coin-types [Figure 2.2], makes it clear that many of the Italians in the centre of the peninsula still hated Rome, and they very briefly established the independent state of Viteliu (Italy), with its capital at Corfinium on the other side of the Appennines; at the same time the rebels wanted the imperial privileges that came with Roman citizenship (Appian, *Civil Wars* 1.34.152).[33] This 'inconsistency' is no harder to understand than, for example, the mixed aims of the Basque ETA or the Italian Lega Nord in contemporary politics. When the Romans compromised on the citizenship issue (90), the rebellion was doomed; a further century of Romanization followed. In the next chapter we shall see what effects this incorporation had on Rome's internal affairs.

But to return to the period before 241: another innovation, about 300, was coinage, an idea taken over from the Greeks and soon put to wider and wider use;[34] new officials, additional quaestors, seem to have been appointed to deal with minting from 267 onwards. The initial advantage was probably a more efficient system of paying the state's military suppliers, and the civilian ones involved in public works; later on in the third century it facilitated the payment of the soldiers' wages. This, however, was more a matter of catching up with the other major Mediterranean states than overtaking them. (In earlier times, soldiers received booty but no regular pay, and since they had to provide their own equipment they were drawn from those who met a minimum property qualification. As the state grew richer, regular pay was introduced, perhaps about 280, and later the property qualification was reduced, until it was effectively abolished by the consul C. Marius in 107).

An ancient Mediterranean state demonstrated its military power above all by its ability to mobilize large and effective naval forces. Rome owned some warships by the late fourth century, as we already noted, and the

[32] On Hannibal's mixed reception in Italy, see Salmon 1982, 78–89.
[33] Notwithstanding the useful study of Mouritsen 1998.
[34] A new chronology has been proposed by Coarelli 2013.

notion that the Romans were still at that time innocents at sea (traceable to Polybius 1.20) is seriously misleading. Such events as the colonization of the island of Ponza (Pontiae) in 313 are unintelligible without naval resources.[35] It is clear, however, that Rome became a great naval power quite abruptly once it decided, from 264 onwards, to challenge Carthage. The two states committed no fewer than a combined 680 warships to the Battle of Ecnomus off the south coast of Sicily (256), which made it the largest naval battle of the war and one of the largest ever fought in antiquity.

While residing in a British prison, Nehru once wrote that the Romans, whose history he knew quite well, were (like the English, in his opinion) 'singularly devoid of imagination', but at least in the military, political, and religious spheres of Roman republican life, what is striking is rather the reverse: the ability to build a durable imperial structure and devise mechanisms for maintaining social cohesion – at enormous costs in human suffering.

World power, 241–146 BC

After the decisive engagement of the first war against Carthage was fought off the Aegates islands in western Sicily in 241, Rome always retained naval superiority in the western Mediterranean. In the years 216–214, in spite of intense difficulties in Italy, it found the resources to force the king of Macedon out of the Ionian Sea. Having virtually eliminated the remaining Carthaginian navy by means of the peace treaty of 201, the Romans turned much of their attention to the east, and in 190 scored twin naval and land victories over King Antiochus III of Syria at the Battles of Myonnesus (off the Asia Minor coast between Smyrna and Ephesus) and Magnesia. The treaty they imposed on him, the Peace of Apamea (188), forbade the king to own a real navy ever again (see Polybius 21.43.13), and it did so effectively.

What accounts for all this success at sea? Partly of course those same qualities that made Roman land forces so formidable (we shall return to this question shortly). Sheer economic resources, plus the willingness to use them, also weighed heavily. The only Mediterranean states that possessed timber and money in sufficient quantities to resist Rome successfully at sea for any length of time were Carthage and the Seleucid

[35] See further Harris 2007, 312–13. No doubt a considerable proportion of these resources were provided by Italian 'allies' (cf. Polybius 1.20.6).

Empire. What also stands out of the narrative of the naval campaign of 190 against the Seleucid navy was the vital role played by Rome's old allies the Rhodians, famed for their skill at sea: it was they who defeated a Seleucid fleet at the Battle of Side (off the south coast of Asia Minor), and they were essential at Myonnesus too (see Livy 37.22–25 and 30); in other words, diplomacy counted mightily on the Roman side.

Rome's expansion between 241 and 146 falls roughly into six phases, which one can set out as follows. (1) The first was an era of beginnings between 238 and 202, with Roman wars in Northern Italy, Spain, and Illyria, and war with – though not in – Macedon. This was all interrupted by the long years of Hannibal's invasion of Italy, which led to dreadful casualties (one-quarter perhaps of Rome's adult male citizens lost their lives, including eleven consuls or former consuls), culminating in the Carthaginian's defeat deep inside Carthage's own territory (the Battle of Zama, 202) and the effective hobbling by treaty of possible Carthaginian resistance in the future. (2) There followed another period of rapidly expanding power (wars in Spain and Northern Italy again, and against Greek states and Macedon, and then against King Antiochus III in Greece and Asia Minor), 201–188, ending in the oppressive Treaty of Apamea between Rome and Antiochus III. (3) Then came a period of steady but less dramatic military success (Spain and Northern Italy, 186–172). Not that this was a period of complete inactivity in the east – it appears, for instance, that in about 179 Rome established 'friendship' with both Pharnaces king of Pontus and the Chersonitans in the Crimea (*IOSPE* I^2 402).[36] (4) The next act was the deliberate destruction of the Macedonian monarchy, 172–168, one of the three major states in the eastern Mediterranean. (5) There followed another period largely devoted to wars in Northern Italy, Spain, and Dalmatia (166–150).[37] (6) Finally there came the last war against Carthage, together with a decisive settling of accounts in Macedon and Greece, all this leading to the physical destruction of both Carthage and Corinth in 146.

Polybius was obviously right to say that the Battle of Pydna – the decisive victory over Perseus, the last king of Macedon, fought in Macedon itself in 168 – gave Rome command over the whole (Mediterranean) world, in the sense that no one could afterwards afford to disobey. A famous incident that took place in Egypt later that same year illustrated the new reality

[36] With the chronology of Will 1966–1967, II, 244–5, and Heinen 2005.

[37] Rich and Shipley 1993, 48, should not have referred to the years 167–154 as a 'peaceful interlude', still less have implied that there were other substantial ones in this general period. That the depth of Rome's military commitments varied from time to time did not need saying.

(Polybius 29.27): when King Antiochus IV of Syria, invading, had reached Pelusium in the eastern delta of the Nile and was no doubt quite pleased with himself in consequence, he was met by an ex-consul, C. Popillius Laenas, the practically unarmed emissary of the Senate; Popillius gave the king a senatorial decree ordering him to withdraw, and when the latter asked for time to consult his advisers, the Roman drew a circle round him in the dust and bluntly told him to consent before he stepped out of the circle. Antiochus had to comply. As has often been pointed out, power rises to a new level when no immediate threat is needed to get one's orders obeyed; such was the case here.

It is not my intention in this book to provide a full military-political narrative of this pan-Mediterranean expansion. It is a gripping story, which thanks mainly to Polybius, Livy, and Appian we can follow in considerable detail. Various modern works retail the narrative with a high degree of accuracy: best in English is the second edition of the *Cambridge Ancient History*, volumes VII and VIII. There are, however, two serious defects in all such accounts, one unavoidable, the other avoidable but seldom avoided. In the first place, what we read is in effect victors' history: even Polybius, though he sometimes criticized the Romans, was deeply co-opted, and became an active collaborator after 146 if not before. Furthermore we know that the Romans and their allies filled the air with self-serving lies in their conflicts with other states.[38] That is quite normal of course, but it makes the political part of the story, in particular, difficult to write. The second trap is that even the best kind of narrative has a tendency to mask both patterns and causes. Here by contrast I want to answer the crucial questions directly. Before coming to them, however, a few words about three issues that I consider to be distractions, red herrings.

It used to cause historians of Roman imperialism some puzzlement that while Roman power grew quite rapidly throughout the period down to 148 BC, it was only in that year that Rome actually annexed its first province in the eastern half of the Mediterranean (Macedonia).[39] In reality there is nothing here that is hard to explain, since for a long time, while they of course knew which areas they ruled directly, the Romans lumped together those foreign communities that were their subjects and those that were their subordinate 'friends'.[40] Their conception of their dominion was a realistic one: it consisted of the 'allies' and the *provinciae et reges*,

[38] See, for example, Harris 1985, 227–33, on the case of the war against Macedon in 172–168.

[39] The classic absurdity that resulted from this confusion is the claim that mid-republican Rome 'reject[ed] opportunities for the extension of power' (Badian 1968, 1).

[40] Cf. Richardson 2008, 188.

the provinces and the kings. In practice Rome's empire comprised on the one hand the territories Rome controlled directly, which in this period were Sicily (from 241 onwards),[41] Sardinia (238), Corsica (236), and Hither and Further Spain (197 – these two provinces were gradually expanded down to 133), and a group of 'client' states, not all of them actual monarchies, where the strength of Roman power naturally varied.[42] To equate the Roman Empire with the area delimited by the external frontiers of the provinces is a mistake, throughout the Republic and the Principate. As the geographer Strabo remarked at the end of his great work (17.839):

> Of all the land that is subject to the Romans, some parts are ruled by kings, but the Romans hold others themselves, calling them provinces … There are also some free cities, some of which came over to the Romans on friendly terms at the beginning, while others they set free as an honour. There are also some subjects who are local rulers or tribal leaders or priests.

In other words, the Roman Empire was partly 'formal' and partly 'informal', a distinction introduced long ago into the history of nineteenth-century imperialism and popular in that field since the 1950s.[43] In the informal empire, the degree of power exercised by the imperial power obviously varies.

Another misunderstanding, less important here, concerns the term 'imperialism'. We can say that no large empire was ever built without great quantities of ruthless bloodshed. Those who, for whatever reason, are unwilling to face this aspect of Roman imperial expansion sometimes, even now, attempt to exclude the term imperialism itself, often with the excuse that its common use in this context is a mere 100 years old, or with the excuse that it is a term subject to abuse and to divergent definitions – like 'democracy' or 'dishonesty' or countless other abstract nouns. Two scholars have even preferred the evasive euphemism 'state-building process'.[44] (We shall see in Chapter 3 how the Romans often revised the nature of their state during the whole period). A decent simple definition of imperialism might run as follows: 'imperialism is the activity by which a state or its surrogates impose its power, which it subsequently exercises and maintains, far beyond its previous boundaries, as part of a

41 The entire island only from 210 onwards.

42 For the unsuitability of the 'client' metaphor, see Kaizer and Facella 2010, 16–22. But the expression has become part of the language, and the term 'vassal' state, which I sometimes use, is no better.

43 Cain and Hopkins 2001, 26–9.

44 Eich and Eich 2005. They provide no justification for their preference except the claim that republican Rome was no more belligerent than 'most' other states, which is false (see below), and in any case hardly relevant, since no one has equated belligerence with imperialism.

long-lasting policy of expansion'. That is undeniably what Rome did, over several centuries. It may not be a fair description of Rome's behaviour prior to the 320s, but that does not alter the overall picture (see above, p. 26, for the Romans' growing ambitions in the 320s and 310s).

It is to be hoped, finally, that no one will argue yet again that the Romans cannot have been imperialistic or aggressive because they did not 'plan' the expansion of their empire,[45] as if the ancient Persians, the Muslim Arabs, the Spanish, the Ottomans, the British, or anyone else ever brought a large empire into being by means of a plan. But when it mattered, when they were praying to the gods, the Romans of the middle Republic were quite explicit about their desire for a constantly growing empire.[46] And when major conflicts were in prospect, they thought ahead; we are told on good authority that the Senate decided on the war against Perseus (172) and the last war against Carthage (149) well in advance, and according to custom kept the decision to itself.[47]

Questions and controversies

Now for the most important questions. I will briefly address six of them:

(1) *What caused Rome to behave, in general, so aggressively?* Scholars occasionally claim that no state is more aggressive than any other,[48] a point of view that has a spurious worldliness to it, but such authors never seem to consider the counter-examples in any detail and never seem to take into account the fact that some states, such as mid-republican Rome, persistently take great risks (as in 264 against Carthage) and persevere in spite of terrible losses. Few in fact, if any, of the Italian peoples of the fourth century BC could match Rome in this respect – consider the Etruscans, Veneti, and Greeks, not to mention smaller populations. Carthage itself did not reach Rome's level.[49] Indeed the theory of uniform aggressiveness assumes a uniformity of human rationality and of psychological make-up that is in the highest degree implausible.

[45] See Harris 1985, 107. Strange things continue to be written on this point, e.g. Brélaz 2005, 23. Mattern 1999, 214, alleges that Polybius attributed the growth of the Roman Empire to 'a deliberate and grandiose plan', but he says nothing of the sort.

[46] See the evidence gathered in Harris 1985, 117–30.

[47] Preparations for the First Punic War: Harris 1985, 183–4. The decision to make war against Perseus: Appian, *Macedonian War* 11.3–4. The Third Punic War: Polybius 36.2.1.

[48] For example, Eich and Eich 2005, 1 (in fact they hedge a little). Scheidel's hypothesis (Scheidel 2009b) that imperialism is based on the desire for reproductive success is a sophisticated variant. See further below.

[49] See further Harris 1985, 1–2.

Figure 2.4. Denarius of 211 BC or later. The reverse, like many other types of the period 211–136, shows the mounted Dioscuri (Castor and Pollux), the heroes of the Roman knights. Obverse: head of Roma. Crawford, *RRC* 53

What then drove the Romans forward? In 264, when Rome first fought outside the Italian peninsula, Roman life was to a great extent centred on warfare, and there were dangerous enemies within a few days' travel. Two generations of dramatic military success had nourished the natural aggression of a rugged and relatively uncouth population. The senatorial order was dominated by a military ethos centred on glory and honour that was in practice highly functional, in that it promoted both the Senate's and the senators' own political power and their economic well-being. The struggle for glory (*certamen gloriae*) among members of the governing class was central. Their heroes were the twin Dioscuri [Figure 2.4], equestrian warriors who constantly appear on Roman coin-types until the 150s,

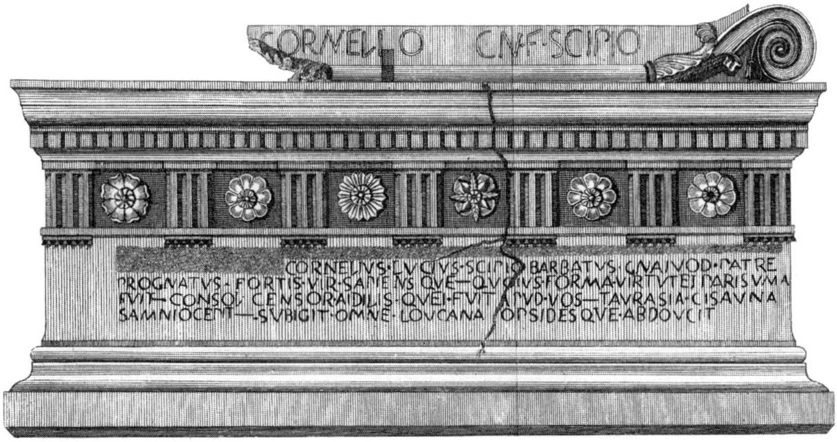

Figure 2.5. The aristocratic sarcophagus of L. Cornelius Scipio Barbatus, consul in 298 BC (the sarcophagus, however, is generally thought to be several decades later), commemorating his military achievements (for the text see *ILLRP* 309). The erasure is unexplained. An accurate eighteenth-century engraving. The original is in Rome, Musei Vaticani

a medium which also strongly suggests the governing class's obsession with military victory [Figure 2.5].[50]

Meanwhile the ordinary citizens, brought up in military traditions, could expect to benefit materially from successful campaigning. The strength of these factors appeared very clearly during the first two very long and painful wars against Carthage (264–241 BC, 218–202). Before 151 we only hear once (the sources, it is true, are not abundant) that the citizen assembly balked even temporarily at a foreign war, and that was in 201 when it was a question of initiating a war against King Philip V of Macedon immediately after the unparalleled exertions of the war against Hannibal.[51]

In ordinary times, the leading men looked around for external opportunities and provocations, sometimes reacting with overwhelming force to relatively minor or even fictitious provocations (the case of Dalmatia described by Polybius 32.13 provides a vivid example). But the aggressive pattern went still deeper: after Hannibal's surprise invasion of Italy, it might have seemed obvious in the following years that all Roman troops

50 The Dioscuri: Crawford 1974, 861–2. 'Victory' types last all the way through the Republic: Crawford 1974, 869–70.

51 Harris 1985, 218.

were needed in the peninsula, but instead Rome kept an army in Spain throughout the war, and sent another to Greece long before Hannibal had been driven out – in other words, there was a risk-taking strategic boldness about Rome that finds few parallels, especially in non-monarchical states. This is in fact an extra reason not to think of mid-republican Rome as a democracy (see the next chapter).

The economic drive of which we have already spoken was always present in one form or another.[52] Prior to the Second World War, in an era in which most historians of Rome were citizens of imperial states, one might have forgiven a certain fogginess of thinking on this subject; some of those historians believed, naturally enough, that only noble motives could have been at work in the construction of an empire. Now there is no such excuse, and while there will always be those who for whatever reason want to cleanse the Romans – of all people! – of any possible economic motives they do not need lengthy new refutation.[53]

It was never of course even faintly plausible that ordinary Roman citizens were little interested in their own economic advantage, and the extension of Roman power served them very well in this respect, over the whole period covered in this chapter. The plundering and enslavement of defeated enemies were integral parts of warfare, and the results were paraded in every triumph. In an economy based mainly on farming and warfare, Rome's ability to seize land from its enemies, from the fourth century onwards, very visibly improved the lot of ordinary citizens. It must have been because of the consequences of victory that in 313 Rome was able to abolish the condition of citizens' debt-bondage (*nexum*), which had previously been a major affliction (p. 73).

No wonder that the Romans, as soon as we know anything about their outside reputation, were notorious for their greed[54] – in a world in which others too robbed the defeated. Eventually more peaceful means of exploitation became popular, and Roman and Italian traders multiplied under the wings of military power: this was already happening in the third century.[55] All these advantages meant that Roman citizens and Latins, and

[52] North 1981; Coarelli 1984; Harris 1985, chapter 2 (with different nuances). For a succinct re-statement of the case, see Eich and Eich 2005, 21–8.

[53] Dmitriev 2009 bases his counter-argument mainly on the entirely arbitrary claim that economic imperialism can only exist under capitalism (shades of Lenin), and on the alleged absence of evidence, brazenly failing to consider the fairly abundant evidence that has been adduced, or the methods that a historian should use in analysing motives.

[54] See *SIG*[3] 593 = Sherk 1969 no. 33 (translated in Lewis and Reinhold 1990, I, 332) (197–194 BC), I Maccabees 8.3, Polybius 6.56.

[55] Harris 1985, 65.

many non-citizen Italians too, were inevitably aware that victory and fearsome power were often enough highly beneficial.

The attitudes of the mid-republican aristocracy were in harmony with this world-view. The leading men obviously knew that successful warfare would add to their wealth. Their status naturally required them to spend a good proportion of what they gained, but we have clear testimony that in this aristocracy, at least, the profits of war were a respected pursuit. The funeral oration delivered in honour of L. Caecilius Metellus, who had twice been a consul during the First Punic War, in 221, includes 'acquiring great wealth by respectable means' as one of the conventional ambitions that Metellus fulfilled (Pliny, *Natural History* 7.140). Wording and context show that this can only refer to the material benefits of war.[56] No one will suppose that Roman aristocrats were capitalist vampires, and they clearly had other motives too, in particular the 'struggle for glory', but economic motives predisposed them to go constantly to war.

The state benefited too of course. In some ways it was still, in the mid-second century BC, a rather rudimentary state, but there had long been a *res publica*, a public sphere. It can scarcely be argued that the senators who determined the war policy of the state are likely to have gone to war because they calculated that the state would benefit financially, but as soon as we ask what benefits they saw accruing from the influx of new revenue, and how they are likely to have reacted, we can see that they were conditioned to favour an aggressive foreign policy. They saw victorious commanders building new temples in profusion; they saw more and more public works paid for by the state, especially after 184; they saw public revenues steadily increase; they presided over the first large-scale adoption of coinage in Italy, and in 167 over the ending of the direct taxation of Roman citizens.[57]

The leaders of mid-republican Rome often attempted to justify their wars for external audiences, and occasionally (more often than we know, no doubt) for internal ones too. Sometimes they claimed that they were fighting to keep promises they had conveniently made to allies, sometimes – but not in fact often – that they were fighting in self-defence. Historians of the nineteenth and early twentieth centuries, partly it may be conjectured out of sympathy for the imperialism of their own days, created from such material an enormous myth which we may

[56] Harris 1985, 67.

[57] For a useful survey of the indemnities and plunder acquired during the first half of the second century, see Kay 2014, 21–42.

call 'defensive imperialism'.[58] It is true of course that imperialist expansion, in any era, occasionally runs into enemies who hit back and have to be resisted; the two great instances under the Roman Republic were Hannibal and Mithridates, king of Pontus. The Gallic invaders of 225 were another case.[59]

After the defeat of Carthage and Hannibal at Zama (202), there was no power anywhere in the Mediterranean that could stand up to a prolonged Roman onslaught, and in short order the Battles of Cynoscephalae (197), Myonnesus (190), and Magnesia (190) demonstrated Rome's superiority over the Macedonian and Seleucid monarchies. Rome's characteristic behaviour did not change at first, though in the years 151–146 we can probably see Roman citizens becoming more reluctant to fight tough and unprofitable wars, while the last war against Carthage (149–146) and the destruction of both Carthage and Corinth in 146 suggest a still more ruthless Rome.

The above, it seems to me, is what a historian can say with reasonable confidence about Roman aggressiveness in mid-republican times. Yet one may be haunted by such evidence as Polybius' account of Scipio at New Carthage (above, p. 16). Polybius also remarks (1.37) that 'the Romans use violent force for all purposes', and one may feel a pathological violence in many of their practices, not only in war itself, but in their military discipline, in their love for gladiatorial combat (which can already be detected in 174 BC, Livy 41.28.11, but was hardly new then), and in their treatment of their slaves.

There is little need, I think, to add comments about the contribution of a scholar who subscribes to a particular brand of American political science doctrine known as 'realism' (bizarrely named, since the doctrines in question are not actually realistic at all). He slips deceptively from the vague and banal claim that all ancient Mediterranean states were 'ruthless[ly] self-seeking' (without even noticing how relative ruthlessness may be) to the silly historical falsehood that all large and medium-sized states were 'ferociously aggressive and militarized' (most small states too).[60] The counter-examples are innumerable, and they include most – though not all – of Rome's fourth- and third-century enemies. As for the classical Greeks, Simon Hornblower is plainly right that 'Roman militarism …

[58] I attempted to exorcise this ghost in Harris 1985, 163–254.

[59] On the latter event, see Harris 1985, 198–9.

[60] Eckstein 2008, 8 and 9. For a forceful critique from a political science perspective, see Tröster 2009. On Eckstein's 'hidden agenda', see Hölkeskamp 2009, 213. For the fallacies involved in this kind of realism, see further Hobson 2006 (showing that even Mann has not been immune).

was certainly more marked than in any Greek state', even Sparta.[61] There were of course other aggressive states or at least rulers – Antiochus III is an obvious case. What is without parallel in the ancient Mediterranean is a centuries-long history of almost unremitting warfare.[62] It is not hard to see that the self-styled 'realists' who write about Roman history are actually trying to provide coverage for the foreign policy of the contemporary United States – a policy that may possibly be defensible, but preferably not by means of pseudo-history.

(2) *What, in this period, made the Roman military so formidable?* Much is imponderable, with respect to morale, logistics, and even tactical skill and equipment. No doubt the legions often had their enemies thoroughly frightened even before the fighting started (cf. Livy 31.34.4 and Appian, *Syrian War* 19, both referring to the 190s and both based on Polybius). When Polybius says that the Romans quickly adopted the superior kinds of weapons and armour used by the Greeks, he was showing a certain amount of Greek conceit, but his final comment is supported by other evidence[63] and is convincing:

> they swiftly imitated them [Greek arms], for the Romans are better than anyone at changing their practices and emulating what they see to be better (6.25.11).

The Roman soldier, says Polybius, is adaptable and can fight on his own as well as in a unit (18.32.11). But what impressed the historian most was a combination of meticulous organization and draconian discipline. The best examples of Roman military organization, he thought, were the method of enrolling the soldiers and the construction of the legionary camp. We may be equally impressed by Roman logistics: it was apparently normal practice, for instance, to supply the troops even in distant theatres of war with wine (e.g. Livy 37.27.2). Punishments on the other hand were quite often capital, even for stealing in camp (Polybius 6.37). The most extraordinary practice was 'decimation': a unit that abandoned a position in the face of the enemy would have a tenth of its members, selected by lot, dishonoured, and put to death (Polybius 6.38). How and why such stern methods were effective can be discussed at length,[64] but it is evident that both shame and fear of authority played larger parts than they would in a modern army, and larger parts than they did in most ancient armies.

[61] Hornblower 2007, 30; cf. 39.
[62] Macedon was probably Rome's nearest rival in this respect.
[63] Walbank 1957, 75; it is unlikely that this notion was original with Polybius.
[64] Cf. Rosenstein 1990, 95–8; Harris 2006, 308; and above all Phang 2008, esp. 243–8.

Long-distance overseas expeditionary forces had not worked perfectly in the first war against Carthage: Rome had succeeded quite well in Sicily, but not in Carthage's home territory. Rome gradually learned to operate in highly hostile surroundings: Scipio Africanus' campaign in Carthaginian home territory (204–201) was impressive by any standards. Once again, the Roman military was able to learn.

A combination of factors is thus the answer. The Roman soldier was a tough fellow, thoroughly inured to slaughter, very commonly a brutal killer (and rapist).[65] He was unlikely to desert or surrender. He was relatively well-looked after and equipped, he knew that his fellow soldiers were unlikely to run away, and that his officers were not cowards either. Tending to believe that the gods were on Rome's side (see further below, p. 49) he expected to win, and he expected to be rewarded for winning. At the same time, he knew that any failure might be repaid with shame and punishment. This combination worked extremely well. Meanwhile enlistment, logistics, and communications also functioned well (literacy and numeracy were sufficient though not over-abundant). Historians of republican Rome take all this for granted, quite naturally; to appreciate its importance fully, it is worth comparing these men with their late-antique counterparts, whom we shall discuss in Chapter 6.

How far the vitally important Italian 'allies' shared these characteristics is largely a matter for speculation.[66] The high level of trust they inspired in Roman commanders by the second century suggests that they were mostly regarded as being of similar quality. By Polybius' time, select allied troops called *extraordinarii* were singled out for special positions in the camp and on the march.[67] Which leads to the next question.

(3) We return to the vital matter of the '*organizational techniques*'. How did Rome make its victories outside peninsular Italy into permanent dominions? Rome over a long period adapted its city-state institutions reasonably well to the ruling of empire, as it had to the ruling of Italy itself (though in the end not well enough to enable a republican form of government to survive).

In the era of Italian expansion, a constitutional and political stumbling-block had been removed (326) when a consul had his *imperium*

[65] On the psychological and military training these men received, see McDonnell 2006, 182–4.

[66] Rosenstein 2012 discusses the extent to which Roman and allied troops were integrated on campaign.

[67] Polybius 6.26.6–9, 31.2–3, 40.4–8; Patterson 2012, 217. But it is noteworthy that after decisive victories Rome demanded the return of deserters, some or all of whom are likely to have been disaffected allies (cf. Appian, *Numidian War* 3, for example).

continued beyond his year of office, which made more ambitious campaigns possible. The major innovation after 264 was the creation of 'provinces' outside peninsular Italy and of extra high-level annual magistracies (praetorships) in order to provide these provinces with continuous supervision. The term *provincia* originally meant, and continued to mean, a sphere of responsibility, but it took on a territorial meaning from 227 when the number of praetorships went from two to four and the number of quaestorships from six to eight, the new officials having the jobs of ruling Sicily and Sardinia. In 197 the creation of two regular Spanish provinces led to the addition of two more praetorships and perhaps two more quaestorships. All these officials operated with small personal staffs, except of course when they were in command of substantial military forces.

But this is only the most obvious part of the story of overseas control: equally important was a level of diplomatic activity that was already quite intense by the 220s, involving communication with cities and peoples in the provinces, and the maintenance of the informal empire of vassal states outside.[68] On the Roman side, expertise was concentrated in the Senate, which received foreign delegations and dispatched its own members to instruct, investigate, or negotiate according to current needs. Details are quite often known from Greek epigraphical records as well as from literary evidence. The earliest surviving document of this kind is a letter written between 197 and 194 by the proconsul T. Quinctius Flamininus [Figure 2.6] to the small Thessalian town of Chyretiai, which Rome had 'liberated' from King Philip V of Macedon.[69] One of the editors of this text rightly describes the return of confiscated property that Flamininus announces in it as 'a very practical and clever maneuver to convince the wealthy classes that Rome will look after their interests'.[70] Rome also developed appropriate diplomatic language, including the broad category of 'friends [*amici*] of the Roman people', peoples who might be provincials or inhabitants of vassal states but were in any case implicitly Rome's subjects.[71]

From the earliest days of expansion the Romans had known how to make use of local elites: as early as 194 we find Flamininus replacing democratic governments in Thessaly, which was not yet part of a Roman province ('he chose the [local] senates and judges mainly on the basis of

[68] The Illyrian cities subdued in 229–228 and 219 did not yet become part of a province but were recognized as Rome's subjects (Polybius 7.9.13, with Rich 1989, 121–2).

[69] See n. 54 for references to this inscription.

[70] Sherk 1969, 213.

[71] See briefly Harris 1985, 135–6.

Figure 2.6. After T. Quinctius Flamininus (consul in 198) defeated King Philip V of Macedon and (196) proclaimed the freedom of the Greeks, he was so popular with them that he was extravagantly honoured (Crawford 1974, I, 544), with *inter alia* his portrait on gold staters. No later republican Roman aroused such enthusiasm. Reverse: Victory holding a wreath and palm branch. Crawford, *RRC* 548

property', Livy 34.51). But an important new phase began when Romans began to make use of the institutions and cultures that they found in foreign territories. By the late third century there were senators who could converse in Greek, a few anyway (a hundred years later it was commonplace), but it was more significant when Flamininus made effective use of the Greek slogan 'freedom' at the panhellenic gathering at the Isthmian Games of 196,[72] and when L. Aemilius Paullus, the victor at the Battle of Pydna, erected, or rather appropriated, a victory monument at Delphi in 168. Yet this sort of initiative is most visible in the Greek world, and few Greeks were deceived: most Greeks clearly continued to think of the Romans as 'barbarians' (the collaborator Polybius was naturally too polite to refer to them thus, though he gets close to doing so at 12.4b.2). That naturally did not prevent them from honouring relatively sympathetic Romans (cultic honours for Flamininus and so on).[73]

Rome had no compunction at all in what might well be regarded as a barbaric practice, the wholesale removal of defeated populations. This was the classic basis of Roman colonization and settlement, and the main victims in

[72] See in particular Walsh 1996.

[73] See among others Tanner 2000, 38–45 (though he greatly exaggerates the role of *clientela*).

the period 241–146 were the inhabitants of certain regions of northern Italy, in particular Liguria and the territory taken from the Boii (which enabled Rome to found Bononia, Mutina, Parma, and other settlements). Afterwards there were few if any Boii remaining except as slaves (Strabo 5.213 and 216 is the most valuable source here). Picenum also suffered (Strabo 5.251).

Tax-gathering and law enforcement were largely left to local authorities, until during the late Republic private contractors based in Rome itself (the *publicani*) got their hands on much of the work of taxation.[74] The system allowed ample room for Roman profiteering by officials and private individuals alike.

As applied to mid-republican times, the concept of 'provincial administration' conjures up the wrong image of Rome's empire (and even later it is problematic).[75] In the first place, the governor was not rigidly limited to action within precise frontiers: he might make war on neighbouring populations. Secondly, he had a small staff (though it was not minuscule, for there were swarms of slaves involved), and could not attend to many issues, even by later Roman standards.

The written word was also in a sense an organizational technique, and empires depend on it. The beginnings of this technology of domination can easily be seen in mid-republican Rome: the census kept track of military manpower, and the army already made extensive use of written documents.[76] Literacy was very limited by modern standards, but it was sufficient for the essential needs of control and exploitation.

Control and exploitation are not quite the whole story, however. Prominent Romans had patronage ties with provincial communities,[77] and there already grew up in the first half of the second century BC the idea that provincials could in certain circumstances gain redress at Rome. In 171 Spaniards complained to the Senate about the greed and cruelty of certain Roman magistrates, and they obtained a hearing if not much satisfaction.[78] In 149 a law was passed, the *Lex Calpurnia*, establishing a court to try greedy provincial governors, but the plaintiffs probably had to be Roman citizens,[79] and since the juries were to be made up of senators, no one was ever convicted.

[74] On this complex story, see Lintott 1993, chapter 5.

[75] The best short account of republican Rome's control over the provinces is to be found in Lintott 1993, 22–32, 43–107; more detailed but less perceptive is Schulz 1997.

[76] Harris 1989a, 166.

[77] Braund 1989.

[78] Harris 1985, 78.

[79] Richardson 1987.

Was there already an ideological component in Rome's power over outsiders, as there certainly was later? Ideologies have to be *sets* or *systems* of ideas, and it would perhaps be overstating it to see the complex of ideas that the Romans of these times expressed about their relationship to the outside world in such terms. The source material does not, for instance, permit us to know how openly Rome's leaders appealed to the class interests of their counterparts in other states. On the other hand it is plain that they already in the third century claimed for themselves some particular forms of justification for their armed attacks, if not for their power more generally,[80] in particular *fides* ('good faith'), which could be invoked whenever an ally of however recent vintage was involved in actual or potential conflict. King Hiero II of Syracuse complained to Roman envoys in 264 that the Romans 'harped on their good faith [*pistis* = *fides*]' in order to justify intervention (Diodorus the Sicilian 23.1), and they went on doing so.[81] Romans also knew by the time of the Hannibalic War how to use the language of justice in their relations with other states.[82] But such notions only received a degree of theoretical elaboration in the age of Cicero.

In short, Rome was able to devise the 'organizational techniques' that were necessary for the growth and maintenance of what we might call a 'Mediterranean Plus' empire; it is hard to say how they could have done so more effectively.

(4) *What did Roman power overseas mean in practice?* and (5) *What was the perspective of Rome's subjects?* After the initial death and destruction, the extension of Roman power meant indemnities and taxes, and – sometimes at least more onerous still – the private enterprise of senatorial officials and their associates. We do not know how heavy the tax burden was, but provincial revenues enabled the Romans to cease paying direct taxes themselves after 167 (the sources, however, attribute this to the influx of plunder from the war against Macedon). In the short term, Rome's impact on local social structures was probably not great except in Greek states that had previously been democratic, and there was as yet very little formal colonization (Carteia, a Latin colony founded in 171 on the bay of Algeciras in Spain, was an exception[83]). Economic opportunities attracted settlers of

[80] The war-declaring procedures of the fetial priests seem, by now at least, to have been intended for purely internal consumption (Harris 1985, 171).

[81] For the use of *fides* language in the external affairs of the middle Republic, see Gelzer 1962–1964, III, 70; Badian 1984, 408–13; Ferrary 1988, 72–8; *Fides* received a temple on the Capitoline about 250 (for the religious context see below, p. 72).

[82] Harris 1985, 171–3.

[83] On this and other Roman foundations in Spain, see Harris 1989b, 128–9.

various kinds, especially in Spain and in Sicily, where we know that there were Roman landowners by the 130s – not recent arrivals, one would think.

Rome's overseas subjects reacted in normal ways: some cooperated more or less eagerly with the invader, the best-known individual case being Polybius.[84] Others, in Spain especially, rebelled, or would have done so if Rome had not been so daunting: even when we make allowance for the Roman tendency to see any resistance as rebellion, it is clear that there were several serious revolts in parts of Spain that had already been subjugated.

(6) *What successful imperialism did to the Romans themselves* is another complex story, to be continued in the next chapter. Power brought wealth to the state and to the elite and to some of the ordinary citizens; it also brought, certainly by the second century, a degree of financial corruption.[85] Two other results of vast importance were the change in the structure of Roman society that resulted from the influx of slaves – Rome thus probably became more slave-dependent than any large state had ever been before –, and the linking up of the Roman commercial economy with the Hellenistic world, with the consequence that in the second century Mediterranean trade intensified as never before. (One might say roughly that the Romans supplied the capital and the Greeks supplied the financial sophistication). The scale and nature of this slave economy we shall consider in the following chapter; here it need only be noted that the huge mobilization of the citizens for war throughout the third and second centuries, was made possible by the fact that a large amount of the actual work, including farmwork, was being done by slaves.

Did the Romans of this period (prior to 146 BC) reflect much about their imperial power? One might speculate about this question at some length (we have noticed above that already in the third century they boasted about their good faith and their justice), but the important point is probably their religiosity.[86] Empire-builders normally suppose that divine powers have given them crucial help, and almost as soon as we have a documentary record we find the Romans attributing their success to their piety towards the gods (for early documentary evidence see an inscription of 193 BC, Sherk 1969 no. 34, line 13). This was indeed partially true, in the sense that their self-consciously meticulous attention to the state religion (for which see the next chapter),[87] combined with a long record of success,

[84] On Polybius as a collaborator, see Baronowski 2011, chapter 7.

[85] Cf. Crawford 1974, 695, on the mysterious disappearance of large quantities of public funds.

[86] Cf. Harris 1985, 123.

[87] Scheid 2007a.

can be presumed to have bolstered the determination of those Romans who were of religious temperament (how many they really were, we cannot tell, but in any case a significant number). Religion helped Rome to survive serious defeats in battle, as when for example the dictator Fabius Cunctator explained in the Senate that the defeat suffered at the Battle of Trasimene in 217 (Hannibal's great victory in Etruria) was due to the ritual error of the commanding consul C. Flaminius even more than to his tactical imprudence.[88] With sufficient religious effort, the gods' good will could always be regained. It is striking too that Rome's political elite – atypically – filled all the main religious offices of the state (below, p. 81); that 'most important religious action was taken by the magistrates';[89] and that such great resources were devoted to temple-building. Polybius (6.56) claimed that Roman public religion was the state's greatest strength, and though his meaning is not wholly clear, he was probably right to be impressed by the solemnity of the whole business. But if religious observance was one of the strengths of the growing Roman Empire, can it also have been one of the weaknesses that brought about its decline? To this question we shall return.

Almost irresistible

Here, as a basis for a discussion of Rome's further expansion all the way down to the major change under Tiberius, is a list of Rome's new provinces from 146 onwards, interspersed with some other details about the territorial extension of Roman power (these are the indented items in the following catalogue). A comprehensive list of military campaigns, since they continued to be almost annual, would of course be much longer.

Achaea (146 BC)
Africa (initially the northern half of modern Tunisia) (146)

  146f.: increased Roman influence in Numidia
  141f.: Roman incursions into Thrace

Asia (western Asia Minor), including Pamphylia (133)[90]

  129f.: occasional Roman incursions into northern Illyria

[88] Livy 22.9.7–10. It was convenient to blame Flaminius, and his personal responsibility, as well as the importance of religion, was underlined by the prompt decision to build a temple for *Mens* (Prudence) (for the religious context, see the next chapter). How Livy can have known what Fabius said on this occasion is a question we can leave aside.

[89] North 1986, 257.

[90] Some scholars used to imagine that Rome was slow to take action in 'Asia' in 133, but two new inscriptions published in 2003 show that this was not the case: see esp. C.P. Jones 2004.

Phrygia, added to 'Asia' (122)[91]
Gallia Transalpina (but only the southern part, roughly speaking Provence) (121)

Lycaonia (in southern Asia Minor) (about 116)

113f.: some Roman military presence in Noricum
111–105: Roman power in Numidia re-asserted
107: first known Roman intrusion into Gaul outside the above-mentioned province
105: Cimbri and Teutones, migrant peoples, heavily defeat Roman forces at Arausio in Provence

Cilicia (further east in southern Asia Minor) (100?)

96: Cyrene bequeathed to Rome but not yet annexed
96 or 95: installation of a client king in Cappadocia
91–89: the 'Social War' against some of Rome's Italian allies

Gallia Cisalpina (northern Italy) (89), already long under Roman control

89: Roman-sponsored invasion of Pontus, home territory of King Mithridates VI
88 or 87: Egypt bequeathed to Rome but not yet annexed[92]

Illyricum (east coast of the Adriatic) (76), initially as part of Gallia Cisalpina
Cyrene (75)
Bithynia (in northern Asia Minor) (75/4)

69: army of L. Licinius Lucullus invades Armenia and captures the capital Tigranocerta; (some of) his troops refuse to go further.

Crete (67).

66: all Asia Minor effectively under Roman control; Cn. Pompeius Magnus' [Pompey's] army victorious in 'Iberia' (Georgia-Azerbaijan)

Pontus (in northern Asia Minor) (64)
Syria (63).

63: first Roman capture of Jerusalem
61: Pompey triumphs over 'Asia, Pontus, Armenia, Paphlagonia, Cappadocia, Cilicia, Syria, the Scythians, the Jews, the Albanians,

91 For the date, see Ramsey 1999.
92 Cf. Harris 1985, 155–8.

Iberia [both of these peoples lived in the Caucasus], Crete, the Bastarnae, King Mithridates and Tigranes'

Gallia Transalpina (the balance, that is) (58)
Cyprus (58)

55: first invasion of Britain
53: Parthians overwhelmingly defeat a Roman army at Carrhae

Numidia (46)

44: Caesar plans to conquer Parthia
35–33: Octavian extends Roman power in Illyricum

Egypt (30).

29–28: pacification of Thrace
26–19: completion of conquest of Spain
26–25: military expedition through Arabia to Yemen

Galatia (in central Asia Minor) (25/24)

25: Mauretania a client kingdom
24–22: campaigns in Ethiopia

Noricum (16)

Raetia (15)

12f.: invasion of Germany. There was no province of Germany east of the Rhine, but Germania as a province west of the Rhine may have come into being in these years.[93]

Pannonia (8)
Moesia (6?): now often considered to be an acquisition of post-Augustan date, but good sources suggest that Rome was already in effective control by about this time.[94]

Paphlagonia (6), as part of Galatia
Judaea (AD 6), as part of Syria

AD 7: Tiberius celebrates triumph over Germans

[93] On this controversial matter, see most recently Ausbüttel 2011.

[94] Wilkes 1996, 556, claims that Moesia became a province under Claudius, but the sources he cites do not say that. Cassius Dio 55.29, referring to 6, suggests that Moesia was by then under Roman control; cf. Strabo 7.303. AD 12 is the latest possible date for the province: see *PIR*² P 847.

AD 9: annihilation of a Roman army under P. Quintilius Varus in Germany
AD 16 : Tiberius, now emperor, gives up on conquering all of Germany.

It was warfare that brought almost all the new provinces under Rome's control. This applied even to 'Asia', Cyrene, and Bithynia, which were bequeathed to Rome by rulers who were intent – in vain, as it turned out – on trying to prevent a violent kind of Roman takeover. The large and challenging rebellion of the recently provincialized inhabitants of Illyricum and Pannonia in the years AD 6 to 9, may suggest why Rome's expansion slowed down soon thereafter – but explaining this change needs further discussion (see Chapter 4).

Let us now repeat for the late Republic the six questions posed in the previous section.

(1) *Roman aggressiveness.* The attack on the Achaeans that led to the destruction of Corinth in 146 was a typically exaggerated Roman response to a foreign obstacle, and this pattern continued down to and including the era of Augustus. The component parts of this aggressive attitude changed somewhat, however. By the 120s, participation in war, previously a requirement for members of the senatorial elite, had begun to be a little more optional, at least for men who had the ability to stand out in other ways (but that was very difficult for a man who was not born into a consular family, and the brilliant advocate Cicero, whose father was a mere knight, was one of the few true civilians who got right to the top). The first man we know of who reached the consulship without a proper military background was L. Licinius Crassus, consul in 95, and even he tried to get himself voted a triumph after some relatively minor warfare in northern Italy. Thus the senatorial elite came to participate rather less in foreign wars, but it almost unanimously supported them. Popular support seems to have been widespread too, and still was under Augustus. Actual service was another matter, and the frequently heavy demand for soldiers in the late Republic created some strain. However, the only tribune of the people who is known to have complained about the burdens of military service in these years was the relatively extreme Licinius Macer in 73 (Sallust, *Histories* 3.48.17–18).[95]

The old Roman appetite for savage violence persisted: among innumerable instances during the first century, one might cite the case of T. Didius, consul in 98, who the following year in Spain tricked the inhabitants of a town that had previously helped Rome into surrendering, on the grounds

[95] When an Augustan poet belittles military conquests (Propertius 3.5.11–18) it is a straw in the wind.

that they had been practising 'brigandage' because of their poverty; he promised them land, trapped them in a Roman camp, and slaughtered them to the last woman and child. He did so with the support of the ten-man senatorial commission that was arranging the affairs of Nearer Spain at the time, and on his return to Rome the Senate awarded him a triumph (Appian, *Iberian War* 100).[96]

In all these circumstances it is hardly surprising that Rome often attacked foreign peoples without serious provocations: this applies, for example, to the wars in southern Gaul in 125–120, the war in Illyricum in the mid-70s, many of the frontier campaigns of Lucullus, Pompey, and Caesar, and so on and so on.

Having built such a large empire by the early first century, and having made so many enemies, it was inevitable that the Romans sometimes had to defend their provinces. Their most effective enemy by far in the late Republic was King Mithridates VI of Pontus, who, with Rome still in 89 labouring under serious difficulties because of the rebellion in Italy, invaded and soon took over all of Rome's possessions in Asia Minor, much to the satisfaction of most of the locals. In 88 he invaded Greece, and it took Rome two years to throw him out again. But it was mostly Roman aggression that had started all this, as the sources reveal in spite of their Roman bias. The king had spent 'twenty years ... backing away from Rome',[97] in fact nearly thirty years. The individual aggressors were the future dictator L. Sulla in the mid-90s, and more decisively M'. Aquillius (consul in 101) in 89. Mithridates captured the latter and put him to death in a symbolically appropriate manner, by pouring molten gold down his throat. So much for Roman greed. The Greeks of western Asia Minor, encouraged by the king, took the opportunity to kill all the Romans and Italians they could lay their hands on (Appian, *Mithridatic War* 22–3).[98]

By this time the financial tentacles of influential Romans extended into all areas within the range of Roman power, especially perhaps in Asia Minor: by 88 King Nicomedes III of Bithynia was already deeply in debt to Roman military commanders and to others in their entourages (Appian, *Mithridatic War* 11).[99]

[96] The other sources: Broughton 1951–2, II, 7.

[97] Hind 1994, 144 (who gives what is probably the best existing account of the Mithridatic wars); see also Madsen 2009.

[98] For disputes that had fuelled Greek resentment, see Wallace 2014, esp. 71.

[99] See further Goukowsky's notes (2001) and Harris 1985, 95–7.

It was apparently in the 50s BC that leading Romans occasionally began to question the justice of some of Rome's wars,[100] and began to speak of *pax* with foreign nations as desirable[101] – but *pax*, it must be remembered, is not, in the Latin of this period, peaceful co-existence, but the happy condition that ensues when the foreigners have been vanquished. Meanwhile all the so-called 'great men' of the late Republic built their careers on extensive military victories, which brought spectacular wealth and still conferred great prestige. Nowhere is this last truth more evident than in the campaigns of the rival leaders Octavian and M. Antonius in the 30s, when a 'rational' modern calculation would have led them to concentrate on each other rather than on largely unnecessary foreign wars.

With Octavian's victory over M. Antonius at Actium in 31, the whole nature of Rome's political decision-making changed forever. But it was not simply 'path-dependence' that made Augustus engage in nearly forty years of military expansion: it was expected of him and it added to his authority (see *Res Gestae*, chapters 26–7, 30); there can be little doubt that it was also intended to add to Rome's revenues (cf. Suetonius, *Divine Augustus* 25 end; Strabo 4.200–1). We can trace the close connection between his foreign wars and his political needs within the Roman state.[102] None of this should be taken to mean that he wanted to break with tradition. What was new was the big lie, only possible under one-man rule, that he had conquered the Parthians (this is implied in *Res Gestae* 29.2, and on coin-types, and on the breastplate of the emperor's famous Prima Porta statue [Figure 2.7])[103] – as Caesar had intended to do –; whereas in reality his representatives had made a pact with them (in 20 BC) that enabled him to concentrate most of his forces in Europe. It is wholly untrue that there was a 'cessation of military conflict' under Augustus.[104] And there was now free rein for fantasies of loyal subjects: Horace looks forward to the emperor's conquest of China (*Odes* 1.12.56).[105]

When, at the end of his life, Augustus advised his successor to 'maintain the empire within its existing boundaries' (Tacitus, *Annals* 1.11),[106] we

100 Harris 1985, 174.

101 Harris 1985, 36.

102 See Rich 2003, 345–57, who, however, slightly overstates his case.

103 For the coin-types, see H. Mattingly 1976, Augustus nos. 10–11; for the breastplate, Zanker 1988, 188–92 (but in this case the conquest claim is interestingly weaker).

104 Rose 2005. 33. He follows the perilous procedure of inferring Augustus' attitude towards the Parthians in 19 BC from a reconstruction of the lost Arch of Augustus (on which see Nedergaard 1993) derived from coin-types, while substantially ignoring the textual evidence.

105 The Romans underestimated the remoteness of the 'Seres': Nisbet and Hubbard 1970, 167.

106 One wonders whether he considered the Rhine or the Elbe to be the boundary between Rome and the Germans.

Figure 2.7. On the breastplate of the Prima Porta Augustus, a monumental marble statue found in a villa belonging to the emperor's wife Livia, we are shown, symbolically, one of the leader's claims – that, thanks to him, barbarians (personified on the right) had returned to the Romans legionary standards that had been lost by other Roman generals (cf. *Res Gestae* 29). The scene is usually interpreted as a reference to Augustus' fictitious victory over Parthia. Rome, Musei Vaticani

cannot be sure whether he was mainly reacting to the temporary crisis brought about by the Illyrican-Pannonian rebellion and the Roman defeat in Germany in AD 9, or whether he had more structural considerations in mind. Since many of his successors more or less followed this advice, we must suspect it was the latter.[107]

(2) *Military effectiveness.* In 107 the consul C. Marius, in need of legionary troops to fight in Numidia, accepted men from the poorest class of Roman citizens. This became the general practice. For various reasons the number of qualified citizens was not in 107 keeping up with imperial requirements: military service had no doubt gradually lost some of its attractiveness (one might think that few wars could by now arouse fervent patriotism or even greed, though both these instincts still had a long Roman future), and in consequence of the encroachments of large landowners (below, p. 87) there were fewer small farmers who met the property qualification. The effect was to change the army's social composition, with momentous consequences for the internal affairs of the state. Marius improved military training, however, and the army's sheer military effectiveness was not harmed in the late Republic; the occasional serious defeat, such as the one inflicted at Arausio in Provence in 105 or Crassus' disaster at Carrhae in northern Mesopotamia in 53, is virtually inevitable even in the most effective of military systems. Incompetent generalship appears to have been the usual cause.[108] In fact the armies of the late Republic, particularly perhaps those of the 60s and 50s, performed extraordinary feats.

Whether the same could be said about the Augustan army – which admittedly conquered large swathes of difficult territory – is slightly less clear. We should like to account for Quintilius Varus' absurd defeat in AD 9 as well as the army's frequent successes. According to Syme, Augustus' German policy had been based on 'an excess of optimism',[109] but that is largely a guess. The incompetence of Varus and his staff officers seems to have been the immediate cause; the skill of the German commander Arminius must also have contributed.

The sheer terror that the Roman army could bring continued undiminished, however:[110] when Germanicus led Roman troops into Germany in AD 14, 'they devastated the country with fire and sword for fifty miles

[107] See Chapter 4.
[108] For an original view of Carrhae, Rome's first fight with the Parthians, see Traina 2010.
[109] Syme 1988, 243 = 1991, 389.
[110] Campbell 2002, 169.

around. No pity was shown to age or sex. Religious as well as secular buildings were razed to the ground' (Tacitus, *Annals* 1.51); there were special circumstances, but such behaviour seems to have been quite common and no doubt many neighbours of the Roman Empire lived in fear as a result.

Mann was in error to say that 'class struggles contributed much to the military effectiveness of the Roman Republic',[111] though they may have contributed to the success of Roman colonization. It is remarkable, however, that if strife between rich and poor was a major element in the political struggles of the late Republic (as it was; see the next chapter), the military efficiency of the state was not greatly impaired. Within the military, the command structure generally stayed intact; by an established tradition, a sacred oath (*sacramentum*) tied the soldiers not to the state but to their individual commanders,[112] and a good commander made sure that he was on cordial terms with his centurions, who were the sails that really carried the boat along. Some of Caesar's soldiers apparently wobbled a bit in 58 (*On the Gallic War* 1.39–41, Cassius Dio 38.35),[113] but in foreign wars (it was different in wars between citizens) Roman soldiers generally seem to have obeyed orders much as before. Discipline remained ferocious: even commanders who were in effect competing for popularity in the 30s applied 'decimation' (above, p. 43) to units that were held to have retreated out of fear or otherwise failed in the face of the enemy.[114] Discipline was still a well-protected tradition.

Whether the rank-and-file Roman soldiers were better armed and equipped than their opponents in this period is not altogether clear, but in relation to their European opponents, such as the Gauls and Germans, this must generally have been the case; and they were certainly well supplied. More of them must also have known how to read and write, which was a serious advantage.

The prompt movement of troops and their impedimenta was vital. First there had been the trunk roads in Italy, including the Via Aemilia and the Via Postumia in the plain of the Po and the Via Popillia (132) in the north-east; now the provinces too were involved, with the Via Egnatia (*c.* 130) from the Adriatic to the northern Aegean, the roads built (most remarkably) by M'. Aquillius in Asia Minor in 129–126 – the

111 Mann 1986, 1, 252.
112 Campbell 1984, 19.
113 See Chrissanthos 2001, 67.
114 Suetonius, *Divine Augustus* 24; Frontinus, *Stratagems* 4.1.37; Plutarch, *Antony* 39; Appian, *Illyrian War* 26; Cassius Dio 48.42, 49.27, and 38.

father of the M'. Aquillius mentioned earlier –;[115] and the Via Domitia (*c.* 120) along the coast of Provence. There had never been anything like this, not even in the empire of Persia.[116]

(3) *Organizational techniques.* Roman provincial administration in the late Republic has a poor reputation, understandably. It was a magnificent system of larceny. Roman governors and their subordinates lost almost all sense of shame in this regard (most modern accounts are too squeamish).[117] Tacitus (*Annals* 1.2) can easily be believed when he writes that the provincials were pleased that Augustus eliminated the greed of the republican officials (naturally the new administrators were not saints either, and Augustus' aim was orderly exploitation of the provinces).

The governor's main official activities, apart from repressing overt opposition to Rome, involved hearing major legal cases (Roman senators assumed that such power was vital) and making sure that taxes were paid. The art lay in balancing the competing interests of the Roman state and of individual Romans against the interests of the locals, who could expect to suffer but who might be able to activate influential Roman patrons,[118] all this while feathering one's nest but not too flamboyantly. The classic texts on this subject are Cicero's prosecution speeches against Verres and Piso, his defence speeches for Fonteius and Flaccus, and his letters from Cilicia – all these texts to be read with plentiful grains of salt. Various efforts were made from time to time to regulate what governors could and could not do (for instance by a *Lex Porcia*, best dated about 121), but central control remained elusive, partly for practical reasons, partly because the Senate was often indulgent towards the known sins of its own members such as Verres.[119]

Extortion charges such as were levelled against Verres had a complex history for the remainder of the Republic: the point here is that whether they resulted in convictions or not, they helped to keep the imperial system itself in good health. As no doubt did the (certainly not insincere) protestations of Cicero that his younger brother should rule the province 'Asia' with *comitas* – 'good manners', we might say, to be combined of course with *gravitas*, 'firmness' (*Letters to his Brother Quintus* 1.1.23; Cicero

[115] Sherk 1984, 43. Incidentally, this man helped along his military campaign by poisoning the wells of several cities (Florus, *Epitome* 1.35, disapproving).

[116] The courses of these roads can be followed in Barrington.

[117] See Badian 1983, chapters 4–5, Harris 1985, chapter 2.

[118] Even the poor fishermen on the tiny Aegean island of Gyaros hoped to gain tax-relief by appealing to a powerful Roman (Octavian): Strabo 10.485.

[119] Harris 1985, 77.

expands on this principle at length). And maintaining Roman order could be portrayed as something helpful to the provincials themselves: thus a coin-type of 71 BC (Crawford, *RRC* no. 401) showed the moneyer's grandfather M'. Aquillius (the consul of 101) helping up a personified Sicilia, which he had done by suppressing a slave revolt; Sicily, admittedly, was now treated with more respect than most other provinces.

All this larceny and extortion should not distract us from the fact that in this period, as before, Rome successfully adapted its organizational techniques to the very great challenge of ruling an expanded empire. This in spite of the fact that from the 130s, for slightly more than a century, Rome itself was often in an extreme state of internal turmoil, amounting several times to large-scale civil war. Rome succeeded in maintaining central control over its provinces partly because of methods that were traditional: readiness to use force, and alliance with local elites. Augustus undoubtedly increased efficiency by appointing 'procurators', even in the provinces he did not administer directly: they looked after his huge and growing property holdings but also served as his eyes and ears.

There were, however, two fresh developments in this period of enormous importance. The first was the extension of Roman citizenship to Rome's Italian subjects and their partial incorporation into the Roman state (see above, p. 31). This steadily increased the involvement of the previously non-Roman Italians in the affairs of the central state, at a time when their local identities as Etruscans, Samnites, and so on were weakening. A handful of such Italians may even have made it into the Senate.[120]

The other development was a new wave of colonization, most importantly under Sulla in Italy, and under Caesar and Augustus in both Italy and the provinces. Sulla's colonies in Etruria and Campania – at least eight in number[121] – consolidated Roman power, while also showing soldiers what they could expect if they supported a successful usurper.

As to whether it was Augustus who put Roman imperial power on a stronger foundation, or whether Caesar had already made major changes, there is some disagreement. Since Caesar was in overall control for only a year (45–44) prior to his assassination, his potential long-term effects are unknown. There had been a small number of 'colonies' in the provinces in earlier times, and it may be that in greatly increasing their number[122] Caesar was thinking more about the citizen beneficiaries than

[120] Harris 1971, 319–25; Wiseman 1971, 188–90.
[121] Harris 1971, 259–67.
[122] Brunt 1971, esp. 255–9.

about strengthening imperial control. But it had for some time been his policy to extend full Roman citizenship to the inhabitants of Italy north of the Po,[123] most of whom were of Gallic or Venetic descent, and as dictator he put this plan into effect; he probably also intended to make the Sicilians, who were predominantly Greek, into 'Latins' (cf. Cicero, *Letters to Atticus* 14.12).

Caesar certainly founded or planned quite a number of overseas colonies, from Spain and North Africa to Corinth, Lampsacus, and Sinope in the Greek world, at least ten and perhaps as many as twenty, comprising as many as 80,000 colonists according to Suetonius (*Divine Julius* 42). The triumvirs who ruled from 43 onwards continued this policy, as did Augustus. The latter showed a more restrictive attitude towards Roman citizenship – except in one respect.

It was an age-old Roman custom to make use of foreign mercenaries, and when they had done important fighting they had sometimes been rewarded with Roman citizenship. Some of Caesar's cavalry in Gaul had even been German (*On the Gallic War* 7.13). Non-Roman troops were heavily involved in the spasmodic civil wars between 49 and 30. Nonetheless it was a notable innovation, a new organizational technique, when Augustus began to make use of provincials in the legions themselves,[124] and regularized the provincial 'auxiliary' forces, who were now paid almost as much as the legionaries.[125] Both changes led to the spread of citizenship, since provincials could only serve in the legions if they were 'naturalized', while auxiliary troops, recruited from rugged rather than Romanized surroundings, were awarded citizenship after their discharge. By AD 14, in consequence of these changes, there had been a dramatic increase of the number of provincials, some of them not at all deeply Romanized one must suppose, who were full Roman citizens.

Romans of the political class gradually grew used to this kind of incorporation; they probably did not theorize it much in the period we are considering (it depends in part whether Pseudo-Sallust's letters to Caesar were written now or later). There were always good pragmatic reasons, and Greeks in particular could also be well connected at Rome. In non-Greek places Romans showed scant interest at the high official level in making any accommodations with local cultures. Augustus showed a little more flexibility, but only a little, permitting the Egyptians to portray him in

[123] Gelzer 1968, 94–5.
[124] Forni 1953.
[125] Speidel 1992. But see further Alston 1994.

the form of a pharaonic ruler,[126] and allowing some Celtic elements into the celebration of the cult of Rome and Augustus in the Galatian capital Ancyra (Ankara) (but Roman and Greek traditions predominated) (*OGIS* 533[127]). Such developments favoured his personal dominance.

Augustus was responsible for two other concrete innovations that solidified imperial power: a special treasury for paying golden handshakes to retiring soldiers, to be supported by new taxes;[128] and a system of 'vehicles' (not merely horses) stationed along the empire's trunk roads for sending and receiving official messages (*Res Gestae* 17.2; Suetonius, *Divine Augustus* 49).

(4) *What did Roman power over non-Romans mean in practice?* The classic late-republican texts illustrating exploitation by officials are mostly, as mentioned above, tendentious in one way or another, but no one should doubt that provincial administrators were generally ruthless, with a tendency towards violence. The best that could be said for Roman rule in this era was that, until the civil wars began in earnest in 49 BC, it usually prevented war (and it was right, so Cicero said, that the provincials should pay for this blessing, *Letters to his Brother Quintus* 1.1.34); not that protection was always perfect, and pirates were much more than a little local nuisance, especially between 74 and 67 (they effectively destroyed the important port of Delos in 69).[129]

Roman rule sometimes encouraged the resolution of disputes between local communities (the case of Contrebia in the valley of the Ebro provides an example[130]). Roman rule generally also aimed to make property more secure (see the passage of Cicero just mentioned) – in so far as this was consistent with Rome's perceived interests. The colonization under Caesar and Augustus normally meant the dispossession of local people. Under the first emperor, however, while provincial communities were more often called upon to protest their loyalty (to 'Rome and Augustus'), most of them probably saw their financial burdens decrease.

The Romans of this period, even the most cerebral ones, seem to have given little thought to anything we might call Romanization, while following practices that tended to push the process along both in Italy and in the western provinces, by insisting for example that all official

126 Herklotz 2007.
127 With Mitchell 1993, I, 109–10.
128 This was in AD 6. In reality it is not clear what the advantage of the innovation was thought to be.
129 See De Souza 1999, chapters 4–6.
130 Richardson 1983.

communications should be in Latin. The thoughtful probably took it for granted that the men of substance in such places would become more and more Roman. There was no cultural policy as such, however: when Vergil wrote of Rome's mission he summed up its peaceful aspect with the words 'pacique imponere morem' (*Aeneid* 6.852), which has nothing to do with culture or with morality (the phrase has often been misunderstood): it means 'to impose order on the pacified world'.

Vergil and the other great Latin poets of the Augustan age epitomize Rome's cultural victory in Italy and the western provinces, both European and African. In the time of Augustus much of this was still to come, but the imperial power was already busy co-opting the men of talent to hold local office, and even to ascend the Roman social hierarchy itself (see below), while so engaging writers such as Vergil, Horace, and Livy, whose grandparents must have had quite other cultural identities, in such a profound change that they were recognized as the Roman nation's best spokesmen.[131]

(5) *What was the perspective of Rome's subjects?* Armed resistance continued in most if not all regions, often for a long period after the initial conquest. We have seen that Rome managed to keep hold of peninsular Italy even during Hannibal's invasion, but more than a century later, in the so-called Social War (91–89), many Italian peoples attempted to set up an independent state based on a bitter rejection of Rome. Mithridates VI found eager helpers among Rome's subjects in both Greece and Asia Minor. 'Words cannot express', said Cicero in 66, 'how much we are hated among foreign nations because of the wanton and destructive conduct of the men we have sent to govern them', greed being the central problem (*In Favour of the Manilian Law* 65). After Baetica had been under Roman rule for well over 150 years, Augustus still had to 'pacify' it (*ILS* 103). When his stepsons Tiberius and Drusus conquered Raetia in 15 BC, they deported most of the men of military age because 'it seemed likely that they would rebel' (Cassius Dio 54.22); this was what you expected of new subjects; three years later in Pannonia Tiberius 'sold most of the men of military age into slavery, for deportation' (Cassius Dio 54.31).

There were also of course those who did well out of collaborating with Roman power, at all social levels. The extreme case was L. Cornelius Balbus, born a citizen of Gades (Cadiz): Pompey made him a Roman citizen in 72, but he later sided with Caesar and in 40 became consul – a

[131] For the spread of Romanness in southern Gaul, see especially Woolf 1998.

sign of what was to become normal 150 years later. But in every province there were less spectacular cases of accommodation to the new conditions, including at the end of the Republic and under Augustus the military recruitment mentioned above.

(6) *What successful imperialism did to the Romans themselves.* It might be said that for a prolonged period the effects of imperialism on the structure of the Roman polity were remarkably slight. In the end, however, the successes of the aristocratic leadership created two interconnected threats: popular aspirations, and super-powerful generals, with pretensions almost too great for a consensus republic. Marius, who obtained his Numidian command by means of an unprecedented tribunician law (the *Lex Manlia* of 107: Sallust, *Jugurthine War* 73), and later Sulla lighted the path. And after Pompey – who in the end gave his life to preserve the existing system – had put up the following inscription in Rome (about 61), a Caesar figure could not be far behind:

> Cn. Pompeius Magnus, conquering general, having completed a thirty-years war [an exaggeration, as no doubt is much of the rest], having routed, scattered, killed or received the surrender of 12,183,000 people, having sunk or captured 846 ships, having received the capitulation of 1,538 towns and forts, having subdued the lands from the Maeotians [i.e. the eastern shore of the Sea of Azov] to the Red Sea, faithfully fulfils his vow to Minerva (Pliny, *Natural History* 7.197).

But the spread of Roman power also led to the Hellenization of the Roman elite, which, whatever it may have amounted to in the second century, was by the time of Sulla, Pompey, and Cicero much more than a surface veneer (it was already in progress a century earlier[132]). We will consider in the next chapter what effects this had on the struggle for power within the Roman state, and there were indeed such effects. Most historians, however, reject the notion that Greek ideas seriously weakened the republican system of government, while believing that empire somehow undid the governmental system of the rulers. The conventional view is that a large empire from time to time necessitated huge military commands, which had the effect of putting strong and more or less devoted armies into the hands of men such as Sulla and Caesar who could not resist the temptation to use them to establish themselves as dictators. Empire undoubtedly had two effects of huge political significance: it necessitated the recruitment of impoverished soldiers who had little reason to support

[132] Rawson 1989.

the political status quo; and it created an enormous (by ancient standards) capital city – incomparably wealthy and grand, and also well endowed with slums – which by the 60s (indeed two generations earlier) was no longer willing to acquiesce in conservative aristocratic control. One-man rule was the logical outcome.

How had Roman ideas about Rome's external power changed in the late Republic and under Augustus? The belief that Rome now ruled the whole world, previously expressed by Polybius, was now articulated by Romans too. Our earliest evidence concerns a speech of Ti. Gracchus in 133 (Plutarch, *Tiberius Gracchus* 9), and by the 80s if not earlier the idea was commonplace; Roman coin-types in the 70s sometimes give visual expression to it by including globes among symbols of Roman power (Crawford, *RRC* nos 393, 397 [Figure 1.3]).[133] Embassies sent to Augustus by remote rulers, such as the Indian king Porus (Strabo 15.719, who describes his exotic gifts; cf. *Res Gestae* 31) and Queen Candace of Ethiopia (Strabo 17.820–1), must have encouraged this idea.

Another idea that probably developed more in the first century, though it may possibly have been expressed before 146, was that Rome had not only fought just wars but had acquired its empire justly, 'by defending its allies' (Cicero, *On the Republic* 3.35). Not that this precise view seems to have been much voiced.[134] Another, less well-known rationalization can be glimpsed in Cicero's early work *On Invention*, the only surviving text in which a republican Roman defines inter-state power: he distinguishes power (*potentia*) from security (*incolumitas*) by saying that while security is the 'established and untrammelled maintenance of well-being', power also includes 'command over suitable resources for reducing the possessions of another [sc. state]' (2.56.169).[135] It may be implied here that Rome had acquired its *potentia* in order to resist powerful enemies, and if that was Cicero's meaning, he was probably influenced – he was writing in the 80s – by recent events (the Social War and the attack of Mithridates).

Finally, Augustus, hardly more boastful in spirit than Pompey, was able in virtue of his unprecedented power to formulate actual policies: 'I undertook many civil and foreign wars by land and sea throughout the world ... When foreign peoples could safely be pardoned, I preferred to preserve rather than to exterminate them ... I extended the territory of all those provinces of the Roman people on whose borders lay peoples not

[133] Such claims have been reasonably common in other empires: S. Reynolds 2006, 155.
[134] Cf. Harris 1985, 164–5.
[135] There is a minor uncertainty in the text here.

subject to our government' (*Res Gestae* 3 and 26). The long-term implications will become visible in Chapter 4.

Conclusion

What stands out most plainly throughout this chapter is a deep devotion to merciless war, spread all across Roman society but especially strong in the social elite (the fuller significance of this point will emerge in the following chapter), together with great creativity in imposing permanent control over the peoples and lands that Rome subdued. These two factors together enabled an astonishing expansion of power. Rome's devotion to war evolved, however, in the period from the 70s BC onwards into a more normal imperial acceptance of war as a professional activity less integral to the identity of senators (though it was still of vital importance to the major leaders). To what extent this change determined the deceleration in imperial expansion that took place after AD 16 is another question for Chapter 4.

There are naturally a number of similarities here with what happened during the expansion phases of the British and Chinese empires, among others. One such similarity is a propensity for establishing zones of informal empire as well as zones of directly controlled formal empire.[136] That may lead to the question whether Rome too, as many contend was the case with nineteenth-century Britain, imposed informal control whenever possible, and formal rule only when it was necessary. But the differences in the two cases between what constituted control (economic exploitation? limiting the power of rival states?) and what constituted 'necessity' prevent the comparison from throwing much historical light.

Another similarity is that Rome, like Britain, was ruled by a more or less aristocratic oligarchy during crucial periods of expansion (from about 400 to 49 BC in the Roman case, from 1688 to 1902 in Britain), with a high degree of popular support for such expansion. The oligarchies in question were very different in structure, but there is some contrast with the failure of democratic fifth-century Athens to retain its power over a long period. Athens was only a democracy in a limited sense, and it was led into its crucial disasters by aristocrats, but in any case the contrast is not very illuminating. A close-knit governing class such as that of Rome can establish and maintain the sort of links with local elites that are useful for imperial success, but most empires have been built by strong-willed

[136] For the British case, see Ferns 1953; Robinson and Gallagher 1961; Cain and Hopkins 2001, 26–9, 243–74, 362–8.

monarchs, from Darius to Alexander to the Qing emperors of the eighteenth century.

What most distinguishes the Romans of this period is what Stanislav Andreski would have called their higher MPR, military participation ratio, that is, the proportion of the citizens who were regularly under arms.[137] This was much higher under the Roman Republic, until the enfranchisements of 90 BC, than it ever was in imperial Britain or in Qing China: the Qing emperors never seem to have maintained an army as large as that of Augustus,[138] though the population they ruled was between four and ten times as large. Similar levels are probably to be sought in two populations who much later had lethal effects on the late Roman Empire, the Germans of the early fifth century AD, and the Muslims of the seventh century.

This high level of citizen participation in warfare was linked to another distinctive aspect of Roman expansion: their constant policy of enslaving large numbers of prisoners of war, a constant over the four centuries covered in this chapter. While it is possible to debate the numbers at length, it remains obvious that Rome was only able to mobilize so many of its citizens and allies for warfare because it largely replaced their labour with that of slaves; this was never a large-scale policy in China.[139] And while slavery was an important element in British economic growth in the eighteenth century, it was not essential to the manpower needs of the growing empire's army.

[137] Pfeilschifter 2007, 28–9, applies this approach to the whole population of Roman Italy.
[138] See Perdue 2005.
[139] On slavery in China in the Warring States/Qin and Han periods respectively, see Yates 2001 and Wilbur 1943.

CHAPTER 3

The Romans against each other, from republic to monarchy

Inside an aristocratic society

Republican Rome was ruled by a patriarchal land-owning and slave-owning aristocracy. In each of its last three years, 51–49 BC, one of the consulships was held – it so happened – by a Claudius Marcellus, members of a family that had held twelve previous consulships as well as innumerable other offices since 331 BC.[1] In mid-republican times, say down to the 140s BC, political, religious, military, social, and economic power remained within the same social stratum, and even when there were fortunes outside it, they were closely linked to the old ruling families. But the consuls of 51 and 50, as they were more or less aware, held office in a political system that was on the point of exploding, as duly happened in January 49.

Rome's aristocratic government co-existed with a degree of citizen power, which is not to be confused with democracy. The legitimacy of the authorities – some of whom also had coercive powers and could provide material rewards as well – derived from established convention, that is from the *mores maiorum* ('the customs of earlier generations'). There was also a vital admixture, in limited quantities, of a kind of mass approval that has largely been forgotten by democratic modern theoreticians because it was provided by the better-off male citizens not by the population in general. (The inadequacy of Max Weber's theory of legitimacy for the Roman republican case needs no extra comment here.)[2]

In this chapter I will first describe the mid-republican evolution of this system, then how it was challenged from both inside and outside the

[1] For the ancestry of the late-republican consuls, see Badian 1990; Hölkeskamp 2010, 89.

[2] For a critique of Weber's categories, as applied to Rome, see especially Lendon 2006. Roman magistrates combined both 'legal' and 'traditional' authority, and consuls had some charismatic authority in Weber's sense (but Weber undoubtedly knew all this). I return to Weber near the end of this chapter.

aristocratic consensus during the late Republic, and finally how Augustus and others established a new hybrid system that combined monarchical power with the power of a land-owning elite somewhat different in character from the old aristocracy (though if it had not been for an accident of illness, Augustus might have been succeeded by yet another Claudius Marcellus, son of the consul of 50 BC). And we shall see how the authorities gradually came to employ new claims to legitimacy.

Foucault maintained that 'relations of power ... necessarily extend beyond the limits of the State ... first of all because the State ... is far from being able to occupy the whole field of actual power relations, and further because the State can only operate on the basis of other, already existing power relations. The State is superstructural in relation to a whole series of power networks that invest the body, sexuality, the family, kinship, knowledge, technology and so forth'.[3] The terminological reminiscence of Marx suggests that we consider what in this case is superstructural and what is basic. In the case of Rome, it seems obvious that the family is logically prior to the state (cf. Aristotle, *Nicomachean Ethics* 8.12; contrast *Politics* 1.2), in the sense that there could be no state without disciplined families. And heads of households long remained relatively powerful.[4] But it would not be illuminating to say that the state was superstructural: let us rather say that the Roman state and the Roman family worked in tandem, with *patria potestas* (the legal rights of the *pater*, the head of the family), and the myths that surrounded it, tending to foster the quality that the expanding *patria* needed most of all, namely military discipline. These myths taught, for example, that a citizen should be willing to sacrifice even the life of his own son for the sake of Rome.[5]

To measure gender relations within the Roman family accurately against those that prevailed in other pre-modern patriarchies, we would need to know much more about, among other things, women's work and domestic violence [Figure 3.1] than we can possibly know – and this applies almost as much to other periods of Roman history as to the middle Republic. Women could, however, own property, make wills, and receive legacies – in fact they probably had equal rights with their brothers in cases of intestate succession; but there were also restrictions on their private-law rights, and there can be little doubt that they generally had to marry in their mid-teens and were generally kept in informal subordination.

[3] Foucault 1980 [1977], 122.
[4] This line of thinking is interestingly developed by Linke 2006.
[5] Harris 1986.

Figure 3.1. Denarius of the moneyer L. Titurius Sabinus (89 BC), who was intent on showing the importance of the Sabines in Roman history. The reverse image shows two Roman men abducting Sabine women ('The Rape of the Sabine Women'), which at least suggests an unworried Roman male attitude towards sexual violence. Crawford, *RRC* 344/1

In any such society, women's possibilities of exercising informal power will depend on their economic rights, on their religious functions, on their legal and customary rights within marriage, and not least on what we can call their sociability (do they socialize with men and express their opinions about significant issues?). The mid-republican story is mixed. Vestal Virgins occasionally exercised some political influence, but women had no other major religious functions; Cornelia mother of the Gracchi is the only woman who gets into the pages of conventional histories and it is not clear that she really belongs there. Rich women actually lost some economic power by the *Lex Voconia* concerning testaments of 169 BC (no one was permitted to leave more than half his estate to a woman). The best that can be said is that few Roman men seem to have divorced (some did), and that women could express their opinions in front of men (cf. Polybius 10.4.7–8, 31.26.8, etc., and the evidence of Plautus).[6]

Let us continue with Foucauldian power for a while, since historians seldom ask how the power of knowledge and technology operated under the middle Republic. Certain kinds of knowledge and pseudo-knowledge

[6] The latter as analysed by Rei 1998.

conveyed a hard-to-define degree of power and were largely or partly the preserve of the social elite – literacy, equestrian skill, and religious expertise in particular. We should see these skills not exactly as the basis of power, but as integral parts of the system of the elite's dominance. If the elite ever had a near-monopoly of the use of written texts, it had in fact lost it by the fourth century BC.[7] But in that same period the cavalryman's skills became more important;[8] and the elite's control over religious expertise, though it was challenged from time to time by the arrival of new cults, continued to be firm.[9]

In certain fields, however, there was expertise outside the elite (I leave aside the vital knowledge of experts in, for example, metallurgy that were too closely involved with manual labour to be 'respectable'): hence there are interesting questions as to how effectively the social elite controlled the scribes employed by the magistrates, or the *haruspices*, Etruscan soothsayers. The scribes' operations are largely hidden from us, but with the major exception of Cn. Flavius in 304 (see below) they seldom seem to have kicked over the traces.[10] The *haruspices* were non-official experts in prophecy who had probably already enjoyed some repute at Rome when Etruria was still free; on occasion in the second century some of them even exercised a certain influence over war-making decisions,[11] but whether they were really independent is unclear.

What was basic was the possession of land. No one was paid for holding office, and in practice only substantial landowners could afford much political participation. Every male citizen was assigned to a property class,[12] which determined the extent of his political rights, to the great advantage of the well-to-do. Large landowners had dependants, small ones debts. Most of the political strife of the middle Republic, when it did not concern the technicalities of political life, revolved around debt and the acquisition of land. This theme will therefore recur.

But what about the power of ideology in mid-republican times? Nothing so systematic existed, but certain prevailing values came close to doing so. Some of these we met in the previous chapter, in particular *fides*, good faith, which supported contracts and social obligations in an era when most contracts were unwritten. That *fides* really was considered

7 Cf. Harris 1989a, 152–5.
8 McDonnell 2006, 193.
9 Beard, North, and Price 1998, 1, esp. 103–4.
10 Cf. Purcell 2001.
11 MacBain 1982, 43–59; Beard, North, and Price 1998, 1, 20, and 102.
12 See Lo Cascio 1988; Rathbone 1993.

important is demonstrated by the fact that it was the first 'virtue' to receive a temple at Rome (unless we count hope as a virtue), during the First Punic War. But the numerous other 'abstract' deities who received temples during this period reveal a whole set of ideals. These were temples vowed and built by magistrates for their own glorification as well as for the good of the Roman people. *Concordia* and *Salus* ('Security') may have been the first to be dedicated (304 and 302 BC). There followed, among others, the temples of Victory (294), *Fides*, Hope, Honour and Courage [*Virtus*], Intelligence or Prudence [*Mens*] and, in 181, Loyalty [*Pietas*]. Successful generals spent the proceeds of war on such projects, and other officials spent money raised from fines (such fines were an indication of a stronger state).[13] This was at a time when the state's other non-military expenditure was minimal. The habit of building new temples began to flag somewhat after 191, and more definitely after 173 (because national self-assurance had increased?).

Among all these abstract qualities, *virtus*, courage or manliness, undoubtedly had a special role.[14] The great heroic figures of the past, for Roman males who lived in the period of the Italian wars, were Horatius Cocles, the soldier who had protected Rome from the Etruscan invader Lars Porsenna (Polybius 6.55, etc.), together with the generals who had celebrated triumphs and the young officers who, by tradition, volunteered to undertake combat-by-champions – like David against Goliath, except that the Roman Davids were knights not shepherds.[15] The war against Hannibal produced three heroes who lived on in Roman memory: M. Claudius Marcellus (consul in 222 and in four later years) – the ancestor of the late-republican Claudii Marcelli already mentioned – Fabius Cunctator, and Scipio Africanus. The most conspicuous of these for personal courage was Marcellus, and it was he who in 222 had vowed *Virtus* her temple, together with *Honos*. *Virtus* was expected of Roman soldiers of all ranks,[16] but at the same time it was a special quality of great military leaders and a major basis of the aristocracy's claim to rule.

Libertas was also very important, though its exact role in the middle Republic is hard to define (later on, it was an ideal taken over by dynasts and emperors).[17] It marked off the boundary between the free citizen and

[13] Cf. Ziólkowski 1992, 258–61.
[14] Well analysed by McDonnell 2006.
[15] On this practice, see Oakley 1985.
[16] McDonnell 2006, 59–71.
[17] For the flexibility and importance of this concept now and in the late Republic, see Mouritsen 2001, 9–14.

the slave, a boundary that had only become entirely firm and definite when debt-bondage (*nexum*) was abolished in 313 (the probable date).[18] The headquarters of the censors, the senior senatorial officials who every five years supervised the registration of the citizens, were in the *Atrium Libertatis* (The Hall of Liberty). Some Romans, the majority in all likelihood, felt that their freedom needed defending against the men of privilege. There was a temple of *Libertas* on the Aventine hill[19] – it had been to the Aventine, according to tradition, that the Roman *plebs* had decamped in protest in 449. In equally archaic times the *plebs* had begun to elect its own officers, the 'tribunes of the people' (see below), who at some point obtained the right to propose legislation – a right which in the middle Republic they seldom if ever used on behalf of the masses. The *plebs* decamped again in about 287, this time to the Janiculum, and on this occasion the conservative leaders of the state were compelled to concede that the 'plebeians' – that is to say, the citizens not born into the patriciate – could by themselves pass laws (*plebiscita*),[20] a change which did not, however, have major repercussions for another century and a half. But the ideal of *libertas* survived: to take one example from many, when the Roman *plebeii et pauperes* (ordinary poor folk) are portrayed on stage, they harp on the fact that they are *liberi* and not at the beck-and-call of anyone (Plautus, *Poenulus* 520–523 – whether they could have been quite so loud-mouthed about it in real life is a fine point).

The *libertas* of the ordinary Roman citizen did not by nominal modern standards amount to very much.[21] Citizens could be compelled to undertake military service (but when has that not been true?), and they were forbidden to address meetings on political subjects unless invited to do so by a magistrate or by a tribune of the people. The *ius provocationis* ('right of appeal') was considered a major right, even though it merely gave protection against condemnation to death or flogging by a single magistrate.[22] Yet the ideal of the *libertas* of the citizen was by no means dead, and there were occasional rumblings of citizen discontent even in the long period of almost uncontested senatorial domination that ended in the 130s.

[18] The sources concerning the abolition are listed in Broughton 1951–2, I, 146.
[19] Supposedly founded in 246, but much is uncertain here; cf. A. Clark 2007, 59.
[20] On the problematical *Lex Hortensia* that contained this provision, cf. von Ungern-Sternberg 1986, 367–70, though he unduly diminishes its importance.
[21] See Brunt 1988, chapter 6, for a lucid statement of a more optimistic view.
[22] See Cloud 1998.

The form and nature of the polity in the middle Republic

Political, military, economic, and religious power remained mainly in the hands of the aristocracy throughout the middle Republic – though, as we shall see, the better-off citizens outside the aristocracy possessed not inconsiderable political weight, which it will be important to measure. During the 1980s and 90s a certain number of British and other scholars attempted to show that republican Rome was after all a democracy.[23] This was a perversion of the fact, well known to nineteenth-century historians such as Mommsen, that Rome was an aristocracy with certain elements of *citizen* power – something rather different. Henrik Mouritsen effectively wrote the obituary of the revisionist view.[24] Fergus Millar heavily emphasized the legislative power of the 'tribal' assembly (see below, p. 80), but this only became an instrument that citizens could use against the perceived interests of the aristocracy when ballot laws began to be passed in 139 (see below, p. 88).[25] Mouritsen showed in particular that in the middle Republic the participation of the ordinary poorer citizens in formal politics can only have been minimal. Constraints of the time and spaces employed for voting show that it is most unlikely that *at the very most* 3,000 or 4,000 men voted on any single occasion in the tribal assembly.[26] The 'democracy school' did well, on the other hand, to bring out the element of class conflict in the political struggles of the late Republic, when conditions had radically changed. And it did not fall into the trap of supposing that democracy is merely a mean of 'managing power relationships to minimize domination', a weak definition (in both senses) that allowed its American author to remain hopeful that the USA might count as a democracy.[27]

The major weakness of most accounts of Rome's polity in both mid- and late-republican times is that they take insufficient account of the military and imperial context, which included constant warfare, the gradual differentiation of Rome from every other Mediterranean state, and the spectacular enrichment of the few, among a number of other relevant factors.

23 See especially Millar 1984, 1998, 2002.

24 Mouritsen 2001. See further the lengthy rebuttal by Hölkeskamp 2010, whose own account of the political structure of the Republic seems, however, too static.

25 Millar in fact recognized that the 130s were a 'new phase' (1984, 18).

26 Cf. Mouritsen 2001, 18–25.

27 Shapiro 2003, 3. This was before *Citizens United* (*Citizens United v. Federal Election Commission*, 2010) and the permanent enthronement of plutocracy.

In the fourth century BC, state-formation had already progressed a long way, as in some other Italian city-states. Political institutions were in place. Executive officers – the 'magistrates' – were elected every year. There are major uncertainties about the development of these magistracies in the half-century prior to 367 – the era of the 'military tribunes with consular power' – but they do not much concern us here.[28] The fourth-century state extracted taxes and could mobilize the population effectively for war,[29] and private armies were almost entirely a thing of the past. The state founded colonies on land taken from other Italian peoples. Even before the Via Appia (312), its building activities, which included the 'Servian' Wall (some of which is still standing), put it on a level with all but the grandest of western-Mediterranean cities (Carthage, Syracuse) (see Map 3). On the other hand, there was little written law (and the so-called Laws of the Twelve Tables were for the most part transmitted orally), criminal justice was rudimentary, and the state had nothing to do with welfare of any kind. It had very few employees.

The aristocratic system was itself of a peculiar kind. While bloodlines were important, and the caste of patricians retained a major political privilege as late as 173 BC (the first year in which both the consuls elected were non-patricians; it was not till 131 that both censors were non-patricians), there were of course no titles of nobility. Much more importantly, a tacit consensus ensured that all public offices would be passed around among members of the leading families, with no one getting much out of line. Consuls, praetors, aediles, quaestors – the executive officers of the state – all held office for twelve months only. At some point, probably as early as a *Lex Genucia* of 342, there were accepted rules establishing in effect that an individual could only hold the consulship again after an interval of ten years.[30] The censors, normally senior ex-consuls with important functions to which we shall return, lasted for merely eighteen months. And all these officials were elected by citizen assemblies, though in a highly undemocratic fashion (to be described shortly). A so-called 'dictator', an emergency supremo appointed by the consuls, had only a six-month term. The whole elite seems to have agreed that though one man might be pre-eminent for a time, that time had to be short.

[28] The issues are well summarized by Oakley 1997–2005, I, 367–79, and IV, 502–7.

[29] As to how it did that, see Tan 2015, 211–12, with references to earlier literature.

[30] See Livy 7.42.2, 10.13.8, and Oakley 1997–2005, II, 24–6, who argues that the *Lex Genucia* is genuine, though it was quite often ignored 'in critical periods' of the fourth and third centuries.

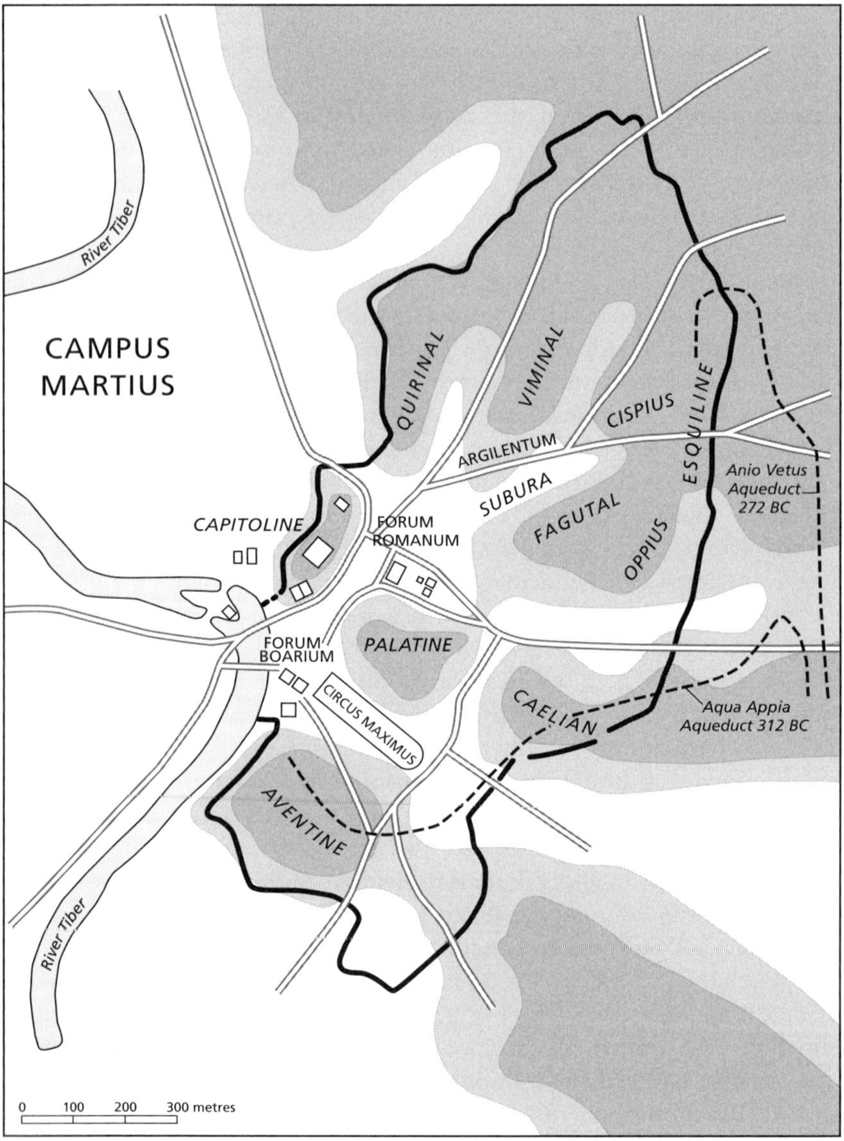

Map 3. The 'Servian' Wall of Rome

As Rome's external power grew during the fourth century BC, the patrician caste struggled unsuccessfully to go on excluding well-to-do plebeians from public office, and the leading plebeian families gradually became the other half of the aristocracy. The intriguing anomaly that, according to Roman tradition, 'plebeians' had previously dominated the chief magistracy of the state in isolated years (399, 396, and 379) should not obscure the fact that the patricians had generally been in political control, for several generations at least. A law successfully proposed by two of the tribunes of 367 (C. Licinius and L. Sextius) required one consulship each year to go to a plebeian, or at least permitted this.[31] The first plebeian 'dictator' held office in 356, the first plebeian censor in 351, the first plebeian praetor in 336. In 300 the plebeians gained access to the major religious offices. As to why and how they succeeded in doing all this, there are various theories, but two factors stand out: the patricians with sufficient resources to compete in politics diminished slowly in numbers,[32] since one could become a patrician only by birth, and secondly the rising families were by the standards of the time rich. Who then were the plebeian Sextii, Licinii, Genucii, and so on who began to hold high office in the generation after the Licinian-Sextian laws? They probably owed something to successful military service,[33] but what mainly gave them confidence and clout – and encouraged more frequent intermarriage between patricians and plebeians – was probably added wealth derived from the military expansion (especially at the expense of Veii) that was achieved in the previous generation; this wealth was quite moderate by later standards but substantial for an ancient city-state.

The young men of these leading families, both patrician and plebeian, all performed ten years of military service, though this was mostly seasonal until the Hannibalic War. Then they were free to compete for public office, attempting to rise from one rung to another, a system that was formalized in various respects between 198 and 180.

The assemblies that did the electing were to modern ways of thinking by no means democratic: the censors, consuls, and praetors were elected by the 'centuriate assembly', in which the votes were cast not by individuals but by voting-units known as centuries, with the votes of a few

[31] The supposed terms of the Licinian-Sextian Laws are deeply suspect, but it is likely enough that they concerned the magistracies as well as debt and state-owned land. For detailed discussion, see Oakley (1997–2005), I, 652–61.

[32] I am supposing that they largely practised partible inheritance.

[33] Cf. Raaflaub 1986a, 206.

men of property vastly outweighing those of the masses, who in all likelihood were unable and unaccustomed to attend in substantial numbers.[34] Another restrictive or conservative factor was that the presiding officer, a consul, was entitled to decide who was a proper candidate. Yet another was that the votes of the elderly (those aged 46 and over – remember that ancient life-expectation was short) outweighed those of the younger members. Furthermore all voting in this period was public, subject, that is, to the scrutiny of the men of power; secret balloting was introduced in the 130s. And finally, it appears that under the *Lex Hortensia* of about 287 electoral assemblies could no longer meet on market-days, the natural time for an agrarian population to go to town.[35]

Another power reserved to the centuriate assembly is sometimes supposed to be strong evidence that mid-republican Rome was democratic, namely its power to decide on war, peace, and treaties (for which see Polybius 6.14.10–11).[36] But the assembly normally accepted the Senate's lead about war-decisions with little or no demur. The only occasion when its decision was decisive – in favour, in effect, of war with Carthage – was in 264, when the senators were divided. When in 200 it voted the 'wrong' way, in favour of peace, the Senate pressured it into reversing itself (Livy 31.6–8). After 171, this secondary role shrank still further. The only occasion when the assembly is known to have rejected peace terms agreed to by a magistrate was in 241, when it insisted on imposing severer terms on defeated Carthage (Polybius 1.63).

The consuls commanded the principal armies in the field, except when these were being led by proconsuls; they presided over the Senate and the centuriate assembly, and could arrest other citizens; with the tribunes, they had a virtual monopoly of the right to preside over public meetings (*contiones*) and to propose legislation. In practice, they were in a position to lead the state into war-decisions. During their year of office they were like kings, as Polybius remarked (6.11.12). He might have mentioned that when the presiding magistrate announced the names of the new consuls, he did not mention how many 'centuries' had voted for them or the names of the other candidates: there was in appearance no opposition. As if they were kings or emperors, the consuls' years of office were named after them ('in 205 BC' was thus 'when P. Cornelius Scipio and P. Licinius

34 On the voting procedure, see Hall 1998; on the numbers who are likely to have attended, see further Mouritsen 2001, 26–32.

35 Michels 1967, 103–6.

36 On this power, see Rich 1976; Harris 1985, 263–4.

Crassus were consuls'; hence few adult Romans are likely to have known their exact age). The consuls' power was symbolized by the twelve uniformed lictors who always accompanied the senior consul, carrying *fasces* (bundles of rods), which vividly indicated to all who saw them their right to carry out punishments.

The censors and praetors also had very important powers. The censors (a pair of whom were normally elected every five years) drew up the lists of members of the Senate as well as of the citizen body, exercising their own discretion within limits. They enjoyed a wide and undefined right to interfere in what we consider private life in the face of what they personally considered to be irresponsible or luxurious. They may well in fact have used this right mainly to regulate the senators and knights,[37] and what is most striking is that the upper orders normally accepted such supervision. The censors' most important field of discretionary activity, however, was making state contracts, for such items as arms, military clothing, and public construction. As the state's revenue increased enormously in the second century this responsibility grew heavier, and in the years for which we have relatively good sources we know that many of the censors were accused of corruption, probably for good reasons.

The censors, together with the financial officials, the quaestors, must gradually, because of the complexity of their work, have created another centre of power, in the shape of an embryonic bureaucracy. We have almost no direct information about the staffs of these officials in the middle Republic, and even in the late Republic we know little. I am not concerned here with attendants but with the *scribae* and others who kept the registers, wrote the contracts and made the payments. For the late Republic we have a well-known story about the younger Cato, who, in order to serve as a quaestor (about 64 BC), nonplussed the regular staff of the treasury by actually learning about its procedures and taking charge: normally, says Plutarch, the staff would surrender none of their power to the young and inexperienced quaestors (*The Younger Cato* 16–18). *Mutatis mutandis* (the censors were more authoritative figures than the quaestors, and the affairs of the *aerarium* had been simpler in earlier times than they were in the 60s), we should suppose that powerful backroom technicians were already in existence at the time of the First Punic War if not earlier, and constantly gained strength thereafter.[38] While Republican

[37] This latter view was urged by Astin 1988.

[38] Our evidence is slight, but see A.H.M. Jones 1960 [1949], 153–7; Nicolet 1976, 91 (on the censors); P. Eich 2005, 54–66.

Rome always preferred methods of tax collection that 'placed minimal demands on the administrative capacities of the state',[39] there were important tasks that could not be shrugged off.

But we return to the elected officials. The praetors were in effect, after 367 at least, deputy consuls (their power being symbolized by six lictors). At first there was only one at a time and he commanded armies and stood in for the consuls when they were absent. Livy (6.42.11) says that from the first they had the job of giving justice; they may not really have acquired this function until the time, about 244, when a second praetorship was created (John the Lydian, *On Magistracies* 1.38),[40] but from then on for the rest of the Republic it was the praetors who presided over the increasingly sophisticated legal system. Since statute law, still based on the archaic Laws of the Twelve Tables, was thoroughly inadequate for both the civil and criminal law needs of the evolving Roman community, the praetors enjoyed wide discretion, which it would be plausible to suppose that they used not only to settle disputes but to protect the interest of the social class to which they all belonged; prior to the late Republic, however, we have virtually no details.

It is a delicate question whether the more junior senatorial-rank officials that were elected by the 'tribal assembly', namely the curule aediles and the quaestors, had to win elections that were actually somewhat more democratic. There is really no sign of it. Cicero, later, takes it for granted that a single well-motivated and influential citizen can normally decide which candidate a tribe will vote for (*On Behalf of Plancius* 48). Which strongly suggests that what made Roman elections undemocratic was not so much the procedures, though they certainly helped, as informal social control assisted by bribery and by low participation levels.

The tribunes of the people, on the other hand, elected by virtually the same body (meeting, however, as the 'Council of the *Plebs*'), occasionally showed a more independent spirit, even before the office began to reveal its potential as a vehicle for reform in the 130s; we can trace this pattern back at least as far as C. Flaminius, tribune in 232, and Q. Claudius in 218:

> Gaius Flaminius was the originator of this popular policy [of dividing Gallic and Picene land on the east side of the Appennines among Roman citizens], which we must pronounce to have been the first step in the demoralization of the Roman people... (the opinion of the conservative Polybius, 2.21.8).

[39] Tan 2011, 64.

[40] For a full discussion, see T.C. Brennan 2000. Bergk 2011 usefully discusses the much-debated development of the praetorship in the fourth and third centuries.

The powers of the tribunate – the most remarkable of Rome's public offices – offered a confident young man wide possibilities (and it was relatively easy to get elected, since there were ten slots a year). They had an ill-defined right to protect citizens from mistreatment by the 'magistrates'. They had the major right, as mentioned above, of summoning and addressing public meetings. They could in theory veto legislation, election results, and senatorial decrees, and from 287 onwards they could propose laws. In fact most mid-republican tribunes cooperated with the establishment (thus effectively depriving the ordinary citizen of the possibility of speaking in public); but they were not made senators until some unknown date generally thought to have been in the second century.[41]

A few words more about the Senate before we consider the social and economic relations that made this state machinery work. At one time the consuls of each year seem to have nominated or re-nominated every member, and it was a mysterious *Lex Ovinia* that gave the power of nomination to the censors (Festus 290 Lindsay), perhaps not long before the censorship of the equally mysterious patrician Ap. Claudius Caecus in 312–311.[42] This change gave each member of the Senate a minimum of five years, and must greatly have increased that body's *de facto* power. In the middle Republic the Senate dominated the management of foreign affairs and exercised great domestic power as well; it controlled the state's finances and often made important decisions about religion.[43] The rapidly increasing complexity of Rome's external relations clearly fortified the Senate's position from the late-fourth century onwards, and even more so when Rome came to be heavily involved with the tangled world of the Greeks; expertise was needed. The Senate always in this period had the good sense to keep its proceedings to a great extent confidential (unfortunately for us).[44] It formed a social as well as a political elite, and its members wore purple-bordered togas and distinctive shoes – which made them especially noticeable in a society that favoured austere costume, at least for the male.

The senatorial elite also occupied the major religious offices, a very elaborate grouping that reflected widely shared superstitions. Priests

[41] Kunkel and Wittmann 1995, 442.
[42] On Caecus, see the exhaustive treatment of Humm 2005 (the problem of the *Lex Ovinia*: 188–95).
[43] Beard 1990, 33 (referring to the republican period as a whole): the Senate was 'the principal, but not the only, focus of mediation between gods and men'. Within the household the *dominus* sought a similar monopoly (Cato, *On Agriculture* 143).
[44] Harris 1985, 255.

(*pontifices*), augurs, the major *flamines*, fetials,[45] *decemviri sacris faciundis* (the 'Ten Commissioners for Performing Sacred Rites'), and Vestal Virgins – a total of some fifty-seven persons in the third century BC – had functions that were essentially civic as well as religious. (At the same time, the consuls and censors had religious duties as well as secular ones). Once co-opted – and they were usually chosen young – these religious officials held office for life, and in almost all cases they could hold high political office simultaneously. Members of aristocratic families – and all the leading families took part – thus possessed the almost exclusive right to interpret the will of the gods (the *haruspices*, soothsayers, were marginal by comparison). The only religious official who was actually elected in the middle Republic was, paradoxically perhaps, the *pontifex maximus*, but it was far from being a democratic election.[46]

As for the actual power of such religious officials, the sources give the impression that what mattered was that they gave sanction to secular authorities – and that it was seldom withheld (the consuls of 162 were compelled to abdicate because of a technical religious fault in their election – actually a dire prodigy in the eyes of Roman senators; but they were both re-elected in later years).[47] There can be little doubt, however, that the performance of the elaborate rituals of the state religion, together with the custom of interpreting military successes and failures in a religious key, added incalculably to the hold that the senatorial elite exercised over the rest of the population.[48] I will return shortly to the matter of controlling non-state religion.

It was the citizen assemblies that made statute law in mid-republican Rome (though by modern standards there was little legislation, just as there was little civilian administration). The consuls or very occasionally the praetors made proposals to the conservative centuriate assembly, or alternatively the tribunes, normally acting in accord with at least part of senatorial opinion, made proposals to the 'tribal assembly'; so there was no space for radical measures, or so it seemed. It is true up to a point that 'democracy never materialized at Rome because the popular assemblies could not function as autonomous institutions'[49] – but most of the time they were not really 'popular', and such an explanation is in any case too abstract.

[45] For the precise meanings of these terms see Beard, North, and Price 1998, I, 20–30.
[46] See Lintott 1999, 184.
[47] On this affair, see Linderski 1986, 332 = 1995, 487.
[48] Cf. North 1989, 156.
[49] Cornell 1989, 401.

A Greek who analysed a political system could scarcely escape from the classic triad of constitutional forms – monarchy, aristocracy, democracy. Polybius succumbed to this type of analysis, and concocted a theory that Rome's constitution was a fair and balanced one, whatever that might mean (6.11.11). Its democratic element was a significant amount of criminal jurisdiction (6.14 – discussed below). He knew perfectly well, however, that in the main the political system was aristocratic, as he explicitly states further on (6.51.6–8, 23.14.1–2; he took this to be obvious) and implicitly demonstrates throughout his account of Rome's external expansion.

Aristocratic power was based on both competition and consensus within the senatorial order and on vertical ties with the rest of the citizens, also with the Latins and the Italian 'allies'. Rivalry for political office, best described, though in very generic terms, by Sallust (*War of Catiline* 7–12), never led anyone to undermine the system itself (well, hardly ever),[50] even when more or less discreet bribery came to have more influence after the Hannibalic War. Buying votes naturally tended to be repugnant to the aristocracy.[51] At the same time, it was vitally important that there was room for vigorous newcomers (who were often helped upwards by powerful nobles): they seldom got as far as the consulship in their first senatorial generation (Cato, in 195 BC, was an exception), but their sons found that easier. Members of well-known families were at an advantage, and such families paraded their past office-holding at funerals by dressing people up in carefully preserved wax masks.[52] Polybius says of such funerals that 'the young men are inspired [by them] to endure everything in the public interest, for the sake of achieving the glory that attends good men' (6.54.3). These funerals were also the occasions when, starting in 264, aristocratic families organized public fights between pairs of gladiators. (Polybius diplomatically passes over this detail).[53] A century later, if not before, these had become very popular and took place in the city's central place, the forum.[54] Meanwhile, starting apparently in 338 (Livy 8.13.9), the leading families had gradually stuffed the forum with life-sized statues of their more distinguished members.[55]

How the careers of individual aristocrats benefited from their relatives and friends is little known. Brothers could be important (see Livy

[50] For a somewhat different view, see Cornell 1989, 394–401.
[51] Daube 1969, 126; Gruen 1991, 255–7.
[52] Flower 1996, chapter 4.
[53] Fourth-century tomb-paintings from Paestum demonstrate, however, that the Romans cannot take the credit for inventing this form of entertainment: Pontrandolfo *et al.* 1998.
[54] The wholesale slaughter of wild animals for entertainment had begun in 186: Livy 39.22.
[55] Giuliani 2008.

40.17.8, for example), and marriage alliances too (such as the alliance between Ap. Claudius Pulcher, consul in 143, and his son-in-law Tiberius Gracchus: Plutarch, *Tiberius Gracchus* 4 and 9). But most modern accounts have underestimated the political importance of a man's personal reputation, which was to a very great extent gained or lost in war.

As to vertical social ties, the story is clear only in outline, as far as the middle Republic is concerned. How exactly did the leading families, or the members of the senatorial order more generally, seek to control their fellow-citizens, urban and rural? The matter is quite contested. Men of power all had 'friends' of lower social rank, they also had ties of hospitality and clientship (*clientela*). It is the importance of this last institution that is most debated. It would be a mistake to suppose that the entire citizen body could be controlled from above by the obligations of *clientela*.[56] Sallust, however, was alluding to a major and traditional instrument of power when he makes the new man C. Marius refer to the 'numerous client-relationships' of the nobles (*Jugurthine War* 85.4).[57] Patronage of this kind mattered in public and private life alike – yet we can scarcely measure the political influence of patronage in this period against the effects of military prestige or material largesse. And it is easy to exaggerate: Peter Garnsey, for instance, in an otherwise excellent account of patronage in this period and later, writes of the 'responsibility of private patrons for the material welfare of their clients',[58] but it would be hard to show that such a responsibility ever amounted to much. Ordinary citizens had *collegia* (in a diluted sense 'guilds') that were more or less based on occupations such as smithing, but they could apparently use them little if at all to forward their common interests, until this changed in the Republic's last decades.

With about 300 members, the Senate was by modern standards large in relation to the overall citizen body, for in the half-century prior to 140 the number of adult male citizens registered by the censors was always in the range between 258,000 and 337,000 (multiply by about four to reach the total number of members of citizen families) – fewer than 5,000 citizens per senator therefore. Outside the Senate were the other 'equestrian' families, some 1,800 in number in the third and second centuries, who still in that period performed real cavalry service.[59] These were

56 See Brunt 1988, chapter 8, but he somewhat overstated his case.
57 Mouritsen's attempt to discount this passage (2001, 96) does not convince me.
58 Garnsey 2010, 44.
59 The standard work on the *equites* in this period is Nicolet 1966.

relatively well-to-do folk whose economic and political interests, in this period, largely coincided with those of the senators. Thus it may be imagined that the tentacles of the men of property reached quite easily into the lives of most of the ordinary citizens.

These tentacles extended into popular religious activities, which were evidently felt to have important implications for the well-being of the state. The most famous incident was the repression of the worship of the Greek and Italic god Bacchus in 186 (resulting in many executions), but the suppression of religious books (213 and 181) and the expulsion of 'Chaldaeans' and Jews from Rome and Italy (139) reveal a recurrent urge on the part of the upper orders to keep contacts with the supernatural under their own control (meanwhile Cato happily recommended the use of magical spells, *On Agriculture* 160). The Ten Commissioners for Performing Sacred Rites had overall charge of imported religious practices.

How did the power of the Roman upper class play out in criminal law more generally, and in civil law? As far as civil-law proceedings are concerned, such evidence as there is suggests that the men of property will have been at an advantage[60] – no surprise. Yet the ordinary citizens had some rights, and after a certain Cn. Flavius in some sense or other made the required procedures known to them in 304 (Livy 9.46.5, etc.),[61] a greater number of them could go to court, though there were still financial barriers.[62] The interesting test of the power of law itself is rather whether it is regularly and fairly applied between litigants: praetors with specialized knowledge were a help, but expert administration came only in the last half-century of the Republic.

As for criminal law, its effectiveness in this period is highly dubious, since prosecution (not to mention investigation) depended on private persons and the law itself was rudimentary. The adequacy of the homicide laws is in particular highly debatable.[63] But there were public courts presided over by the tribunes and aediles, and in theory every citizen could participate – whereas in the late Republic the upper class, as we shall see, took the whole matter into its own hands. According to Polybius (6.14.4), the *demos* (by which he meant the citizens rather than the masses) had all power over 'honour and punishments' (in Greek it makes a nice

60 J.M. Kelly 1966.
61 See Purcell 2001, 635–7.
62 Kelly 1966, 81–4.
63 Gaughan 2010 points out that there seems to have been no law against murder as such, as distinct from family-murders and some specific forms of murder, but she engages in too much special pleading, and the issue needs revisiting (cf. Kroll 2012).

alliteration), 'by which alone', he adds in an almost Foucauldian way, 'both states and human life in general are held together'. Observe that Polybius refers to 'punishments', not 'law-courts'.

The important point to notice, however, is that there is little justification for thinking that the people ruled through the courts. In Polybius' time the *tresviri capitales* (Three Capital Commissioners), about whom we know very little, handed out punishments to ordinary people, while important persons were sued before the centuriate assembly. There is in other words precious little sign of democratic control.[64] When the magistrates deemed that large-scale repression was necessary, as in the case of the cult of Bacchus in 186 just mentioned, they used their powers of *coercitio* (summary jurisdiction), which allowed them to inflict virtually any punishment they liked on a Roman citizen, except death, and death too on a non-citizen.[65] (Some time in the 190s, however, a *Lex Porcia* had forbidden the magistrates to flog Roman citizens).[66]

Meanwhile the state made no pretence of guaranteeing the physical safety of the ordinary citizen (no one in fact entertained this notion prior to the Enlightenment), and such safety was the prerogative of the well-to-do.

What is largely missing from traditional analyses of the power-structure of mid-republican Rome is in fact structure, in the sense that they do not say how the political power that we have been considering related to economic power.[67] The first point to emphasize is that the economy of mid-republican Rome, even in its most developed form, was agrarian and military. The men of power were both landowners and, intermittently, generals. In the latter capacity they dispensed booty to their soldiers after victorious campaigns. In the former capacity they conditioned the economic lives of the smaller farmers to a certain degree even in the fourth century; then, with the influx of slaves that gathered speed from that century's last decade and continued for the next 300 plus years, Rome became the classic ancient Mediterranean slave state. Year after year, with brief hiatuses, Roman armies enslaved tens of thousands of defeated enemies. When Rome enslaved some 150,000 people from Epirus in northern Greece in 167 BC, its own official citizen numbers were only 313,000

64 See Gruen 1991, 262–5.

65 In such cases they seem to have relied on civilian volunteers, all of whom will have had military experience. See Finley 1983, 20–3; Kunkel and Wittmann 1995, 149–76. There are many problems here.

66 De Martino 1973, II, 427.

67 But see De Martino 1973, II, 299–310; Brunt 1988, 68–74.

(males of military age), but the Roman slave market absorbed the new slaves, that is to say put them to productive use, without any apparent indigestion. The bulk of this new labour force worked on the land, above all on the estates of the large senatorial and equestrian landowners.

The effects of this process on power relations within the mid-republican citizen body cannot be followed in detail, but they are plain enough in outline. Colonization in Italy had steadily reduced the political weight of the ordinary citizens, such as it was, by removing them to distances that effectively denied them political participation. Now competition from slave labour, together with bullying from powerful neighbours (Appian, *Civil Wars* 1.7.29), acted negatively on small farmers,[68] driving them off the land and into the towns and especially to Rome itself. This competition became all the more intense in the second century as large landowners showed more and more interest in efficiency (Cato's handbook on agriculture is the best-known evidence, but there is more).

A possibly unique feature of this slave-system was the way it exploited freedom: what was unusual was not that the slave-owners used the prospect of manumission as an incentive to good behaviour (balancing it against vicious punishments for bad behaviour), but that freed slaves automatically became full citizens, subject to certain limitations; by the late Republic the wealthiest ones were even a constituency worth canvassing.[69] The effect was to make the condition of slavery slightly less hopeless, and at the same time to buttress both the political and the economic domination of the well-to-do, not least because freedmen did disproportionately well in craft occupations. The importance of this practice for Rome's supply of manpower has already been remarked on.

Meanwhile Rome and some at least of the towns of Italy grew steadily more prosperous on the back of second-century imperialism: revenues flowed in; empire provided manifold business opportunities; and labour must have been cheap. By 140, however, though the senatorial elite may well have seemed more powerful than ever, an earthquake was building up.

Late-Republican discontents

The nature of the earthquake that brought the Republic to an end and left Rome once again securely in the hands of an autocratic ruler has been

[68] Sallust, *Jugurthine War* 41.8, is important confirmation of this.

[69] Quintus Cicero, *Essay on Canvassing* 29; for some background, see Brunt 1988, 339; for a different view, see Mouritsen 2011, 75.

much debated and much misunderstood. It is probably symptomatic that as acute a commentator as Michael Mann, though he absorbed many of the most important modern histories of the subject, got the matter somewhat wrong, failing to explain why Sulla, Caesar, and Octavian behaved in untraditional ways or why 'the army could not be held together by the state'.[70] And modern views of Caesar, in particular, are very often guided if not determined by the historian's recognized or unrecognized political preferences.

First, let us be clear that truly major changes really did occur between 140 BC and the reign of Tiberius (AD 14–37). The Roman Empire was larger than ever at the end of this period, and was still ruled in a partially similar fashion; most of the old institutions survived (the 'dictatorship', however, was incompatible with the new monarchy). Military forces – gradually becoming more professional – had also become the ultimate arbiters of internal power from the 80s BC onwards, and they still were under the Principate, even though, as we shall see, emperors more often than not, over many generations, managed to succeed other emperors without warfare. But the new system (1) built up a near-absolute monarchy; (2) eliminated such political power as the ordinary citizens possessed, with the important exception of local power; (3) replaced the old senatorial aristocracy with a new, more plutocratic and politically less powerful, senatorial class; and (4) set about absorbing the provincials not in sporadic cases but on a vastly ambitious scale. This last change, most analysts agree, was the principal reason why the Roman Empire lasted as long as it did.

The first sign of serious trouble that we can detect appeared in 151 BC when the tribunes, in a dispute with the consuls over the draft, actually imprisoned them.[71] It was in the 130s, however, that several different discontents came to a head. A series of three ballot laws enacted between 139 and 130 introduced secret balloting in electoral, judicial, and legislative assemblies.[72] The purpose of these laws was not democratization in any strong sense, but the Cassii Longini saw the *Lex Cassia* of 137, which one of them had proposed, as a liberation from slavery (see the coin-type Crawford, *RRC* no. 266 [Figure 3.2]) and the *Lex Papiria* of 130 may have helped C. Gracchus to get his reforming laws passed in 122. The point was rather to give an extra degree of power to those propertied and more-or-less literate citizens outside the elite who were already in the

[70] Mann 1986, 1, 256–9, at 258.
[71] Livy, *Periocha* 48; Appian, *Iberian War* 49.
[72] Harris 1989a, 167–70; Williamson 2005, 306–9.

Figure 3.2. Denarius of C. Cassius, 126 BC. The figure of *Libertas* on the reverse, holding the *pileus* or cap of liberty in her right hand, alludes to the *Lex Cassia* of 137, a ballot law successfully proposed by the moneyer's relative L. Cassius Longinus Ravilla. Crawford, *RRC* 266/1

custom of voting but could now do so with a better prospect of confidentiality [Figure 3.3].[73] It was just these citizens, one may suppose, who most favoured the *Lex Domitia* of 103, which laid down that future additions to the priestly colleges should be elected not co-opted.[74]

A quite different group of malcontents was made up of slaves. Serious rebellions occurred in Campania in 143 and 141, and in 140 or 139 the slaves in Sicily, led by a charismatic Syrian named Eunus, and in parts of southern Italy initiated an uprising that lasted until 132. This was easily the longest slave revolt of all Roman history. It did not cause the Republic to totter, but there was more to come, down to the defeat of

[73] There has been much recent discussion of these laws: see Mouritsen 2001, 76; Feig Vishnia 2008.

[74] Broughton 1986, 82–3; North 2011.

Figure 3.3. Denarius of P. Licinius Nerva, 113 or 112 BC. The reverse shows a scene of voting after the ballot laws, with voters on the 'bridge' that isolated them; the one on the left receives a ballot from an attendant, the one on the right places his in a ballot-box. Crawford, *RRC* 292/1

Spartacus' rebellion in 71 [Figure 3.4], and at the very least we can say that in the late Republic fear of slaves and of slave-revolts periodically raised the political temperature.

But it was the needs of the poorer citizens, now at last championed by reform-minded members of the senatorial order, that set the Tiber on fire. When Tiberius Gracchus (son and great-grandson of consuls) made use of the tribune's right to propose legislation in order to recover 'public land' from the rich and share it out among the citizens (133),[75] the conservative senatorial majority resorted to murder, led by the chief priest, the former consul P. Cornelius Scipio Nasica. The same fate overtook the younger Gracchus and his supporters twelve years later; this time the Senate

[75] On what had happened to this land since the Roman conquests, see especially Roselaar 2010.

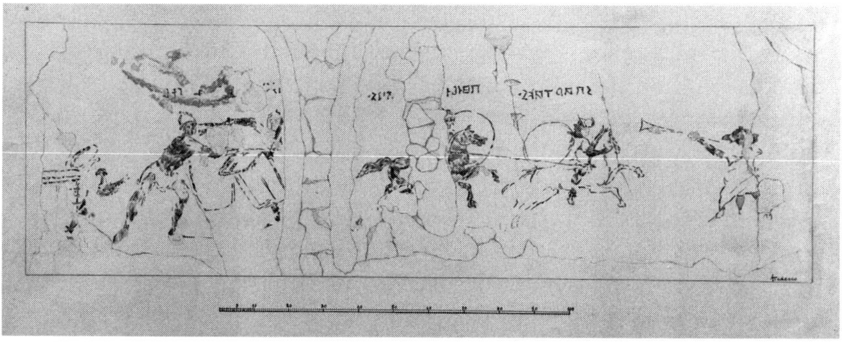

Figure 3.4. This badly preserved but unique image of the rebel Spartacus ('Spartaks', written right to left in Oscan) comes from the House of the Priest Amandus at Pompeii, a town where Spartacus must have caused great dismay among the slaveholders. The identity of 'Spartaks' is confirmed, if it needs to be, by the detail that in his final battle he was wounded in the thigh (Appian, *Civil Wars* 1.120), as here, and is not seriously weakened by Plutarch's tale (*Crassus* 11) that Spartacus killed his own horse before the fight. Discovered in the 1920s, the painting is still *in situ*, covered in plexiglass, but faded to illegibility

considered that the killing of the reformers was legalized by a decree of its own 'that the consuls should see that the state suffered no harm', the so-called 'final decree of the Senate', *senatus consultum ultimum*. Lacking a large-scale police force, the consul in question, L. Opimius, made use of unspecified soldiers and a force of mercenary Cretan archers who happened to be present (Plutarch, *Gaius Gracchus* 16).

Troublesome tribunes were then slaughtered one after another over the next two generations, Appuleius Saturninus, Livius Drusus, Sulpicius Rufus, P. Clodius Pulcher (killed six years after his tribunate) – as also was Catiline (a patrician ex-praetor). The Senate used the 'final decree' as a cover for violent repression on some seven occasions between 121 and 43.[76] On the other side, the worst anti-aristocratic violence in the city itself seems to have consisted of throwing stones at magistrates, as happened to a consul in 67,[77] and to the younger Cato as tribune in 62.[78] Rural protest could apparently be a degree more violent (see below).

[76] Finley 1983, 3–6, shows how many modern historians have more or less consciously adopted the point of view of the violent leaders of the senatorial elite.

[77] Asconius p. 58 Clark; Dio 36.39; people also broke his official *fasces*, as they did those of the consul Bibulus in 59 (Dio 38.6).

[78] Plutarch, *Cato the Younger* 28. The senatorial tradition, followed by all modern authorities, maintained that Saturninus was responsible for the death of the consular candidate C. Memmius

The discontents that the radicals gave expression to chiefly concerned land, basic subsistence – Gaius Gracchus initiated grain subsidies for the citizens –, and relief from debt.[79] Tribunes successfully proposed agrarian laws against the wishes of senatorial conservatism in 103, 100, 99, and 59. And other politicians too had to take notice: the most radical debt-relief law ever passed was in fact the work of a patrician consul (L. Valerius Flaccus in 86), and in 57 the richest and most powerful man in the state, Pompey, was given by law extraordinary powers for five years to take care of the city's grain supply. The Roman people had not by any means forgotten about *libertas* (Clodius tried to dedicate a shrine to *Libertas* on the site of Cicero's house after the latter had been driven into exile in 58[80]), but they usually had clear-cut material interests to worry about.

Meanwhile the basis of politics was changing: the new army of landless or virtually landless men created by Marius did nothing at first to subvert the constitution,[81] but when a political dispute arose between two men of power, Marius and the consul L. Cornelius Sulla in 88 (characteristically over who should have the privilege of making war against the formidable King Mithridates), each of them could use legions to fight against other Romans. For the first time, large and lasting groups formed around individual leaders, the 'Mariani' and the 'Sullani'. When Sulla succeeded in overthrowing the legitimate government by military force (83–82) and became dictator both in name and in fact, he rewarded his troops not with land overseas but with land he appropriated in Italy from people who were now (barring technicalities) Roman citizens.

Shortly before this, in 90, Rome had in principle conceded its citizenship to large numbers of the inhabitants of peninsular Italy (by a *Lex Iulia*), and combined with Sulla's colonization that gave further impetus to Romanization, both in the sense that local men of power might now have more influence at Rome and in the sense that quite a number of Etruscans and Campanians were displaced. The senatorial elite, already in possession of a network of personal ties in 'allied' Italy, adapted without great difficulty to this new political reality; the danger for them was that the tripling of the citizen body dramatically increased the number of the discontented (including the victims of Sulla's confiscations) who

(*RE* no. 5) in 100, but Memmius is himself well attested as a bitter enemy of the nobility (Sallust, *Jugurthine War* 27).

79 None of these ideas was in fact new in the Gracchan period.

80 Dio 38.17; cf. Cicero, *On his House*, 132; Mackie 1992; Arena 2013 212–14.

81 But the law that gave him his Numidian command (above, p. 64) gravely controverted traditional practice.

were now within the system. But while the upper elite co-opted a number of men from previously allied Italy during the late Republic, as indeed it had in a few cases prior to the Social War, they did not form a distinct group. To some extent they eventually favoured Caesar, and he them.[82] How much clout the formerly allied cities and the municipal bigwigs who governed them possessed in the politics of the late-republican capital is open to debate.[83]

When Sulla seized power by force of arms in 83–82, he inflicted more violent death on the Roman elite than they had ever suffered before in a short time: apart from those who died in the actual war, the 'proscriptions', which involved confiscations of property as well as executions, affected considerably more than forty senators and some 1,600 knights (Appian, *Civil Wars* 1.95.442–4); perhaps one-third of the members of the Senate died altogether. Sulla also attempted the most radically reactionary shift in power the Roman Republic had ever seen, effectively emasculating the tribunate of the people (the tribunes lost their right to propose laws, and they could never run for higher office), but also, with a much longer-term effect, handing over large areas of the criminal law to six new 'perpetual courts', one per criminal charge (one such court already existed, for 'extortion' [see above, p. 47]) in which the juries were made up exclusively of members of the social elite). There is unfortunately no fully satisfactory account of the origin of these courts or of their effects on the distribution of power, for legal historians seldom give any thought to the jurors' social class.[84]

Sulla tried in a quite systematic way to give decisive power to the Senate and the social order from which it was drawn.[85] In the short term, therefore, his innovations exacerbated existing tensions. He had killed his immediate opponents, but his programme had not convinced many of his senatorial allies, and new leaders stepped in to represent the discontented. Sulla was scarcely dead when the patrician consul of 78, M. Aemilius Lepidus – an enigmatic figure for us – attempted to undo vital parts of his handiwork. By 70, all that remained was fresh memories of violence between citizens (the *Mariani* and *Sullani* continued to exist more than a decade after both Marius and Sulla themselves were dead – see for example Plutarch, *Caesar* 6) and – also very important – the effects of forcible Sullan seizures of land.

82 Wiseman 1971, 167.
83 For a sceptical view, too sceptical I think, see Mouritsen 2001, 118–23.
84 See for the time being David 2007.
85 See among recent accounts Gotter 2008, 214–16, who draws on Hantos 1988.

It must be significant that some of the poorer citizens supported the slave rebellion led by Spartacus (73–71).[86] When Cicero associates popular politicians with slaves, that may be mere libel, but Clodius at least does seem to have achieved something in the way of organizing the common people of the capital by means of the *collegia*, the guilds (the evidence mostly comes from Cicero and is therefore poisonously hostile).[87] Clodius' very frequent use of public meetings[88] shows the closeness of his ties with the city *plebs*.

The desire of many twentieth-century scholars to exclude popular discontent from the reasons why the republican constitutional system ultimately failed led to serious distortions.[89] It is true of course – but not very important – that popular discontent seldom found leaders who were not themselves members of the senatorial elite (the former centurion C. Manlius in 63–62 being the major exception); by the late Republic the political career was very expensive,[90] quite apart from the other barriers to public office. It is also true that it was legions under arms, not civilians, who overturned the system in 49. But as all intelligent contemporaries recognized, the central political struggle, from 133 till 48, was between those who defended the aristocratic and senatorial status quo on the one side, and the ordinary citizens of Rome on the other. Cicero knew this:

> There have always [only in fact since the mid-second century] been two kinds of men in this community who have been active in politics and have striven for public distinction. One kind has wanted to be and to be considered *popularis*, the other the *optimates*: those who wished their deeds and words to be pleasing to the masses [*multitudini*] were considered *populares*, those on the other hand who aimed to have their policies approved by all the best people were considered *optimates* (*On Behalf of Sestius* 96),[91]

and on the other side so did Caesar: he marched into Italy, he says, 'to reclaim liberty for himself and for the Roman people oppressed by a faction of the few' (*On the Civil War* 1.22.5).

This was not merely a matter of a new style of conflict between members of the governing class,[92] for as we have seen the concrete interests of the ordinary citizens were involved, and we cannot deny them agency

86 Appian, *Civil Wars* 1.116 and 117, *Mithridatic War* 109.
87 See Mouritsen 2001, 58.
88 Tan 2008, 185–6.
89 See Wiseman 2002; also Flaig 2011.
90 See, for example, Cicero's account of the duties of an aedile: *II Verr.* 5.36.
91 Cf. *On the Agrarian Law* 1.22, *On Behalf of Milo* 95, *On Behalf of Plancius* 86.
92 As argued by Mouritsen 2001, 131 ('the political upheavals in this period would … seem to reflect a breakdown of elite cohesion rather than of social control').

simply because they lived inside a given culture or because their voting rights were constricted; they had others ways of expressing their feelings.[93]

What mattered most perhaps was the steady encroachment of the rich in the countryside (well-to-do people could also be among the victims),[94] where the tribunes could do nothing to help.[95] No wonder the soldiers were willing to fight for Caesar against the reactionaries. In him the poorer citizens finally found a leader who was able to win a consular election (for the year 59) and was for a long time too powerful and too astute to be assassinated. He brought down the republican system with wide popular support across much of Italy. (His inner motives are a distraction we need not be concerned with here). The years 59 and 58 (58 was the year of Clodius' tribunate) were the false dawn when popular power was briefly in the ascendant. When Clodius later ran for the praetorship, he had to be assassinated (January 52), and all his civilian supporters could do, eloquently enough, was to burn down the Senate-house.

The new army was the most important factor of all in bringing the Republic to an end. Syme wrote that the soldiers 'were ceasing to feel allegiance to the State',[96] but a more precise formulation would say that the social stratum that was called upon to serve in the legions from 107 onwards had never in fact had any strong reason to feel allegiance to the traditional way of organizing the state. Caesar, the victorious and (thanks to his military victories) vastly wealthy general, could in any case rely on both the ordinary soldiers and the officers who had fought with him in Gaul. This remains true even though Caesar ran into cash-flow problems during the Civil War, partly because he could not of course afford to allow his soldiers to plunder the property of the provincials.[97]

The aristocratic oligarchy had gone a long way over the previous seventy years to undermine the institutions that had long served it well, starting with the 'Final Decree' of the Senate in 121 and the killing of citizens without trial which the consul of that year L. Opimius carried out under its protection. They used it again in 100. Many of them supported the Sullan insurrection and dictatorship, then later the extraordinary powers given to Sulla's follower and pupil Pompey in the 60s and 50s (not that their support was anything like unanimous in either case). When Cicero as praetor in 66 told the Roman people that it was a splendid thing that a private

93 For the importance of agency in this context, see Tan 2011, 8–9.
94 Brunt 1971, 551–7.
95 Wiseman 2002, 98.
96 Syme 1939, 15; cf. Finley 1980, 119–20.
97 Cf. Chrissanthos 2001, 70.

citizen (Pompey) had raised and commanded an army (*In Favour of the Manilian Law* 61), he was playing with fire (encouraged no doubt by his ties with the provincial tax-gatherers) – and foreshadowing the language that Augustus used in the *Res Gestae* (1) to justify his own usurpation.

Pompey's whole career down to 70 had been illegal at every turn, and, though in the 60s he performed important services for the state, he remained unconvincing as a defender of the republican system of government. When Tacitus (*Histories* 2.38) said that he was 'more devious [*occultior*], but no better' (than Marius and Sulla), he was a little unfair on both counts. But Pompey's career showed that the old senatorial elite to which he belonged was not capable of maintaining any longer the old system of dividing up the political and imperial spoils.

By the 50s BC this political elite had become more sophisticated in various respects than it had been a century earlier, but it had lost its political cohesion. A possibly symptomatic change was the increasing public prominence of women, a complex process that began well before the overt political influence of certain well-born women at the end of the Republic (it is from 102 BC, for example, that we know that women too could have the elaborate aristocratic funeral[98]). There was no official role of course, but it is plain that a good deal of unofficial power was wielded by Clodia (the tribune's sister), the Porcia who was involved in the conspiracy to assassinate Caesar, and after the Ides of March by Fulvia, Octavia, and Livia.[99] There is no reason, on the other hand, to think that the lives of ordinary Roman women changed one whit.

Many of the leading men supported Caesar when, imitating Sulla, he invaded peninsular Italy in 49 BC and made himself 'dictator', or they quickly joined him (almost half the individual senators whose allegiances in the Civil War we can identify). Personal ties, opportunism, and a certain desire for strong leadership all had some influence. Caesar combined a policy of reconciliation (*clementia*) with military efficiency. The forces of the Republic retreated across the Adriatic to Thessaly and were defeated at the Battle of Pharsalus (48), which marked the end of a political system. But having prevailed in a long and bitter civil war (there was much fighting to do after Pharsalus), Caesar turned out to be mostly on the side of property-rights after all (cancellation of a year's rent was probably his most

98 Flower 1996, 122.

99 Clodia was the linear descendant of at least seven consuls; Porcia of Cato the Censor; Fulvia was the wife of Clodius and later of M. Antonius. The latter later married Octavia, Octavian's sister. We shall return later to Livia. See in general and for the time being Bauman 1992, chapters 6–8.

extreme measure).[100] Those of his supporters who pressed for truly radical measures, M. Caelius Rufus as praetor in 48 and P. Cornelius Dolabella as tribune in 47, were both firmly reined in. And his restrictions on the *collegia* (Suetonius, *Divine Iulius* 42) must have been a disappointment to his rank-and-file supporters. Caesar was now 'dictator' for an unheard-of ten-year term (April 46), then 'perpetual dictator' (early 44). Republican traditions be damned!

To conclude this late-republican section, I will add five brief vignettes to illustrate five kinds of power that need further comment: the power of the rich; the power of the Romans in the provinces; the power of the Senate and magistrates in matters of religion; the power of the written word; and the power of freed slaves. In each case there were limits, but where?

1. *The landowner.* In 49 BC, one of Caesar's opponents, L. Domitius Ahenobarbus, who had been consul five years before, enlisted as soldiers in Etruria some of his slaves, freedmen, and tenants (*coloni*) (Caesar, *On the Civil War* 1.34). A landowner could send his tenants to war – but it was an emergency, and Ahenobarbus was technically a proconsul, and Caesar's report was probably meant to be denigratory.
2. *The Roman magistrate in the provinces.* In the 50s, the young M. Iunius Brutus – the champion of liberty who afterwards helped assassinate Caesar – lent money, at usurious rates, to the city of Salamis in Cyprus, which found it impossible to pay. One of Brutus' agents obtained a 'prefecture' and some cavalry from the provincial governor, Ap. Claudius Pulcher (the other consul of 54), and besieged the town-councillors in their council house; five of them starved to death (Cicero, *Letters to Atticus* 6.1.6). Proconsuls were willing to use force to assist the financial interests of individual Romans, even if it meant the death of some local dignitaries – but Cicero disapproved (in a private letter) and refused to renew the prefect's mandate.
3. *The government and religion.* Several times in the late Republic (in 58, 53, 50, and 48 at least) magistrates acted against the practitioners of the cult of the popular Egyptian goddess Isis in the city of Rome,[101] concentrating on destroying her cult-places; attempts to control her cult continued later. But in the long run the senatorial order lacked the resources, if not

[100] But he found himself relying to some extent on men whom he must have known to be politically unreliable, such as the consul of 51 Ser. Sulpicius Rufus, who was made governor of Achaea (I am supposing that the sentiments Sulpicius expressed in Cicero, *Letters to his Friends* 4.5, were genuine).

[101] Tertullian, *Apologeticum* 6, etc. See Coarelli 1996, 112–13.

the will, to prevent the cult from spreading and even establishing itself on the Capitol.

4. *The written word.* The functioning of the Roman Empire and the Roman army depended on written documents, that is obvious, but it is a delicate question how much power the written word exercised in a world of oral communication and limited literacy. The difficulties are nicely illustrated by the fact that it is between 46 and 30 BC, not before and not again until much later, that we hear of attempts to propagandize ordinary legionary soldiers by means of written texts (*biblia*, pamphlets?), with at least some success (Dio 43.5, etc.).[102] It remains unclear whether it is an accident of the source-material that the evidence is concentrated in this period, and whether anyone expected that the majority of the soldiers in question would easily be able to read for themselves.
5. *Freed slaves.* While we cannot determine with any precision what chances a slave had of legally gaining his or her freedom, freedmen and women sometimes prospered greatly in the late Republic and under Augustus. One thinks of Chrysogonus, the favourite of Sulla, or Tiro, the favourite of Cicero, or the super-wealthy C. Caecilius Isidorus (for whom see below, p. 106). But 'in the eyes of the [freeborn] Romans a freedman could never become equal to an *ingenuus*',[103] and if he grew too rich he was subject to criticism. He could not hold office, normally not even municipal office, and his voting rights, though they existed, were limited in various ways.[104] Since the influence of freedmen on political figures was exercised in private, it is impossible to judge how much power they really exercised,[105] and it may be that such men were more likely to enrich themselves than wield political clout.[106]

One-man rule and its effects on wider power-relationships

Four years after the Battle of Pharsalus, on the Ides (15th) of March 44, republican-minded senators, many of whom had benefited from Caesar's *clementia*, assassinated the man who was now 'perpetual dictator'; but it is probably not mere hindsight to suppose that their cause was hopeless.

[102] See, briefly, Harris 1989a, 253, where inscribed sling-bullets should have been mentioned too.
[103] Mouritsen 2011, 66.
[104] Mouritsen 2011, 75–9.
[105] For some discussion, see Mouritsen 2011, 100–3.
[106] Cicero alleges that Chrysogonus was 'perhaps the most powerful young man in the country at this time' (*On Behalf of Sextus Roscius of Ameria* 6; cf. sects 138–41), a strange description in itself, but the very fact that Cicero could attack him so vigorously renders the claim suspect.

They could rally sizeable and formidable forces to oppose the successors of Caesar, M. Antonius and Octavian, at the Battle of Philippi (42), but they were decisively defeated. A recent writer has shown that Sextus Pompeius, the younger son of Pompey, also continued to be a serious threat to Octavian until his defeat at the Battle of Naulochus (off the north coast of Sicily) in 36,[107] but if Sextus ever, after Philippi, imagined that the republican political system could be restored (and there is no evidence to that effect) he would have been dreaming. Political power was now definitively in the hands of those who could command the steadfast loyalty of legions.

Octavian was eighteen when his great-uncle Caesar was murdered. The very young man's rapid rise to power in 44–43 showed extreme astuteness and determination ('his sense for realities was unerring, his ambition implacable'[108]). Quasi-monarchical power such as Caesar's could potentially be passed on by inheritance. The older man adopted the younger by testament, so that he became C. Iulius Caesar Octavianus instead of plain C. Octavius, and Caesar bequeathed him a large proportion of his vast estate. Crucially, Octavian understood from the first how to win over the veterans of the dictator's legions. In the summer of 43 a delegation of his soldiers demanded that the Senate should make him consul, contrary to all the rules, and, when the senators delayed, the centurion in command of the delegation showed the hilt of his sword and said 'This will do it if you don't' (Suetonius, *Divine Augustus* 26). Shortly after this both Antonius and Octavian took a further step towards overt monarchy by minting coins with their own portraits (Crawford, *RRC* nos. 488, 490), something which even Caesar had only done in the last months of his life (Crawford no. 480). (But the 'liberator'-assassin M. Iunius Brutus soon did the very same thing).[109]

Octavian did not hesitate to shed blood: massive proscriptions followed the formation of the Caesarian triumvirate in November 43, bringing death to an indeterminate number of senators, probably more than 200 out of some 900.[110] The aim of this triumvirate (M. Aemilius Lepidus, consul in 46, as well as Octavian and M. Antonius) was to eliminate the republican enemies who were part of their inheritance from Caesar, but after doing so at the Battle of Philippi they inevitably contended with

[107] Welch 2012. She amply demonstrates that Octavian's success was far from inevitable.

[108] Syme 1939, 113.

[109] Crawford, *RRC* nos. 506/1, 507/1, 508/3 (the famous coin-type with two daggers and a cap of liberty on the reverse).

[110] Sulla had increased the number of senators to 600, Caesar to 900.

each other. The three-man directorate had been given a legal form (43), but it was a division of spoils not a system of government.

The Battle of Actium (31), with the forces of Octavian on one side, those of M. Antonius on the other, makes it seem inevitable that the Roman Empire would be ruled by one man (it might perhaps have been divided). Each of them, during the preceding thirteen years, had practised the arts of accumulating power both in traditional ways (patronage, largesse, publicizing victories over foreign enemies) and in less traditional ones: they used pamphlets to work on each other's soldiers, as we have seen, and in 32 Octavian arranged for Italy and the western provinces to swear a personal oath of loyalty to himself (*Res Gestae* 25.2). Another innovation was Octavian's 'tribunician power',[111] which he probably took for himself in two stages in 36 and 30, an implicit – and fraudulent – claim that he was on the side of the *plebs*.

Octavian's consolidation of his monarchical power was not always smooth going, since it would have been very difficult to dispense with the old aristocracy, or so he thought. A number of its members had been on the losing side at Philippi, or were in any case reluctant to accept the new reality. There were awkward moments in 27, and even more in 23–22 and in 19. There was still opposition, or at least resentment.[112] But Augustus (to give him the name he took in 27) had two very powerful assets, and gradually acquired a third. These were, first, his victorious, amply rewarded and no doubt grateful army, which was largely settled in twenty-eight colonies in Italy, an event with vast local as well as political effects. Another asset was his own and his friends' political ingenuity. A fine example was the claim in his political testament the *Res Gestae* that he ruled in virtue of his superior *auctoritas* (prestige) (34.3);[113] a 'crafty tyrant' indeed, as Gibbon called him. The third asset was simply time: those who could remember the Republic steadily died out while Augustus lived on (Tacitus, *Annals* 1.3).

That monarchical power was now the order of the day must after the year 31 have been clear even to the most somnolent. Major decisions were in the hands of one man, and ample monarchical symbolism was on display: the regal mausoleum started in 28 [Figure 3.5], the chatter about Octavian as a new Romulus (see Dio 53.16), and in January 27 the unprecedented new name *Imperator Caesar Augustus* (roughly 'Sublime

[111] Brunt and Moore 1967, 10–13.
[112] The best account is in Syme 1939, chapter 31.
[113] See Scheid 2007b, 91. I do not find Rowe's revisionist view (Rowe 2013) persuasive.

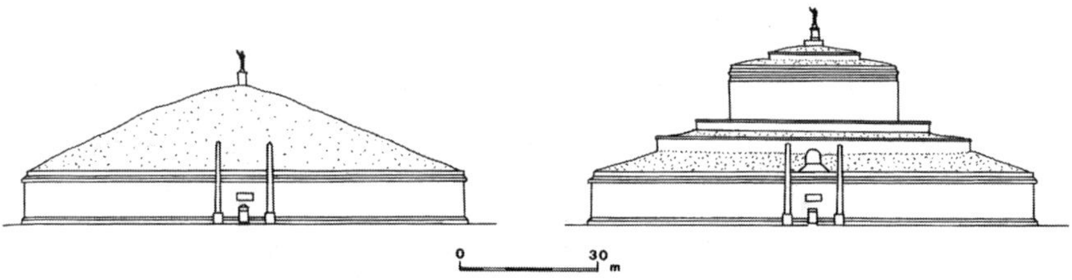

Figure 3.5. Two reconstructions of the Mausoleum of Augustus, the core of which still survives. Construction began in 28 when Octavian was not yet Augustus. The grandiose scale of the monument, contrary to republican tradition, hints plainly at how he conceived his role (but interpretation is complicated by other grandiose tombs of the period, such as Caecilia Metella's on the Via Appia)

Victor Caesar'). Various mechanisms ensured the supreme command of the legions, which were duly stationed on the frontiers and in the less docile provinces (but here there was a potential weakness, for the legions tended to love the generals who had actually led them to victory, which Augustus never did again after 24 BC). The praetorian guard, effectively established, so it seems, by 27 (Dio 53.11) and gradually increasing in number (nine cohorts by Tiberius' reign), secured the capital, assisted by the 'urban cohorts' and the *vigiles* (see further Suetonius, *Divine Augustus* 49). Augustus governed Spain, Gaul, Syria, Cilicia, Cyprus, and Egypt directly though usually without going there, and so too the provinces he created later, the 'Germanies', Raetia, Noricum, and Pannonia. He thus governed most of the provinces where legions were stationed – by AD 14 there was only one legion outside his line of command (in Africa).[114] Very soon the ruler also gave instructions, when he saw fit, that applied to the 'public' provinces.[115] It is pointless to discuss his 'legitimacy', partly because the term has been used in very varied ways, partly because Augustus, though he had a great deal of it, subverted the main institutions of the Roman state.

The *princeps* (first citizen), as he styled himself (*Res Gestae* 13, etc.), allowed the political institutions of the Republic to function, in so far as they were consistent with one-man rule. The assemblies elected the magistrates, as before: Augustus even distributed bribes to make elections seem authentic (Suetonius 40), and indeed from the praetorship downwards there was some genuine competition. Later on, Tiberius simplified matters

[114] Talbert 1984, 425.
[115] Lintott 1993, 114–16.

by effectively moving consular and praetorian elections to the Senate (Tacitus, *Annals* 1.15). Senators had of course always been men of property, but Augustus introduced a formal financial qualification (1 or 1.2 million sesterces, the sources are contradictory) as a form of political insurance. As for provincial government, ex-magistrates ruled as before, though those who commanded armies were directly responsible to Augustus. The latter appointed 'legates' to rule the provinces and legions under his direct control, while the 'proconsuls' who governed the public provinces were chosen by lot from among the eligible senior ex-magistrates.

Meanwhile Augustus lived in a less-than-regal house (though it gradually became part of an imposing complex[116]), and behaved with a certain moderation towards members of the upper class who were loyal (he sometimes slept with their wives, but his friends excused this by saying that he simply wanted to discover his enemies' secrets: Suetonius 69).

It was in any case a monarchy all right. The *princeps*, once established, seems to have minimized the number of personal enemies he put to death, but the proscriptions and civil wars, plus a purge of the Senate in 29 BC, had already eliminated most of the potential opposition. He could and did kill men off when he thought it necessary – the Fannius conspirators in 22 BC, subjected to a sham trial *in absentia*, and others four years later.[117] He purged the Senate again on at least three more occasions (*Res Gestae* 8.2 does not tell the whole story).[118] It is evident that he was also the source of all new legislation, though some of it bore the names of others. No one outside the imperial family was allowed to celebrate a triumph after 19 BC (the triumph in that year of the younger L. Cornelius Balbus, who had advanced far into the Sahara, must have been an extraordinary affair, perhaps a little too extraordinary for the *princeps*).[119]

Another mark of monarchy was the relatively overt power of a woman, Livia, the emperor's wife. It is true that some late-republican women belonging to leading families had exercised political power, Fulvia, for a time the wife of M. Antonius, being the extreme case, but with supreme power concentrated in the hands of one individual, a single strong-minded woman could be an important member of the innermost circle. Measuring her influence is impossible, even with the help of the

[116] See Gros 2009.

[117] Suetonius, *Divine Augustus* 19, states that he suppressed quite a number of conspiracies (*complures*) and gives some details.

[118] See Cooley 2009, 138–9.

[119] Balbus' triumph: Pliny, *NH* 5.36–8.

iconographic evidence, which is fairly extensive.[120] But an informed foreign ruler who wished to curry favour concentrated on the imperial family, including Livia, plus the emperor's friends and freedmen, as Herod did when he made his will (Josephus, *Jewish War* 1.646).

The great loser in all this was of course the Senate, but for most of its members the loss was an acceptable price to pay for peace and stability. They in any case retained their social role and a very large part of their role in provincial government. Senators administered the treasury and formed the committees that Augustus created to look after the capital's grain supply and its aqueducts and the public roads, among other needs.[121] This was an era of bigger government. Meanwhile knights, not senators, commanded the new military units in and near the capital, and knights, not senators, ruled Egypt on Augustus' behalf.

That supreme power was to be dynastic gradually became more obvious, but there was some awkwardness about it. Republican tradition could not complain that Augustus employed his family-members to form political alliances, but openly designating a political heir was another matter. He had only one legitimate biological child, Iulia, and apparently no urge to create any more. The first potential successor, his nephew and son-in-law Marcellus, died in 23 before he reached the age of twenty. The role of son-in-law went next to Agrippa, the real victor at the Battles of Naulochus and Actium, but he was about the same age as Augustus and died in the year 12 BC. It was to Agrippa's two sons by Augustus' daughter, C. and L. Caesar, that the *princeps* turned next, adopting them as his sons (already in 17) and piling up their honours. They seem to have been included in the loyalty oaths which Augustus extracted from a number of provincial cities in the period 5 to 2 BC.[122] But these heirs too died young, in AD 4 and 2 respectively, which left Augustus' stepson Tiberius as his only close and competent male relative. From 6 BC to AD 2 the latter was in semi-voluntary exile in Rhodes, but then he had to be recalled and marked out as the future ruler; by AD 13 his nominal powers equalled those of Augustus.

The reader may wonder what happened to the seething discontent of the late-republican *plebs*. Augustus worked hard and quite successfully to disarm it. While feeding and entertaining large parts of the population of the capital, he arranged for *vicomagistri* to operate in the newly organized city-wards (7 BC), where they made dedications to 'The Spirit [*genius*] of

120 Bartman 1999. For a detailed discussion of Livia's role, see Barrett 2002, chapter 7.

121 See Crook 1996, 124.

122 Cf. Le Gall 1990, 166–7, and *AÉ* 1988 no. 723.

Augustus';[123] in the towns of Italy, meanwhile, 'Augustales' looked after honouring the supreme leader's name. One thing that distinguishes the *Res Gestae Divi Augusti* from the so-called *Res Gestae Divi Saporis* is that Augustus, unlike the king of the Persians, at least claims to have performed benefactions for his own people.[124] And the official story was that all the citizens of Rome joined in honouring him: in 2 BC 'the Senate, the equestrian order and the entire Roman people gave me the title of Father of the Country' (*Res Gestae* 35). But following this statement, an appendix of the *Res Gestae* lists his immense public benefactions – the near-divine ruler also needed to pay.

The violence of Augustus' rise to power was matched by ideological excess. It is perhaps meaningless to speak of consensus when freedom has been removed, but Augustus did his utmost to persuade his subjects that his rule was both glorious and beneficent. This process was already far along by 29:

> [The Senate] ratified by oath all his acts on the very first day of January... they further determined that he should be included in their hymns equally with those of the gods ...; that he should wear the triumphal crown at all the festivals; that the senators who had participated in the victory should take part in the triumphal procession ...; that the day on which he entered the city should be honoured with sacrifices by the whole population and be held sacred for ever; and that he might choose priests beyond the regular number ... as many as he should wish ... (Dio 51.20).

Fortune bestowed on him the two finest poets who ever wrote in Latin, Horace, and Vergil, and the latter's work in particular had relatively wide diffusion by pre-print standards. Both did their best, though not without the occasional note of ambiguity, to raise the new ruler above the normal run of mortal magistrates. Since 42 Octavian had been able to call himself *divi filius* [son of a god], Caesar having been declared one of the gods of the Roman state, and already in the *Eclogues* (1.6–7) Vergil named him a god himself (while also presenting in the poem as a whole a far from serene background).

Augustus and his agents steadily built up his religious status, using different strategies in different contexts, on such a scale that we can almost speak of 'the restructuring of the religious system around the person of the emperor'.[125] In the capital, he was not formally deified till after his

[123] Lo Cascio 2007.

[124] For the *Res Gestae Divi Saporis*, see below, p. 113.

[125] Beard, North, and Price 1998, 1, 196; this is all right as long as we remember that there was a lot of religion in the Roman Empire that was outside the official system.

death (Dio 51.20 comments on the difference between the centre and the provinces), but while he was still alive his *genius* (divine spirit) was the object of cult;[126] in the provinces his cult was normally joined with that of Rome (Suetonius 52, confirmed by inscriptions). In other words, he and his agents let it be known that he was to be treated as a being of superhuman status. Scholars like to say that there was no single thing we can call the 'imperial cult', but it would be naïve to suppose that the important aspects of the matter were not carefully regulated from the centre. And his religious reach was long: as far as he could, he suppressed prophetic writings (Suetonius 31). Yet it is difficult to know how much any of this added to Augustus' authority. Like the monumentalizing of parts of the capital, the main effect may have been to demonstrate to the political class that the regime was strong and stable. How the provincials reacted privately is, as noted earlier, quite unclear.

Another ideological excess was Augustus' claim to be the champion of old-fashioned morality, and again it is an intriguing question whether it in fact helped him to consolidate his power (a Roman tyrant who died in his bed, like Augustus, must be assumed to have had excellent political judgement). The main events in question date from 18 and 17 BC: laws criminalizing adultery and penalizing the unmarried were followed by Horace's paean, written for the Secular Games: 'now trust and peace and honour and old-fashioned modesty and neglected manliness [*virtus*] dare to return' (*Carmen Saeculare* 57–9). This was obviously a complete sham, but sung with proper solemnity it necessarily had some effect – on the more impressionable minds in the capital.

Charismatic power, economic power

Should the *princeps*, now or in later centuries, be considered a charismatic Weberian leader? So it has sometimes been claimed by well-informed scholars.[127] The concept is widely considered by historians and sociologists to be too vague to explain anything, but it can reasonably be applied to Augustus, since he not only claimed superhuman status but operated to a great extent outside the pre-existing institutions (his successors, on the other hand, so it will be argued in Chapter 5, were caught in a dangerous dilemma – essentially whether to govern or to rule).

[126] For the altar of his *numen* (divine will) set up in Rome during the last decade of his life, see Palombi 1996.

[127] Most recently by Phang 2008, 22–4, and Sommer 2010, 134–6.

If we define charismatic power as something that an individual or a group may obtain outside an institutional context, we will not look to Sulla, Pompey, or even Caesar, but to real outsiders, to the great slave rebels Eunus and Spartacus, and possibly to Sertorius (even though the latter had held public office: after his praetorship in 83, he rallied the anti-Sullan opposition in Spain; Plutarch considered him important enough to merit a biography). All three stood up to the military power of the Roman state with remarkable success, and one wants to know how they succeeded in winning ascendancy over, and maintaining discipline among, such heterogeneous followers. Eunus and Sertorius exploited supernatural connections (Eunus was a wonder-worker who claimed to be in touch with the gods: Diodorus the Sicilian 34/5.2.6–7 and 14; so too the later slave-leader Athenion in Sicily, 104–101 BC; on Sertorius, see Gellius, *Attic Nights* 15.22). And presumably Spartacus offered something more than an escape from slavery, since as we have seen he had free followers as well as slaves.

A discussion of slavery leads to the matter of economic power. How did it evolve in the late Republic and under Augustus? The question can best be answered if we consider the changing composition of social classes, and the dynamics that operated between capital and labour. (Gender and the divide between Italians and provincials complicate the story). For the great majority of people in Italy, slave and free, the system changed very little, even when Roman citizenship spread all over the peninsula (a process completed by Caesar in 49). The return of domestic peace in 36 BC after some fifty-five years of spasmodic but agonizing internal warfare and displacement made no structural difference. The treatment of slaves was probably as brutal as ever (occasionally they could get their own back: see Philodemus, *On Anger* 5[128]). Big property was if anything more secure (there were no more actual or threatened agrarian laws). The rich upper-class grew much more variegated, however, as individuals accumulated new fortunes, often benefiting from imperial power; and the super-wealthy freedman now emerges – such, to take an extreme case, was C. Caecilius Isidorus, a contemporary of Augustus who may well have been the wealthiest person in the Roman Empire of his time, apart from the *princeps* himself (see Pliny, *Natural History* 33.135[129]). And it was the wealth of the emperor that was the main new factor: inheritance, booty, confiscations, and exactions of one kind or another provided him with

[128] Translated in Harris 2002, 322.
[129] With Brunt 1975a, 625–6.

a vast patrimony and a vast network of dependants spread across virtually all the provinces.[130] He stated in his will (AD 13) that in the previous twenty years he had received 1.4 billion sesterces in the wills of friends, but that he had spent most of it 'on the state' (Suetonius, *Divine Augustus* 101). This economic power permitted the largesse we have mentioned before, some of which even did some good.

The main beneficiaries of the Augustan regime, outside his immediate circle, were the provincials (cf. Tacitus, *Annals* 1.2 end). The late Republic had permitted extremes of exploitation: it was characteristic of the Senate that even though it had got wind of Verres' rapacity as governor of Sicily, it extended his term of office.[131] Some of the provincials were rewarded by Octavian/Augustus for their service in the civil wars, which clearly brought home their potential as soldiers; the distinction between provincial and Italian was also getting blurred as a result of Italian emigration. The *princeps*, unlike republican governors, had an obvious long-term interest in the provincials' prosperity; and we shall see in the next two chapters how Roman attitudes towards the provinces, as well as the provinces themselves, progressively changed, and that to a certain modest extent the rapacity of Roman officials was curtailed.

Did women gain or lose power in late-republican and Augustan times? We have already said something about the upper class. Cicero complained in 63 that lawyers had found ways around the traditional institution of *tutela mulierum* (*On Behalf of Murena* 27), which limited women's freedom in financial affairs, and it certainly looks as if there is some truth in this, at least as far as the upper orders are concerned.[132] Yet Augustus apparently thought that by offering women exemption from *tutela* if they reared three children (Gaius, *Institutes* 1.145, 194), he would persuade a significant number of them to do so; therefore *tutela* must have been a burden (perhaps Augustan judges had made it more so, perhaps *tutela* was more of a nuisance to the middle classes than it was to the rich or to the poor). But outside the imperial court itself little if anything seems to have changed.

Internal power, External power

Monarchy eliminated republican government, and the new authorities added to their claims to authority both sacredness (Sulla, Caesar,

130 Maiuro 2012 concentrates on Italy. For the provinces, see briefly Rathbone 1996, 315.

131 Harris 1985, 77. This admittedly may be further evidence that Cicero's allegations against Verres were exaggerated.

132 Cf. Dixon 2001, 78.

Augustus – a crescendo) and personal qualities (the Senate and People of Rome dedicated a golden shield to Augustus in the Senate-house 'because of my manly courage, *clementia*, justice and piety', *Res Gestae* 34: such imperial virtues had a long history awaiting them). What caused this change? The most popular explanation is essentially structural. It states that the growth of the empire led to military commands of unprecedented size, Sulla and later Pompey against Mithridates, Caesar in Gaul. The needs of empire also led Marius and his successors to recruit from the poorest classes, thereby hastening the professionalization of the military but also creating legions that looked to their individual commanders for economic security. These commanders could afford to pay their soldiers even when the treasury at Rome was not available (Sulla, Caesar briefly, Octavian for a while, Antonius). The state lacked effective protection against internal enemies, and eventually almost everyone concluded that, in Tacitus' words, 'it was in the interest of peace that all power [*potentia*] should be bestowed on one man' (*Histories* 1.1).

This view is largely convincing, but it simplifies and distorts the matter of agency. In the first place, the revolutionary soldiers came from a class that had much to complain about, and they had much to gain from redistributions of property. Not that one should simplify their behaviour – or that of aristocrats. Not only Sulla and Caesar, but their upper-class followers too, were apparently happy to subvert the old system. Two other factors were new, in addition to the stirrings of the dissatisfied: the perceived diminution of outside risks, especially after the destruction of Carthage in 146 (this theory was dear to Sallust), and Hellenism.

Many ancient theorists believed that decisive victory over foreign states had a corrupting effect on the victors,[133] and Sallust (*Jugurthine War* 41) among others applied the theory to Roman politics: 'the habit of parties and factions, with all their attendant evils' originated, he argued, with the final victory over Carthage.[134] Modern historians have understandably reacted against the moralistic and exaggerated aspects of this diagnosis.[135] And as we have seen, Rome sometimes had serious enemies after 146. It remains plausible, however, that the conscious or unconscious awareness of Rome's Mediterranean-wide dominance opened the way for the first-century escalation of civil war.

[133] Harris 1985, 127.

[134] See also *Histories* 1.12 Maurenbrecher, with McGushin 1992, 78–9, who lists later Romans who accepted versions of Sallust's theories.

[135] See, however, von Ungern-Sternberg 1982.

Modern historians have perhaps also underestimated the effects of Hellenism, which is indeed hard to evaluate – but the fact is that the leading men of the late Republic included in their Greek education a good working knowledge of the arguments that Greek philosophers had used for and against every possible form of government. When the common people began to cause trouble, these men knew how to justify a violent reaction: one symptom is Cicero's speech *On Behalf of Milo*, another is the passage in his work *On the Laws* (3.33–9) in which, blending Greek theory with Roman class-consciousness, he justifies the past domination of the aristocracy and advocates that the people should be satisfied with 'the appearance of liberty'. There were those who preferred to die for the anti-democratic cause rather than compromise (*ibid.* 34). Meanwhile the Epicureans had 'conquered the whole of Italy' (Cicero, *Tusculan Disputations* 4.7), and though Epicureanism in Italy did not necessarily entail political indifference, as in theory it should have done, it certainly encouraged it.[136] At the same time the expensive new Greek education served to deepen the divide between the social elite and the masses.[137]

AD 14 showed that the Senate (which Augustus had repeatedly purged) did not have the will to contest monarchical power. The tyrant, being old and sensible, had made it crystal-clear the previous year who should be his successor, by having *imperium* equal to his own bestowed on his adoptive son Tiberius. And the Senate had no legions (Tiberius promptly wrote to them all [Dio 57.2], showing who was in charge). Augustus' other adoptive son, Agrippa Postumus, was quickly assassinated. What the new ruler feared was his own assassination or a military uprising, neither in fact very likely – but better safe than sorry. The dangerous men seemed to be the surviving aristocrats, and this meant that a rash of treason-trials was virtually inevitable. It was thus Tiberius who 'broke the back of the Roman aristocracy'.[138] As we shall see in Chapter 5, the regime was becoming steadily more regal. Meanwhile the army was a source of anxiety, and this had a profound effect on Rome's relations with the outside world.

How finally should we summarize the mutual effects of Rome's internal and external power relations? Let us start with the effects of internal

[136] For the Epicureans in late-republican Italy, see Sedley 2009.

[137] Latin education too was getting more demanding, and hence had a similar effect; spelling now mattered more – Augustus reportedly dismissed a high official for a mistake, though he was a careless speller himself (Suetonius, *Divine Augustus* 88).

[138] Yavetz 1996, 121.

power relations on the state's external relations. The position of Rome's aristocracy was not precarious in the fourth or third centuries BC, but it was to some extent contested. Its leaders contended with each other for military prestige but also attempted to satisfy both their own ambitions and the needs of the mass of the population by fighting constantly against neighbouring states. Agricultural and workshop slavery made it possible to meet the ever-increasing need for military manpower. When Rome's internal politics became more sharply contested, reaching a crescendo in the period 63 to 31, this had in a sense surprisingly little effect on the state's ability to maintain and indeed greatly increase its external power, partly because powerful enemies were by now few and remote, partly because expansionist and exploitative imperial policies served the interests of everyone at Rome who counted. Attitudes towards warfare – warfare between citizens as well as foreign conflicts – were changing, but for a long time this had little effect on external relations. Imperial revenues were quite sufficient in the late Republic, and even under Augustus, to maintain the military forces that were needed for immediate purposes.

The new dictatorship had complex effects on Rome's external relations. The regime engaged in constant external wars, with a significant pause in the last years of Augustus' life. But it was less and less obvious that the interests of the *princeps* were served by aggression, and while many members of the senatorial order still undertook military service, and benefited from doing so, there was less and less to be gained in that way. For senators and indeed for most of the rest of the population, it made more sense to exploit the opportunities that the existing empire already provided. Meanwhile the provincials themselves gained in influence and were exploited somewhat less.

What about the reverse effects, those of Rome's external relations on its internal power structures? This chapter and the previous one have supplied something of the answer: simplifying, but not excessively, we might say that for a long time foreign conquest and imperial success promoted political and social stability but in the end undermined them. The remarkable political stability of the Roman state, lasting arguably from the 360s BC to the 80s, was due in part to the fact that all kinds of Romans could expect to satisfy their various ambitions, and their proclivity to violence, in the external world. In so far as there was a Roman theory that explained why this happy state of affairs came to an end, it claimed that what had kept the Romans in order was their fear of Carthage, a fear that must have declined after the defeat of Hannibal in 202 and finally evaporated after 146 – the idea being, obviously, that as long as they had frightening foreign enemies they would not risk tearing their own polity apart.[139] Late-republican conservatives also tended to blame the ambition of the *popularis* tribunes, while others blamed the aristocratic warlords and in particular Sulla. The notion that Rome's no longer having fear-inspiring enemies led to unrestrained quarrelling among the Romans themselves makes excellent sense, but it needs to be supplemented by reference to the other effects of successful imperialism, the economic and cultural effects in particular, that we have already noted. And, as has often been remarked, the continuing foreign wars of the late Republic necessitated the creation of both super-commands for the likes of Pompey and Caesar and of a partly new kind of army that was prepared, in certain conditions, to fight against other Romans.

Did external events also contribute to the political stability that appeared to return with the victory of Octavian/Augustus in 31 BC? The new ruler certainly made much of the supposed fact that he had defeated a dangerous foreign enemy, Cleopatra (Dio 51.19, etc.). Modern historians tend to assume that contemporaries saw through this story as readily as we do, but Augustus' supporters came near to monopolizing public means of communication, and some part of the acquiescence that he managed to engineer presumably depended on his being perceived as the man who restored the integrity of the vital eastern part of Rome's empire.[140]

[139] Above, p. 108. This theory had Greek antecedents (Harris 1985, 127), but that does not make it fallacious.

[140] Not many will have agreed with M. Brutus' belief that it was better to surrender the empire than submit to one-man rule (for which, see Quintilian, *Institutio* 9.3.95).

CHAPTER 4

The Romans against outsiders, AD *16 to 337*

'Everything worthy of you, most invincible rulers, is yours, and for this reason it is permitted to you to look after the interests of individual areas equally, since you hold them all' (Anon., *Panegyrici Latini* 8.20, AD 297 or 298).

Expansion slows and ceases

Who is inside, who is outside? The Romans may seem confused to us because they often said that the whole world was under Roman control[1] even though the governing class knew that this was false, and indeed often indicated, at least down to a certain date, that plentiful outsiders were still there to be conquered – thus Tacitus, writing in the 110s, criticizes Tiberius for being 'uninterested in expanding the empire' (*Annals* 4.32 end), with a fairly clear allusion to his own times. Meanwhile for a long period Roman writers frequently referred to provincial populations as *exterae gentes*, external peoples.[2] The confusion was probably intensified by the fact that, as before, Rome counted the 'client kings', who were a standard part of their periphery, as being part of the empire.[3] And it was quite common in this era for Roman troops to be stationed outside the provinces.[4] This still happened on the northern frontier under the 'tetrarchs' (Diocletian and his three fellow-emperors) and Constantine.[5]

Furthermore, many of those who lived inside the Roman Empire were still in the era of Tiberius (14–37), and long afterwards, outsiders in several senses: they were not Roman citizens and they were neither Romanized

[1] Brunt 1990, 433–4; the practice continued in the fourth century: Ando 2000, 333–4.

[2] Richardson 2008, 188; the latest author he refers to for this practice is Suetonius. It is thus scarcely surprising that Suetonius referred to the suppression of the Illyrian revolt of AD 6 as an 'external' war (*Tiberius* 16).

[3] Richardson 1991; cf. Harris 1985, 105, 135–6.

[4] Cf. Isaac 1992, 398–9. An extreme case, from near Baku: AÉ 1951 no. 263 (under Domitian).

[5] Elton 2012, 342.

nor Hellenized. Nonetheless they were more or less willingly Rome's subjects, and in AD 212, after a long period of gradual and partial cooption,[6] virtually all of the remaining non-citizens except the slaves were incorporated into the citizen body. From time to time various subject peoples had rebelled, without success, and meanwhile a wider, informal, process of incorporation continued. Whether that produced a real Roman nation is a question that will be addressed in the chapter that follows after this one. Here we shall be concerned with those Romans who interacted with the outside world on behalf of the state – the emperor, the elite, the military – and what they knew, what they desired, what they did; and we shall of course be concerned with the outsiders themselves.

'The outsiders themselves': throughout this chapter we shall be the prisoners of Roman sources, and that is a great stumbling block. No lengthy text conveys the unmediated perceptions of the Parthians or the Sasanians, still less of the Roman Empire's other neighbours. We occasionally know about factual divergences: King Shapur I's famous trilingual inscription of about 270 naturally puts the military performance of Roman emperors, Philip the Arab for example, in a more negative light than they did themselves.[7] But what we need are wider perceptions of Roman strength and weakness. One might, for instance, guess that outsiders distinguished less than we do between Roman state power and the traders who flourished under its wings, but that is only a guess.

My initial questions, in any case, will be about the ideology of conquest and what became of it, and about the financial constraints on expansion. Then we will come to the interests of the emperor, the elite, and the military, and the enemies and potential enemies. All this changed as one generation gave birth to another. Then we shall consider what the Romans knew, the violence and the diplomacy they directed towards outsiders, and some of their characteristic ways of behaving. And how did all this set of relationships with the outside world affect the Roman Empire's internal power relationships?

In AD 337 the Roman Empire was considerably larger than it had been in the year 16, and almost as large as it had ever been. Our task is to explain this growth and this extraordinary stability, and more particularly why

[6] New research by R.R.R. Smith 2012 and by Myles Lavan (forthcoming), based on wholly different approaches, strongly suggests that on the eve of Caracalla's edict a hefty majority of the provincials were still not Roman citizens.

[7] *Res Gestae Divi Saporis* ed. Huyse, for example, sects. 8.3 and 9.3. For the accompanying relief, see Ball 2000, 120. Whether Shapur and the Romans differed as to how Gordian III met his end, as is often supposed, remains unclear (Huyse 1999, 47–50).

expansion slowed and ceased, and why the Romans, after having failed to defend themselves adequately for several decades in the third century, were largely able to recover, territorially at least, in the era of Diocletian and Constantine.

To prepare the way, here is a summary chronological account of the relevant military and political events. The turning points, in so far as they can be isolated, occurred under Hadrian (117–38), at the death of Philip the Arab (244–9), and, more arguably, under Aurelian (270–5). (Map 4 shows the main locations mentioned in this chapter).

Starting with Tiberius, imperial expansion decelerated quite dramatically. Roman power did spread to new areas in the subsequent two centuries, but this expansion was by earlier standards slow and limping. The crucial change came in the year 16: at the end of his adopted son Germanicus' season of campaigning in Germany, Tiberius sent him 'numerous letters' (Tacitus, *Annals* 2.26) instructing him to return home to celebrate a triumph, which was taken to mean that the war between the Rhine and the Elbe had been completed (*Annals* 2.41). It was never seriously resumed. That did not in the least mean that Tiberius was reluctant to annex new provinces when it was advantageous to do so: the death of the vassal king of Cappadocia in 17 led to the annexation of this substantial territory, and Commagene to the immediate east was provincialized in the following year. The taxes paid by the Cappadocians allowed Tiberius to halve the one per cent tax on auctions. What he was opposed to was major wars of conquest. In practice, his successor Caligula was too, though it was probably he who recruited two new legions (XV Primigenia and XXII Primigenia), with the half-hearted idea of conquering Britain. Claudius (41–54) began by easily annexing Mauretania, a vassal kingdom whose ruler Ptolemy son of Juba had recently been murdered by Caligula (who happened to be Juba's cousin – they were both grandsons of M. Antonius). Claudius then succumbed to the temptation to invade Britain, after a generation of only minor military activity: he sent four legions there in 43, soon following on their heels. The first phase (43–9) established control over most of the south and the east (roughly from the River Severn to the Humber), but later attempts, under the Flavians and their successors, to advance the frontier further were never completely successful.

The other tempting regions were mainly beyond the Euphrates and beyond the lower Danube. Rome eventually abandoned Augustus' policy of avoiding war with Parthia, and between 55 and 63 conquered and reconquered Armenia. Conquest of Parthia itself still lay beyond the practical possibilities. There were other projects too at this time, for example in 'Ethiopia' – actually the Sudan – under Nero (Pliny, *NH* 6.181, Dio 63.8.1–2), but they were never quite considered worthwhile.

Domitian (81–96) presented himself to his subjects as a great general,[8] but most of our sources loathed him and belittled his achievements. He in fact seems to have created a new and stronger Roman position in south-west Germany. What is in question is the establishment of some sort of 'fixed' frontier.[9] The only evidence for such a thing in Domitian's time concerns areas of Germany (the Taunus hills and the Agri Decumates in the south-west) where Roman forts begin to appear in territory which could not be controlled without them, but we have scant reason to think that they represented a strategic change (the only relevant text we have, Frontinus, *Stratagems* 1.3.10, is enigmatic). In Dacia meanwhile, where Domitian's army fought periodically from about 86 to 92, his achievement is difficult to measure. His forces probably weakened local resistance, so that when Trajan invaded later (101–2 and 105–6) the fight was fairly one-sided, and by the end of 106 Trajan could send the head of the Decebalus, the king of Dacia, to be exhibited in the capital. This war is famously represented on Trajan's Column in Rome [Figure 4.1] and on the Adamklissi monument in Romania. Dacia became a province, and Rome may also in the next few years have gained temporary control over the kingdom of the Roxolani further to the east.

Dacian gold solved Trajan's financial problems, but he was by no means satisfied. He aspired to the largest expansion of Roman power in the Middle East since the days of Pompey. The death of the Nabataean king Rabbel II led in 106 to the annexation of his realm as the Roman province of Arabia, and by 111 Rome was building a highway from Bostra, Rabbel's capital, down to the Red Sea. The strategic significance of this road is unclear,[10] but it made it much easier to move troops and supplies from Egypt up to the Syrian frontier. In 114, Trajan began his attack on the Parthians, and at first it was a rapid success: he deposed the king of Armenia during the first season and made the kingdom a province, then in the following two seasons moved down the Euphrates all the way to the Persian Gulf, creating two more provinces, 'Mesopotamia' and 'Assyria' (southern Mesopotamia apparently). A friendly king was placed on the

[8] Griffin 2000, 63.
[9] See Thorne 2007, 231.
[10] Isaac 1992, 121.

Map 4. The Roman world AD 96–284

30°E
40°E
50°E
60°E
50°N
40°N
30°N
SARMATIA
Olbia
BASTARNAE
Uspe
REGNUM BOSPORI
Sarmizegethusa
CIA
ROXOLANI
ALBANIA
IBERIA
Danube
Durostorum
Adamklissi
Abrittus
MOESIA INFERIOR
Nicopolis ad Istrum
Abonuteichos
THRACIA
BITHYNIA ET PONTUS
SANNOI
DONIA
Nicomedia
GALATIA
Ancyra
CAPPADOCIA
ARMENIA
MEDIA
Pergamum
ASIA
Tyana
COMMAGENE
Sardis
Smyrna
LYCAONIA
Samosata
OSRHOENE
Carrhae
Tigris
Athens
ACHAEA
Ephesus
Aphrodisias
Lystra
Tarsus
Hatra
Tralles
CILICIA
Euphrates
Loukou
Stratonicea
LYCIA ET PAMPHYLIA
Antiochia
SYRIA COELE
Dura
Ctesiphon
Palmyra
Misikhe
PARTHIA
SYRIA PHOENICE
CYPRUS
Damascus
Caesarea
Bostra
SYRIA PALAESTINA
Aelia Capitolina (Jerusalem)
ARABIA
NABATAEA
Alexandria
Fayum
Philadelphia
Oxyrhynchus
AEGYPTUS
Nile
El-Khargeh oasis
Thebaid

Map 4 (*cont.*)

Figure 4.1. Yet another Roman conquest, this time Dacia. Decebalus, King of the Dacians, cuts his own throat as the Roman cavalry reach him. To a modern sensibility he seems heroic, but what did the artist (an anonymous genius) and the Roman viewers think? See especially Coarelli 1999, 31. Trajan's Column, Rome, *in situ*

throne of Parthia. But Roman control was fragile, as was the emperor's health. After Trajan's death in 117, Hadrian withdrew Rome's troops from all the territories beyond the Euphrates, including Armenia. No emperor initiated another foreign war of any significance for eighty years.

Hadrian to some extent inaugurated a new policy, not that his successors were obliged to follow it. Hadrian's Wall, though its exact purpose is much disputed, symbolizes clearly enough that here, for some time to come at least, was the edge of the Roman Empire [Figure 4.2]. In Algeria, too, it was Hadrian again who seems to have initiated the so-called *fossatum Africae*, a set of ditches and forts, although this too is disputed.[11] His soldiers strengthened the frontier in south-west Germany with a wooden palisade.[12] None of this made the empire into a walled city (that

[11] See Cherry 1998, esp. 45–7. The function of the *fossatum* is also unclear: see Vanacker 2014, esp. 204.

[12] Birley 2007a, 358.

Figure 4.2. A section of Hadrian's Wall at Walltown Crags, Northumberland, as it is now

existed only in the imagination of rhetoricians),[13] and there continued to be informal zones of Roman power, incomplete power of course, outside the school-atlas frontiers. The texts make it clear, however, what Hadrian had in mind. He attempted to attribute his non-aggressive policy both to the elder Cato (*Augustan History*, *Hadrian* 5) and to Augustus (see below, p. 130), the greatest authority figure of all. The *Augustan History*, a reasonably well-informed document as far as Hadrian is concerned, says in the context of Hadrian's visit to Roman Germany, that 'he was more eager for peace than war' and that he concentrated on the troops' training and discipline (*Hadrian* 10.2; and see 12.6 for defensive frontier engineering). 'For the most part he lived at peace with foreigners', says Dio (69.9.5), because they saw Roman preparedness and were terrified – and he paid some of them off.

[13] Aelius Aristides, *Orations* 26.82–4; cf. Herodian 2.11.5.

Hadrian's successors were insufficiently intimidating. In addition to repressing rebellious provincials, Rome experienced serious attacks on both the Parthian frontier and the Danube (what these attacks tell us about Rome's military preparedness we shall see later). Having annihilated a Roman legion (perhaps IX Hispana) in Armenia, the Parthians invaded Syria about the time Marcus Aurelius and Lucius Verus became co-emperors in 161, and Verus, the less unmilitary of the two, spent four campaigning seasons restoring the status quo. His subordinates seem to have done most of the work, and he barely deserved the title *propagator imperii*.[14] A Roman army had sacked Ctesiphon and made an incursion into Media, but the Parthians retained their independence. Similar events occurred on the Danube. Germans, provoked or unprovoked, assailed the provinces of Pannonia and Dacia in 166 and 167. Marcus Aurelius eventually reacted, and crossed into 'barbarian' territory in 170, with disastrous results. Invading forces (Marcomanni from Bohemia) evaded him and reached northern Italy, while others (from east of the Carpathians) raided as far south as Attica. Roman forces finally managed to defeat the Marcomanni at the Danube in 171, and Marcus campaigned in the area beyond the middle Danube from 172 to 175, and again, after a necessary visit to the eastern provinces and to Rome, in 179, without adding any new territory, though it was probably his genuine intention to create provinces called Marcomannia and Sarmatia.[15] Commodus gave up all such pretensions.

The Severan emperors, understanding no doubt how useless Marcomannia and Sarmatia would have been, concentrated their aggressions on the eastern frontier once again. Septimius invaded Mesopotamia in 195 and created the small new province of Osrhoene, and in 197 attacked Parthia and re-captured Ctesiphon. Once again, like Trajan, he established a province of Mesopotamia, though only a relatively small part of that territory as we understand it. But Septimius, whose home town was Lepcis Magna in Libya, also took the initiative in 197–202 in advancing Roman control southwards into the Sahara, all the way from Tripolitania to Mauretania. The governor of Numidia who was in charge of this effort, Anicius Faustus, is scarcely mentioned in the literary sources, but inscriptions and material remains reveal a new line of forts further forward.[16]

[14] For which, see *CIL* XIV.106.

[15] On this point see *Historia Augusta*, *Marcus* 24, and other sources, with Birley 2000, 184. The contrary argument of Kovács 2009, 256–9, has little substance.

[16] Cherry 1998, 49–53.

Septimius campaigned in north Britain in 208–10, and Caracalla, now sole emperor, in the Rhineland in 213; these were punitive expeditions. Caracalla initiated another Parthian campaign in 216, but he was assassinated before it could achieve anything, and it led only to a humiliating and expensive peace agreement two years later (for which see Dio 78.27). Alexander Severus was equally ineffective in Mesopotamia in 232. A large-scale German raid in the fortified *limes* area of the Black Forest brought him back to the west, but the Roman reaction to this raid, led by Alexander's murderer and successor Maximinus (235), was also a punitive expedition not an attempt at conquest. (The contemporary but unreliable historian Herodian says, 7.2.9, that he 'threatened' to conquer the whole of Germany up to the North Sea… .) Internal power-struggles prevented Rome's forces from any concerted attack on external enemies for many years thereafter.

Meanwhile the more active of these enemies took their opportunities: the new Sasanian king Ardashir seized several of the main towns of Mesopotamia, including Carrhae, which was dangerously close to Syria (236), and the fortress of Dura on the right bank of the Euphrates (239) [Figure 4.3]. The forces of the youthful Gordian III won back this territory, but he himself was defeated by Ardashir's son and successor Shapur I at Misikhe on the Euphrates and died in the battle or shortly afterwards (244). The Roman Empire was significantly larger than it had been in the year 16, but its growth had slowed since Trajan to a virtual halt. The Sasanians now threatened long-established Roman domains all across the Middle East.

With the central government gravely weakened by rival candidates for the imperial office, who often fought with each other to the harm of Rome's soldiers and civilians alike, power along the frontiers was greatly diminished for a period of some three decades.[17] But Gordian III's successor Philip [Figure 4.4] ransomed the prisoners taken by Shapur for the not unreasonable price of half a million *denarii* (which scarcely justified his taking the title 'Parthicus maximus').[18] When the Carpi invaded Dacia and Lower Moesia (244/5), Philip was able to push them out again, and return to Rome to celebrate the city's notional 1,000th birthday (248) in proper style. His general Decius was equally successful, it seems, in pushing

[17] For a more detailed narrative of the foreign wars of 244 to 284, which is inevitably very sketchy given the brevity and poor quality of the sources, see Potter 2004, 236–80.

[18] Shapur was pleased (*Res Gestae Divi Saporis* 3), but the sum in question was probably equivalent to a year's pay for no more than 370 legionaries (cf. Alston 1994, 115 – unless these *denarii* were gold).

Figure 4.3. The Palmyra Gate at Dura Europos, Syria, a major Roman fortress on the River Euphrates which was largely destroyed *c.* AD 256. Dura, *in situ*. No information is available as to its present state

Quadi, Goths, and others out of the middle and lower Danube provinces in 248/9. It was Decius, however, not the barbarians, who was the graver threat at this juncture. Proclaimed emperor by his troops – the first of many Illyrian emperors –, he marched on Rome, and his army defeated Philip's near Verona; Philip was the first emperor to die in battle (with the possible exception of Gordian III) and it was against a *Roman* army.

Decius (249–51), however, and his successor Trebonianus Gallus (251–253) effectively lost control of the lower Danube frontier. Goths inflicted a major defeat on the Romans at Abrittus in Bulgaria in 251, killing both Decius and his son, possibly with the connivance of Trebonianus.[19] Within a few years warfare spread to provinces that had long been essentially peaceful such as Bithynia, Macedonia, and Numidia.

Antioch, the fourth or fifth city of the empire, was occupied by King Shapur in 252/3 (being welcomed by the local poor according to one

[19] Sources in *PIR*² M 520.

Figure 4.4. Bust of Philip the Arab, emperor 244–9, found on the site of a coastal villa south of Rome. A soldier emperor who presents himself in civilian dress. Rome, Musei Vaticani

account).[20] Shapur took the emperor Valerian prisoner in 260, a dramatic and unprecedented Roman failure, and kept him in captivity.[21] Between 259 and 267 no major region of the empire except Africa Proconsularis was free from warfare. Invasions, together with wars between imperial pretenders, seriously damaged at least thirty of the forty plus provinces, and Italy too. Northern Italy was raided by Iuthungi from across the Danube (259–60), and several times by Alamanni in the years 268 to 271. Aurelian (270–5) decided that the capital city had to have a serious defensive wall, which had not been needed for nearly half a millennium.

Gallienus (253–68) put some useful military changes into effect (see below), and he, Claudius Gothicus (268–70) and more especially Aurelian succeeded in re-establishing central, though fragile, control over almost the entire empire. Their successors down to Probus (276–82) continued to have serious frontier troubles from time to time, but only when Roman forces were distracted by internal squabbles.

In all this it is important, and difficult, to distinguish between regions that suffered from damaging raids and civil war, and those that seemed to be slipping from Rome's grasp for good: the latter group comprised Mauretania Tingitana,[22] Dacia, the two Moesias, and perhaps Syria. Dacia was abandoned, probably in 273, as was an important area of south-west Germany between the Rhine and the Danube. But without Dacia to defend, Aurelian and his successors were able to hold the line of the Danube. To the east, Shapur never showed any sign that he actually intended to wrest Syria permanently from Rome,[23] and after his death in 272 Persia in any case became less formidable for several decades. In spite of various troubles within Roman territory, the emperor Carus, possibly helped by an internal revolt in Persia,[24] had captured the wretched city of Ctesiphon, as Septimius Severus had done, shortly before his death in 283.

By the summer of 285 Diocletian was in command of all provinces of the Roman Empire, soon co-opting a fellow officer, Maximian, to share his rule. The frontiers required constant vigilance and activity, but he and his fellow 'tetrarchs' (for whom see Chapter 5) protected them effectively. Their greatest achievement was against the Persians: the war conducted by Diocletian and his deputy Galerius in 296–8 led yet again

20 Petrus Patricius fr. 1; cf. Downey 1961, 256.

21 It seems to have been at this time that the Sasanian kings began to claim that they ruled the non-Iranians as well as the Iranians: Alram 2008, 21.

22 MacMullen 1988, 275, n. 23.

23 Isaac 1992, 31.

24 Frye 1983, 128.

to the occupation of Ctesiphon but more impressively to a treaty with King Narses (299) that apparently set the Tigris as the boundary between the two empires (Petrus Patricius fr. 14, but this is a sketchy account), at least for the time being. Civil wars followed (308–13, 316, 323–4), but the reigns of the tetrarchs and Constantine maintained the existing frontiers. Constantine reorganized the army, so that fewer troops were stationed on the actual frontiers. The historian Zosimus (*New History* 2.34), hostile to Constantine, claimed that he thereby 'allowed the barbarians unhindered access to Roman territory', but whatever the justice of this complaint the ill effects were apparently not felt during Constantine's own lifetime. The Danube campaigns of 322, 332, and 334 mostly involved fighting beyond the frontier; there is no sign that the Sarmatians or Goths thought that they had 'unhindered access'.

Thus there really was a major change in the behaviour of the Roman state, which contemporaries approved, justified, or blamed according to their interests and temperaments. It was in the age of Hadrian and his successor (117–61) that this change really took hold. We should not be distracted by the fact that later emperors quite often invaded Mesopotamia (Julian did so in a serious fashion as late as 363, and even Heraclius' army got there much later still [p. 247]). Those who have argued[25] that much of the old attitude towards foreign conquest long persisted are correct up to a point, but seriously mistaken to suppose that Rome was persistently aggressive towards the outside world as it had been under the Republic (this may well come from insufficient familiarity with the extreme behaviour of just those earlier Romans). A significant number of emperors showed no interest at all in such expansion, and even those who did hope for such conquests in the east or in Germany mostly neglected to mobilize the resources that all serious military men knew would be necessary. And this change can be explained – indeed there are almost too many possible explanations.

Desires and reasons

We can begin with the ideological superstructure, one of the factors whose importance it is hardest to assess. Foreign conquests continued to be a matter of pride and boasting. Claudius put up a triumphal arch in Rome

[25] Most conspicuously Isaac 1992 (372: 'the frontier policy of Rome in the East intermittently but persistently aimed at expansion. This is clear from actual Roman behaviour at least till the age of Diocletian').

after the initial victories in Britain, claiming that he had defeated eleven kings there 'without any losses' (*ILS* 216), and to commemorate his victory gave his young son the extra name Britannicus. The statues set up, not long before or after this, in the north portico of the Sebasteion [the Augustus or imperial shrine] at Aphrodisias in Caria catalogue in effect the places that Augustus had conquered or reconquered.[26]

Ideas about what the empire was for, and how the centre should relate to the provinces, began to change visibly under the Flavians and later (see Chapter 5), and at the same time the ideology of conquest weakened somewhat, but it emphatically did not disappear. It might have to be justified: when Domitian defeated the Germans, so Frontinus says, the emperor was acting for the good of the provinces (*Stratagems* 1.1.8) (this was an old theme refurbished). The younger Pliny's official panegyric lauds Trajan's military career (*Panegyric* 14–17), though what is most striking in that text may be the claim that the emperor was not aggressive ('you do not fear wars or provoke them'). Trajan naturally made a great deal of noise about his Dacian, Arabian, and Parthian conquests, and Dio is quite credible if somewhat simplistic when he says (68.17.1) that the emperor invaded Parthia 'out of a desire for glory'.[27] From Claudius to Caracalla, most of those emperors who lasted for more than a few years quite frequently had themselves proclaimed as *imperator*, that is to say as a great victor, after real or inflated victories (Domitian did this twenty-three times); the exceptions were Hadrian and Antoninus Pius. Trajan's Column, a phallic symbol of unprecedented dimensions, and the twin column in honour of Marcus Aurelius set up by Commodus commemorated wars of conquest, or in Marcus' case attempted conquest.[28] Marcus, typically, took resounding titles: 'Imperator Caesar M. Aurelius Antoninus Augustus Armeniacus Medicus Parthicus Germanicus Sarmaticus Maximus', that is to say conqueror of Armenia, Media, Parthia, Germany, and Sarmatia, though this was a charade as well as a ridiculous exaggeration, since he himself, as we shall see, certainly did not set much store by conquering barbarian peoples [Figure 4.5]. But the outward forms were important. The Senate and People of Rome dedicated the famous arch of Septimius Severus in the forum to Septimius and his older son 'on account of their having restored the republic and expanded the empire of the Roman people' (*ILS* 425). Septimius had prevailed in a four-year civil war and needed

[26] R.R.R. Smith 1988; R.R.R. Smith 2013.
[27] See further Sommer 2013, 36–8.
[28] Mattern 1999, 194–5, discusses representations of emperors trampling upon barbarians.

Figure 4.5. Gloriously taking women and children into captivity in Marcus Aurelius' German wars, which the Germans may genuinely have initiated. Column of Marcus Aurelius (probably erected under Commodus). The brutality and violence depicted on this column go beyond what we see on Trajan's Column (Coarelli 2008, 66). Rome, *in situ*

to emphasize his credentials. Coin-types, among other media, guaranteed that the emperor's military glory also had some resonance in the provinces. But the Severan arch was, as far as we know, the last monument in Rome to claim that emperors had made the empire grow larger.

The claims that emperors made often involved a good deal of chicanery. Most of those who took 'victory names' such as Germanicus (first awarded to Drusus, the step-son of Augustus) did not deserve them.[29] Claudius' claim 'without any losses' indicated both that the emperor could tell foolish lies and that the Roman people was losing its historic appetite for warfare; such a claim was first made, as far as the surviving record goes, by Velleius Paterculus (2.97.4) on behalf of his master Tiberius' campaigns in Germany.

The precise degree of influence exercised by this ideology cannot be gauged. Septimius is still said to have acted out of a desire for 'glory', and it is often supposed that emperors sought to legitimate themselves by means of foreign conquests. Two of the three emperors who might be thought to have most needed legitimation in this period and lived long enough to mount major wars (Trajan and Septimius, but not Vespasian, who was already sixty years old at the end of 69 and had in any case demonstrated his prowess by defeating the rebels in Judaea) rapidly did so, and both, unlike very many others, died natural deaths.

But who was impressed? In the second century the attitude of the upper class underwent a certain change: the old language of conquest co-existed with a prolonged period of inactivity, and senators did not greatly complain. Nor apparently did the soldiers. The Romans in the capital, especially exposed to imperial self-glorification, and emotionally linked to the emperors, at least down to the Severans (see Chapter 5), may have been relatively enthusiastic, but their main passions were very different, and when Commodus opted for peace and returned to Rome, ignominiously in the eyes of some, the city gave him a warm welcome (Herodian 1.7.3–4). In the rest of the non-elite population, indifference probably ruled, especially perhaps in places where the barbarians were far away.

Under the middle Republic, the citizens showed their relative eagerness for conquest by undertaking heavy military service. The people of the imperial Roman Empire showed no such desire. Aspiring members of the senatorial elite, who under the middle Republic had done at least ten competitive years of real military service, now served as military tribunes for a brief period, often a single year, during which it was normal and

[29] On this phenomenon, see Kneissl 1969.

quite unembarrassing not to have seen active service (cf., for example, Pliny, *Letters* 1.10.2, 7.31.2); even this came to an end in Severan times. The new military elite was professional and was not much in the business of impressing civilians.

Did the ideology of conquest survive into the period after 180? Herodian (1.6) describes a bitter conflict in Commodus' court in 180 between a conquest party and a peace party vying for the emperor's assent. Peace won, for the moment. Victory, however, and especially the victories (real or fictitious) of individual emperors, continued to be a constant and banal theme. Conquest was something else, and later propaganda tended to emphasize that the whole world (*orbis*) was Roman. Commodus received the titles *pacator orbis* ('pacifier of the world') and *invictus* (some time, neatly enough, in the three weeks prior to his assassination) (*ILS* 400), the latter term ('unconquered') having a curiously negative tone to it.

Even the aggressively expansionist Septimius Severus could boast to provincials that he had established 'universal peace' (by having defeated 'the barbarians who were ever attacking the empire').[30] *Invictus* gradually became a common title, especially (of course) after 235; Aurelian liked such titles as *restitutor orbis*, and by 285 such language was the common currency of imperial propaganda.[31] The emperors – military men – congratulated themselves in 301 on their military victories, but also on the 'tranquil condition of the *orbis* [understood to be the *Roman* world], which is wrapped in the embrace of the most profound calm' (*ILS* 642). This may be, indeed it should be, accounted a sensible ideal, but in the long term the tone had changed.

To what extent were the slowing-down and cessation of Rome's wars of conquest determined by administrative, financial, or economic considerations? It is important here not to assimilate the rationality of Roman emperors or their advisers to that sometimes attributed to modern leaders – though few indeed of the major wars of the last hundred years can be said to have been brought on by anything resembling rational thought about financial or even economic considerations. By Tiberian times, in any case, everyone who counted probably believed that Rome already ruled over the best parts of the inhabited world, as Strabo says (17.839), giving details of the three continents as he saw them. This became a commonplace, but it was a commonplace with some significance.[32]

[30] Oliver 1989, no. 217 (an inscription from Nicopolis ad Istrum, AD 198).
[31] See also, for example, *P.Oxy.* 63.4352, quoted by Bowman 2005, 67.
[32] Contrary to the view of Cornell 1993, 146, who sets up a false dichotomy between 'a rhetorical conceit' and 'a rational statement of policy'.

It is an unanswerable question whether the Roman central government would actually have been able to administer a much larger empire than it actually ruled in the second century, but Rome had always adapted its instruments of governments to increased possessions and there is really no reason to think that anyone doubted that it could continue to do so.

More significantly, there seems to have been a new propensity for assessing expansionist policies in primarily financial terms. When Suetonius attributes to Augustus the saying ('he used to say') that people who sought small advantages [in war] at great expense were like a man fishing with a golden hook (*Divine Augustus* 25), he was probably inventing or embellishing a story to justify the new defensive frontier policy of his master Hadrian – as he certainly was when he claimed, absurdly, that Augustus was far from desiring to expand the empire in any way or to increase his military glory (chapter 21). Yet Augustus rather obviously did weigh the fiscal consequences of his military policy. The armed forces were always the government's largest single expense,[33] as all agree (and the government could not, or at least did not, borrow). With twenty-eight or more legions to support, not to mention roughly 200,000 professional 'auxiliary' soldiers, plus the navy, the praetorian and urban cohorts, and the *vigiles* of Rome (and all the above required lump sums on retirement), the emperor had huge bills to pay. Even before Septimius Severus' extra recruitment, the military forces contained upwards of 350,000 men. A new tax, a 5 per cent tax on certain kinds of legacies, had to be invented in AD 6 to pay for the soldiers' golden handshakes (Dio 55.25), to the general distress of the well-to-do.

A fascinating passage of Strabo (4.200; likewise 2.115–16) probably reflects the way that the imperial court was increasingly beginning to think: all of Britain, he says, is already virtually Roman property and:

> furthermore [the inhabitants] submit so easily to heavy customs-duties on their cross-channel trade … that there is no need to garrison the island, for one legion at least, with some cavalry, would be required to exact tribute from them, and the expense of the army would offset the tribute-money; in fact the customs-duties would decrease, and there would be dangers if force were applied.

Now, such calculations were not altogether new: Strabo (16.780) says of Augustus' reasons for sending an expedition to Arabia that it was also a

[33] Duncan-Jones 1994, esp. 45–6; but see further Rathbone 2007, 175 (his 'ideology of low taxation' is a figment, however).

consideration that the inhabitants were reported to be wealthy (details follow), 'for he expected either to deal with wealthy friends or to master wealthy enemies'. And such calculations could be set aside, as Claudius demonstrated in the case of Britain (cf. Tacitus, *Agricola* 12, on Britain's valuable metal-ores; they should be seen as at most a secondary incentive to invade). In due course it became obvious that conquering Dacia would be profitable, because of its gold mines (there is no definite proof that Trajan knew of these in advance, but given the extent of prior Roman interest in the area, he probably did). Conquering Germany, on the other hand, or the Arabian Peninsula, Ethiopia or the Sahara might well be thought of as a waste of resources. Meanwhile the army was often needed for maintaining order in the existing provinces. The historian Appian, who worked as a senior official in Rome, also seems to have seen imperial policy in primarily financial terms (*History*, Preface 7.24–7; this was written under Hadrian or his successor),[34] and no doubt many officials thought likewise. In this generation and the next such thinking is echoed by several other sources.[35]

A historian who put the case against the importance of financial factors[36] underestimated the need for new legions if major wars of conquest were to be attempted. Trajan already had to raise two new legions, II Traiana and XXX Ulpia, during his second Dacian war, and he took at least eight legions with him to the Parthian War, plus an equivalent number of auxiliaries,[37] which might have been enough (Caesar thought that he would need sixteen) – but he largely did so by taking troops from places where they were needed, as troubles in Egypt soon demonstrated. Marcus had to raise two more legions (II and III Italica) to replace the troops that Verus had taken from the Danube to the east. Septimius Severus expanded the army still further, increasing the total number of legions from thirty to thirty-three, with titles (I, II, and III Parthica) that reflected the task for which he eventually employed them; but it seems reasonably clear that he did not intend to hold even southern Mesopotamia as a Roman province (Dio 75.9).

[34] 'I have seen some [of the penniless and impoverished barbarians], on mission at Rome, offering themselves as subjects, and I have seen the emperor refusing men who would have been no use to him.'

[35] Mattern 1999, 159.

[36] Cornell 1993, 147–9. This article was in effect the first full discussion of the reasons for the historical change being examined here.

[37] Bennett 1997, 192–3.

At home there were the bean-counters. Dio shows that many senators thought the matter should be assessed in financial terms, and concluded that Septimius' eastern campaigns were not worth it: 'he [Septimius] used to say that he had annexed a large territory and made it a bulwark of Syria; but it has been proved by the facts themselves to have been the cause of constant wars for us, and great expense, for it yields very little and costs an enormous amount…' (75.3). The only territorial addition in these years was the small and unprofitable province of Osrhoene, annexed by Septimius.

The Great Pestilence (the Roman Empire's first smallpox epidemic, generally known as the Antonine Plague), brought about a widespread population decline.[38] Together with its recurring appearance in the third century, and the civil wars of the 190s and 230s, it diminished the tax-base. It should be noticed incidentally that there is no substance to the persistent claim that the tax burden which the provincials carried under the Principate was a light one.[39] And the further debasement of the coinage from Marcus' reign onwards[40] strongly suggests that the state was hard pressed to balance its budget (this mildly anachronistic terminology will do no harm here).

Diocletian and Constantine greatly strengthened Rome's ability to collect tax revenue, but according to some historians they also vastly increased the size of the military. This is one of Roman history's most important factual problems, bearing as it does on the military catastrophe that occurred two to three generations after Constantine's death. The sources, such as they are, disagree, and while we know roughly the number of legions the tetrarchs commanded, some sixty-seven,[41] we do not know how many of them contained the old number of effectives (5,280 in theory) and how many had only a 1,000 men, as some of Constantine's legions certainly did.[42] Some units were already seriously undermanned under Diocletian, 116 men for example in a unit that in previous times would have had a complement of 500.[43] For financial reasons in particular, it strains belief in any case that the regular establishment in this period can have exceeded the army of 450–475,000 that Septimius Severus commanded.[44] John

[38] The severity of its impact: Harris 2012, discussing a variety of recent studies.
[39] See Harris 2011b, 35.
[40] Duncan-Jones 1994, chapter 15, for the period down to Severus Alexander.
[41] Campbell 2005, 122–3.
[42] Cf. Elton 2012, 327.
[43] Duncan-Jones 1990, appendix 4. Our evidence is regrettably fragmentary.
[44] Harl 1996, 216: 'probably the Roman army's peak during its entire history'.

the Lydian is not a very reliable source of numbers, but there is some plausibility to his assertion (*On Months* 1.27) that under Diocletian there were altogether 389,704 Roman soldiers (though the precise-seeming number is no guarantee of accuracy). One could hardly say that at this date the Roman Empire did not have enough soldiers to defend itself. Their quality is another matter. But while it is evident that by Diocletian's time many soldiers were conscripts (cf. *Theodosian Code* 7.22.1 on compulsory service for the sons of soldiers), none of Rome's neighbours was yet capable of defeating a Roman army in an evenly matched fight if the Roman commander was competent. Vast new conquests, however, would have required a degree of mobilization of men and resources that no one wanted.

Emperors and their rivals

The logic of the emperor's own position was the most important factor of all, though it was conditioned by ideology and finance (usually pushing in opposite directions), and to some extent by the wishes of others.

Did emperors in fact formulate frontier policies? Most of them did so, at least in broad outline, except when they were preoccupied by civil wars. We must incidentally avoid the trap[45] of supposing that emperors *either* followed a 'grand strategy' *or* reacted piecemeal to events; no, the truth is somewhere between these two poles – most emperors had some general ideas about how to deal with foreign enemies and most of those ideas were inherited. As under the Republic, commanders in the field had a degree of discretion unthinkable in a world of modern communications, but without instructions they did not go beyond restoring order in territory that Rome already regarded as its own.[46]

There were elements of policy continuity, but they are not to be exaggerated. When Benjamin Isaac wrote that 'Rome had long-standing ambitions to acquire parts of the Persian empire and frequently made attempts to realize them',[47] pointing to but exaggerating the periods of major warfare between the two states,[48] he was in a sense correct, but that does not mean that we should interpret every action that Roman governments took

[45] Fallen into by e.g. Wheeler 2007, 237; Le Bohec 2010, 6.
[46] Mattern 1999, 10–12, may exaggerate their independence. When P. Vellaeus campaigned in Thrace under Tiberius (Tacitus, *Annals* 3.38–9), he was in a 'client state'.
[47] Isaac 1992, 52.
[48] For example, a period of 'major warfare' did not begin in AD 52–4, merely a localized conflict over Armenia, largely conducted by proxies.

to strengthen Rome's power on the eastern borders as part of an expansionist policy. Rome's attempts to expand in that direction were not only, to say the least, discontinuous, they were usually half-hearted: no Roman with any knowledge of military history or Parthian affairs can have doubted that the forces Rome committed were insufficient – except, arguably, in the case of Trajan – to ensure the acquisition of any new territory across the Euphrates larger than Osrhoene. Rome always regarded Parthia as a potential enemy, but no first- or second-century Roman is likely to have taken seriously the ambition of King Artabanus III, attributed to him at least by Tacitus (*Annals* 6.31, AD 35), to regain the lands once ruled by Cyrus and Alexander; and what to do about Parthia itself – as distinct from Armenia – was always a matter of choice.

Emperors were chronically insecure: the life-expectation of a Roman ruler was the shortest of any known monarchy in world history (see Chapter 5). It was often a palace plot that terminated the emperor's existence, but military rebellions were always a danger and the Civil War of 68–9 showed that a senator of a relatively undistinguished family, Vespasian, could win the supreme prize if the legions he commanded far from Rome supported him. Tacitus famously remarks (*Histories* 1.4) that the crisis disclosed to everyone the secret that you could become *princeps* without being in the capital. Relatively successful generals therefore, such as Domitius Corbulo under Claudius and Nero and Agricola under the Flavians, made the emperor nervous. That meant that large wars of conquest had preferably to be led by the emperor in person, who might like that idea but usually did not. In 47 Claudius ordered Corbulo not to prosecute a war with Germans. When Tacitus (*Annals* 11.19) says that the emperor's motive was fear of the general's success, that may admittedly be an anachronism or the historian's well-known cynicism; and when Nero eventually ordered Corbulo to kill himself, it may well have been because the emperor really believed that he was involved in a conspiracy. However, Corbulo reportedly said in 47 that 'in former times Roman generals had been lucky men', that is to say they had not been hindered from conquering foreign nations; but Roman generals would never again be allowed to do that. Under Nero, T. Flavius Vespasianus could be entrusted with suppressing the revolt in Judaea because of his relatively obscure origin (Suetonius, *Divine Vespasian* 4), but even that turned out to be no guarantee at all.

It was not only the emperor's insecurity that was in operation on such occasions, but his desire to concentrate glory and victory in his own person. In the late Republic, and still under Augustus until about 20 BC, Roman commanders had often benefited from a good deal of *de facto* autonomy, extending wars of conquest further than anyone had expected.[49] This now ceased.

Much therefore depended on the emperor's own temperament. Active military command evidently suited Trajan and Septimius Severus, but others less. At Hadrian's accession, he was both objectively and subjectively insecure in his hold on power: he soon arranged (or, according to some, permitted) the execution of four ex-consuls with military credentials.[50] It may be that peace suited Hadrian's pleasure-loving temperament (but he had commanded a legion during Trajan's second Dacian War and was certainly no sort of pacifist). Foreign adventures were altogether unnecessary – the Parthians now knew how dangerous Rome could be – and put the emperor's own position at some risk. The man who rebelled against Marcus Aurelius, Avidius Cassius, was a successful general. It is noteworthy that usurpers attempted to unseat even such apparently well-established emperors as Antoninus Pius (one Cornelius Priscianus attempted a revolt in Spain in 145) and Marcus.[51]

From 172 to 175 Marcus had fought every year beyond the Danube, but while he was there he wrote, presumably for his own benefit, derogatory remarks about military achievements, and implied very clearly that those who made war on the Sarmatians were simply bandits (*leistai*):

> the spider is proud of having caught a fly, a man is proud of having caught a hare, or an under-sized fish in his net, or boar-piglets, or bears, or Sarmatians. Are not all of these people just bandits, if you examine their principles? (*To Himself* 10.10).

This was not a mentality that was likely to produce effective military action, but for the time being the machine worked quite well by itself.

It was indeed the general rule that emperors who wanted to fight wars of conquest, even on a fairly modest scale, thought that they needed to take command in person. After 244, they were almost all experienced soldiers, but even when, from the 290s, they once again had freedom of choice, that did not lead them to be aggressive expansionists of the pre-Tiberian type.

[49] See above, pp. 51–2, and Mattern 1999, 10.
[50] Syme 1958a, 244–5.
[51] For Priscianus, see Birley 2000, 154. On Avidius Cassius, see below, p. 184.

Nor I think would they have had much support from the rest of the governing order of society if they had wanted to do so. Even under Tiberius, the incentives that had once driven Roman nobles to invade foreign lands had drastically weakened.[52] Even under the late Republic, those who held *imperium* were gradually coming to spend much more of their energies on civilian government. And whereas the members of the republican aristocracy had competed with each other in the military sphere, and had often benefited dramatically from victory, from Tiberius' time onwards members of the Senate had much less to gain from military service. Many of them still served (it was only in the third century that they lost most of their military responsibilities), and many of them approved in principle of further imperial expansion, but the fierce drive of mid-republican times had gone. It is quite believable that Marcus' 'friends' often recommended him to leave the war beyond the Danube behind (*Augustan History, Marcus* 22.8) (though that does not necessarily mean that they wanted to bring the war to an end). Many senators, like the younger Pliny, now had exclusively civilian interests. It is the contrast with the republican era that gives all this significance. Of course one cannot say what would have happened if senators had in fact retained their old military passion.

Furthermore the governing class had now widened out to include local elites (see the next chapter), and there was very little to induce such people to favour aggressive wars.

We must not write history from anecdotes, but when, during Septimius' unsuccessful siege of Hatra in Iraq (much to the east of Osrhoene), Iulius Crispus, a tribune in the praetorian guard (a senior officer), subversively quoted lines from Book XI of the *Aeneid*, lines in which one of Turnus' soldiers bemoans the war in which he is compelled to fight for the benefit of the ruler (Dio 75.10, referring to *Aeneid* 11.371–3), everyone got the point, and Crispus was executed. The incident strongly hints at the doubtful morale of the Severan officer corps when it was engaged in fighting far from home on the personal initiative of the emperor. Yet if Septimius' aims included keeping his army in fighting form (and there is some evidence that this is why he fought in north Britain: Dio 76.11.1), his reasoning was sound. For in fact the Roman Empire needed to initiate frontier wars quite often, for both internal and external reasons. An excessively peace-loving elite endangered imperial security: the soldier-emperors of the third and fourth centuries were a necessary evil.

[52] Cf. Cornell 1993, 165–6.

Military strength and weakness

The gradual changes in the nature of the Roman army between the time of Tiberius and 235 certainly affected both Roman society and the empire's internal power-struggles. Did they also affect Rome's strength at the periphery? The really big changes were three, though they had all started well before Tiberius' accession. The first was the regular organization of 'auxiliary' troops into quasi-permanent units in which they would normally serve for twenty-five years before being made Roman citizens on discharge, a system set up by Augustus and refined by his successors. As in centuries past, such troops often outnumbered the legionaries, and their effectiveness was of profound importance.[53]

That leads, secondly, to the matter of recruitment. In the era of the civil wars of 49 to 31 BC, and under Augustus, provincials had entered the legions in large numbers. Recruits came from Roman-colonial or Romanized communities, but also from others: thus an inscription of the early Principate (*ILS* 2483) shows that almost all the soldiers in the two legions stationed in Egypt had been recruited in non-citizen communities in the eastern provinces (their lingua franca was Greek). All over the empire, the more Romanized provinces provided more and more of the legionaries, while Italians – who made up the bulk of the better-paid praetorian guard – provided fewer and fewer. The authorities were now quite willing in practice to recruit non-citizens, giving them citizenship when they were sworn in. This 'provincialization'[54] probably reflected some Roman/Italian reluctance to serve (Italy was too prosperous) but also some intention on the emperors' part to bring provincials into the mainstream. From Hadrian's reign on, the normal pattern (though not in Britain) was to recruit legionaries in the provinces where they were needed, but from relatively Romanized/Hellenized elements (and legionaries were more likely than 'auxiliaries' to be literate).[55] This was by and large a well-organized and disciplined force;[56] and fighting spirit was probably not lacking either, at least down to Trajan's time – when battle-commanders chose to entrust the initial impact of the fighting to 'auxiliary' units and keep the legionaries in reserve, a procedure that is

[53] As to the frequent occasions when 'auxiliary' units bore the brunt of the fighting, see Haynes 2013, chapter 17.

[54] For which, see above all Forni 1953 and 1992, 11–141.

[55] On the last point, see Harris 1989a, 253–4.

[56] The strictness of Roman discipline can be judged from the fact that surrender was considered treason (*Digest* 48.4.3). For military record-keeping practices, cf. Speidel 2007.

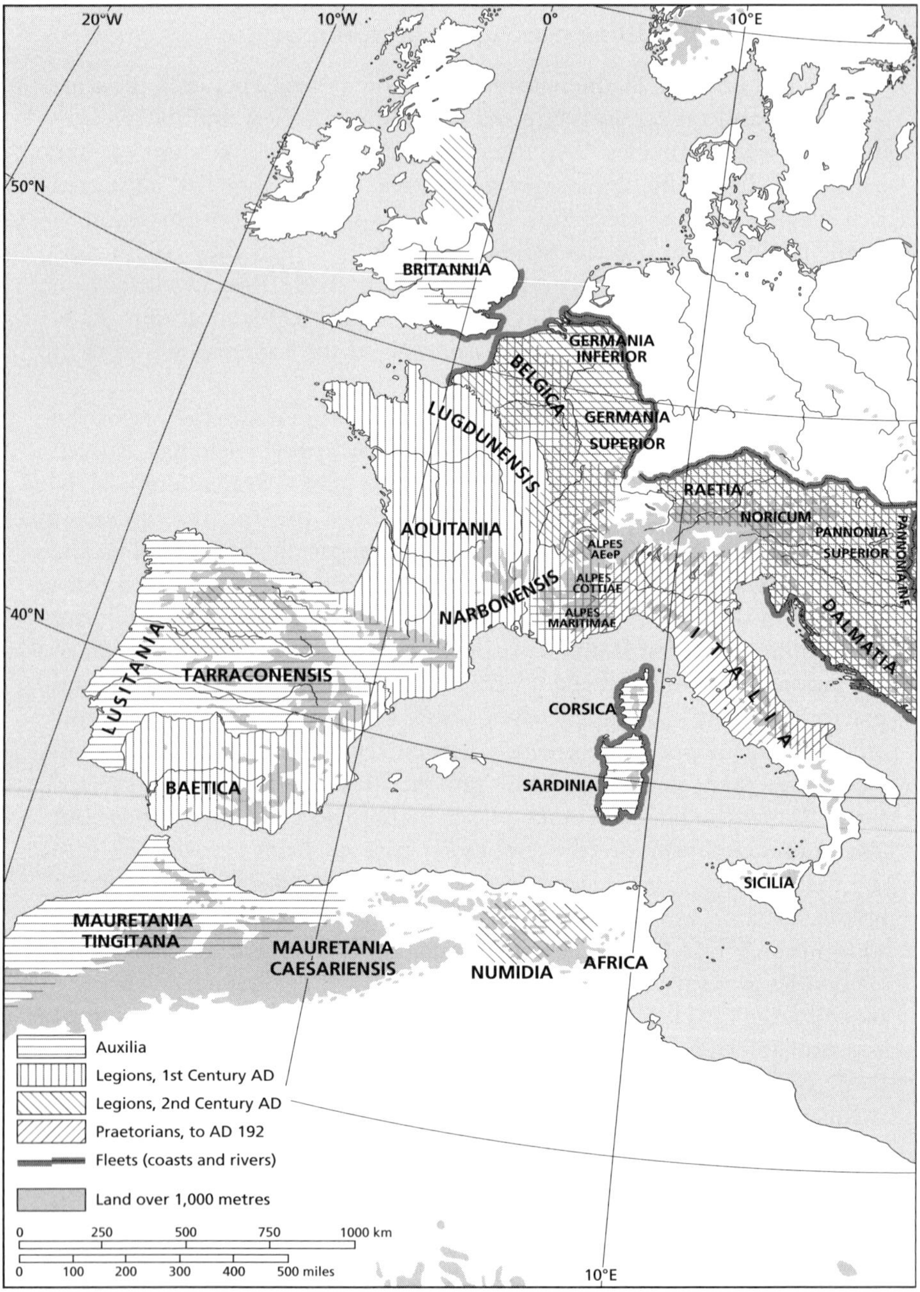

Map 5. Military recruitment under the early emperors, down to AD 192

20°E
30°E
40°E
50°E
60°E
50°N
40°N
30°N
DACIA
MOESIA SUPERIOR
MOESIA INFERIOR
ILYRICUM
THRACE
MACEDONIA
EPIRUS
THESSALY
ACHAEA
PELOPONNESE
CRETE
MYSIA
ASIA
BITHYNIA
PONTUS
GALATIA
CAPPADOCIA
ARMENIA
CILICIA
PAMPHYLIA
CYPRUS
SYRIA
SYRIA PALAESTINA
PARTHIA
ARABIA
CYRENE
AEGYPTUS
20°E
30°E
40°E

Map 5 (*cont.*)

first attested in a major battle at Idastaviso in Germany in AD 16 (Tacitus, *Annals* 2.16.3), there could be a variety of tactical reasons.[57]

'Auxiliary' recruitment was quite different: the government concentrated on fringe areas such as Iberian Galicia and Thrace, simply supplying officers from the core area of the empire; such units were commonly posted away from their home areas, Britons for example in Upper Germany,[58] while the *auxilia* in Britain itself might, for example, be Batavian or Syrian. Eventually, but unfortunately we do not know when, Rome also began to employ soldiers who are unlikely to have felt themselves to be Roman subjects: Marcus sent 5,500 cavalry of the Transdanubian Iazyges, whom he had just subdued, to serve in Britain (Dio 71.16). There were Goths garrisoning Arabia in 208,[59] and Goths later took part in Valerian's war against the Persians.[60] This was probably an increasing trend, but it is hard to tell how much the armies of, say, Constantine and Licinius were really dependent on Goths or Arabs, whom they are known to have made use of.

The other military change of potentially great importance in the period prior to 235 was not so much that many units in the Roman army became 'sedentary' from generation to generation, becoming deeply involved in essentially administrative duties, but that many Roman soldiers never experienced battle. This army had never been invincible, but its deplorable failure to protect the Danube frontier in 170–1 suggests significant changes for the worse. Enemy forces reached northern Italy for the first time in some 270 years, while others, as already mentioned, raided as far south as Attica. Our sources on all this are poor, but it may be conjectured that a shortage of officers and soldiers seasoned by warfare had a great deal to do with Rome's failure, and this in turn was the indirect result of conscious policy. In other respects, the Romans were normally at an advantage: throughout this period they were superior to their opponents in important areas such as artillery[61] and engineering ('the soldiers are always practising bridge-building', Dio 71.3).

Temporary causes admittedly contributed, and the Danube line still had a long future. Marcus Aurelius, as we have seen, had had to raise two new legions about 165 to replace the three which his co-ruler Verus had taken from the Rhine and Danube to the east in order to fight the

57 See Gilliver 1996.
58 Birley 2007b, 314.
59 *AÉ* 1911 no. 244; cf. Bowersock 1983, 120. For outsiders in the Roman army in the 230s, see Herodian 7.2.1.
60 *Res Gestae Divi Saporis*, ed. Huyse, sect. 6.
61 See Bishop and Coulston 1993.

Figure 4.6. Sestertius of Marcus Aurelius, AD 172 or 173. Obverse: the emperor, with philosophical beard and the legend M ANTONINVS AVG TR P XXVII; Reverse: Germania, seated beneath a trophy; the legend reads GERMANIA SVBACTA IMP VI COS III S C. Mattingly 1940, Marcus Aurelius 1432

Parthians. Shortly thereafter, the Roman military in the north suffered seriously from the Great Pestilence, as recent studies have demonstrated.[62] Marcus himself had had no military or even provincial experience before 168 – and it showed. Imperial coin-types furthermore had often exaggerated the emperors' military achievements, and there was a risky deception involved when coin-types absurdly declared in 172–4 'Germania subacta' – 'Germany has been vanquished' [Figure 4.6].[63]

Few historians have really tried to evaluate the Severan army, and the evidence is slippery. Even republican armies sometimes mutinied, and

[62] Eck 2012.
[63] H. Mattingly 1940, Marcus Aurelius nos. 1,413–15, etc.

there were whole rhetorical topoi about undisciplined soldiery. But an army stationed in Mesopotamia that was mutinous enough to assassinate the provincial governor (about 227, Dio 80.4.2) was a very negative symptom (and see below on the year 235).

We have quite a lot of information about how the Roman army changed between Severan times and Constantine, but assessing its ability to do its job is nonetheless difficult. On the one hand it never, unlike the republican army, won battles it might well have lost, on the other it never, unlike the late-antique Roman army, lost battles that it ought to have won. We have little option but to judge it by its results, though these may be mainly attributable not to its own qualities but to those of its generals, or its logistics, or its enemies, or to any combination of these factors. Recent accounts of Rome's military performance in this 100-year period[64] are unsatisfactory, but our sources are admittedly tenuous to a degree, whether it is for the defeat at Abrittus in 251 (see above) or the battle nine years later in which, or after which, the Persians captured the emperor Valerian (some Roman sources naturally preferred to claim that he was captured by trickery).[65]

Tiberius already knew that it was worth keeping two legions in Dalmatia partly in order to back up the legions on the Danube (Tacitus, *Annals* 4.5).[66] Later Roman emperors eventually concluded that the long-standing dispositions of the Roman army, with the great majority of the soldiers stationed on or near the frontiers, were ill adapted to resisting major invasions that might come from different directions. It had always been necessary to balance the needs of the Danube frontier and the Euphrates frontier, but both became more dangerous in late-Severan times. Once Rome surrendered the initiative, the distances involved presented an almost insoluble problem: it took something over two months, for example, for troops to travel from Rome to Cologne. The best that could be done was to create a reserve army that could be sent wherever it was needed without weakening some vital garrison. It appears to have been Gallienus who created a central cavalry force (cf. Zosimus, *New History* 1.40, Cedrenus, 1, p.454 Bekker).[67] The development of these *comitatenses*, as they came to be called, is impossible to follow in any detail,

[64] Sabin *et al.* 2007 ignores the whole problem; Ziólkowski 2011, 128, asserts that the Roman soldiers of this period were 'vastly superior' to those of the Republic!

[65] What really happened is exhaustively discussed by Glas 2014, 170–7.

[66] Thorne 2007, 229. This arrangement lasted until the reign of Nero.

[67] But there are signs of something similar under the Severans: Strobel 2007, 271. See further Glas 2014, 225–9.

but Constantine apparently expanded their role (Zosimus 2.21.1 may refer to such troops),[68] while also centralizing the command structure of the army by means of an overall infantry commander (the *magister peditum*) and a parallel cavalry commander (the *magister equitum*). Nonetheless it remained difficult to counter any large invasion once it had passed the northern or eastern frontiers. An enterprising governor might raise a local militia (*populares*: *AÉ* 1993 no. 1231b shows us a governor of Raetia doing this in 260), but they would be largely untrained and untried.

The reliefs on the Arch of Constantine distinguish between his Roman and his 'barbarian' troops,[69] which raises again the complex question of whether Rome was now relying too much on troops who were merely mercenaries. According to the emperor Julian (*Caesars* 329a), Constantine 'practically paid tribute' to the barbarians, and modern accounts suppose that he and his rival Licinius made Rome significantly more reliant on German and other non-Roman troops than any previous ruler; but the ill effects do not yet seem to be visible.

The strength of the Roman Empire's numerous and various neighbours to the north, east, and south can only be judged, once again, by the results, their aims likewise. From Tiberius' time to Trajan's, those who kept their freedom from Rome and their territorial integrity were doing well; this applies mainly to the Romans' failure to advance far beyond the Rhine and to hold on to Mesopotamia. The incursions of the 160s–70s and of the 240s–60s showed a great deal of vigour. The invaders' goal was often plunder, including human beings, which the Roman Empire offered in abundance. Dio (71.16) asserts that the Iazyges had taken far more than 'ten myriads' of prisoners in Roman territory – a five- rather than a six-digit number, one might think. (Some of the third-century booty has been recovered from the bed of the Rhine, rafts having apparently sunk).[70] Not even Sasanian Persia, the most powerful external enemy Rome faced in this period, showed any determination to hold on to any Roman province, and in fact it had no reliable means of protecting its own core area against Roman forces that were always relatively near. But northern peoples had already in the second century extracted territorial concessions of a sort, obtaining lands within the Roman frontier. This practice went back to Julio-Claudian times. Initially the advantages to

[68] Cf. Elton 2012, 331–2. P. Brennan 2007 plays down Constantine's role.

[69] Hoffmann 1969/70, 135. Not that there is any reason to think that Constantine increased the number of barbarians in the army (see Campbell 2005, 129).

[70] References in Todd 2005, 442.

Rome probably outweighed the disadvantages; whether that continued to hold true in and after Marcus Aurelius' time we shall consider in a moment. It certainly looks like a major surrender to strong outside pressure. Purchasing the docility of outside enemies by means of payments, unless it was a short-lived tactical expedient, was likewise a recognition of real enemy strength: this started with Domitian, but involved Trajan, Hadrian, and many later emperors.[71] Yet from a Roman point of view, this was by no means an irrational policy, within limits.

Fundamental changes had taken place by the time the conglomeration of Germans known as the Alamanni ('All Men'), who are first attested in a Roman source in 213, inflicted quite serious harm in 232–3. This was nothing less perhaps than the birth of a new national formation.[72] What made a difference here was probably in the end quite simple: such a new grouping, like the Franks from about 260, could put larger forces into the field than any single German people. But the tetrarchs and Constantine could always, it seems, defeat the northern peoples on the battlefield.

Knowledge and methods

In some ways, the Roman Empire was rather ill equipped to deal with its external enemies. A considerable number of the emperors of the pre-crisis period lacked the military experience that would have helped them to understand the condition and capacities of their own military forces, let alone those of the enemies: that applied in particular to Claudius, Nero, Antoninus Pius, Marcus, Commodus (he had accompanied his father on campaign but was only eighteen at the moment of his accession), Alexander Severus, and Gordian III (reigns amounting to exactly 100 years out of 230); of course some of them, especially Marcus, were compelled to learn about military affairs on the job.

The knowledge that matters most to an imperial power concerns its own resources and the resources and likely behaviour of its powerful enemies. Whether it possesses elaborate information about the peoples and geography of foreign peoples years in advance of actual conflicts clearly matters much less; there is no reason to suppose that the Roman republican governing class knew much in detail about, for instance, Spain, Gallia Comata, the interior of Asia Minor, or Egypt, before

71 Mattern 1999, 121.
72 This is much discussed: see among others Kulikowski 2012, 348–54.

deciding to seize power there. They simply knew that those territories were desirable possessions.

When we make proper allowances for the sheer physical and cultural obstacles that stood in their way, we should probably judge that down to Severan times Roman emperors and their entourages were rather well informed about the civil and military affairs of their own realm. Too much fuss has been made about the probable unavailability of maps. Provincial censuses continued to function until the mid-third century (in Egypt, where we know most, the census of 257/8 was the last until the tetrarchy), and the record-keeping of the Roman army is almost legendary. How well this system survived in Constantine's reign it is hard to tell, but the army in Egypt was still generating a great deal of paperwork in that era, as is implied by some of the documents in the Abinnaeus archive.[73]

The sources scarcely reveal to us how well the Romans knew their main enemies. It is evident, however, that even some quite moderately competent Roman emperors took an interest in the functioning of the Parthian and later the Sasanian state (see, for instance, Herodian 6.7.1 on Alexander Severus).[74] From Claudius' reign to Hadrian's there is also evidence of serious official interest in among other areas the Sudan, the Sahara, and the eastern Black Sea.[75] Cassius Dio's sources knew the names of a number of the Transdanubian rulers under Marcus Aurelius, and even something about their internal politics.[76] There is no evidence whatsoever to back the assertion that Commodus and his advisers 'profoundly' underestimated the distance between the Danube and the Baltic.[77]

On a tactical military level, the Roman army under the Principate seems generally to have kept itself well informed (Varus' defeat was highly atypical).[78] But there may have been some deterioration even before the great crisis: when Ardashir defeated Alexander Severus' invading army it was apparently because the whole Persian force caught the Romans off guard (Herodian 6.5.9). Later on, Decius' demise seems to have been precipitated by inadequate reconnaissance (Zosimus, *New History* 1.23.3).

73 See Bell *et al.* 1962, 13. Abinnaeus joined up in about 304.
74 See further Mattern 1999, 67–71.
75 Nicolet 1988, 241–3; Isaac 1992, 45.
76 Dio 71.3.1a, 71.11, 71.13.3–4, 71.16.
77 Thus Mattern 1999, 4, referring to Herodian 1.6.5. See instead Syme 1988; Rives 1999, 139–41. Pliny, *NH* 37.45, had given the distance from Carnuntum to the Baltic as 600 Roman miles, a good approximation.
78 For a collection of material about military intelligence, see Austin and Rankov 1995.

The whole system of external power rested on terror. What was necessary was not only, as Hadrian thought, military preparedness, but what an Israeli officer has drily referred to as 'cutting the grass', that is to say periodically doing violence to significant external enemies to prevent them from getting strong enough or bold enough to cause serious trouble. Antoninus Pius and Marcus Aurelius were too complacent to understand this, but the best generals of the first century, and the emperors Septimius, Caracalla, and Maximinus seem to have understood it well. So did the tetrarchs.[79] Most modern accounts give too little attention to what are euphemistically called 'punitive expeditions',[80] partly because they were often too insignificant to get much attention from our literary sources.

For a long period Roman preparedness could be guaranteed to terrify the outsiders, to varying degrees; Roman brutality also contributed. We shall see in the next chapter how rebellious provincials were treated, but terror was a weapon on the margins as well, as for example at Uspe in the Krasnodar region of southern Russia in 49: the inhabitants offered to surrender, but the Romans preferred to seize and slaughter the inhabitants in order to instil terror in the rest of the region (Tacitus, *Annals* 12.17). During the siege of Jerusalem Titus, the Roman commander, had thousands of civilians tortured and crucified outside the walls to induce the besieged to surrender (they were provincials, but the rebellion had taken on the dimensions of an all-out war); the soldiers amused themselves by crucifying the victims in a variety of positions (Josephus, *Jewish War* 4.451). The savage Roman treatment of the 'barbarians' depicted on the column of Marcus Aurelius[81] probably reflected actual practice with reasonable fidelity [Figure 4.5]. Any population perceived as rebellious was always likely to undergo the same fate (such as the Caledonians in 210/11: Dio 76.15). When Maximinus 'devastated the whole countryside' in south-west Germany, 'set fire to the villages and gave them to his army to plunder' (Herodian 7.2.3), he was behaving normally – and rationally.

It must be emphasized that this was not rogue behaviour, for it was approved at the highest levels. Hymning Trajan in the Senate, Pliny congratulates him on terrorizing foreign nations and invokes battlefields covered in (enemy) dead (*Panegyric* 12). The still more brutal author of a later panegyric addressed to Constantine says admiringly that the emperor threw so many Frankish prisoners to the wild beasts in the arena at Trier

79 For an outline account of their frontier wars, see Wilkes 2005, 229–31.

80 But see Goldsworthy 2007, 91–3.

81 Coulston 2003, 410.

that the animals grew tired (*Panegyrici Latini* 6 (7).12.3). The same writer rephrases the classic line 'let them hate as long they fear' (Suetonius, *Caligula* 30). What matters is the almost routine nature of all this: all imperial states commit atrocious acts from time to time, but at Rome it was policy, and policy that the military cheerfully put into effect. This violence was without doubt related to the violence of internal power that we shall be examining in Chapter 5.

That does not mean that Rome did not frequently use diplomacy – more or less high-handed diplomacy. Augustus had maintained the traditional policy of making use of client kings, and his successors did so likewise (on the continuing use of client kings in the second century, see Appian, *History* Preface 7.27; cf. 4.15). There were still client kings under Caracalla (see, for instance, Dio 77.12.1). But they now seemed to play less of a role, presumably because a century after Trajan's victories the Roman Empire instilled less fear and deference in its neighbours, especially in the east once the Sasanids came to power in Persia (226).

Negotiating with other states seems at first sight to be out of keeping with Rome's arrogant attitude towards the outside world, all the more so since major questions were now settled not by the Senate but by the emperor (with the advice of his entourage of course).[82] In practice Rome was periodically driven to negotiate. Quite apart from endless interactions with Parthia/Persia, there are many other cases: Marcus made an agreement with the Iazyges (Dio 71.17), and Commodus with the Marcomanni (73.2).[83] A set of eleven inscriptions from Volubilis records the negotiations between the governor of Mauretania Tingitana and the leaders of the Baquates and other peoples in the Middle Atlas from 169 to 280.[84] Many other such negotiations carried out by provincial governors have disappeared from the record. But we could say that Rome never succeeded very well in playing the German peoples off against each other, by contrast with their successes in the Greek world and North Africa under the Republic.

Something more needs to be added about the imperial frontier. There was such a thing, even though, as already explained (p. 36), Roman power usually extended beyond it in most directions. The Rhine and Danube frontiers were clear, and from Domitian onwards there seem to have been some relatively fixed land frontiers, at least in a few areas. None of this meant an

[82] For this centralization, see Sidebottom 2007, 6–7.
[83] For many other such occurrences under Marcus, see Stahl 1989, 300–7.
[84] Shaw 1986 = 1995.

unchangeable line or a mainly defensive attitude towards the outside world; the historical problem should not be posed as a simple dichotomy: either Rome wanted a fixed defensive frontier or it was still an expansionist power – for neither of these views can be sustained in a pure form.[85] The Rhine, Danube, and Euphrates provided some of Rome's frontiers for a very long period, but they did not prevent or even, as far as one can see, greatly discourage further expansion. By the early fourth century, however, few if any Romans thought about territorial expansion, and the tetrarchs built more and more frontier forts, especially it seems in the east.[86]

Aelius Aristides' image of the empire as a walled city is all the more problematic because Roman authorities had periodically settled large numbers of 'barbarian' outsiders in the provinces. Ti. Plautius Silvanus, a governor of Moesia in the 50s or 60s, boasted in his epitaph that he had brought more than 100,000 men across the Danube, 'with their wives and children and kings and chieftains' (that is to say perhaps 300,000 or 400,000 people altogether), and had settled them in Roman territory 'to make them pay tribute' (*ILS* 986), Rome having perhaps made some space there by slaughtering the earlier inhabitants. Much remains obscure about this event, but it was something to be proud of. Silvanus was not the first to have carried out such an operation, though no one seems to have done it on such a scale before.[87] After this, we hear of nothing similar until the reign of Marcus, who even brought some Germans to Italy, though he later turned them out again when they caused trouble (Dio 71.11); evidently the Romans maintained control. A great deal more of this happened after 250, and it becomes more probable that the settlers felt little or no loyalty to Rome and paid little tribute. It is impossible to believe that all the Burgundians, Vandals, Bastarnae, Franks, and Goths settled in various provinces by Probus[88] became reliable Roman subjects. When an imperial panegyrist claims under Diocletian that this was all splendid – enemies had become farmers (*Panegyrici Latini* 8 (5).1, 6, 9, 21) –, we must be sceptical. But Constantine persisted with this settlement policy, and therefore it must still have been seen as being less perilous than leaving such people outside. All the same, one result was that Roman power decreased in Britain, Gaul, the German provinces, Pannonia, Thrace, Macedonia – in other words, all across the European provinces – and probably elsewhere too.

85 For this supposed dilemma, see Whittaker 2004, chapter 1.
86 Lewin 2002 ('Diocletian restored the imperial presence moving his troops into the pre-desert', 96); Elton 2012, 340.
87 De Ste Croix 1981, 510, who gives the fullest account of the whole phenomenon.
88 De Ste Croix 1981, 512, lists the sources.

But Constantine did one other thing besides reforming the army that conduced to military strength, and that was the foundation of a second capital at Byzantium, nearer to some of the most vulnerable frontiers.

Conclusion

We set out to explain imperial growth and stability. The old incentives to imperial expansion – the material, political, and psychological gains accruing to those who determined the comportment of the Roman state – had already lost much of their force by the time Tiberius' government made its dishonest claim to have conquered Germany. Some of the impetus was still there, however, and down to Trajan's time at least it was still felt in the upper class. Even after that, the great majority of emperors continued to rejoice in taking credit for extending the frontiers (the arch of Septimius) and defeating foreign enemies. But it was increasingly hard to claim that it made financial sense to initiate large foreign wars, and such thinking, though not new, seems now to have carried more weight than it had even in Augustan times. As we have seen, the personal interests of the emperor, and sometimes his lack of military experience, were crucial factors in limiting wars of conquest all the time from Tiberius to Philip the Arab, and even when internal stability of a kind returned in the 280s internal factors told heavily against any major attempt at expansion.

The astonishing stability of the Roman Empire as an empire in this period rested firmly on military power and its intelligent use. But these 300 plus years of mostly stable frontiers need further explanation, all the more so because of the formidable internal convulsions of AD 68–9, 193–6, 235–84 and 305–24. The frontiers were always vulnerable, especially when the imperial power was, for whatever reason, not intimidating. But the empire itself was not vulnerable – not yet. Its manpower and financial resources were still sufficient to maintain power over the great bulk if not all of its existing territory. The Roman army sometimes performed its frontier-defence tasks poorly even in the second century, and it evolved in various ways, as we have seen, but it was still under Diocletian large and reasonably well equipped and led, as well as being properly trained. (Whether the seeds of future weakness – besides recruiting difficulties – were already present will be discussed in Chapters 5 and 6).

But there was another element in the Empire's durability, an internal factor that is hard to describe accurately but of great importance nonetheless. A large section of the population not only believed in the Roman Empire's destiny but believed in its unity. After the death of Alexander the

Great his vast empire split into four main sections. The Roman Empire was also subject to centrifugal tendencies, and in the third century there were short-lived quasi-states within the state, one in Gaul (258–74), the other based in Palmyra (*c.* 261–72). An emperor who was strong enough to repossess these territories – namely Aurelian – naturally did so, but what made it natural was not only personal ambition but the widespread Roman identity of those who over many generations had been incorporated into the Roman possessing class. Hence it did not matter, or rather it was a positive advantage, that between the reign of Septimius Severus and that of Decius equestrian officers displaced senatorial ones,[89] for this was a wider group of men who nonetheless were normally well-to-do,[90] saw themselves as Romans, and identified with the Roman state. That immense structure could of course only defend itself as long as it could extract sufficient revenue from its citizens and its enemies, but it also needed, and in 337 still possessed, enough competent and committed administrative and military manpower deployed more or less in the right places. The men in question needed to be devoted, at least to a reasonable degree, to the idea of Rome. How far this devotion went is a problem we shall return to in the next chapter, but we can already say that it went far enough to make the Constantinian empire reasonably secure against all imminent enemies.

[89] For the fact, see Strobel 2007, 271.
[90] Cf. Cooley and Salway 2012, 215.

CHAPTER 5

The Romans against each other: from empire to nation?

Durability and docility: the historical problem

'Against each other': that phrase may obscure much that was functional if not harmonious in three centuries of Roman life. But consider this. In AD 61 L. Pedanius Secundus, the city prefect of Rome, was murdered by one of his slaves. Law and custom required the execution not only of the perpetrator but of all the slaves who were 'under the same roof', which meant in this case, Pedanius having been wealthy, some 400 persons. Some of the city population vigorously protested, and they had sympathizers in the Senate. But a senatorial majority approved the massacre, and Nero sent soldiers to provide security: the sentence was carried out (Tacitus, *Annals* 14.42–5). The law in question lived on (Ulpian and others, in *Digest* 29.5).

This chapter is not primarily about the exercise of brutal power over slaves, but slavery is the water in which everything else floats. To varying degrees it conditions the economic life and the psychology of virtually the whole population. But the slaves do not get together and rebel a great deal, however much they may rebel as individuals. They are too weak, and they know that it is usually hopeless: Pedanius' slaves were no match for the praetorian guard. So although there is much to say about slaves, and though we shall soon meet some very powerful freedmen, I shall deal first with power relations among the free (both Roman citizens and others), and come later to the nature of Roman slavery.

For the principal aim of this chapter is to explain how a system characterized by harsh and exploitative kinds of power – in rapid flux, furthermore, between the 250s and 310s – could remain so stable. What in fact needs to be explained is a double mystery: the durability of the Roman Empire and its high degree of docility; and both of these features seem all the more puzzling when we consider that by the standards of other monarchies both Roman emperors and Roman dynasties were relatively short lived, thus unstable. These questions will form the framework for what follows, leading first to a discussion of political power in all its main manifestations, then to social and economic power and the effects of class and gender on many aspects of life, then to the power of beliefs and ideas.

We must not regard the durability of the Roman Empire down to the time when it first fragmented in a major way, in the first decade of the fifth century AD, as by any means automatic. It is true that in major divisive crises, such as had occurred under the 'Second Triumvirate' and were to occur again in AD 69, 193–6 and periodically between 235 and 284, the empire always held together. New rulers and their armies, imbued with a deep sense of the majesty of the Roman Empire as well as of their own interests, almost always took it for granted that there should be a single central government ruling in the name of Rome.[1] And that this government would, by and large, most of the time, be obeyed both by soldiers and by civilians. Meanwhile, as we have seen, Rome's military forces were extremely effective, most of the time, in controlling the more restive provinces and in guarding the frontiers: and what was most extraordinary about the military failures of the third century is that the Roman Empire made an almost full military recovery.

This stability is made all the more impressive of course by the immense size of the Roman world. The distances were large, and communication was slow and inefficient. Not that one should exaggerate the importance for the ruler on the Palatine hill of knowing quickly what was happening on the lower Danube or in Alexandria, or on the most distant frontiers: this was the condition of all imperial rulers until the spread of the long-distance telegraph in the 1860s. The most dangerous gap in Roman knowledge always concerned the enemies' intentions, and that was only in part a problem of distance.

Within the empire, Roman governments did their best, within their technological limits, to facilitate official communication and the movement of troops. The justly famous system of road construction already appeared in Chapter 3, and it continued to grow vigorously down to the time of Trajan. Except in times of internal military crisis it really did allow the emperor, using the system of vehicles and animals established by Augustus, to receive and send out great quantities of messengers and messages.[2] This was merely one of the effective 'organizational techniques' by which Rome maintained its power over soldiers and civilians alike. Any good set of maps of the Roman road-network (the *Barrington Atlas* is the

1 Cf. Béranger 1953, 228–9.
2 See especially Kolb 2000.

best) shows that immense care was taken to make troop movements as efficient as possible within the limits of the available technology.

The long-term trend in imperial government was a gradual shift from the somewhat haphazard methods of republican times to a more systematic and routine-based set of procedures. Increasingly, as we shall see later in this chapter, these procedures were operated by expert officials – at least until the military crises of the mid-third century.

As for provincial obedience, it was quite imperfect, and there were many rebellions: the point is that they were always repressed, and for a long time without the slightest concession, unlike what had happened in Italy in 91–89 BC. Even when south-western Germany and Dacia were abandoned in the third century it was because of external pressure, not because the indigenous population had rebelled. The most restive provinces were efficiently garrisoned until the 250s and most of the time after that, and the mystery lies in the more quiescent regions. A speaker in Josephus' *Jewish War* (2.373) brings out the problem, though not the answer: how is it that the Romans control Gaul with 1,200 soldiers when Gaul has almost that number of cities (he evidently did not attribute much importance to the rebellion of Iulius Civilis – on which see below – in the chaotic years 69–70)?[3] Vast tracts of territory that were still capable of riot and even rebellion – Gaul, much of Spain and north Africa, most of Asia Minor, Greece, Dalmatia, and the Alps – were very lightly garrisoned most of the time. In Egypt, most of the gradually diminishing number of legionary troops were stationed near to Alexandria. Not that we should exaggerate the sparseness of military force: while Pliny governed the peaceable province of Bithynia-Pontus, there were at least two cohorts of *auxilia* stationed there (Pliny, *Letters* 10.21).

It is true that by any modern standard the central government did not impinge much on the life of most of the peaceful provincials,[4] apart from exacting taxes – but the vital problem remains: why did the provincials pay their Roman taxes, and in sufficient quantity to enable the Roman Empire to maintain and defend itself? Tax-gatherers could sometimes be violent, and rational fear of Roman retribution was a major reason why many tax-payers obeyed. But that is clearly not enough of an explanation. All the less so because there really is no substantial reason to believe the

[3] Josephus evidently underestimated the mobility of the Roman army. Tacitus, better informed, knew that the Rhine legions had been meant to keep the Gauls as well as the Germans in check (*Annals* 4.5).

[4] Lendon 1997, 2.

current myth that the Roman Empire in general was a low-tax regime: the burden varied greatly but was often oppressive.[5]

Historians have answered these twin questions in a number of more and less convincing ways. The multivalent concept 'honour' has little explanatory value here,[6] for it was the common currency of innumerable pre-modern societies.[7] The main consensus doctrine is in brief this. Rome succeeded in assimilating and winning over significant portions of the local population, especially but not only the local elites, in literally every part of the empire. Patronage relationships between emperors and other important figures linked the centre with Italy and the provinces. As for the mass of the population, the central government employed 'bread and circuses' in the capital, and in the provinces, where bread and circuses were left to the local leaders, ordinary people could be consoled by the idea that in the last resort the emperor might respond positively to their appeals over the heads of lesser authorities – and occasionally he did so. But in general local elites cooperated with the central government and its agents. In return they received imperial backing for their own authority as well as marks of distinction. Slave and peasant revolts were now less common than they had been under the late Republic, at least until the third century, though Greek cities in particular were given to disorder.

Characteristically, emperors committed imperial forces to help slave-owners in searching out runaways (Marcus Aurelius and Commodus are cited in *Digest* 11.4.1.2).[8] When ordinary people began to lose rights under the Antonine emperors,[9] receiving the label *humiliores*, 'Lower People', the members of the local elites, along with senators, knights, and army officers, were classified as *honestiores*, 'Better People'. Meanwhile the army fulfilled a triple function: it faced the outsiders; it helped, as we shall see, to administer the less mature provinces (mature, that is, from a Roman point of view); and by recruiting men from outside the citizen body on a very large scale and making them into Roman soldiers, it promoted Roman identity.

This doctrine is broadly convincing, but it needs to be made both more historical and, crucially, more sociological. Later on in this chapter

[5] See D. Mattingly 2011, esp. 134–6; Harris 2011b, 35. Exactions could be particularly oppressive if Roman army units came by: Rossignol 2012, 110–11. But on the difficulty of defining high and low levels of taxation, see Monson and Scheidel 2015, 9.

[6] Contrary to Lendon 1997.

[7] Harris 2005, 26–7.

[8] See in detail Fuhrmann 2012, chapter 2.

[9] This label will recur: it refers to those who ruled from 138 to 192.

I will provide the wider social context. Here I will sketch some historical changes.

It is obvious that the above explanation works least well if it is applied to the period before a great deal of assimilating and winning-over had taken place, especially therefore with respect to Julio-Claudian times. This was when the emperor's monarchical power, coupled with his control of the armed forces, showed its vital importance. When Tacitus, somewhat reluctantly, pronounced that one-man rule was necessary, he said that it was 'in the interest of peace' (*Histories* 1.1) – that is to say of tranquillity within the empire as well as the cessation of civil wars – that this should be the system of government. It was Augustus, Tiberius, and Claudius (the latter two often underestimated by historians because of the resentment of the senatorial order transmitted by Tacitus) who put Rome on the path to massive incorporation.[10]

In Tiberius' time, Roman citizens still perceived the empire as existing for the benefit of Rome or at most Italy. Tiberius said that he wanted his sheep to be 'shorn, not flayed alive' (Suetonius, *Tiberius* 32; a slightly different version in Dio 57.10), but in any case the provinces were the sheep. Claudius would probably not have disagreed with this formula, but he also, in a speech to the Senate, famously articulated a doctrine of incorporation – to the effect that defeated former enemies could become patriotic Romans, after they had re-made themselves culturally (Tacitus, *Annals* 11.24).[11]

The earliest clear expression of a Roman 'civilizing mission' appears in Pliny's *Natural History* (3.39) in the AD 70s: speaking of Italy (interestingly, not of Rome itself), he says that it was chosen by the gods to:

> unite scattered empires, to make manners gentle, to draw together in converse by community of language the jarring and uncouth tongues of so many nations, to give mankind civilization [*humanitatem homini dare*], and in a word to become throughout the world the single fatherland of all peoples.

These notions probably reflect a significant current of thinking in the Roman upper class of this period, and although they are deeply imperialistic

10 And even Caligula deserves a mention. See in general Syme 1958a, 589–90, and on Gaul Woolf 1998, esp. 37–40 (the latter brings out the extent to which this process included displacing local people with Roman colonists).

11 'It was the ruin of Sparta and Athens that although they were powerful in war they treated their subjects as aliens and kept them at a distance.' That Claudius really did address the Senate in such terms is guaranteed by an inscription (*ILS* 212). Tacitus makes it plain, however, that there was serious opposition (chapter 23).

they differ at almost every point from older Roman thinking. None of this prevented the current emperor, Vespasian, from squeezing the provincials when necessary: he 'increased, in some cases doubled, the tribute exacted from the provinces' (Suetonius, *Divine Vespasian* 16; see also 8).[12]

Since the late Republic Roman public art had depicted provinces and foreign nations. Augustus constructed a *porticus ad nationes*, a portico to display the peoples of the [Mediterranean] world, and it has sometimes been suggested that such monuments show the provinces as being 'equal' in some sense to Italy.[13] It was much too early for that. But a more subtle change set in under the Julio-Claudians: what is perhaps most interesting about the statues of recently defeated peoples set up in the Sebasteion at Aphrodisias in Caria (see above, p. 126) is that they were set up in a province. We may suppose that the authorities expected, or at least hoped, that this provincial audience (in a favoured city) would see the victories in question as serving their own interests as well as those of the imperial power.

Small touches show that attitudes were changing. There is space to mention only a few, and that only in a cursory fashion. One of the most fascinating documents of early imperial government is the Edict of the Prefect of Egypt Ti. Iulius Alexander of AD 68, which seems to reveal extensive abuses permitted by his predecessors but claims in great detail that he is correcting them (the focus is Alexandria, but the text was evidently circulated throughout the province). How hard he tried we can scarcely know, but the emphatic ambition to provide good government in Egypt is remarkable.[14]

By defeating the Germans, Frontinus says, Domitian acted for the good of the provinces (*Stratagems* 1.1.8). For Tacitus, writing some two decades after Domitian's death, the people of Tiberian Spain were still 'barbarians' (*Annals* 4.45), and he imagines Seneca apologizing for his provincial origin (14.53),[15] but it would be hard to find any Roman referring to the people of a comparable set of provinces in these terms at a later date. And at almost the same time, Trajan (98–117) and Pliny were exchanging letters in which they profess their concern for the well-being of the Greeks of Bithynia (e.g. in Pliny, *Letters* 10.18). Hadrian's extensive 'province coinage' – coin-types

[12] For details, see Duncan-Jones 1994, 12.

[13] Cf. La Rocca 1994, 290.

[14] The text is known from an inscription at the El-Khargeh oasis, some 650 kilometres from Alexandria: Chalon 1964, translated in Levick 2000, 188–92.

[15] In *Annals* 15.20 Tacitus seems to endorse the view that the provincials should know their (subordinate) place.

depicting personifications of regions and provinces[16] – while hard to interpret precisely, suggests that the places in question (eastern and western alike) were now viewed from the centre with at least a certain respect.

Such attitudes co-existed somewhat uneasily with recognition that the empire was in a loose sense a system of slavery (Plutarch, *Political Precepts* 19 = *Moralia* 814f; Florus, *Epitome* 2.21.12 – naïve, but all the more revealing).[17] And they co-existed with the contempt of non-official Romans such as Juvenal for Greeks, Egyptians, and Jews – but even Juvenal seems to take a more favourable view of the Gallic and African provinces.[18]

It was part of the same system that under the early Principate the Senate, and from time to time the emperor himself, spent long hours judging charges of 'extortion' levelled by collectives of provincials, powerful ones of course, against former governors (Tacitus and Pliny – e.g. *Letters* 2.11 – give us ample details).[19] Meanwhile the rules under which governors operated grew more strict.[20] The fact that the defendants, though men of power, were often punished demonstrates that emperors and senatorial opinion were prepared to go to considerable lengths to satisfy the grievances of the most Romanized of the provinces.

It is uncertain, as we noted in the last chapter, what proportion of the population had obtained Roman citizenship prior to the general grant by Caracalla in 212,[21] but without much doubt it was only a minority. What is most noteworthy is that, though the sources are generally hostile to Caracalla and in some cases impugned his motives, claiming that the aim was to raise more tax-revenue, no one, as far as we know, objected to the incorporation of so many provincials, many of whom were of course far from being Romanized. A proclamation of Alexander Severus in 222 shows that by this date provincial governors, very many of whom were provincials themselves, were supposed 'to show unflagging consideration and care' for the provinces they ruled.[22] The welfare (*utilitas*) of a province was now a recognized principle (Ulpian in *Digest* 1.16.10 pr.). Italy meanwhile steadily lost its privileged position. By the time of Diocletian's Price Edict (301), the emperors spoke simply of 'our provincials' – and taxed them all, including the Italians.

16 For this material, see H. Mattingly 1966, 341–52, 504–26.
17 Lavan 2013, 101–5, shows how pervasive this view is in Florus' work.
18 Isaac 2004, 397.
19 Bang 2012, 209, gives a misleading account of this matter.
20 Robinson 2007, 79.
21 For a translation of the decree, see Lewis and Reinhold 1990, II, 380, or Potter 2004, 138–9.
22 *Select Papyri* II.216, but better read in Levick 2000, no. 214.

Assimilation and identity

Who then was assimilated and won over (the sociological dimension of the problem), two processes that were to some extent independent of each other? Josephus once again points to a crucial truth when he observes (*Jewish War* 2.338) that in Judaea in 66 the men of property wanted peace. Of course: for them the Roman Empire was a guarantee of tranquillity and property rights. Since the time of Rome's conquest of Italy centuries before, Rome had always tended to favour the men of property, normally landowners, in any foreign community, rewarding them with political privileges and bringing them into the Roman orbit. 'There is no need of garrisons to hold the acropolises [in the unarmed provinces]', wrote Aelius Aristides (*To Rome* 64), 'but the greatest and most powerful men in every city guard their own fatherlands for you'; for once, he was accurate.[23]

This alliance was the bedrock of the Roman Empire. Rome had always favoured oligarchic government in the cities, and by Flavian times if not earlier few vestiges of democracy were to be found anywhere: the members of the local senate or council held office for life and were not answerable to the ordinary people. Rome considered that it was better to admit the under-age sons of the *honesti*, the 'honourable men', to a local council rather than let in the *plebs* (Pliny, *Letters* 10.79.3). Citizen assemblies continued to exist in many places, but their powers were limited and their composition was sometimes at least restricted.[24] Where we have evidence – mostly in the Greek cities of Asia Minor between the Flavian and the Severan emperors[25] – there are ample signs of social tension, which is likely to have 'encouraged' the philanthropy of the well-to-do, but the latter remained firmly in command.[26]

Aristides and others claimed that the empire was under the rule of law, which was true in the very limited sense that the men of property had a system of legal remedies regularly available to them. It was not in any case easy to know the law,[27] but members of the economic elite would characteristically have a degree of access both to the provincial governor and to armed force. Papyrus documents from Egypt – such as the first-century

[23] Cf. Lendon 1997, 7.
[24] Cf. *SEG* 51 (2001), no. 1832 (Lycia, AD 45), referring to the 'undiscerning crowd' that is excluded from elections.
[25] Much of the evidence comes from Dio Chrysostom (cf. C.P. Jones 1978, chapter 11).
[26] The orthodox view that the assemblies were now quite powerless has been elaborated by Zuiderhoek 2009, 60–6, but challenged by Vujcic 2009. See further Fernoux 2011.
[27] See Millar 1990, 213–14.

archive of Nemesion son of Zoilos of Philadelphia[28] – show us how this system worked in detail, but *mutatis mutandis* it operated everywhere.

The economic decline of the third century hurt the 'curial order', that is to say the social group that all over the empire provided city officials and councillors, as well as hurting the rest of the population.[29] The 'curials' were now less able and willing than before to pay for the burdens of public office, though the imperial government still tried to help them from time to time, in its own interest of course (see for example *P.Oxy.* 33.2664 for Egypt under Philip the Arab). But through all the troubles of the third century, the established social order of urban centres, landowners, peasants, and slaves persisted, sustaining the structure of the Roman state.

But to return to the matter of cultural assimilation. The spread of Roman identity over many centuries made an oceanic difference to who exercised power in the Roman world and who it was exercised upon. The 'provincialization' of the governing class and of the army put different people in power; meanwhile 'Romanness' itself evolved.

The lop-sided nature of the evidence makes any overall cultural history of the Roman Empire quite hypothetical. Certain regions are poorly known, and more importantly the relevant evidence about the mass of population is, except in Egypt, very thin indeed. This remains true in spite of the vast amount of archaeological evidence for every area. For a study of power in the Roman Empire needs to judge how far the peoples of the Roman Empire came to *feel themselves* to be in any strong sense Roman, with the further complication that the dominant culture was Greek as well as Roman.[30] And while *we* may see certain cultural changes as marks of Romanization (an indispensable term, as long as it not understood to refer to any comprehensive policy),[31] they may not have been felt to be specifically Roman. This may apply, for example, to a whole range of phenomena, from Roman forms of urbanism to the spread of gladiator fights all over the western empire and to parts of the east [Figure 5.1]; it may also apply to the massive spread of Roman-style artefacts – many of them of ultimately Hellenistic origin – terracotta lamps, the red-glazed pottery known as *terra sigillata*, glass, etc., etc., throughout the western empire.

[28] Bagnall 1995, 40–1.

[29] For a good overview, see Carrié 2005.

[30] This bipolarity of Roman and Greek culture probably contributed to the durability of Roman power. It permitted the simultaneous flourishing of different kinds of humans in somewhat different spheres, while imposing enough cultural unity to serve as a basis for a diffused elite.

[31] Too much fuss has been made about this term, mainly by British scholars who apparently suppose that using it would show sympathy for colonialism (for a recent instance, see Haeussler 2013, 20–2). For good discussions of the concept, see Wallace-Hadrill 2008, 9–14, Ando 2011, 34–47.

Figure 5.1. Marble relief from Halicarnassus (western coast of Asia Minor), *c.* AD 200, commemorating the retirement of two female gladiators named Amazon and Achillia (Robert 1940, 188–9). Gladiator fighting gradually spread to the Greek East. In 200, however, Septimius Severus banned women from taking part. London, British Museum

But some changes were much more obviously linked to national identity, in particular perhaps language change. Local languages survived in most provinces throughout this period,[32] and not only in remote parts of the countryside: Lycaonian was the main language of the town of Lystra when Paul was there (*Acts of the Apostles* 14.11), while all of its inscriptions were in Greek and Latin, showing the limitations of such evidence. In the Hauran in Syria during its period of prosperity in the second and third centuries the inscriptions are in Greek, but the population spoke a form of Aramaic or Arabic.[33] The graffiti of the potters of La Graufesenque in south-western Gaul combine Celtic and Latin.[34] There is a great deal

[32] Harris 1989a, 175–90.
[33] Hoffmann-Salz 2014, 298; she nonetheless shows how Roman identity spread in that area.
[34] Marichal 1988.

more such evidence, and in many cases, Cappadocian and Neo-Punic for example, there is ample proof that such languages were still spoken in the fourth century.

Meanwhile bilingualism came to be quite widespread, at least in the towns (Greek being of course the lingua franca in the eastern provinces).[35] Many governmental practices, including the custom of recruiting large numbers of soldiers in relatively unromanized and unhellenized provinces such as Lower Germany, Thrace, and Cappadocia, contributed to a degree of language-change and indeed of acculturation more generally.[36] It can be argued that the Roman government achieved approximately as much acculturation as it wanted, by concentrating on the most important provincials. When Tacitus describes how Agricola, as governor of Britain, concerned himself with the Roman education of the sons of the leading natives, the *principes* (*Agricola* 21), he was recounting what an efficient governor probably did in any such province.[37] Knowledge of canonical Roman texts such as the *Aeneid* spread through the social elite in the empire's Latin half. And while local religious practices had sometimes suffered very severely in the course of and in the aftermath of the Roman conquest (Britain, Judaea), local deities usually survived reasonably well even though syncretized with Graeco-Roman ones. How far the Latin language eventually spread we can tell, very roughly, from the fact that the languages of Portugal, Spain, France, and Romania owe infinitely more to Latin than they do to any linguistic substratum. And as Roman citizenship spread, before and even more after the Edict of Caracalla (212), so Roman law spread too;[38] but local law was what mattered to most of the provincials prior to that date, and even afterwards (though the matter is debated) it is clear that in many places it formed part of the legal system.[39]

Dress too can matter. Do we provincials look like Romans, whatever that may imply at a given time and place? Funerary monuments in many areas, for example in the Moselle region of the Rhineland, show how in some cases local populations in the western provinces adopted Roman costume, while in others they held on to their own traditions or devised compromises.[40] In Spain, toga-wearing was a major sign of acculturation (Strabo 3.166).

35 Adams 2003 is the definitive study, but he seems not to discuss the likely rural/urban difference.
36 For the role of Latin in Roman thinking in the early empire, see Dench 2005, esp. 302–5.
37 For the case of Gaul, see Tacitus, *Annals* 3.43.1.
38 Cf. among others Millar 1993, 528.
39 Cf. Arjava 1996, 49; Sommer 2009, 239–42.
40 On the Moselle region, see Rothe 2009.

None of the cultural change cursorily summarized here (the great book on the subject has yet to be written) necessarily signified provincial loyalty – the history of the twentieth century was crammed with examples of colonized elites which were thoroughly imbued with the dominant culture but resisted the colonial power politically. And it is not hard to find signs of resistance to this particular colonial power, ranging from outright rebellion to hard words to half-concealed resentment (social resistance not specifically directed at the imperial power will receive more attention below). The major rebellion led by Iulius Civilis in 69–70 involved not only Batavians like himself but northern Gauls from among the Treveri and Lingones who had been subject to Rome for over a century. His chief Gallic ally, Iulius Classicus, had been the commander of a Roman cavalry unit. One scholar has catalogued some sixty or more armed disturbances initiated by provincials between AD 16 and 192.[41] Such incidents are often obscure, as with the outbreak in Achaea under Antoninus Pius (*Augustan History*, *Ant.Pius* 5). When in later times a little bit more is known about large-scale lawlessness within longstanding Roman provinces, such as the banditry of the 'Boukoloi' ('herdsmen') in Egypt under Marcus and the rebellion of the Bagaudae in Gaul in the 280s, such movements were not apparently nationalistic in character, although they were in some sense anti-Roman.

Those who actively hated Rome, exemplified by the author of *Revelation* and by the Sibylline Oracles of the second and third centuries (see for example *Sibylline Oracles* 8.31–42, 91–5, 121–9), were perhaps no more than a minority, and indeed Christians were a small minority until late in the third century. The Judaean Jews were exceptionally recalcitrant to Roman domination, and in the Bar-Kochva revolt suffered near-genocide in consequence [Figure 5.2]. 'They [the Romans] destroyed fifty of their most important forts and 985 of their most considerable villages, and slew 580,000 men … so that almost the whole of Judaea was made into a desert…'. (Dio 69.14). (These numbers are problematic, but the slaughter was undoubtedly devastating.)

It is also striking that even a pro-Roman Greek such as Plutarch can refer to the Roman Empire as a system of slavery, while Aelius Aristides, a man of privilege famous for the Greek panegyric of Rome that he delivered in the Senate, probably in 143, can be seen on a careful reading to have nursed continuing resentment of Roman power.[42]

[41] Pekáry 1987, 138–45.
[42] Pernot 2009.

Figure 5.2. Masada, the last place to fall to Rome in the Judaean revolt of 66–74. This is what remains of the enormous ramp that the Roman besiegers built in order to assault the fortress rock some 150 m above them.

We may think of the Roman Empire outside Italy as roughly divided into two or perhaps three zones that do not appear on any map.[43] In the 'inner' regions, not always tidily identifiable with provinces, there were no significant bodies of Roman troops, and members of the social elite, who were quite often of at least partly Italian descent, cooperated with Rome and in some cases entered the equestrian and senatorial orders; urbanization went relatively far and so did acculturation (allowing for the differences between the Latin West and the Greek East). Baetica and south-eastern Tarraconensis in Spain are examples, likewise Achaea and the province called 'Asia' in the east.

In the 'outer' regions, by contrast, though there were always towns and the local elites were meant to cooperate, troops were stationed, acculturation was slow, and few if any men made their way into the upper Roman elite. There might be less law and order, particularly if there were mountains

[43] For a similar distinction, see Brélaz 2005, 328–9.

hospitable to banditry. Such 'outer' regions included, for instance, Cantabria and Sardinia, and in the east Cilicia and Judaea, but also quite numerous areas in other provinces, as for instance the mountains of the Sannoi in eastern Pontus, who, Arrian indignantly reports in the 130s, have ceased paying their taxes to Rome (*Voyage around the Euxine* 15).[44]

The ideal, from the point of view of the central government, was that provinces would gradually shift from the second category to the first, or at least to an intermediate position, as Hispania Tarraconensis did (three legions were necessary for most of Augustus' reign; after 62 one was enough, which meant, with auxiliaries, perhaps 8,000–10,000 troops for a very large territory), and likewise Egypt (three legions under Augustus, only two by AD 23).[45] After 62, all the other legions (25, later 27, later still 30 and 33), were stationed on the frontiers, until the system went into crisis in 235. But if a region offered no major risk to imperial tranquillity (being situated well away from the frontiers) and paid its taxes, and was deemed uninteresting by the Roman elite – Sardinia, for example – it might be much more neglected.

Most provincials cooperated with Rome most of the time, of course. For the upper classes, 'they, the Romans' eventually became 'we, the Romans'. This happened quite quickly in the 'inner' provinces of the west,[46] where local traditions had been delegitimized. In the Greek world, the historian Cassius Dio (a Bithynian born *c.* 164), twice consul, is an extreme example, but the trend in the whole propertied class of Asia Minor was towards Roman nomenclature and presumably a certain degree, at least, of identification with the imperial power. It would be reasonable to assume that this self-incorporation took place in synchrony with the admission of various provincial populations to senatorial and equestrian office (of which more below). But promotions to Roman office did not guarantee universal contentment: Aelius Aristides was still somewhat disgruntled while living a secure existence in a province which had already sent senators to Rome for the best part of a century.

One long-term change which assisted the incorporation of 'colonial elites' and possibly a higher degree of professionalism was the gradual growth and empowerment of equestrian officials (for the origins of the knights' role in government see above, p. 103). Equestrian rank was a

44 For similar territorial gradations of power in the Ming and Qing empires, see Santangelo 2014, 41–2.
45 For the changing nature of the province Syria in the first and second centuries, see Gebhardt 2002.
46 Syme 1958b, who, however, implicitly underestimated the importance of the incorporation of people outside the senatorial and equestrian orders.

conferred honour, riches being a necessary but not a sufficient condition.[47] In AD 16, a few provinces, of which Egypt was the most important, were governed by knights, the praetorian prefects were knights, and so were the senior non-senatorial army officers; almost all these men were Italians. From Flavian times onwards the knights' positions in the civilian administration, financial but not only financial, multiplied; it has been estimated that there were some 110 such positions at the end of Hadrian's reign, about 200 by the third century. There was an equestrian career, with a simple salary scale. By Hadrian's time the majority of the knights were probably provincials.[48] Under the Severans, knights increasingly started to rule provinces and command legions that had previously been entrusted to senators. By the 240s it was being an equestrian that mattered most of all, not being a senator.[49] Gallienus in 262 effectively pushed senators out of military commands (Aurelius Victor, *Caesars* 33.33), and the change became permanent (but it cannot be good for any state if members of the upper social elite lack any sense of personal responsibility for its effectiveness in war: see the next chapter). None of this represented a large shift of social power, for most equestrians were of landowning families, as far as we can tell; however it was also possible for a few men to start in the lower ranks of the army and advance into the equestrian order. In short, there was an added degree of social mobility.

The social elite that made up the senatorial and equestrian orders gradually took in more people of provincial origin. The first provincial to reach the consulship under the emperors was Valerius Asiaticus from Vienne, suffect in 35. Even during Nero's reign, the provincials in the Senate were still relatively few, and they largely came from the most Romanized parts of Gaul and Spain, though a few came from the Greek world too. The subsequent civil war meant that there were many gaps to fill, and it is evident in any case that Vespasian and his sons were intent on change.[50] Yet most senators from the western provinces were at least partly descended from Italian settlers.[51] The first consul from the Greek world was Ti. Iulius Celsus Polemaeanus from Sardis,[52] suffect in 92, whose wealth can be roughly gauged from his huge funerary monument

47 Duncan-Jones 2006.
48 Duncan-Jones 2006, 189.
49 Potter 2004, 232.
50 Cf. Eck 1995, 1, 149–50.
51 Cf. Shaw 2000, 373. On the difficulties involved in determining a senator's geographical origin, see Krieckhaus 2006, 169–75.
52 *PIR*[2] I 260.

(the 'Library of Celsus') in Ephesus. He apparently owed his senatorial promotion to the part he had played as an equestrian army-officer in prevailing on the legion III Cyrenaica in Egypt to support Vespasian's usurpation in 69. We have no up-to-date statistics, but according to older numbers nearly half of the senators whose geographical origins are known were by Hadrian's time provincials, and soon afterwards senators from the Greek-speaking world made up about half of this provincial contingent.[53] The equestrian order went through a similar evolution. But it is to be noted that all of the new arrivals were men of Latin or Greek culture; they also belonged broadly speaking to the same social class as their predecessors – they were rentiers.

To what extent the free inhabitants of the third-century and the Constantinian empire identified with Rome is a delicate question, to which we shall return again at the end of this chapter. All knew that they were Roman citizens, and alienated persons such as Tertullian (a Christian apologist from Africa Proconsularis) assume that everyone (except of course the Christians) belongs to the same state or community (*civitas*) (*Apologeticum* 1.7), the Roman one.[54] There was in truth not much for the alienated to hold on to except fringe religions. Such alienation only began to matter about the time when Decius attempted to exterminate Christianity, and later when its numbers began to snowball.[55]

As for the soldiers, the great majority of the men who fought for Rome in the second and third centuries were provincials, and there is no reason to doubt their Roman identity – or proof that it was unconditional. They very seldom seem to have supported any anti-Roman cause, and when they mutinied or deserted it was for reasons entirely mundane, such as unpaid wages.[56]

The emperor

It is time to look more closely at those who exercised political power, beginning at the top. Absolutism, in so far as it was possible in a pre-technological society, came out into the open with Tiberius. He not only decided on war and peace, commanded all the military, effectively

53 Hammond 1957, 77.

54 In fact the common Christian attitude in the first three centuries was that they were a *third* nation, separate from both the Romans and the Jews: Harnack 1908, 1, 266–78; see further Gruen 2013, 19–20.

55 On Christian numbers, see Hopkins 1998.

56 Cf. Phang 2008, 330.

chose the consuls, and initiated all legislation (all this might be said about Augustus too), but also connived in the explosion of treason trials and accusations, and ruled from a pleasure-dome away from the capital (a telling sign of absolute power). Down to Marcus Aurelius, later emperors often ruled from their country-palaces.[57] Tiberius no longer went through the formality, observed by Augustus as late as AD 13, of getting the Senate to renew his powers. He brought the larger part of the praetorian guard, which had previously been stationed well away from Rome, into a permanent camp in the city, 'which', in Gibbon's view, 'for ever riveted the fetters of his country'.[58] And it seems to have been under Tiberius that the concept of 'the imperial house' (the *domus Augusta*), an implicitly monarchical notion, gained wide currency.[59]

This was how the future would be. The personal decisions of the emperor were all-important, whether they were based on good information or caprice. But his intimate circle, including his freed slaves, was also extremely powerful, especially but not only if his character or his intellect was weak. We can even speak of a kind of oligarchy. The key members of this court (*aula*) were naturally the emperor's immediate family and favourites, alongside secretaries as well as public office-holders such as the praetorian prefect.[60] This latter official, from the time of Sejanus (d. 31) until the reign of Constantine, was usually the most powerful man in the Roman Empire apart from the emperor; ideally, as an *eques* of respectable but not the most exalted origin, he served as a counterweight to the senators.

Most of the actual work of governing was done by a staff of freedmen and slaves, the most important of whom had formal titles, especially from Claudius onwards. They might be in charge of the emperor's correspondence (the *ab epistulis*), his accounts (the *a rationibus*), the petitions he received (the *a libellis*), or his more intellectual activities (the *a studiis*), but at any given moment there were hundreds of imperial freedmen, many of them working for the emperor, many others pursuing occupations of their own while still having financial obligations to the man at the top. Not surprisingly, the emperors' freedmen could accumulate enormous power and wealth, the extreme cases being Pallas and Narcissus

57 See Millar 1977, 25–8.
58 Gibbon 1776–1788, chapter 5. On the military presence in the city, see Busch 2007.
59 Cf. Braund 1985, no. 551; Corbier 2006, 188–94.
60 For the emergence of the imperial court, see Winterling 1999; Paterson 2007. As to who should be considered its members, see below.

in the court of Claudius, who supposedly amassed between them a sum equal to one-and-a-half times the annual military budget of the Roman state.[61] The important positions just named were so desirable that under the Flavians they fell into the hands of influential knights: presumably emperors now saw that knights were no more difficult to control than clever ex-slaves and did less harm to their image. This was not a modern bureaucracy (no such thing ever existed even in late antiquity), but its apparatus of soldiers, freedmen, and slaves was fairly elaborate. This statement is scarcely quantifiable, but the stratification within the imperial 'household' is indicative.[62]

Like all men of power, the emperor also listened to his more trusted acquaintances, his 'friends', who in the high empire would almost all be senators or knights; and he would consult those he considered the 'leading' men of both orders.[63] Any idea that there should be a formal cabinet of advisers (a *consilium*) was put on the shelf by Tiberius, but what happened later is disputed. It depended, so it seems, on what had to be decided. If the question was legal, as it often was, it came before a standing *consilium*, at least by Hadrian's time; Hadrian added legal experts (*Augustan History*, *Hadrian* 18). When the emperor addressed other issues, fiscal or military ones for instance, there is no sign that he consulted any formal body (the best counter-evidence, Herodian 7.1.3, concerns the anomalous reign of Alexander Severus), but the consultation of friends could nevertheless be a somewhat formal matter (otherwise the satire in Juvenal 4.72–154 would have been pointless).

The correct model is a court, not a cabinet.[64] The imperial court was a natural consequence of the concentration of a great deal of arbitrary but routinized power. One suggested image is a series of concentric circles,[65] but it might be better to think of a single circle, changeable according to circumstances, all of whose members had external links of their own. Marcus Aurelius lists as the members of Augustus' court his wife, daughter, descendants, ascendants (which is odd: both his parents were dead by 42 BC), and sister, then Agrippa, Augustus' relatives, household members and friends,

[61] Rathbone 1996, 312.

[62] Cf. Weaver 1972, esp. 295, Boulvert 1974, 143–9; but more research is needed. C. Kelly 2004, 111, speculates that there were 'perhaps up to 10,000 slaves and seconded soldiers performing administrative duties throughout the empire' in the first and second centuries. Much depends on what is meant by 'administrative duty', but the true figure for the second-century empire could easily be twice as high.

[63] For the emperor's friends, see Millar 1977, 110–22; Paterson 2007, 143–8.

[64] 'It was in essence still an aristocratic household', Mouritsen 2011, 94; not quite – it was too large.

[65] Levick 1990, 53; Paterson 2007, 140.

Areius (a philosopher), Maecenas, and finally his doctors and soothsayers (*To Himself* 8.31).[66] All this leaves it regrettably unclear how the later *consistorium* evolved. This was a formal all-purpose advisory body; we first meet it under Diocletian (*CJ* 9.47.12), and it may well have been his invention.

The emperor was the main source of legislation, though (confusingly) it often took the form of a senatorial decree[67] and sometimes even of an old-fashioned *lex*. Down to and including the reign of Marcus Aurelius, sensible emperors thought it best to treat the Senate with a certain respect. Most emperors attended its meetings fairly frequently, at least until the reign of Marcus.[68] It is often said that the Senate became much more a collection of senior officials than a deliberative body; it was prestigious, but it certainly never got to decide anything of world-shaking importance. The emperors that it appointed (anomalously again) in 238, Pupienus and Balbinus, only lasted for ninety-nine days, and it had no part in the major decisions of later times. That is all true, but the Senate did conduct important trials as well as acting as a sounding-board for the emperor, and its decrees could have real effects on provincial administration, as in the case of the rules for the administration of Egypt known as the Gnomon of the Idios Logos (the Rule of the Private Account) (*Select Papyri* II.206).[69] And in the mid-third century the Senate still counted for something with military emperors such as Philip and Aemilianus.[70]

Imperial laws as such, known as 'constitutions', could take various forms – edicts, rescripts to officials or cities, instructions to high-level state officials, and so on.[71] They were often reactive and concerned with local or minor problems. But as Graham Burton has shown, the surviving evidence gives a misleading impression in this respect, obscuring the fact that the centre must have given extensive rulings about matters such as census-taking and tax-collection.[72] However, the impression we receive from the surviving evidence that imperial legislation was at its height from Trajan to Caracalla,[73] and again under Diocletian and Constantine, is

66 The implication is that the court of other emperors was similarly composed. The favoured freedmen were of course household members.

67 Talbert 1984, 438–50.

68 Talbert 1984, 179–81.

69 See further Modrzejewski 1974.

70 For the latter, cf. Zonaras 12.22.

71 For a formal statement, see *Digest* 1.4.1.1 (Ulpian). See further Hauken 1998, 298–303; Burton 2002, 252.

72 Burton 2002, esp. 259.

73 A change under Trajan is to be associated with a certain sense on Trajan's part that his rule both was and ought to be superior to that of his predecessors: see Pliny, *Letters* 10.1.2, 10.97.2, *Digest* 48.22.1; cf. Bleicken 1982, 24.

probably correct. These were the emperors who really tried to make use of the legislative power at their disposal.

From Tiberius onwards the early emperors, helped by natural causes, eliminated the descendants of the old aristocracy. Tacitus, in an undervalued analysis, claimed that the latter, through their extravagance, contributed to their own demise (*Annals* 3.55). After Nero, in any case, leading senators very seldom belonged to families with many generations of consular rank behind them: a man such as C. Calpurnius Piso, a consul in AD 111 whose consular ancestors went back to 180 BC, was a very rare specimen (but the family continued: its last known consul held office in AD 175).[74] In spite of their social conservatism, emperors did not create a new aristocracy. There has been some dispute about this: Hopkins and Burton argued in detail that 'during the first three centuries AD membership of the Roman senate was to a large extent not hereditary'.[75] The statistical basis for this statement is inevitably fragile, but the contrast with the mid- and late-republican Senate is clear. So is the main reason for it: a relatively rapid turnover suited the interests of the emperors. They dispensed patronage, sometimes they identified talent, and increasingly they brought in provincials, so that in the second century all the more assimilated parts of the empire, including the Greek cities, had produced a significant number of senators and even consuls. Others have argued that in the Antonine period the consulship was hereditary, which is a highly misleading way of describing a situation in which some 27 per cent of consuls were the sons of consuls.[76] There were inherited social privileges, obviously – very few 'ordinary' Severan consuls (the more prestigious kind) were the sons of men who had not even been in the Senate;[77] but an aristocracy properly so-called both dominates in the present and passes on much of its power to the grandsons of its grandsons.

As the power of the Senate waned, it became thinkable that a powerful military man of equestrian rank could hold the imperial power. The first was the short-lived Macrinus (217), who had been commander of the praetorian guard. From Maximinus Thrax (235–8) onwards, emperors with long military experience became more and more necessary, and non-senatorial origin became the norm.

[74] See Syme 1958a, 575–8.
[75] Hopkins and Burton 1983, 194.
[76] See Burton 1995, responding to Hahn and Leunissen 1990.
[77] Five out of some sixty-five whose origins are known: Leunissen 1989, 107–8. The period considered includes the reign of Commodus.

But eliminating the old aristocracy did not make the emperors personally secure. Scheidel has shown that the reigns of Roman emperors were the shortest among all the thirty-one highly various monarchies he took into consideration (Byzantine emperors were also relatively short lived).[78] Roman dynasties did not last long either. Of the 72 men who can reasonably be classified as *Augusti* and not merely minor usurpers between 14 and 337, 50 died as a result of Roman military actions of one kind or another. Their life-expectation was especially low between 211 and 284.

It is scarcely surprising that the military origins of the monarchical system would return to haunt it unless emperors were shrewd, vigilant, and fortunate. But more is in fact needed to explain the high rate of 'premature termination' (Scheidel) among Roman emperors than the availability of armed force and the Roman proclivity for bloodshed, important though these factors were. The armed forces were never tamed: Septimius Severus' death-bed advice to Caracalla and his brother is famous – 'Don't disagree with each other, give money to the soldiers, and despise everyone else' (Dio 76.17.4). As for the proclivity for bloodshed: in what other nation would Caracalla have been widely believed to have plotted the death of the father Septimius, who had made him co-emperor [Figure 5.3]?[79]

An additional destabilizing factor was the understandable tendency to approve of the assassination of a tyrant, an inheritance from a partisan optimate doctrine of the late Republic:[80] according to Suetonius, himself a former high official, it was right that Domitian, whom in some respects he portrays favourably (*Domitian* 8), was murdered, because of his 'greed and cruelty' (*Divine Vespasian* 1).[81] The emperor was supposed to behave well from the point of view of the elite (to some extent an inheritance from both republicanism and Augustus), and if he did not do so he could properly be removed – and there was only one way to do that. What led to the assassination of Alexander Severus? The soldiers thought that he was dominated by his mother and had been ineffective as a military leader; they also hoped to be rewarded by his successor (Herodian 6.8.3).

78 Scheidel forthcoming. Veyne 2002 noticed the problem, but his explanation, to the effect that emperors depended on a popular mandate (p. 50), makes little sense.

79 Birley 1988, 187–8.

80 On this doctrine, see Pina Polo 2006.

81 The courtier Seneca naturally claimed that the tyrannicide M. Brutus, who was still much respected in senatorial circles, had acted contrary to Stoic teaching (*On Benefits* 2.20).

Figure 5.3. Murderous relatives. Caracalla (bottom right), with his parents Septimius Severus (whom he was suspected of murdering) and Iulia Domna and his (erased) younger brother Geta (whom he certainly murdered and dishonoured with *damnatio memoriae*). Painted wooden tondo *c.* AD 198. Berlin, Antikensammlung

Imperial questions

While much more can be said about the power of the emperors, seven questions stand out. I am not much concerned here with their supposedly 'charismatic' power (cf. above, p. 106), which either means prestige, which is less vague, or a combination of fame and extra-institutional power – such as was possessed by the 'false Neros', usurpers who pretended to be

Nero after his death.[82] We will come later to some charismatic persons who were not emperors or imperial claimants.

(1) *The loyalty of the military.* Emperors did their best to keep the military out of politics,[83] but the support of the soldiers was crucial to them. How did they manage to ensure loyalty in ordinary circumstances? The soldiers in the capital, namely the praetorian guardsmen, were naturally the most important: they were paid three times as much as legionaries, or more.[84] It was also vital to select the senior officers of the legions well and to make sure that they remained loyal, for the armed services were of course hierarchical (a crucial moment in Vespasian's rise to power came when Ti. Iulius Alexander, the prefect of Egypt, 'led' the legions there to swear loyalty to him: Suetonius, *Divine Vespasian* 6). The list of consulars who rebelled or thought about doing so is quite long.[85] In the third century it was the loyalty of the higher officers that slipped, first in 217 and later on many other occasions. Equally obvious was the need to pay the soldiers promptly and provide them with donatives and assorted opportunities for gain.

But all that was only part of the tool-kit. There was an image to project, and there were mechanisms to bring into play. When the soldiers renewed their oath to the emperor on the anniversary of his accession they did so in the presence of his portrait, and such oaths do really seem to have had a certain force.[86] It was also better for the emperor if he personally led his soldiers to victory; next best was visiting them in camp and flattering them, as Hadrian did. By contrast, a reputation for effeminacy made the soldiers scornful – hence trouble for Nero and Elagabalus. 'Had the soldiers been passionately loyal instead of confused or apathetic, no general could have risked a proclamation…'.[87]

When matters went wrong and the disloyal had to be suppressed or the potentially disloyal had to be discouraged, the government minted coin-types advertising 'the concord of the soldiers', 'the good faith of the armies', and so on (thus in 69 and on a number of later occasions). And since the soldiers were always favourable – other things being equal – to entrenched dynasties, it was no doubt partly to satisfy them that emperors made much play with their descent from earlier emperors, especially when it was entirely spurious, as in the case of Septimius Severus and his sons.

[82] Cf. Bowersock 1987, 308–11.
[83] Hopkins 2009, 192–3.
[84] Campbell 1984, 163–4.
[85] MacMullen 1985.
[86] Campbell 1984, 19–32.
[87] Syme 1958a, 440, on Nero.

Thus a complex of factors (money above all, but not only money) kept soldiers loyal or failed to do so. The problem continued: even a strong emperor such as Constantine had to mix ingratiation and privileges with his attempts to maintain discipline among soldiers and veterans (see *Theodosian Code* 7.20 and 22). And Constantine created a substantially new problem by recruiting much of the army with which he warred against Maxentius from among 'barbarians'.[88]

(2) *Ideology.* The Principate rested on a military foundation, but to endure it had to have an ideological foundation too. What did this consist of? The main elements can be summed up as military prestige – the emperor as victor, conqueror, and pacifier –, quasi-divine status, family continuity (which is made more difficult to understand by the difference between Roman adoption practices and our own), and imperial virtues.

I speak of 'quasi-divine status', because the emperor appeared in quite different guises in different environments, while benefiting everywhere from an exalted religious position.[89] In Rome itself, the emperor enjoyed some religious trappings, such as the office of *pontifex maximus* [Figure 5.4], and after his death, if the Senate approved, he became in a loose sense a god. By the time of Claudius, a man on the fringe of the imperial court could refer to the ruler as 'our god' (Scribonius Largus, *Recipes* [*Compositiones*] 163). In most of the eastern provinces he was commonly referred to as a god by people who had a vested interest in so doing, and in many provinces important towns built temples jointly for Rome and Augustus.[90] Most towns in the western empire had their colleges of *Augustales* (see p. 208), largely freedmen, whose responsibility it was to look after the cult of the 'divine spirit' of the emperor. In the eastern provinces, much could be left to local initiative, whereas in the west, where traditions of ruler-cult were lacking, more appears to have been organized from the capital.[91] In short, religious honours proliferated almost everywhere, at city and province level, and sometimes on private initiative. The figure of the emperor dominated visual representations of the central ritual of Roman religion, animal sacrifice.[92]

88 Liebeschuetz 1990, 7.
89 See Hopkins 1978, chapter 5; Price 1984; Fishwick 2002; Gradel 2002.
90 For a very detailed account of how the imperial cult developed in Syria, see Bru 2011, chapters 6 to 13.
91 Fishwick 2002, 213–19.
92 Gordon 1990.

Figure 5.4 Marcus Aurelius about to perform the central rite of sacrifice in honour of Iuppiter Optimus Maximus Capitolinus. The marble relief, one of a series, probably comes from an arch built in the emperor's honour AD 176–180. Rome, Musei Capitolini

The emperor's divinity served several purposes, in addition to gratifying his vanity. It provided a channel for provincial favour-seekers;[93] thus it was typical for an ambitious provincial with money to take on a priesthood of the imperial cult and see his son advance to equestrian rank.[94] Emperor-worship allowed the *princeps* to be coupled with Rome itself as an object of public respect, so that together they formed a focus for possible unity. How much the religious position of the emperor contributed to his personal power, or to the power of Rome, is disputed: it is hard to suppose that a single senator, knight, soldier, or imperial freedman was ever influenced much, even subconsciously; ordinary civilians may well have felt some degree of awe.

Yet a rationalist historian who thinks along these lines is probably missing something, and the emperors who refused divine honours or mitigated them, as they often did from Augustus to at least Caracalla,[95] may well have been mistaken too.[96] Some emperors thought of sparing their subjects expense. They would have done much better, as far as their own security was concerned, to have imposed sacrifices, like mediaeval cathedral builders. Chinese emperors and Aztec rulers, among others, were to some extent protected by their divine status.[97] That is not to say that the security function of the imperial cult was its whole *raison d'être*.[98]

Under Commodus, sacrality spread – the emperor claimed to be under the special protection of Hercules and indeed came close to identifying himself with Hercules, and the consuls of 182 for the first time – as far as we know[99] – referred to a decision of the emperor's as a '*sacred* subscription' (*ILS* 6870 = Riccobono 1941–1943, 1, no. 103), a sacred subscription 'of our master the *sanctissimus imperator*'. (Similar language had long been familiar in the Greek-speaking empire, in keeping with the deification of the emperors there). Epigraphic and iconographic evidence allows us to follow from reign to reign the particular religious associations conjured up by individual emperors.[100] The religious calendar of a cohort of Palmyrenes

[93] See further Price 1984, 243.
[94] Bowersock 1973, 182; Camia 2008.
[95] See Oliver 1989, 14–15, for some examples.
[96] They were following the self-interested advice that the senator Dio (52.35) put into the mouth of Maecenas – avoid 'excessive' honours; that was what senators liked.
[97] On the Chinese case, see Chaussende 2009, 268, 272–3. The exact relationship of the rulers of the Aztecs (Nahuas) to the gods they impersonated and the effects of the impersonation are much discussed: see Klein 2001; Knight 2002, 149–55.
[98] Price 1984, 240, dismissed this function too readily.
[99] Cf. Drew-Bear *et al.* 1977, 360–1.
[100] Rowan 2012 performs this task for the Severan emperors, but focuses too narrowly on coin-types. For the Severan emperors, see Marsden 1997.

stationed on the Euphrates in about 225 happens to be preserved on papyrus (in Latin, for it was applicable everywhere in the empire): it shows us the unit honouring past and present members of the imperial house with sacrifices several times a month.[101] After 244 (the death of Gordian III) the trend seems to have been away from divine honours for the emperor himself and towards close association with recognized deities, including sometimes the deified emperors of the past.[102] From Gallienus onwards, coin-types often claimed select gods as the emperor's 'companion' (*comes*).[103]

As for family continuity, it was assumed by everyone that an emperor who died peacefully would be succeeded by his son or sons, if he had any (whether biological or adopted mattered little, the Romans being accustomed to the adoption of adults).[104] All emperors took the names 'Caesar Augustus'. Breaks in 68 and 96 inevitably brought in different family names. The Severan emperors invented a retroactive family connection with the Antonines and even with Nerva,[105] so that whenever Caracalla appeared in an official text he was not 'L. Septimius L.f. Severus', as nature had intended, but 'Imp. Caesar M. Aurelius Antoninus Pius Felix Aug.', or something similar. In a proclamation of 222 (*Select Papyri* II.216, mentioned above), Alexander Severus typically, and quite falsely of course, refers to Trajan and Marcus Aurelius as his ancestors. Presumably this practice strengthened the authority of the men who made such claims, but for fifty years after 235 it did not help. With the tetrarchs, family links – an inevitable human tendency – came back into play: the joint emperors Diocletian and Maximian appointed as 'Caesars', and later as co-emperors, Maximian's son-in-law Constantius, and Galerius, who at some point married Diocletian's daughter Valeria (hence four joint rulers: the 'tetrarchs') [Figure 5.5]. With Constantine, the son of Constantius, the full dynastic principle returned.

Augustus, as we saw earlier, made much of his supposed virtues, especially 'courage, clemency, justice, and piety'.[106] Later emperors did so too:[107] imperial coin-types harp from time to time on the emperor's justice, piety,

101 The so-called Feriale Duranum: Fink 1971 no. 117; Campbell 1994, no. 207.
102 For the latter point, see the coins of Decius commented on by Potter 2004, 244; cf. Gradel 2002, 367–8.
103 Nock 1947.
104 But Septimius Severus thought that a biological son was better: Oliver 1989, no. 217, line 31.
105 Potter 1994, 112.
106 These terms are approximate translations of the Roman concepts.
107 See Wallace-Hadrill 1981.

Figure 5.5. The joint emperors Diocletian, Maximian, Constantius, and Galerius – the 'tetrarchs' –. shown in military uniform being demonstratively loyal to one another. Statue group in red porphyry, original location unknown, perhaps Nicomedia. Venice, San Marco

foresight, etcetera, and Pliny's panegyric on Trajan 'bombards' the reader with more than thirty virtues.[108] The question here is how much effect such discourse – mostly instantiated on coins and very often concerned with desirable personifications that are not virtues, such as safety, security, and *felicitas* (divinely bestowed good fortune) – had on securing the ruler's power. Much effort went into such propaganda from AD 69 onwards, but it is hard to locate any section of the population that might have been greatly impressed, and the suspicion arises that it was mostly the work of officials who desired to ingratiate themselves with the man in power. From the 260s 'Invictus' (Unconquered) became standard too.[109] The coin-types emphasize in essence that the emperor is a figure of superhuman power,[110] but was anyone listening?[111] Perhaps we should see the use of such coin-types as a secondary type of largely subliminal advertisement.

(3) *Civilian obedience.* How did the emperor prevail on the civilian population to obey, in so far as it did so? Military prestige and the ideological factors just discussed achieved a good deal, but the personal prestige of many emperors was fragile.

An ordinarily competent emperor had in fact little difficulty in controlling the senators and knights, as long as he seemed to retain the loyalty of the military. The carrots were offices, access, and honour and the occasional financial favour (cf. Suetonius, *Nero* 10, for instance), while the sticks were treason trials and death sentences, or exile to an unfrequented island.

Court life was dangerous, and many stories convey the atmosphere of terror that the ruler might engender in the upper elite, heightened no doubt by the fact that in public he was normally accompanied by imposing military guards.[112] Domitian invited the leading senators and knights to dinner:

> he prepared a room that was pitch black on every side, ceiling, walls, and floor ... then he invited in his guests, alone at night without their attendants. And first he set beside each of them a tablet shaped like a tombstone, bearing the guest's name. Next, good-looking naked boys, painted black, entered like phantoms ... every single one of the guests feared and trembled and was kept in constant expectation of having his throat cut the next moment... (Dio 67.9, with further vivid details).[113]

108 Noreña 2009, 273.
109 Cf. above, p. 129.
110 Wallace-Hadrill 1981, 316.
111 See further Levick 1982; Harris 1989a, 213.
112 Millar 1977, 61–6.
113 No doubt this story improved in the telling. It should be set in the context of the (pseudo-)egalitarian tradition of the Roman dinner-party (on which, see D'Arms 1990).

No one was killed that night, but the power relationship was clear (and when Domitian was later assassinated, it was not by a senator or knight). Senators continued to hope for a ruler who was the *princeps* ('first citizen') not *dominus* ('master'), and to express their hope publicly (Pliny, *Panegyric* 45).[114] But they were inevitably disappointed, and senators could be executed, in some reigns at least, for the flimsiest of reasons.[115]

Meanwhile, however, most emperors worked at providing a semblance of good government. They normally spent a good deal of time hearing lawsuits, and might do so even on campaign. They also responded to petitions, mostly, however, to cities not individuals. (Lesser petitioners could apply to lesser authorities). What exactly motivated them to do so is unclear to us and was probably unclear to them, but the more sensible rulers undoubtedly gave thought to the loyalty of the provincials, knowing that these were the populations from which their soldiers sprang. An emperor who did not have wars to preoccupy him was especially likely to deal with the minutiae of provincial governance: Hadrian, in love with Athens, bothered about the regulation of the fish-market at Eleusis (Oliver 1989 no. 77), and he, or at least his chancery, issued instructions about a single house in Stratonicea, a city he had re-founded in Caria while he was on an imperial tour (Oliver 1989, no. 79, lines 10–14).

From Augustus to Constantine emperors proclaimed that they had 'tribunician power', and a useful fiction had it that they were responsive to the most modest of their subjects. But the power of their civilian subjects to affect the government tended to decline still further. It did no harm to humour the population of the capital, which Augustus, it will be remembered, had regimented as far as that was possible.[116] Fronto, intimate of the emperor Marcus, is often quoted. He remarked that:

> it was the epitome of knowing how to deal with Romans [*civilis scientia*] for the emperor not to neglect even actors and the other performers of the stage, circus, and arena, since he knew that the Roman people [he undoubtedly means those of them who lived in the capital] is held fast by two things above all, the grain supply and the games, and that the imperial power [*imperium*] gains approval as much from frivolous things as serious ones (*Introduction to the History* 20 = Fronto ed. van den Hout [1988], p. 213).

114 Amid Pliny's sycophantic language ('we are *subiecti* to you' – a new concept, cf. Thurman 1970, 460), he claims that law also rules (*Panegyric* 24.4).

115 Under Septimius Severus, for example: Dio 76. 8–9.

116 See Millar 1977, 368–75, for a survey of emperors' interactions with the people of Rome.

Fronto was in fact exaggerating in order to justify the emperor L. Verus' taste for actors. And no doubt many Romans could distinguish between the gift and the giver (Martial despised Nero, but liked his baths, 7.34).

More perhaps than in most empires, ordinary people in the Roman Empire seem commonly to have believed that they could obtain redress for their grievances directly from the emperor, above all if he were physically present. So a woman who made a request to Hadrian in the street expected an answer (Dio 69.6; the accuracy of the story is immaterial). The standard technique for ordinary citizens, limited literacy notwithstanding, was to hand in a written petition, a *libellus*.[117] The practice became commoner in the second century, apparently (one wonders why), and down to the Severan period at least, the governmental powers did sometimes respond.

Successful requests to the emperor normally came from towns or collectivities not from ordinary individuals; but they could come from such non-influential people as the fishermen of Formiae and Gaieta, who were, however, at least citizens (they obtained a rescript from Antoninus Pius, *Digest* 1.8.4). In a well-known case the *coloni* on his African estates obtained favours from the lazy Commodus.[118] Even more strikingly, the Goharieni, a tribal population who lived not far from Damascus, took the opportunity of Caracalla's presence in Syria to bring a case before him.[119] Lycian peasants could get the attention of the imperial chancery (*SEG* 48 [1999], no. 1583). In other words, people far from the centres of power could obtain redress from the top: it was evidently an important principle of practical government. But provincial governors were allowed, at some periods at least, to exercise control over who could appeal to the ruler.[120]

Repressive controls were also considered necessary. Senators who were willing to denounce others for treason have received a reasonable amount of attention from historians, but we also need to pay attention to low-level spies. Here is Epictetus (*Discourses* 4.13.5), writing under Trajan but referring quite probably to his own time in Rome under Domitian:

> ...in this fashion the rash are caught by the soldiers in Rome. A soldier in civilian dress sits down by your side, and starts by speaking ill of Caesar, and then you too, just as if you had received from him some guarantee of

[117] Harris 1989a, 214–15.
[118] Potter 2004, 5. This was in the 'sacred subscription' referred to above.
[119] *SEG* 17 (1960), no. 759, with Millar 1977, 38.
[120] See the discussions in Brunt 1990, 73–5; Shaw 2000, 369–70.

> good faith in the fact that he began the abuse, say everything you think – and you are led away in chains.

This argues for an extensive network of spooks.[121] And as Trajan listened to Pliny denouncing informers (*Panegyric* 34–6), he may well have reflected that Domitian and others would have lived longer if their spooks had been more efficient. The underlying premise is that disloyal speech was quite dangerous. The soldiers designated as 'frumentarii', literally 'grain-men', were supposed to search out signs of subversion in the provinces (but we have very little idea of how numerous or efficient they were).[122] Dio (52.37) reflects the practice of Severan times[123] when he makes Maecenas give fictive advice to the emperor to employ a comprehensive set of domestic spies, who are to report on people who think or say anything against the ruler, – but not to believe everything they report. Greeks meanwhile liked to tell stories about how they had been impertinent to emperors and had got away with it, or suffered heroically in consequence.[124]

From Augustus onwards, emperors made frequent efforts to repress subversive talk, particularly if it was prophetic, and to some extent concerned themselves with the written equivalents. Needless to say they were only partially successful, and a notable quantity of more or less subversive literature, much of it Christian, survives. Most of what was committed to writing undermined the emperor's authority rather than challenging it directly.[125]

It will be clear by now that while emperors worked to win and maintain the support of provincial elites, there is no reason at all to think that they succeeded in achieving anything as grand as 'consensus' among the great mass of the provincial population, east or west. There is in fact likely to have been a great deal of variation not only between the 'inner' and the 'outer' provinces but between town and countryside. Towns increasingly carried the emperor's message: from an early date the imperial court seems to have distributed imperial portraits to the principal cities.[126] But most of the population everywhere consisted of farmers and farm-workers, and

121 Cf. Tacitus, *Agricola* 2.3; Suetonius, *Nero* 39; Philostratus, *Life of Apollonius of Tyana* 7.8.

122 See Fuhrmann 2012, 151–7, etc.

123 Cf. Dio 78.17.

124 Harker 2008, 147–51.

125 For subversive literature and censorship, see Harris 1989a, 212 (with bibliography); Lane Fox 1994. A full account remains to be written.

126 Roueché 1993, 145–6; Ando 2000, 232–43; Kolb 2003, 129–32. Some of the evidence goes back to Tiberius, but most of it is second century or later. By the time of Marcus Aurelius, Fronto could say that the cities were full of the emperor's image (*Letters* 4.12.6); similarly, on the late third century, Menander Rhetor (377.26–7). Both were probably exaggerating.

they may not have been much affected by the messages from the centre. The most that emperors are likely to have achieved with the mass of provincials was acquiescence and a measure of identity change.[127] For a long time, that was perhaps all they needed. Later, as Keith Hopkins perceptively observed, the fact that 'the empire as a whole had no effective rituals to give all [its] inhabitants ... a single collective identity' – in sharp contrast with the cohesive citizen body of the middle Republic –[128] helped to make it vulnerable, first to the Christians, later still to the Germans.

(4) *Succession.* Why were emperors unable to institute a stable succession system? It might be argued that there was nothing particularly unusual in this failure until it intensified from 235 onwards, since many other pre-modern monarchies experienced intense succession problems too.[129]

The majority of emperors prior to 211, other than those who ruled briefly in 68–9 and 193, attempted to designate the next ruler. Emperors who had natural sons, even manifestly inadequate sons such as Commodus, wanted to have them as successors. But what happened when the emperor met a violent end?

The first time the succession was unclear, after Caligula's assassination in 41, the praetorian guard decided who should rule (and thereby put an end to senatorial talk of restoring the Republic), and almost always, when there was no established successor, force of arms decided. But quite apart from the fact that, until the third century, no one could become emperor who was not among other things a senior senator, there were forms to be observed that we should not dismiss as pure formalities. When Galba rebelled against Nero, in Spain in 68, he claimed that his authority came from 'the Senate and people of Rome' (Suetonius, *Galba* 10), and the most distinctive of his coins commemorated his late benefactor Livia, the wife of Augustus, with the obvious intent of claiming a sort of quasi-dynastic legitimacy.[130] He apparently asserted that he ruled by the consensus of gods and men (Tacitus, *Histories* 1.15). Yet in 96, when it is commonly supposed that the Senate chose one of its own number as emperor – well-born, sixty-year-old, childless Nerva – the role of the praetorians may have been important (the sources are poor, but the Fasti Ostienses show that he was considered to have become emperor the day before the Senate voted).

[127] Ando 2000 bases his contrary argument on the fallacy that the assent of the local elites, itself far from complete in the second century, is all that matters.

[128] Hopkins 1991, 498.

[129] See Kautsky 1982, 239–46.

[130] Some of his coins also claim that he was restoring *libertas*: H. Mattingly 1976, Galba no. 258.

Rank determined who was eligible, and family continuity was important. But when Avidius Cassius rebelled against Marcus Aurelius, he asserted that he had been 'elected by the most noble soldiers'.[131] This was a new kind of claim, or admission. In 193, another 'year of the four emperors', it was the military again: the exact role of Q. Aemilius Laetus, the praetorian prefect, in the conspiracy that killed Commodus is unclear, but at first the praetorian guard was dominant. After Laetus' nominee Pertinax had ruled for three months, dissatisfied praetorians and bodyguards killed him, and the praetorians famously proceeded to auction off the supreme power. The winner was Didius Iulianus, a senior senator, but he was deluded (as were the praetorians), for still greater power attached to the legions: when Septimius Severus, governor in 193 of Upper Pannonia, arrived in Rome after prevailing in civil war, he dismissed the existing guardsmen and replaced them with legionaries from the provinces. The evil remained, of necessity; in fact the number of troops stationed in the capital dramatically increased – by a factor of four, Herodian claims (3.13.4). Such was the logic of a political system in which military power counted for almost everything.

The praetorian guard was to strike again, in 238, but it was the power of the legions, in most cases more specifically that of their higher-level officers, that determined who would rule throughout the period down to the ascendancy of Diocletian. Gallienus succeeded in retaining power for fifteen years (253–68), at first in combination with his father, but no one else lasted nearly as long; some forty men claimed the title Augustus in the half-century starting in 235, and only one emperor in this time-frame died in his bed (Claudius Gothicus, who died of the plague). How Diocletian and Constantine re-introduced some temporary order into this system we shall see shortly.

For a long time the established method of recruiting senior officers, combined with deference and tradition, had ensured that the successful candidate would always be a leading senator. Macrinus, as already mentioned, was the first exception. Maximinus Thrax, from Moesia, made his way in a similar fashion.[132] The Senate fought back against the rule of army officers, but briefly and in vain. From 244 onwards, senatorial office-holders were the exception among claimants to the throne; equestrian rank was the rule. In other words, the Roman Empire now drew its leaders from a much larger pool of talent.

131 *SB* 10295, with Bowman 1970.
132 See Syme 1971, 188–90.

The difficulties emperors experienced in surviving and in passing on their power to their personal heirs reflect the limits of their power, which we shall return to.

(5) *Imperial women.* First, how much power did they exercise, the mothers, wives, and concubines of the emperors? Our sources are necessarily based to a large extent on gossip, but it is evident that, in such a position, a woman of ability could eliminate rivals and influence appointments as well as obtaining wealth and honours for herself. The highest honour, other than posthumous deification, was the title 'Augusta', 'empress' in effect; this was bestowed on Livia by Augustus, by Claudius on his last wife, the younger Agrippina, by Nero on Poppaea and their infant daughter, and as a matter of routine on every emperor's wife from the reign of Domitian onwards. Mothers too sometimes became Augustae: Iulia Soaemias (the mother of Elagabalus), her sister Iulia Mamaea (mother of Alexander Severus), and Helena (Constantine), and occasionally even daughters did so. In peaceful conditions the emperor's wife could determine the succession: it was Livia's daughter-in-law Antonia who effectively brought down Sejanus in 31, and Agrippina notoriously secured the throne for Nero. Iulia Maesa had an important role in transferring power in 222 from Elagabalus to Alexander Severus.

Vespasian's freedwoman concubine Caenis 'received huge sums from many sources, sometimes selling governorships, sometimes procuratorships, generalships and priesthoods, and in some instances even imperial decisions' (Dio 66.14),[133] this under a ruler who was unusually astute; but Caenis had political experience going back forty years and hence was an extreme case. There were limits: peace, war, taxation, and the very highest appointments seem normally to have been masculine preserves. (But Plotina apparently reined in the fiscal agents of her husband Trajan: Aurelius Victor, *Epitome* 42.21). When Caracalla had his mother Iulia Domna vet his correspondence (with fatal consequences) while he was on campaign (Dio 78.4), that too was exceptional.

All this reflects a society in which there was relatively easy sociability between upper-class women and men (not to be exaggerated, however: Pliny's 247 'private' letters include only three that are addressed to women outside his family), and in which women had relatively extensive legal rights.

(6) *The limits of the emperor's power.* In what ways was the apparently unlimited power of the emperors circumscribed? 'I am the arbiter of

[133] Since Dio is generally favourable to Vespasian, it is unlikely that there is much exaggeration here.

life and death for the whole world, each man's fate and station has been put into my hand', says Nero, as imagined by Seneca – who had a deep practical knowledge of the court (*On Clemency* 1.1). It was a sign of the near-absolute power of the ruler that the emperor's anger was a constant preoccupation, at least in court circles:[134] if the emperor did not realize the value of self-restraint and behave accordingly, there was no other safeguard short of assassination.

When Aelius Aristides explained why he thought (or pretended to think) that the government of the Roman Empire was a democracy, 'under one man who is the best ruler and teacher' (*To Rome* 60), his argument was that it was ruled by law.[135] That was true – though of course only part of the truth –, and conscientious emperors, as already mentioned, spent a large proportion of their time administering justice. And they all, even Caligula, followed established law and practice, most of the time – but not always, for the emperor might prefer 'to be seen to make justice prevail over law'[136] (see Suetonius, *Divine Claudius* 14, for example). And law was no protection against treason trials or against imperial rancour. It pleased Vespasian that a law, which survives, set out his powers;[137] this law has stimulated much commentary, but it was no more than a formal gesture towards the past. When Ulpian declared that the *princeps* 'is absolved from the laws' (*legibus solutus*) (*Digest* 1.3.31), he was essentially repeating what had already been contained in Clause 6 of Vespasian's law, and he was simply giving meaningless sanction to a hard fact. Nonetheless a well-behaved emperor might advertise his conformity with the law (see for example *CJ* 6.23.3, Alexander Severus).

The real limitations on the emperor's power were practical, and they concerned money, information, and time. The emperor's wealth was in principle immense, but so were his expenses, and extravagance or an unexpected war could lead to a drastic shortage of cash (as Nero, Marcus, and Pertinax, among others, discovered). But what was most difficult of all was to know what was happening – on and beyond the frontiers, among the tax-collectors, in the armies, even in the court itself. Imperial procurators and the governors of imperial provinces wrote letters, and the quality of the information they sent may often have been good and reasonably up to date, but much no doubt was self-serving. Pliny's correspondence with

[134] Harris 2002, 249–63.
[135] Cf. n. 96.
[136] Stolte 2003, 268.
[137] *ILS* 244 = Crawford *et al.* 1996, 1, no. 39.

Trajan (*Letters* Book 10) must not be taken as typical – Pliny had been sent to Bithynia because of a perceived local crisis. As we have already seen, however, emperors often showed a strong interest in local detail.

The Roman Empire of this period was probably too large to be ruled successfully, in ancient conditions, by anyone except a man of extraordinary talents. The Romans had in a sense won too many wars for their own good, or rather they needed a more efficient system of delegation – and Diocletian gave it to them. One might say that fully one-third of the emperors who ruled from Tiberius to Alexander Severus were good at it; but it is to be presumed that in the period of generally short and precarious reigns after 211, or least after 235, the power of the emperor was notably weaker. The most important effects were probably fiscal, which leads to the vital matter of finance.

(7) *The emperor and money.* The emperor was in principle immensely wealthy. There is no useful way of measuring this wealth, which in any case fluctuated widely, but major properties in Italy and in every province were the rule.[138] Emperors expected to be remembered in wills, so that Agricola, typically, judged it wise to make Domitian his co-heir (Tacitus, *Agricola* 43). Who exactly regularly did this, and which emperors exercised moderation, are complicated questions,[139] but there is no doubt that the fiscus could by this means accumulate property on a very large scale. The system amounted to an imperial protection racket.

One of the main questions here, apart from the technical problem, quite a severe one, of knowing how the emperor's funds and those of the state related to one another,[140] is to know how much control the emperor exerted over his own assets. We therefore want to know how closely he supervised his *a rationibus* (financial secretary), the roughly two dozen procurators in charge of his provincial properties,[141] the prefects of the Treasury, the *procurator rei privatae*, and other officials. An expert on Roman Egypt concluded that 'the personal involvement of the emperor in his land [was] a constant factor in the history of imperial estates',[142] and occasionally we catch sight of emperors writing to senior financial officials.[143] Marcus Aurelius claims that one of the many things he learned from his adoptive father and predecessor was 'stewardship of the revenues'

[138] For a comprehensive survey, see Maiuro 2012.
[139] See Millar 1977, 153–8; Maiuro 2012, 38–80.
[140] On this, see especially Brunt 1990, chapters 7 and 16.
[141] Eck 2000, 244.
[142] D.J. Crawford 1976, 56.
[143] Millar 1977, 106.

(*To Himself* 1.16). So while it may only have been the most money-oriented emperors, such as Vespasian, who had a really firm grasp of what was going on, most others certainly took a strong interest.

And they needed to do so, because liberality was expected. We have already seen how this applied to the army and the city *plebs*, but it was of much wider importance.[144] From Hadrian's time onwards until well into the third century *liberalitas* was the imperial quality most advertised on coins. And actual liberality began to have a questionable effect. The cities that had succeeded in obtaining tax exemptions had once been few; by the age of the Severi such concessions meant that the tax burden was very unevenly distributed. Listing the cities in certain provinces to whom emperors had awarded property-tax exemptions, Ulpian (*Digest* 50.15) gives the impression that the privilege had spread rather widely (other sources confirm). In the 250s there seems to have been some reaction.[145]

Usurpers in particular needed to be generous. Hence Constantine (but his claim to rule was as good as that of many others) earned a reputation for heavy spending,[146] which he could afford partly because Diocletian and the other tetrarchs had made the system of taxation more effective.

Diocletian and Constantine

How did the emperor's power evolve in the period of Diocletian and Constantine? In many respects, both of them naturally built on ideas that had already taken shape in earlier periods, in civilian as in military affairs. Sanctifying the person of the emperor, for example, was an old tradition, so that when Diocletian and Maximian took the extra names 'Iovius' and 'Herculius' respectively no one can have been surprised. Yet the tetrarchs did most definitely attempt to increase the religious aura around themselves: officially approved flatterers repeatedly referred to them as divine (for example in *Panegyrici Latini* 8 (4) of 297 or 298), and the iconography of their medallions and coins points in the same direction (haloes – technically *nimbi* – had previously been reserved for gods).[147] The aim of all this – how formulated we cannot know – was clearly to increase imperial authority.

The idea of dividing the empire into four (imprecisely defined) segments also grew quite logically out of prior practices; there had several times been

[144] Kloft 1970.
[145] Heather 1994, 22.
[146] C. Kelly 2012, 194.
[147] See Bergmann 1998, 45.

two joint *Augusti*. In some other respects, however, Diocletian was a remarkable innovator, even though some of his ideas were destined to fail, such as his determined effort to prevent price and wage inflation (301) (apparently he was not even able to get his edict promulgated in the west, let alone obeyed).

Diocletian, Maximian, and Constantine lived longer than most emperors, partly no doubt because of a revitalized system of domestic spying. Emperors had long used the so-called *frumentarii* as confidential agents, and it was now apparently that they were replaced in this function by *agentes in rebus* or *agentes rerum* (Aurelius Victor, *Epitome* 39.44–5); what difference that made, we can only guess.[148] The emperors' bodyguards were also numerous.[149] But the ways in which Diocletian strengthened imperial control went beyond the non-trivial achievement of not getting assassinated. Both he and Constantine understood exceptionally well how to retain the support of the soldiers.

Diocletian successfully revived provincial census-taking, an essential basis for effective tax-extraction. The system of personal and property taxation itself was radically reorganized.[150] Privileged communities around the empire seem to have lost their immunity. He also imposed a major reorganization of the provinces, splitting about fifty units into about 100 (in an extreme case, the moderate-sized province 'Asia' was divided into seven). The whole empire was also divided into 'dioceses', each containing eight or nine provinces (these dioceses are not attested till 314, but they were hardly new at that date).[151] Here again the point was clearly to facilitate tax-gathering. Furthermore Diocletian conceived and started putting into effect a major and very valuable reform of the currency.[152]

He and Maximian probably commissioned the first historical, and long overdue, codifications of Roman law, the *codex Gregorianus* and the *codex Hermogenianus*.[153] It also seems to have been Diocletian who reorganized military recruitment by imposing on landowners an obligation to provide recruits, also by conscripting the sons of veterans and by settling non-Romans in the provinces in exchange for army service.[154]

We here approach the problem of bureaucracy, which is going to haunt our whole account of state power in late antiquity. In 288 we meet for the

[148] Giardina 1977. Their number can be roughly conjectured from the fact that a law of 430 attempted to reduce their establishment to 1,174 (*Theodosian Code* 6.27.23).

[149] Elton 2012, 328.

[150] On Diocletian's tax-reform, see Corbier 2005, 376–83.

[151] Barnes 1996, 548–50.

[152] Harl 1996, 148–56.

[153] Cf. Connolly 2010, 41. They were in reality collections of imperial 'constitutions'.

[154] Campbell 2005, 126.

first time a phenomenon that recurs in the fourth century, a high official in Egypt trying for financial reasons to keep the number of subordinate officials under control (*P.Oxy.* I.58); central control had been weak, and with Diocletian in power it may have been getting stronger again. But officials probably multiplied, in part at least for legitimate reasons: there is enough evidence to show that in certain areas where record-keeping had a strong tradition, documentation flourished under Diocletian as never before.[155]

Some of the new officials were eunuchs: it is in 303 that we first hear of allegedly 'very powerful' eunuchs in the (eastern) imperial court (Lactantius, *On the Deaths of the Persecutors* 15.2). There had been isolated eunuchs who were influential at court under the Julio-Claudians, but not apparently since,[156] and one wonders why exactly they now became more powerful; but the question may be wrongly posed – we should rather ask why it took Roman emperors so long to turn for assistance to men who were relatively free of other loyalties.[157] Right-thinking Romans despised eunuchs, but my guess is that Diocletian or one of his immediate predecessors, almost certainly knowing that eunuchs were employed in the Sasanian court,[158] so desperately wanted more security for themselves that they overcame their repugnance. But it was only under the successors of Constantine that the court eunuchs really came into their own.[159]

One of Constantine's first acts after he seized Rome was to abolish the praetorian guard, which had understandably supported Maxentius, the claimant in place in the capital. Praetorian prefects continued in existence, however, with civilian responsibilities, financial and judicial; there were now four or five of them at a time, but they were almost as powerful, in a different way, as they had been before.

Constantine gave two amazing demonstrations of power: he founded an alternative capital of the empire some 1,400 kilometres to the east, and introduced nothing less than a new state religion in place of the existing one. Founding a new capital was in part a recognition of something that had already happened – emperors had seldom needed to go to Rome in recent times.[160] The new foundation gave the *coup de grâce* to the political power of the Senate, but much more importantly gave the empire a capital that

155 Harris 1989a, 291–2.

156 Unless there is some truth in what the *Augustan History* has to say about the court of Elagabalus (*Alexander Severus* 23.6, etc.), which is not impossible. See further Hopkins 1978, 192.

157 On the mutual dependence of the court eunuchs and the emperor, see Hopkins 1978, 188–91.

158 Hopkins 1978,192–3; cf. Dettenhoffer 2009, 98.

159 Whether eunuchs were powerful under Constantine is unclear: cf. Guyot 1980, 130–1.

160 Diocletian built baths in Rome, but the tetrarchs built palaces at Milan, Aquileia, Sirmium, and Nicomedia: Potter 2004, 288–9.

was nearer to some of the most vulnerable frontier areas, the lower Danube and Mesopotamia, which was a net advantage; and in the long term the site turned out to be more defensible (see Chapter 6). Raising Christianity to a position of privilege also of course had, eventually, vast effects on the Roman Empire's internal power structures (see Chapter 7), and even in the short term gave ecclesiastics access to the emperor's attention and liberality. Assessing the secular power of bishops will be important; in 318 they already had the right to try lawsuits between Christians (*Theodosian Code* 1.27.1), a momentous derogation of the power of the state.[161] And few bishops knew much law. However, Constantine seems to have promoted Christians and religious traditionalists without apparent prejudice.

Constantine became more Christian step by step: in 325, the year in which he presided over a 'Council' of bishops at Nicaea, the god Sol Invictus, the Unconquered Sun, appeared on his coins for the last time, and the following year, apparently, he refused to take part in ceremonies at Rome in honour of Jupiter. It was also about 325 that the emperor began to be represented wearing a royal diadem.[162] It may be appropriate therefore that it was in 326 that Constantine executed his eldest son Crispus and atrociously murdered his wife Fausta (in obscure circumstances: Zosimus, *New History* 2.29, etc.).

How much it was Constantine and how much it was his immediate predecessors and successors who changed the shape and titulature of the central administration is not altogether clear. To say that his reign 'saw the emergence of a range of high-ranking officials whose areas of responsibility were systematically consolidated and more clearly defined'[163] is to go far beyond and indeed against the evidence. It was probably he, however, who created the job of 'master of the offices' (*magister officiorum*) to run the central administration,[164] and that of 'quaestor of the palace' for drafting laws and letters. But in so far as Constantine strengthened the central government, it was by surviving for long enough to make sure that the tetrarchic reforms stayed in effect.

One more extraordinary demonstration of power was that Constantine extended the hereditary obligations of the general population, most dramatically on the land (*Theodosian Code* 5.17.1 – quoted below, p. 205), which leads us at last nearer to ordinary Romans.

[161] For the facts: Humfress 2010, 268–9.
[162] R.R.R. Smith 1997, 177–8.
[163] C. Kelly 2012, 191.
[164] C. Kelly 2012, 188.

High and mid-level officials

We want to know how powerful they were, what sort of government they delivered, and what sorts of prejudices and ideas guided their behaviour. The cohort we are considering consists in the first place of the court officials and praetorian prefects we have already met, but more especially of the governors of Rome's provinces, most of them senators but a few of them knights, and the professional army officers of non-senatorial rank who, as we have seen, took over the command of the legions during the third century. In the second place, lower down the scale, we should consider the more variegated category of the local men of power, those who presided over the cities, districts (such as the nomes of Egypt), and peoples.

The garrisoned provinces, being under the emperor's direct control, were governed by his appointees. In the nominally public provinces, the old republican system of selecting the governors by lot among those of suitable rank continued to be the norm until, apparently, the Severan emperors took matters into their own hands by drawing up a list of the eligible senators equal in number to the number of posts to be assigned.[165] The governor's powers were great, but his position was often uneasy: while for practical reasons he often had to take decisions without consulting Rome, his career and even life depended on not angering the ruler. Hence Pliny, while governing Bithynia, consulted Trajan about small matters as well as great – normally for good reasons[166] – even though Pliny had less reason to be nervous about his superior's displeasure than many others. And the provincials, at least in the more acculturated provinces, could complain, and might be encouraged by the governor's rivals at home. Hence the prospect of a possible corruption trial in the Senate.[167]

Within his province, the governor commanded the military, who might be a very large force or a very small one, and administered a system of laws and regulations; he was assisted in the public provinces by a quaestor (procurators did the financial work in the imperial provinces), by legates, military tribunes, and centurions, and like the emperor by 'friends'. His entourage was not immense, but scholars tend to underestimate the numbers of freedmen and slaves who were involved; we almost

[165] De Martino 1975, 813; unfortunately the evidence all comes from unreliable sections of the *Augustan History*.

[166] Sherwin-White 1966, 546–5.

[167] See further Lintott 1993, 120–1.

never have numbers, but when the governor of Macedonia went to Samothrace as a religious tourist in 165 he took 29 people with him who were judged important enough to be mentioned on the commemorative inscription,[168] and there will certainly have been many others with him.

Governors had wide discretion with respect to maintaining order, including of course the power to scourge and execute non-citizens – and he would execute Roman citizens too if he was high-handed enough (Suetonius, *Galba* 9).[169] After the general enfranchisement ordered by Caracalla, governors had the 'right of the sword' over all Roman citizens (Ulpian in *Digest* 1.18.6.9). Greed and cruelty often went quite far.[170] But both governors and their subordinates had to operate within an elaborate framework of patronage as well as law. And there was normally an imperial procurator nearby (for an example of conflict between governor and procurator, see Tacitus, *Annals* 14.38–9). It is clear that when governors such as Marius Priscus or Caecilius Classicus, both known from Pliny's letters, paid the price for their crimes, it was largely because they had upset powerful interests in their provinces (Africa Proconsularis and Baetica respectively). But the system itself probably benefited when such men were prosecuted.

Just as many Romans thought that they could petition the emperor, others, a little more realistically, petitioned the provincial governor, complaining about injustices and presumably with at least a degree of hope that they would be listened to. Aurelius Isidorus, for example, an illiterate but fairly prosperous farmer in the Fayum at the turn of the fourth century, complained at length to the Prefect of Egypt about the abuses of minor officials ('we who are small farmers … we petition you, who fortunately have come to visit our district for the punishment of violent misdeeds … your excellence … your sacred signature … your highness…') (*P.Cair.Isid.* 73); alas, we do not know whether it worked.[171] Normally, however, Egyptian petitions went to the 'strategos', the head of the administration of the district ('nome') in question.[172]

As for efficiency and professionalism, our judgement should be cautious. In the public provinces, terms of office were brief, often a single

[168] Harris 1992.

[169] For parallels, see MacMullen 1986a, 149–50 = 1990, 205–6.

[170] Cf. De Ste Croix 1981, 382.

[171] However, he had petitioned a governor at least once before (*P.Cair.Isid.* 66, 67), some fifteen years earlier, so he may have had reason to be hopeful.

[172] Except that in the Fayum for some reason they generally went to centurions: Whitehorne 2004. In Roman administration we do not expect uniformity.

year. The challenging province of Egypt had a new governor every three years on average, and even more often between 180 and 235.[173] Emperors liked to satisfy the ambitions of as many men as possible, within reason.[174] But modern states have not solved the problem of the ideal term of office for a senior official. And it is highly debatable whether specialized knowledge was an important qualification in the highest imperial ranks; in their greatest periods of success the Romans, at any rate, never set much store by it.[175]

The governor's control over his province ranged from tenuous, in the case of most newly subjugated territories, to placid. At the one extreme, he might face large-scale armed revolt, as in Britain or even more Judaea, but also in other places. Pontius Pilate could not even install Roman standards, with portraits of the emperor, in Jerusalem (Josephus, *Jewish War* 2.169–74). Large cities in the east, Alexandria especially (which got temporarily out of hand in 38–41), could also be troublesome. Rural brigands were a widespread problem. In most provinces, however, while there might be acrimonious disputes between the governor and provincials, he was able to impose his will without recourse to unusual violence.

How effective the central government was in getting its way in the real world we shall be able to judge better when we come to lower-level officials. The evidence is sometimes ambiguous. One historian, contemplating an exceptional piece of evidence, the record of the official correspondence from the Thebaid in upper Egypt in 298 (*P. Panop. Beatty*), says that 'his [the local governor's] frequent refrain is the failure of subordinates to carry out instructions',[176] but one might equally well say that what is impressive is the governor's expectation that his instructions will normally be followed and his insistence in pursuing deficiencies. This was not a modern first-world administration, but until Constantine's time at least, and with exceptions created by warfare, it made valiant and quite successful efforts to intrude into those aspects of its subjects' lives it considered important, as witness the surviving census returns from Egypt.[177]

But the Roman Empire was to a great extent, administratively speaking, an empire of cities and towns (we should think of most of its so-called cities as towns), and wherever possible, if town governments did not exist, Rome brought them into being; it was a preferred organizational

[173] Brunt 1990, 220.
[174] Cf. A.H.M. Jones 1964, 1, 384–5 – though he was too inclined to apply modern Whitehall criteria.
[175] Brunt 1990, 244.
[176] Duncan-Jones 1990, 105.
[177] Bagnall and Frier 1994.

technique. (One result was a set of first-century inscriptions from Spain setting out the rules of municipal government).[178] The effectiveness of Roman government depended heavily on the ability of town authorities to maintain order among the majority of the population that lived in the countryside and to extract taxes from them.

This was a position of privilege and power: as long as a local oligarchy of landowners and other men of substance remained harmonious, it could conduct local affairs largely as it wished. But their position too was uncomfortable: local officials were obliged to make sizeable financial contributions, and they were responsible to Rome for tax-gathering. Representing their communities in their dealings with the Roman authorities could be stressful and expensive. Plutarch gives the following bleak advice to the rulers of Greek cities (*Political Precepts* 17–18 = *Moralia* 813e–814c – the whole passage is fascinating):

> You who rule are yourselves ruled, since the city is set under proconsuls ... you see the soldiers' boots just above your heads ... failure [in public life] brings not merely hissing [like a failure on the stage] ... but many have experienced 'the terrible punisher, the axe that cleaves the neck'... and not only should the local official show himself and his hometown blameless towards the rulers, he should have a friend [i.e. patron] among the most powerful ..., for the Romans themselves are most desirous of promoting the political interests of their friends.

If this kind of nervousness was felt by a well-connected Roman citizen such as Plutarch, one may imagine the feelings of less-favoured city magistrates. No wonder that by about 100, in Italy and elsewhere, it was becoming difficult for some cities to find willing office-holders; later, this became a widespread problem, to which the emperor sometimes had to respond by sending out commissioners (*curatores*).

Yet the strength of these municipal elites was for a long period one of the twin pillars of the whole imperial structure (the other being the army). Roman officials administered justice, but always tended to limit their concerns to major matters of security and finance (and the protection of Roman citizens), thus leaving large amounts of local jurisdiction to local judges.[179] But the useful functions of the local elites went far beyond the narrowly political and juridical. It was they who laid on gladiatorial games and occasional food relief; it was very often they who built

178 See Caballos 1996.

179 For a detailed survey of how this worked in the Greek-speaking provinces down to AD 235, see Fournier 2010.

the public buildings, and took the credit for doing so. And while they kept freed slaves out of municipal office, they co-existed with the prosperous freedmen – who had their own honours within the *Augustalitas*[180] – and accepted upwards mobility by allowing full local honours to the freedmen's sons.

We distinguished earlier between an inner and an outer zone of provincial territory. In some at least of the outer zone, local elites were apparently judged incapable of providing local government. In such cases the army filled the gap, normally in the person of centurions. Thus in Egypt outside Alexandria centurions acted as *de facto* judges,[181] backed up by small detachments of soldiers where necessary. In Britain, there were regional centurions,[182] and they probably had extensive powers. When the imperial procurator had to sort out a conflict between two small communities in Phrygia in the third century, the person who enforced his decision was an *optio*, a sort of assistant centurion (*SEG* 16 [1959], no. 754).

Order and law

It would require a long book to consider in full what sort of government all these more or less powerful officials actually delivered, but two areas require further comment: civil peace and criminal justice. How close did the state come to monopolizing force – a trickier concept than is sometimes recognized?[183] We should be impressed by the fact that Romans were meant to be unarmed in Rome itself, and normally were, and this was apparently the case in every other city too; but travellers between cities, by land or sea, needed to have armed protection. The Roman government did not normally consider it necessary to disarm its subjects,[184] and it would have been impractical to do so, given the persistence of brigandage.[185] And who exactly was a brigand? You do not want to build a country house too close to a main road (a *via militaris*), says the agronomist Columella (1.5.7), because of the 'depredations of the passing travellers'.

Periods of civil war sometimes allowed violence unrelated to the main conflict to break out between provincial communities (Tacitus, *Histories*

180 Above, p. 104.
181 Alston 1995, 86–96. For Palme 2014, 492, this was no more than an occasional procedure.
182 Birley 2007b, 318–24.
183 Cf. Mann 2006, 353.
184 Brunt 1975b.
185 See Campbell 2002, 175–6; also Isaac 1992, 62–99 (on Syria and Palestine); Brélaz 2005, 52–6 (on the Asia Minor provinces).

4.50, gives an example from north Africa).[186] Even in peaceful conditions, as we saw earlier, the wealthy could expect to get away with violence, which historians sometimes euphemistically call 'self-help', especially in the countryside (more so in the fourth century than before).[187] But the evidence about the amount of common or garden brigandage is often ambiguous: we know, for example, that in the second century many provinces in the eastern half of the empire saw the creation of local officials called 'irenarchs', 'Peace Officers'. Is that evidence that 'brigandage in the countryside was becoming serious',[188] or a sign that the relatively ambitious government of the Antonines was trying harder to solve a problem that had long been endemic?[189]

A quiet tranquil province was what a governor should aim for (Ulpian, in *Digest* 1.18.13 pr.). But ensuring tranquillity was normally left to the local authorities, and they might be unable to resist popular protest in times when grain prices rose after bad harvests. Greek cities such as Prusa in Bithynia were especially explosive, and men of wealth such as Dio Chrysostom might run the risk of having their houses burned, with themselves inside. They resisted with violence of their own, and with the threat that Roman authority would intervene (Dio Chrysostom, *Oration* 46.12–14) – also by distributing 'orations' justifying their behaviour.[190]

Effective and transparent criminal justice is an essential feature of any civilized community, but any system of criminal justice is also an instrument of social power. Roman citizens possessed a criminal law system that was highly sophisticated by pre-modern standards, and it offered the ordinary citizen some real remedies. It treated the insane offender more humanely than some modern legal systems.[191] Some provincials evidently believed – the belief was no doubt more widespread in some provinces than in others – that an ordinary member of the community could get the authorities to punish everyday theft and violence. When furthermore an individual weaver in Oxyrhynchus typically petitioned the *strategos* (the provincial governor) for action against an extortionate tax-collector, we do

186 Cf. Fuhrmann 2012, 84.
187 Hopwood 2002, 73–4. See, for example, Aelius Aristides, *Oration* 50.105 (but the aggressors underestimated their victim).
188 So Levick 2000, 47.
189 An argument in favour of the latter view is that the irenarchs seem to have been appointed by the provincial governor (see the inscription published by Brélaz 2011).
190 Cf. C.P. Jones 1978, 24.
191 Harris 2013b, 20.

not know the outcome – but we do know that the weaver thought that it was worth his while to petition.[192]

It can hardly be doubted, however, that Roman criminal justice was to a great extent class justice. Nailing a criminal who possessed social power was possible, but only if he ran up against someone with even more social power and/or if it was in the particular interest of the state, as in cases of maladministration brought against former provincial governors. A criminal defendant of low social status was less likely to get a fair trial, just as a witness of low social status was less likely to be believed.[193]

The distinction between the 'Better People' (*honestiores*) and the 'Lower People' (*humiliores*), which began to take effect under Antoninus Pius – so it appears –, accentuated this discrimination: it meant in essence a loss of rights for those who were outside the elite, the elite defined as consisting of senators, knights, decurions [local senators], and – just to emphasize the military basis of the Roman state – retired soldiers.[194] By the time, therefore, that Roman citizenship was extended to virtually all of the free population in 212, it had lost a good deal of its legal significance. And it was probably in the second century that the state began to use torture on some Roman citizens who were merely suspected of crimes (it had always been a standard weapon against non-citizens and slaves); at first, *honestiores* will presumably have been exempt.[195] When Callistratus, a jurist active around AD 200, ruled that torture should *not* be applied to free men he made an exception for prisoners who gave evidence that was 'inconsistent' (*vacillans*) (*Digest* 48.18.15 pr.), a nice big loophole. By the time of Diocletian, it was perfectly normal to torture criminal suspects unless they were members of the elite, but in practice even the latter were not always exempt.[196] Cruel and humiliating punishments that had once for the most part been reserved for outsiders and slaves spread to the lower-status citizens in the second and third centuries, and later to others: the process is well documented in Book 48, chapter 19, of the *Digest*.[197]

The civil law too favoured those who had social power and money.[198] The wealthy witness was actually believed to be more credible (below, p. 204).

192 *P.Oxy.* LXXIII.4953 of AD 48; the editor cites other similar texts (cf. Bryen 2013, chapter 4).
193 Cf. Macmullen 1986a, 147–50 = 1990, 204–7.
194 Cf. Bauman 1996, chapter 11.
195 For detailed discussion, see Pölönen 2004.
196 See Lactantius, *On the Deaths of the Persecutors* 21.3, probably exaggerating. For criminal law under Constantine, see Humfress 2012, 208–10; torture increased (see, for example, *Theodosian Code* 9.19.1).
197 Cf. Grodzynski 1984.
198 J.M. Kelly 1966, though in truth that was a simplified account.

Before we pass on to the lower officials, we should enquire whether the Roman Empire was heavily bureaucratized. The standard books say not, at least not until the time of Diocletian, partly because there was obviously nothing like the vast bureaucracy of a modern state, partly because we have been led to believe that some other pre-modern states, China in particular, were vastly more bureaucratic than high-imperial Rome. But Weber's well-known contrast between bureaucracy and dilettantism[199] may be too simple for Roman reality. While there was a good deal of amateurism at the highest levels, it seems to have co-existed with a good deal of expertise and routinization lower down. Certain milieux possessed the respect for hierarchy and the love of documentation that are characteristic of bureaucracy; this applied to the army everywhere and to certain provinces, Egypt above all – but also to other provinces with Hellenistic pasts.[200] The imperial household already by the time of Claudius had some markedly bureaucratic features.[201] Historians often seem to underestimate the number of people working at petty administration, partly because much of the work was done by slaves. Patronage operated at all levels, but such a system is not wholly inimical to routine or even efficiency (though it was indeed seen by the emperor Julian as the enemy of merit: Ammianus Marcellinus 20.5): X would ask Y, either the emperor or some other powerful person, for a favour such as an appointment for Z (the request was called a *suffragium*). If Y granted the request, X and Z were gratified; less obviously, X would be ill advised to recommend Z if he were incompetent. Fronto was certainly aware of this when he made requests to Antoninus Pius.[202]

To what extent did merit matter in high-level official careers? A certain level of competence was assumed within the social sub-class concerned. Its members seem to have believed that a gentlemanly upbringing ensured this (cf. Dio 52.26 especially), and emperors seldom if ever gave preference to a possible appointee because of his expert knowledge.[203] The merit that counted was perceived good character, which was no doubt often a cover for a combination of loyalty, good manners, and conventional opinions.

But to return to the matter of bureaucracy. The Roman state created official structures out of military and fiscal necessity. It administered a

[199] Weber 1968 [original edition 1921–1922], 223.
[200] Concerning documentation, see Bagnall 2011, chapter 2.
[201] Wallace-Hadrill 1996, 297–9.
[202] See Champlin 1980, 99; more generally, De Ste Croix 1954; Cecconi 2005, 286.
[203] See the admirable discussion in Saller 1982, chapter 3.

standing army of some 350,000 men, and in order to levy the requisite taxes, it had devised provincial censuses. Such routine matters did not make much impression on the literary sources, and we know that there was no uniformity.[204] The complexity of this system probably reached a crescendo under the Severan emperors. According to a remarkable statement by Ulpian (*Digest* 50.15.4), the tax-payer must declare to his local authorities

> the name of each property, the community, and the *pagus* [the territorial district] to which it belongs, its nearest two neighbours; then how many *iugera* [a *iugerum* was slightly under 2/3 of an acre] of land have been sown for the last ten years, how many vines the vineyard has, how many *iugera* are olive-plantations and with how many trees, how many *iugera* of land have been used for hay for the last ten years, how many *iugera* of pasture there are, likewise of wood for felling. The declarer must give the value of everything [further details follow].

A good deal of effort doubtless went into evading this system, whether by obtaining immunity for one's whole city or by individual cheating, but a jurist of Ulpian's experience probably had reason to believe that the rules could be enforced. And one of the very few criminal charges on which it was permissible to torture the accused's slaves for evidence was making a false census-declaration (*CJ* 9.41.1: a law of AD 196) – in other words, the government was extremely keen that the census should be accurate. That implies a small army of government clerks.[205] Before we can say that the Han Empire was more heavily bureaucratized than the Roman Empire – which may well be true – we need a good estimate of the number of slaves who worked at administrative jobs for Roman officials as well as an accurate estimate of the real total of Han officials (the emperor's 6,000 concubines sometimes get counted).

The officials we have been discussing shared many values and beliefs. What is most relevant in the present context perhaps is their evident confidence in the permanence and inevitability of Roman might (not just power). We should not think of them as tolerant (that virtue requires some intellectual underpinning), but they easily accepted diversity in the non-essentials while imposing the essentials of a governmental system that suited the upper order of society and at the same time gave ample opportunities to the 'middling sort'. Later I will return to the psychological and philosophical aspects of their confidence in their system of power, and

204 For a summary of the evidence, see Eck 2000, 286–8; Carrié 2005, 282–3.
205 The comparisons cited by Miles 1990, 640, do not do justice to the Roman evidence.

what happened when Constantine overturned the religious element in the old ideology.

Lower officials

The lower-ranking officials of the Roman Empire, and soldiers too when they were operating in civilian contexts, exercised fairly unrestrained power within their specific narrow orbits. That may have been inevitable in a society that was neither democratic nor in a modern sense bureaucratic:

> Recently a certain collector of taxes was appointed in our area. When some of the men who were apparently in arrears because of poverty fled in fear of unbearable punishment, he laid violent hands on their wives, children, parents, and other relatives, beating and trampling them and visiting every outrage on them … he racked their bodies with twistings and tortures, and killed them off with newly contrived modes of death …

This is Philo (*On Special Laws* 3.159; cf. 2.92–6), writing about Egypt under Tiberius; scholars like to think that he may have been exaggerating (he was capable of it), but there is as much confirmatory evidence as we should expect. A number of petitions survive complaining about such extortion.[206]

Soldiers were commonly a menace to all but the most privileged civilians. When soldiers supposedly asked John the Baptist what they could do to redeem themselves (the truth of the story is immaterial), he replied, 'Don't take money from anyone by force or by false charges' (Luke 3:14).[207] Epictetus points in the same direction: a soldier may requisition your donkey (so this is advice for those of modest means), and if he does, do not resist or grumble, because that way you will get a beating and lose your donkey anyway (*Discourses* 4.1.79). The higher authorities somewhat disapproved of soldiers who mistreated civilians (cf. Ulpian in *Digest* 1.18.6.6–7), but they could do little about it.[208]

All these tax-collectors and soldiers were from time to time subject to the power of others, but could usually operate undisturbed. And as in most societies, petty tyrannies went right down to the lowest levels of official power. Prison guards, who would typically be public slaves (Pliny, *Letters* 10.19–20), were able to extract bribes in exchange for decent treatment.[209]

206 See *P.Oxy.* LXXIII, p. 139.
207 Cf. Fuhrmann 2012, 232, with an apposite parallel from the Tosefta, *Betzah* 2.6 (third century).
208 See Campbell 2002, 176–8; Fuhrmann 2012, 234–7.
209 Robinson 2007, 113.

Whether conditions changed much in the era of Diocletian and Constantine is unclear. Some documents (*P.Abinnaeus* 47 and 48 of 346) suggest that it was still possible for some people to have criminal officials and soldiers brought to justice at that time. But the 'some people' in these cases were substantial landowners. After Diocletian, people in Egypt wrote fewer petitions and declarations to soldiers,[210] partly at least because Constantine and his successors redeployed the soldiers, which must have had the effect of leaving still greater power to the landowners.[211] That weakened ordinary people still further.

Social and gender power

These fourth-century landowners lead us quite neatly into further consideration of the question of social power, by which I mean the power exercised by those who enjoyed relative wealth and social position (including the advantage of being male). Of course it is somewhat artificial to distinguish state power from social power: much of the time, the same people exercised both. What was different was that, while state power affected everyone, its effects on the individual might be slight or spasmodic (depending on his citizenship, tax obligations, and so on), social power, in the sense given above, affected everyone, all the time.

But how to describe this society, structurally? The essential problem is to know whether we should concentrate on the status distinctions that the inhabitants of the Roman Empire used, or talk about social classes. Be it noted, first of all, that status distinctions such as 'senator' and 'knight' cover only a minute proportion of the population, and that a full account of statuses would have to take into account not only these distinctions but a wide variety of more and less known provincial statuses, such as the 'gymnasial' class in Roman Egypt. Second, Greeks and Romans, and probably every other Roman population too, frequently contrasted the rich and the poor, without defining what they meant any more than we normally do; words for 'poor', in particular, could refer to the working poor or the direly indigent.[212] Now, status obviously affected power relations in the most basic way: above all, much depended on whether you were free, a slave, or somewhere between the two (which might mean being a freed slave – until the third century there were always many of these – or a dependant of some other kind). Many shelves of books have

[210] Aubert 1995, 259.
[211] Cf. Bagnall 1993, 171.
[212] Harris 2011b, 31.

been written about what these life-conditions meant, and we shall consider the most important aspects.

But there is also social class to consider. There is no need to make a shibboleth out of the word itself (we could instead speak rather awkwardly about three kinds of human existence), but in fact it has a great deal of explanatory power.[213] This is not the place for a full theoretical discussion. It is wholly illogical, however, to claim that social class was unimportant because of the vertical links of personal patronage[214] – which characterized virtually every pre-modern society for which we have historical records.

We can usefully distinguish between:

(1) well-to-do persons who, while they might pay careful attention to their financial affairs, had access to all the amenities that existed and had no need to work; they were for the most part landowners. The political class in the capital was of course recruited exclusively from this group.
(2) Those who had very few assets and did not lead a secure physical existence, some because their farms were too small, others because they worked – if they were fortunate enough to find work – for wages or as slaves. The real poor, in short. Note that some slaves fell not into this category but the following one.
(3) Those in between (1) and (2) who possessed enough land to make their physical existence more or less secure, or a skill and a shop that would have the same effect.

A model of this kind has the major virtue that it covers the entire population, including women (see below), and actually says what the basic differences are between different classes (unlike a thoroughly misleading graphic that has often been reproduced over the years to represent the stratification of Roman society).[215] Most important of all, it can help us to think more clearly about the distribution of rights and amenities – and power – across the population of the Roman Empire.

Five claims follow, briefly stated, the last of which is a tentative effort to trace the system's evolution:

(1) The dominant social actor was always the large property-owner, who, however, might have complex economic interests, might in some cases be

[213] Harris 2011b, chapter 1. The chief modern opponent of this idea later had second thoughts (Finley 1983, 3). The counter-arguments of Saller 2000, 824, are easily disposed of in my opinion; he in any case recognizes the great power of the landowners (825).
[214] Alston 1995, 160–1.
[215] Alföldy 1985, 146.

a son of a self-made man or might even be one himself.[216] Six men notoriously owned half of the province of Africa Proconsularis, until Nero executed them and took the land for himself – but what is most important is that our contemporary source for this information, the elder Pliny, takes such a concentration of ownership to be typical of the provinces (*Natural History* 18.35, *iam vero et provincias*). In Asia Minor we are relatively well informed: 'much, if not all of the rural territory of central Anatolia', an expert on that region writes, 'was parcelled out into large estates owned by the local city gentry, wealthy aristocrats from further afield, or by the Roman emperor himself'.[217]

Within the political framework that we have already described, such landowners did largely as they liked. Dio Chrysostom refers to his well-to-do father's *dunamis*, power, in their home-town, Prusa (*Oration* 46.5), and we will not be put off by the translator who turned this into the tame word 'influence'. But perhaps the most extreme exhibit is Herodes Atticus (*c.* 102–77), the richest Athenian of his time, who quarrelled with Roman governors and probably caused the violent death of his wife,[218] but retained the support of Marcus Aurelius. This sort of power was largely informal, but it had its formal side too: it was an admitted principle that a wealthy witness was more credible than a needy one (Callistratus, *Digest* 22.5.3.pr.).

The disparity was even greater in the countryside, which was, in MacMullen's words, 'less observed by the cities' population and therefore … less observant of the latter's values'. He instances unpaid reapers in the *Epistle of James* (5.4).[219] The younger Pliny's letters, notwithstanding their seemliness, reveal other instances of lordly misbehaviour (by our lights) (*Letters* 3.19.6–7, 9.15). Egyptian documents, though they are often *ex parte* statements, fill out this picture.[220]

Since the richest, including the emperor, usually owned property in diverse regions – this is plain from Columella[221] –, many landlords were absentees, and thus their agents and bailiffs could often do some exploiting on their own account. We hear of this phenomenon both from inscriptions (for example, *CIL* 8.10570 and 14464,[222] Africa Proconsularis

216 MacMullen 1986b piles up evidence about 'personal power' in the Roman Empire, but does not ask what those who exercised it had in common.

217 Mitchell 1993, I, 149.

218 Pomeroy 2007, chapter 4. His huge country palace at Loukou in the eastern Peloponnese remains largely unpublished.

219 MacMullen 1988, 84.

220 MacMullen 1974, chapter 1, still gives the best account.

221 See 5.7.1, 6.1.1, 8.17.15, 11.2.56, etc.

222 Translated in Lewis and Reinhold 1990, II, 98–9.

under Commodus) and from the novelist Achilles Tatius (*Leucippe and Cleitophon* 5.17). Both of these stories, as it happens, had 'happy endings'. That was presumably the exception.

Tenants had some rights, it is true.[223] But by Constantine's time there was a legal gulf between landowners and many of those who worked the land, comparable to the situation in Russia before the emancipation of the serfs.[224] The tenants lost further ground under Constantine, as we know from a notorious (though also enigmatic) law of 332:

> *coloni* who meditate flight must be bound with chains and reduced to a servile condition, so that by virtue of their condemnation to slavery they shall be compelled to fulfil the duties that befit free men (*Theodosian Code* 5.17.1).

(2) Slavery was at the heart of the whole social system, even though many free people (more in some provinces than others) could not afford to purchase other humans. In some provinces, Egypt for example, slaves made up scarcely more than a tenth of the population, though in most places the proportion was higher (perhaps one-third in Italy). The old dogma that slave labour was of minor importance in the provinces is unsustainable as far as most regions are concerned.[225] Slavery also had a powerful influence on the free-labour market, even beyond the areas where slaves did a very substantial proportion of the farm-work.[226] Furthermore free men quite commonly sold themselves into slavery in order to obtain desirable jobs,[227] which underlines the fact that well-to-do Romans, from the emperor downwards, satisfied their needs for reliable employees without much use of the freeborn. A few slaves consequently lived well, and had a decent prospect of obtaining their freedom – for the prospect of manumission was an essential incentive to good behaviour. There was indeed a steep and recognized stratification within the slave population.[228] Privileged slaves had slaves of their own, though technically they did not own them.[229]

The lives of slaves were commonly harsh and showed the callousness of internal power corresponding to Roman brutality towards the state's external enemies. Roman law and custom throughout this period permitted

223 Kehoe 2007, rather optimistic.
224 This is implicit, for example, in *Theodosian Code* 11.7.2 (319).
225 Harris 2011b, 61 and 87; Morley's discussion of the problem (Morley 2011, 266–74) is unsatisfying.
226 Harris 2011b, 44–5.
227 Harris 2011b 88–9.
228 Diederich 2007.
229 Bradley 1994, 2–3.

slaveholders to put their slaves to death at will;[230] where provincial laws and customs reigned this was not always so, but later of course Roman law applied everywhere.[231] Fierce corporal punishment was the norm. Where there was extensive agricultural slavery, there were chain-gangs. Few slaves can have enjoyed a stable family life. Sexual exploitation was extremely common.[232]

We must carefully avoid the softening of Roman slavery that infects much modern writing on the subject (translators often make slaves into 'servants'). It is precisely because the slave is in general powerless that the anonymous *Life of Aesop* can make an amusing story out of a slave's constantly outwitting his owner.[233]

There were some minor mitigations. The well-to-do and many ordinary people depended heavily on the cooperation of their slaves. A few home-born slaves, *vernae*, were treated well. A significant number of slaves gained their freedom in high imperial times. Since the slave was commonly compelled to turn over a considerable sum from his/her savings, it might cost the slaveholder little or nothing.[234] But where slaves were numerous or especially resentful they instilled fear (see, among many other texts, Pliny, *Letters* 3.14). One of the reasons why the wealthy Pedanius was murdered (above, p. 151) was thought to have been that he had reneged on the price at which he agreed to sell a slave his freedom. Manumission probably became less common as a result of the economic troubles of late-Antonine and subsequent periods: already under the Severans freedmen almost vanish from the inscriptions.

When emperors, from perhaps Claudius onwards, very slowly began to give slaves some minimal legal protection from maltreatment, it was as far as we can tell largely because they thought that it was in the interests of the slaveholders to do so.[235] (Such regulations probably echoed a certain mild change in ethos – which actually mattered, just because there were so few limits on the slaveholder's power).

The slaves as individuals often fought back, but short of murder their main weapons were doing their work inadequately, malingering, and

[230] Watson 1987, 120.

[231] Constantine's rules (*Theodosian Code* 9.12) apparently meant that the owner was in the clear as long as he could say that death was a side-effect of punishment. See Harper 2011, 232–3.

[232] Harper 2013, 26–30, and cf. Watson 1987, 119.

[233] This text is available in translation in Daly 1961.

[234] Findlay 1975 explained the economic logic of manumission. The freed slave continued to have major obligations to his/her former owner.

[235] Watson 1987, 121–8; Harris 2002, 331. Antoninus Pius forbade the killing of a slave 'without cause', but what counted as a cause?

stealing; all three methods were endemic. Running away was evidently commonplace too.[236]

The economic troubles of the third century probably diminished the demand for slaves somewhat, and 'the middling sort' may have owned fewer of them. But as newly discovered texts (letters and sermons of Augustine) and recent scholarship, in particular the work of Kyle Harper, have underlined, the institution was still little changed under the tetrarchs and under Constantine and even a century after the latter's rise to power.[237] When Augustine wrote that 'nearly all house(hold)s' had slaves (*Enarrationes in Psalmos* 124.7), he revealed his class perspective but also an important truth.

The deeper psychological effects of the master-slave relationship are a subject for speculation, but it is obvious that the huge power of the slave-holders accustomed them to mistreating humans.

(3) Women were of course excluded from formal political power almost everywhere in the Roman Empire. But as far as social and economic power were concerned, the story was quite different: at all social levels women were less powerful than men, but what counted most was, precisely, a person's social level. The period we are considering began and ended, after all, with two influential Augustae, Livia and (the actually much less powerful) Helena (above, p. 185). Upper-class women could exercise enough political influence for a tyrannical emperor to send them into exile (Pliny, *Letters* 3.11.3).

But it should be noted first that, for less exalted persons, locale also made a great difference. Local conditions might mean subjection that was severe even by pre-modern standards: in Tarsus, for example, women had to wear a garment like a burqa (Dio Chrysostom 33.48). Far to the west, on the other hand, among the Cantabrians of northern Spain, 'women ruled' – so Strabo claimed, without clarifying what he meant (3.165; this would have been before Roman influence had been felt much).

The disadvantages of being female began at birth: some populations abandoned more female infants than male.[238] Quite few girls were sent to school, and the paradox that some women were highly educated resulted mainly from private study. Marriage was in any case imposed early: many married at twelve years of age, the majority had probably married by

[236] Bradley 1994, 115–17.
[237] Harper 2011.
[238] Harris 1994, 11.

fifteen or sixteen, and almost all before twenty.[239] First-time brides, as far as we can tell, will normally have had to marry men whom their families had chosen.

Women were generally not admitted to guilds, a significant form of social exclusion. Roman citizen women had extensive property rights, however, and though their financial activities were formally limited by the institution of 'guardianship' (*tutela*), which was no mere legal fiction, they were very often able to escape or circumvent it,[240] and by the time of the Severan jurists it fell out of use in many places. A few women managed to be merchants or doctors.[241] Where Roman law obtained, and no doubt in some other places as well, inheritance rules ensured that a great deal of property came into female hands – possibly as much as one-third of the total.[242] They were correspondingly important as benefactors of the cities, and presumably enjoyed a degree of social power in consequence.

In Roman law, they could initiate divorce,[243] but no doubt it took a strong character to do so; it was definitely uncommon.[244] They could not sue under the criminal law (remember that there were no public prosecutors) except in limited circumstances, and might need to appeal to the emperor himself to get a case heard (Pomponius in *Digest* 48.2.1; cf. Pliny, *Letters* 7.6.8–10).

'Women's greatest potential for exercising power over men was through the manipulation of sexual desire', says one scholar bluntly,[245] and she knows the documents. Power over one's own life, on the other hand, will often have depended on the accidents of inheritance and character.

Some male texts advocate a measure of equality for women, most conspicuously the writings of the Stoic Musonius Rufus. But Plutarch, from this point of view a more mainstream figure, in effect left male dominance in its urban Hellenistic form, which was more civilized than what happened in classical Athens but still male dominance (in favour of female subordination, see especially his *Conjugal Precepts* 11, 19, 22, etc.). A literary genre which may possibly have aimed at a partly female readership,

239 Scheidel 2007 gives a good account of this matter, arguing that we cannot hope to recover the precise facts. See also Hin 2013, 175–9.
240 Gardner 1986, 14–22.
241 Merchants: Harris 2011b, 179; cf. Gardner 1986, 233–7; strangely enough, further work is needed. Doctors: Flemming 2007.
242 This topic also needs further treatment; Hemelrijk 2014 spells out some of the implications.
243 So too the Greeks: Plutarch, *Conjugal Precepts* 41.
244 Gardner 1986, 261.
245 Rowlandson 1998, 355.

the romance (four or perhaps five examples survive intact from this period if we include Apuleius), offers no comfort. As a recent critic observes, 'sexuality in the Greek novels ... typically operates to control women'.[246] The heroine is free to fall in love, but her freedom ends there; that was apparently the way the readers liked it. Nor did women gain much social power from their involvement in religious cults, old or new.[247]

Constantine's main contribution was to make it still more difficult for a woman to obtain a divorce (*Theodosian Code* 3.16.1). The degree to which officialized Christianity altered women's social and economic power is a question for Chapter 7.

(4) An educational system always reflects the power relationships in being, though it may also serve to undermine them. Veblen's *Theory of the Leisure Class*, not Bourdieu, should be the preferred reading here. By the time our period began, the Roman elite had perfected a system that was almost, but not quite, invulnerable. To obtain high office it was necessary to be a member of a social elite that required its male members to acquire an elaborate and largely useless literary education. Useless but not valueless, for the high literary culture to some extent sustained both national consciousness and a certain respect for the great moral-philosophical systems of the past (about which more will be said below). The very great demand for technical expertise was more or less satisfied by on-the-job training (physicians, military engineers). No government, central or local, gave any thought to the education of the masses, and even in the Greek cities that had shown some concern for mass education in Hellenistic times the wealthy philanthropists were not interested; a solitary exception is known, in Lycia.[248] Village schools are unknown in the western half of the empire, and probably not common in the eastern.[249] At the same time, the social system preserved itself by permitting the sons of new money to acquire the high culture if they were willing to pay for it. And even a modest level of education opened up some economic possibilities, at least in towns and in the military.

Anyone who aspired to the independent enjoyment of power needed to read and write with reasonable fluency. The administration of the state, the armed forces, the provinces, and their constituent communities depended

[246] Morales 2008, 54. A more ambiguous reading is possible: Wiersma 1990.
[247] Beard, North, and Price 1998, 1, 296–300.
[248] *SEG* 30 (1980), no. 1535, with Harris 1989a, 244. His foundation may not have been unique.
[249] Harris 2014. A child – or an adult – might acquire literate skills informally, but the assumption always was that you learned your ABCs in a school.

on the written word. Instructions could be issued and responded to orally, and there were diverse intermediaries such as literate family-members and public criers and scribes for hire, but the semi-literate and the wholly illiterate were unquestionably vulnerable to some degree; they were obliged to rely on their memories for every complicated transaction and on the honesty of their interlocutors.[250] The diffusion of literacy must have varied considerably from one milieu to another, but overall it was high by the standards of the Ancient Near East, low by the standards of say eighteenth-century western Europe: perhaps ten per cent of all adults, including women and peasants, could read and write on at least a modest level.[251]

The vulnerability of such an educational system is not so much that it will be discredited as that it will become irrelevant. Macrinus, Maximian, and the third-century soldier-emperors who succeeded them did not need educational respectability. Meanwhile, having failed to absorb the masses into any involvement with the high culture or its ideals, the social elite was shocked to discover, perhaps not long before the persecution by Decius, that a fanatical religion that denied those ideals was gaining a significant number of adherents.

(5) From time to time the Roman Empire experienced in one region or another what might be called social uprisings – and there are the usual problems in deciding whether the actions of bandits and outlaws, such as Bulla Felix in Severan Italy, qualify for such a designation. No one, certainly, could dream of any significant social change within the existing structures. The most important of these uprisings were the revolts of the Boukoloi ('herdsmen') in the Nile delta in the 170s and the Bagaudae in parts of Gaul, beginning in the 280s but continuing off and on into the fifth century; they achieved little, except perhaps in the case of the Bagaudae.[252]

One might say at first glance that the general tendency of the tetrarchic and Constantinian regimes was to make the Roman Empire still more oppressive. At the same time, however, Constantine at least attempted to use his power to alleviate poverty (*Theodosian Code* 11.27.1–2), and even declared, no doubt with little effect, that 'the ears of the judge shall be open equally to the poorest as well as to the rich' (*ibid.* 1.16.7).

[250] See Harris 1989, chapters 7–8; Bowman and Woolf 1994, chapter 1; Woolf 2000.
[251] Kolb 2003 regrettably ignores this matter while discussing the written means by which emperors attempted to reach their subjects.
[252] On whom, see Rubin 1995, 129–65.

The power of ideas

This last observation leads quite naturally to the question of the power of ideas. But historians have no agreed models to help them measure the power of ideas, and there is a real danger that we shall topple over into vagueness; Romanists who have written about 'the power of images' and 'the power of religion' have sometimes fallen into this trap. What I am concerned with here, at all events, is not the power that ideas, such as those of the Stoics or other philosophers or the Christians, may have had to change people's lives – a legitimate subject certainly –, but the power of ideas to reinforce, modify, or subvert political and social-power relationships.

I will therefore concentrate on ideas that can be associated with actual political and social practices. This will mean, for example, that the ideal of *paideia* ('culture') that for better and for worse shaped the way that propertied families educated their sons and occasionally their daughters was of considerable significance, as we have already seen. Conversely it is difficult to identify the effects of the civilizing mission of *humanitas* that gained some ground in the second half of the first century AD (Pliny, *Natural History* 3.39); it comforted the educated upper class, but did it have any other social or political effects?

We have also seen (pp. 174–9) how emperors constructed for themselves something like an ideological framework for one-man rule. Any number of other ideas served to reinforce the existing political and social order, for example the apparently widespread view that the political and social elite could be entrusted with much of the important business of maintaining the benevolence of the gods towards the whole community. The Mithraists, for instance, formed part of this consensus; the Christians did not, but for most of our period they scarcely mattered (see below). The imperial cult was of some assistance, though as I have argued it probably did not go far enough. Then in the early fourth century religious conflict intensified, with consequences that we shall consider in the chapters to come.

Few historians seem to have asked what idea of Rome and its empire the Romans themselves favoured in these centuries.[253] Was there an *idea* that army officers believed in as they slogged through the British or Dacian mud? Yes, in all probability. It was not the high-flown rhetorical idea of Aelius Aristides that the Roman Empire was perfectly organized, but all thinking Romans held that Rome was the great power in the world, that it had inherited glorious traditions, and that it would endure for ever (on

[253] Inglebert 2002 poses the problem, but his approach is too philological.

Figure 5.6. Aureus of Hadrian, AD 134–8. On the reverse, Roma, armed and holding the sun and the moon, with the legend ROMA AETERNA. Mattingly 1966, Hadrian 700–2

this last point, see Aelius Aristides, *To Rome* 108, and the coins of Hadrian and his successors with the legend 'Roma Aeterna' [Figure 5.6]). Anyone who travelled was bound to be impressed at some level by the empire's towns and roads, by its size and majesty.[254]

In 248 Rome celebrated its supposed 1,000th birthday, and no doubt it was a sign of strength that the emperor in charge was a Syrian (Philip). Similarly we might take it as a sign of national cohesion that Constantine was able to create a new physical capital without losing significant political capital. What is largely lacking in the tetrarchic-Constantinian period is any fresh expression of the national myth, which Christianity was busy undermining.

254 Cf. Leyerle 2009, 120–2.

Citizenship was for many centuries a central element in Roman policy and identity. It was a bundle of rights as well as an idea, but there can be no question that in the period AD 16 to 212 it made a considerable impression on that large though still minority segment of the subject population (above, p. 113) that received it.[255] Bringing with it both association with the emperor (the author of citizenship grants) and a change of name (Sparticus the son of Diuzenus, for example, became Ti. Claudius Sparticus), it necessarily tended towards creating a nation. All the more so perhaps, because many of the military grantees had travelled widely and must have had a vivid sense of the immensity of Roman power. And citizenship brought with it the use of the institutions of Roman law, perceived to be on the whole beneficial. What happened after 212 is less clear: it is possible that many of the new recipients of Roman citizenship reacted positively, but it is also possible that the inclusion of huge numbers of people whose forefathers had *not* served in the *auxilia* or otherwise earned the privilege of Roman citizenship in some sense diluted the whole concept.

The set of more philosophical ideas that is widely supposed to have supported the high Roman Empire is late (and watered-down) Stoicism, but the effect of specifically Stoic ideas on power relationships was probably slight. The main achievement of the 'philosophical opposition' of Neronian and Flavian times, apart from its own destruction, was to make life difficult for genuine philosophers such as Epictetus. There is scant reason to think that when the Romans in power treated their subjects or their slaves half-decently they did so for theoretical rather than prudential reasons.

It has been argued that the Stoics attempted to induce the masters of the world to treat their subjects with a degree of humanity.[256] It is true that Stoicism was moralistic, but it also tended to be fatalistic, and very little if anything in the public or indeed private behaviour of Seneca or Marcus Aurelius, both of whom we know well by the standards of ancient history, reflects Stoicism as distinct from the conventional norms of the Roman upper class. It is true that Arrian, the man to whom we owe our detailed knowledge of Epictetus' Stoicism, was himself a Roman official, but did Stoic convictions alter his behaviour? Brunt argued that the so-called cosmopolitanism of the Roman Stoics had no 'practical implications'.[257] On the other hand it seems likely that the notion, widespread by this time,

[255] See further Sherwin-White 1973, 409.
[256] Shaw 1985, 37–43.
[257] Brunt 1975c, 23 = 2013, 294.

that rulers should control displays of anger, had some effect; it had after all a prudential as well as a theoretical foundation.[258]

The subversive ideas with the most power were religious and cultural, not in the first place political, social, or economic, apart from the respect accorded to tyrannicides which we noticed earlier.[259] *Libertas* had been hijacked long before, and as for equality and fraternity, they were known only inside small groups. No one, throughout the period, suggested any idea that would have seriously modified the lives of the slaves.

Since at least the times of Diogenes the Cynic, there had been philosophers who rejected conventional ideas about power and social behaviour. As long as those who in some sense 'opted out' were relatively few, the power-system was unaffected. We considered earlier the possible political effects of Epicureanism during the late Republic. The Essenes opted out, but it made no difference to political or social power, even in Judaea – though they were a powerful example.

Christianity was at first of no general significance, but at some point it ceased to be an occasional annoyance to provincial officials and began to be seen, even though its adherents were still a small segment of the population, as a general nuisance; this may have been in the reign of Decius (249–51).[260] Diocletian's attempt to eliminate subversive sects – the followers of Mani as well as the Christians – failed, and soon afterwards Constantine, when just on the verge of capturing Rome, joined the cause.

In what sense then was Christianity effectively subversive? Like magic and a number of other cults, Christianity offered access to an alternative universe where the emperor and his horrid agents were replaced by quite other powers. The new religion mattered, after 312, in two main ways (Chapter 7 will discuss the years after 337): it gave real-world power to a new hierarchy, the ecclesiastical one,[261] that was mainly indifferent to the interests of the state; and it created an imminent potential for divided religious loyalty inside the one formation where trust in the divine was of practical importance – the army. Both these developments were on display, for instance, when Christians in Alexandria in 335 used soldiers to do

258 Cf. Harris 2002, chapters 9–10.

259 See further MacMullen 1966, 19–41.

260 The theory that Decius' persecution was merely 'motivated by a desire to reinforce Rome's traditional relationship with her gods' (Ando 2000, 207, n. 5) takes no account of the complete lack of precedents.

261 On the emergence of this hierarchy, see Lane Fox 1986, 495–517, and for some of the ways in which third-century bishops exercised power, Lane Fox 1994, 134–7. From an early date bishops had lifetime tenure.

violence to those whose theological opinions they disagreed with (*P.Lond.* VI.1914).[262] To the Christian obsession with 'heresy', and it effects, we shall return in later chapters.

But had the Roman Empire become a nation?[263] The question should be asked more often. We can try to use Weber's definition: 'the concept undoubtedly means, above all, that *it is proper* to expect from certain groups a specific sentiment of solidarity in the face of other groups. Thus, the concept belongs in the sphere of values. Yet, there is no agreement on how these groups should be delimited or about what concerted action should result from such solidarity'.[264]

A quasi-official view of the Roman Empire, expressed by Aelius Aristides, claimed in effect that by the mid-second century Rome had in fact, in these terms, become a nation, and the process continued to unroll after that. Modern scholars, on the other hand, naturally treat such claims sceptically. The empire, it has been claimed, 'seems never to have evoked any active patriotism from the vast majority of its citizens'.[265] How in any case could one tell? A minimalist definition might not require more than that the members of local elites, as well of the upper elite, should share a national self-identification and accept the legitimacy of the central government. We may need to revert to the image of concentric circles alluded to earlier: it would be reasonable to think that by the Antonine period most of the population identified with Rome in such provinces as Baetica, Narbonensis, and Africa Proconsularis. Sherwin-White exaggerated the significance of the fact that in the first and second centuries there were virtually no separatist movements in well-established provinces (rebellion against Rome was a dangerous business indeed),[266] but the degree of apparent acceptance is impressive. As to what happened in the long century between the Edict of Caracalla and the death of the Constantine, the case could be argued either way. The perspective from the capital, perhaps not long after the edict, was that all the inhabitants of the empire were now 'called Roman' (Hippolytus, *Commentary on Daniel* 4.8.7). Even in Greek cities the members of the elite knew that they were Romans. But

262 Bowman 1986, 49.
263 On the period down to 192, see especially Shaw 2000, 361–82.
264 Weber 1968 [original edn 1921–1922], II, 922. Other important comments follow.
265 A.H.M. Jones 1964, II, 1062. The difficulty is not so much that this is overstated as that, as is natural for a democratically minded historian, it gives a degree of importance to mass opinion and behaviour that they seldom possessed in pre-modern times.
266 Sherwin-White 1973, 418. The Nasamones in Numidia rebelled under Domitian; they were exterminated (Dio 67.4).

the development was incomplete. Third-century emperors, even when addressing such favourite provincials as the Aphrodisians, unselfconsciously distinguish them from the Romans.[267] And separatism to some extent increased.

We may end this chapter with some observations about those who from time to time exercised charismatic power in the sense indicated above (p. 106), that is to say without institutional power. It is not Augustus, Trajan, or Constantine that I have in mind here, but Jesus of Nazareth, Apollonius of Tyana, Thessalos of Tralles, and the second-century Paphlagonian Greek Alexander of Abonuteichos – and very few others. This is primarily a question about the acquisition of fame in the ancient world, and it is a particularly difficult one because in the first two of these cases contemporary sources are lacking. We scarcely know what sort of followers Apollonius had, because Philostratus' biography is a century later and full of palpable fiction. But the central point is clear and obvious: that it was men who could play on religious or medical sensibilities or preferably both who established substantial followings in their own lifetimes, Jesus and Apollonius arguably as in the first place miracle-workers, Thessalos as a healer,[268] Alexander as a prophet. It was Alexander who established ascendancy over some men of power, including senatorial officials (on one occasion prevailing on Marcus Aurelius to have two lions thrown into the Danube to bring good luck to the emperor's coming campaign: the lions swam to the other side, where the enemy clubbed them to death – Lucian, *Alexander or the False Prophet* 48). In Lucian's view, Alexander exercised empire-wide influence.[269] One wonders whether it is merely an accident of the evidence that the leaders of such rebellious groups as the Boukoloi and the Bagaudae (above, p. 162) do *not* emerge as distinct figures.

The later equivalents of these men are Christian miracle-workers – none of them more than locally renowned in this period –,[270] and perhaps

267 J.M. Reynolds 1982, no. 20, lines 4–5 (Gordian III), no. 25, lines 8–9 (Decius). Both emperors were of course provincials themselves.

268 On Thessalos, see still Diller 1936: he was a physician and medical writer in Neronian Rome: 'no actor, no charioteer was attended by greater crowds when he walked out' (Pliny, *Natural History* 29.9). His writings were quite well known in Egypt: see most recently *P.Oxy* LIX.4971 and *P. Horak* 2 (information from David Leith). A high degree of aggressivity towards rivals characterized all these figures.

269 See especially C.P. Jones 1978, chapter 12.

270 Yet it has be remembered that our knowledge about who was charismatic tends to concern those who affected the cultural elite to the neglect of those who affected ordinary people male and female (cf. Origen, *Against Celsus* 3.54–5).

men such as Arius (250s to 336), who although a rank-and-file priest in Alexandria was able to exercise wide intellectual influence.[271] But this was outside the sphere of worldly power which is our concern here.

Internal power, external power

How, finally, did the evolution of Rome's external power affect the structures of power within the empire? Those structures developed in complex ways, and for diverse reasons, but four distinctive internal developments were related to some degree to Rome's external strengths and weaknesses (I leave aside here their effect on the Roman economy):

(1) *The insecurity of emperors from Caracalla to Carinus.* While the inability of the emperors who ruled from 211 to 285 to hold on to power had mainly internal causes (above, p. 171), the negative fact that none of them could convincingly construct an image as a great conqueror was also a source of weakness.

(2) *The power of the legions.* They had played a decisive part in politics ever since the time of Sulla. Their power to make and unmake emperors was plain, and sometimes used, even before 235. And the power of the military went well beyond its obvious influence over who became emperor, since it also exercised extensive policing and administrative functions,[272] not to mention the power of the soldiers to terrorize civilians.[273] But there were in fact limits to the army's domestic power: only once in this period do the soldiers seem to have received a genuine pay increase, under Caracalla, and it was quite a modest one.[274] Caracalla's spending on the soldiers required tax increases and other exactions (Dio 77.9–10), which caused bitter resentment among senators (and no doubt many others). What is striking, however, is that most of the time the social elite was to a considerable degree able to hold its own in this conflict.

(3) *Incorporation.* The perceived need for military manpower made it essential to cast the recruiting net widely. The effects were entirely beneficial, from a Roman point of view, as long as the new recruits could be induced to identify themselves with Rome.

[271] A good brief account of Arius: A.H.M. Jones 1964, 1,86–9.
[272] On the former, see esp. Isaac 1992, chapters 2–3.
[273] For some of the evidence, see Alston 2007, 193–5.
[274] Rathbone 2007, 165.

(4) *The slow death of the citizens' rights and freedom* had multiple causes and was well on its way before the tetrarchs and Constantine accelerated the process. But the main confessed purpose of dragooning the population was to raise tax revenues, to be spent for the most part on the military.

How in turn did this internal distribution of power affect Rome's power on and across its frontiers? Rome's gradually widening ability to recruit trustworthy soldiers was clearly a great source of frontier strength down to Severan times and indeed throughout this period. The monarchical system as it actually took shape was eventually somewhat debilitating from this point of view, but what is remarkable is that the disadvantages of that system had a relatively minor effect down to the death of Constantine. Succession problems and the emperors' imperative need to avoid elevating able generals who might become potential rivals might have been expected to do more harm than they did. They in effect prevented any decisive expansion after Trajan's abortive campaigns in Mesopotamia, but left the emperors able to defend all the frontiers except for Dacia and the south-west German *limes*. Rome was fortunate of course to have only one formidable outside enemy in this era.

The Constantinian empire seemed to be robust enough to stand up to any external enemies. To what extent it suffered from internal weaknesses or tensions that were to cause trouble later is endlessly debatable. Four developments were potentially carcinogenic. First, the long series of military coups carried out since 235 made the monarchy highly unstable (and neither the tetrarchs nor Constantine altered that). Second, the separation of the upper social elite from military responsibilities meant that there could be no quasi-national leadership in the face of external threats (in a traditional society, professionalism is not enough). Third, the process of forming a national consciousness seems to have stalled in the generations after the Edict of Caracalla, further impeded perhaps by the fact that the Roman Empire no longer offered the range of economic opportunities that had characterized pre-Severan times. And fourth, there was the shadow of the forthcoming bitter conflict of religions.

CHAPTER 6

The Romans against outsiders, AD *337 to 641*

'A country under attack, unless it is at the height of a social crisis, must defend itself', Victor Serge, *Memoirs of a Revolutionary*, chapter 3.

The crucial decades

The Roman Empire did not end overnight, in fact its decline, like its rise, was a very prolonged affair. One can understand Gibbon's decision to continue the story all the way down to the Turkish occupation of Constantinople in 1453, though it also seems a great mistake, since the Roman-Byzantine state can scarcely be called an empire at any time between the late seventh and the early eleventh century. What is not rational is the decision to write as if the Roman Empire ended as early as the sixth or even the fourth century AD.

There are also those who think that the word 'decline' should be considered taboo in this context, but no thinking historian of political power will hesitate over that issue. The power of the Roman state contracted dramatically, and, though it is a commonplace that all empires end, this particular contraction merits an explanation – or rather, as we shall see, a set of explanations.

The phenomenon we are considering took place in two major phases, the first between the 370s and the 430s – at the outer limit 455 – the second between the 560s and the years 636–41. In both cases, it is possible, and necessary, to consider antecedent causes, but these were the crucial decades. So our questions are the following: why in the first place did the Roman state lose so much of its power in the face of Germanic invasions over two generations between the 370s and the 430s, with the result that the Roman Empire in the west became a kind of ghost empire with very little power within its own former territories? This debate started as soon as the event took place, indeed before it was over, and started again during the Enlightenment.[1] And why did the revived Roman Empire of Justinian, which included at its height Italy, almost all of North Africa and even some Spanish territory, as well as most of the old empire in the east, stumble after his death and finally collapse, as an empire, in the following century?

One central problem is military defeat and withdrawal; the other is the nature of power relations within Rome's surviving domain. And how are these two sets of relationships connected? Should we suppose that the changed nature of power inside the Roman world had a major effect on the Romans' failure, in either of the periods identified above? And conversely, how did these two periods of external failure change the power relations of the Romans with each other?

Western woes

From the 370s to the 430s then.[2] Few things are more difficult in late-antique history than to know why, *in the western half of the empire*, the Roman military and the Roman government failed: the sources and the archaeology simply never tell us enough, and modern historians have invented some unlikely tales (about the size of the Roman army, for example, and about the supposed absence of conflict). We can say very little that is useful about the German invaders: they obviously knew how to make war very effectively, and we may imagine that they had learned some practical lessons from the Romans – but how much any of this was a recent or decisive development is scarcely knowable. And of course we need to understand how the eastern emperors, their ministers, and their armies managed to fare decisively better. Did internal vulnerabilities of some kind make a difference, or were the external forces in the west simply stronger than Rome's enemies in the east?

It is no use arguing that the German invasions were not a hostile takeover or that there was no crisis. The central government in the west gradually lost control of the provinces. When a leading historian argued that there cannot have been much of a crisis because the fall of Romulus Augustulus in 476 had little contemporary impact,[3] it was scarcely probative, since by 476 the

[1] Demandt 1984, 122–69.

[2] Beginning in the 370s is somewhat arbitrary: Ammianus Marcellinus 26.4.5 lists the western regions that experienced invasions after the death of Julian in 363 – the Gallic, Raetian and Pannonian provinces, Britain, and North Africa.

[3] Averil Cameron 1998, 10.

Map 6. The western Roman Empire, AD 370s to 430s

actual western crisis was already over.[4] More recent scholarship, best exemplified by Bryan Ward-Perkins,[5] has re-established the indeed rather glaring fact that the power of the Roman Empire in the west had by 476 largely disappeared. The Vandal conquest of the Maghreb provinces, culminating in the capture of Carthage in 439, made a major recovery impossible, for

[4] For fifth-century awareness of what had happened, see among others Ando 2008, 40–1.
[5] Ward-Perkins 2005 and 2007. The view largely rejected here is summed up in Straw and Lim 2004.

financial as well as military reasons.[6] What is most intriguing here is that scholars lost sight of these facts, from the 1960s onwards, during an exceptionally prolonged period of bourgeois western comfort when the impact of the state's military performance on the individual was relatively limited. In the late fourth and early fifth centuries, by contrast, it was impossible, almost anywhere in the Roman Empire, to be unaffected by war.

The problems that most contributed to military weakness in the 250s and 260s – unstable government at the centre and inadequate funds to maintain larger military forces – had gone into remission, but after 337 they to some extent returned. At least thirteen men claimed the title of Augustus in the forty years after Constantine's death. In the 370s it could be said by an informed observer that 'the vast expenditure on the armies … has thrown the entire system of tax payments into difficulties' (Anonymous, *On Warfare* [*De rebus bellicis*] 5.1, trans. E.A. Thompson, with details; see further Ammianus Marcellinus 20.11.5 on the same problem in 360). But for all the money that was spent on them, these armies failed to defend the empire's western half.

How exactly should we estimate the performance of Rome's military forces over this sixty-year period (370s to 430s)? For several decades now, some contemporary writers have taken to denying – astonishingly – that anything went badly wrong, which seems to have been a curious and distorted echo of the 'explosion' of late antiquity that has occurred in academia over the last half-century. One such scholar writes in an authoritative publication that 'the performance of the army during the decades after 378 was by no means an unmitigated disaster',[7] which invites three main responses. First, you must not write rhetorical history – if the Roman army was not 'an unmitigated disaster' in this period, let us at least admit the obvious fact that it was a disaster. Second, 'the performance of the army' is too narrow a concept to allow us to assess Rome's military effectiveness: we need to include among other factors the political leadership, and those who did not fight but should have fought. And third, no one doubts that there were good soldiers fighting for the Roman state – not enough of them, however, and they were too often fighting against their own side.

The pollyannaish view is indefensible, in fact absurd. Vegetius, probably writing under Theodosius (379–95), knew better (*Epitome of Military Affairs* 1.7, 'so many defeats'). The government of the western

[6] There is a good deal of uncertainty, however, about the speed with which distinctively Roman power diminished in some regions, for example northern Gaul.

[7] Lee 1998, 233; similarly Elton 1996.

empire (based not in Rome now but in Milan, then from 402 onwards in Ravenna) steadily lost control of large parts of its territory from the 380s onwards, mainly to Germans (Map 6 shows the principal locations mentioned in the fourth- and fifth-century sections of this chapter and the next). After the disastrous Roman defeat at Hadrianople in 378 and subsequent events, large sections of the Balkan provinces had to be conceded to Goths whose periodic willingness to fight in alliance with Rome did not make them Roman subjects; the Pannonian provinces (even Savia, quite close to Italy), Lower Moesia, Thrace, and Macedonia were all deeply affected. Theodosius nonetheless accepted them, under their new young leader Alaric, as allies in his war against the usurper Eugenius, which culminated in the Battle of the Frigidus (in western Slovenia) in 394. Being disappointed of a Roman command, Alaric proceeded to do extensive harm in Thrace, Greece, and Epirus.[8] In about 398, in spite of this, the court of Constantinople appointed him to military command of the diocese of Illyricum (Claudian, *Gothic War* 535–9, *Against Eutropius* 2. 214–8, etc.),[9] from which, in 401, he invaded northern Italy.[10] Until that happened, Constantinople had probably seemed to be in more danger from barbarians than Italy was; the Asia Minor provinces were often in almost as much trouble as the ones on the Danube, and there were Goths living in Phrygia by the 390s. But though Alaric was not immediately victorious south of the Alps, Rome's highly competent commander Stilicho [Figure 6.1] was unable to dislodge him.

Alaric's wars in and close to Italy in the years 401 to 410 were by no means always successful, indeed the battle he lost to Stilicho at Pollentia in north-western Italy in 402 may have involved severe Gothic losses (the matter is debated). But the whole peninsula as far south as Rome itself suffered badly during these campaigns. There is really no sign that Alaric was aiming at bringing down the empire of Rome (though Claudian, *Gothic War* 530, may imply such an interpretation); what he claimed in 409 was resources and territory within the empire (Zosimus, *New History* 5.48; cf. Orosius, *History against the Pagans* 7.38.2). But these Italian campaigns of his, combined with the invasion of other very numerous Goths under Radagaisus in 406,[11] left a trail of destruction, most intense in the

[8] For an outline of his career, see *PLRE* II Alaricus 1. For a map summarizing his Balkan campaigns in 395–407, see Heather 1991, 203.

[9] A considerable number of the inhabitants fled: *Theodosian Code* 10.10.25.

[10] Cameron and Long 1993, 329.

[11] The sources agree that Radagaisus devastated many Italian cities before being killed in 406.

Figure 6.1. The military commander Stilicho (half Vandal by descent but deeply Romanized) with his wife Serena (niece of the emperor Theodosius) and their son Eucherius, shown on an honorific ivory diptych *c.* AD 399. Monza, Cathedral Treasury

north. That is plain enough both from the texts and from the archaeological records of the Italian towns and countryside.[12]

None of the western European provinces was secure after 406: Vandals, Alans, and Suebi effectively took control of large stretches of the German and Gallic provinces in 407–8, before moving to Spain. Alaric famously

[12] Cf. Ward-Perkins 1984, 23; Traina 2007, chapter 6.

seized Rome on August 24, 410, and then proceeded south to Calabria. After his death later in that year, his successor Athaulf eventually in 412 took the Goths in question to Gaul. Meanwhile rebellious Bagaudae once more caused trouble in north-western Gaul.[13] The consequences of all this loss of power were severe, and can only be minimized by scholars who are unable to visualize the effects of large-scale invasions. And as the government lost control of tax-paying areas such as Pannonia,[14] so it could afford fewer well-equipped soldiers and thus was less able to defend the old frontiers, which in turn gradually led to still further losses – a vicious circle in short.

In 418 or 419 Rome ceded to the Visigoths an area in the Garonne Valley of south-western France, which the latter steadily expanded over the next two generations until it included much of France and Iberia.[15] In 429 a force of Vandals crossed the straits into the African provinces, and promptly headed eastwards towards the region's greatest wealth, reaching Hippo in 430 and taking Carthage in 439. They used the ships they captured there to raid Sicily and, in 455, Rome itself, with very severe effects,.[16] In 442 Valentinian III had recognized their North African claims. Italy, with Sicily and Sardinia, gradually came into German hands in mid-century. The western emperors who nominally ruled between 455 and 476 – Petronius Maximus, Avitus, Majorian, Libius Severus, Anthemius, Olybrius, Glycerius, and Romulus 'Augustulus' – ruled at most over parts of Italy and Gaul, had very few troops of their own, and had no prospect of improving their position. Romulus was not even worth murdering when he was deposed. The men of power on the Roman side, Aetius (from 435 to 454) and Ricimer (457 to 472), the latter half-Suebian and half-Goth, did not attempt to become emperors; nor did they succeed, in spite of their evident ability, in arresting Rome's military decline.

What the Germanic invasions meant on the ground has to a certain extent been disputed, but at least it is clear that they meant vastly diminished Roman revenues. And there is really ample evidence that in very many districts death and destruction, including the destruction of fixed capital, were widespread.[17] Refugees were evidently numerous, especially

[13] This trouble seems to have lasted from 409 to 417: Zosimus 6.5.3 (with Paschoud's n.); Rutilius Namatianus, *On his Return* 213–16.
[14] For details of this case, see Bratož 2011, who emphasizes the flight of the provincials.
[15] Ward-Perkins 2005, 14–15.
[16] Pani Ermini 1999, 50–1.
[17] Cf. Ward-Perkins 2005, 13–27.

in Illyricum.[18] The effects of the invasions were all the worse because the invaders often fought among themselves (Goths against Vandals in Spain in 413–15, and many other such conflicts in the Iberian peninsula described in the *Chronicle* of the Spanish Hydatius) – thus many places suffered from more than just a one-time conquest. Gaul, Raetia, Noricum, Italy, Spain, Mauretania, and Numidia were all deeply affected. Archaeology trumps any desperate attempt to discount the textual evidence.[19]

The constant trend was for the central government and its agents to leave the local communities to their own devices, as far as defence was concerned: thus Romanus, commander of Rome's forces in north Africa, refused to help Lepcis and the other coastal cities when they were attacked in the 360s by the Austuriani from inland (Ammianus Marcellinus 28.6; not a simple story) (and later see for instance Valentinian, *Novels* 9 [AD 440]).

An attempt at explanation

What caused all this Roman failure? It is not as if Rome had been responding to the more or less coordinated effort of a great power such as Carthage had been in the mid-third century BC. On the other hand, the fighting qualities of the invaders were often formidable, and their numbers were sometimes quite formidable too in relation to the size of the forces that opposed them: Gothic and Vandal armies sometimes it seems ran to 25,000 or 30,000 men. Alaric's forces in 408–10 may well have amounted to 40,000.[20] Radagaisus is even said by a contemporary to have had more than 200,000 followers (Orosius, *History* 7.37.4), though that was certainly an exaggeration.

Internal weakness imposed a strategy of defence even before the Italian and Rhine frontiers fell seriously to pieces after 401 and 406 respectively. A resilient imperial state has to go after its important enemies, as Rome did in the third and second centuries BC, and the Muslims did in the seventh century AD. Julian (sole emperor 362–3) had no doubt sensed this, and if he had been endowed with superhuman foresight he would have attacked the Germans not the Persians. In the late fourth century, by contrast, the main way you flattered an emperor's military wisdom was by

[18] *Theodosian Code* 10.10.25 (408), 7.13.20.1 (410), 6.29.12 (415).

[19] For central Italy, see Marzano 2007, chapter 8, a balanced account. Until recently at least a number of scholars were in denial, e.g. Cracco Ruggini 2004, 37.

[20] Heather 1991, 15–16, 214. But Heather 2010a, 665, n. 87, tends lower: 'the Visigoths who formed around Alaric could certainly field at least [20,000 soldiers]', and 'possibly' between 30,000 and 40,000.

Figure 6.2. Solidus of Honorius, AD 402–8. On the reverse: the emperor holding a standard and a Victory figure, with his foot on a bound captive, with the legend VICTORIA AUGGG (plus mint marks). Kent 1994, 1286–7, etc.

claiming that he had built defensive ramparts such as a long 'adamantine wall' along the frontier, and real effort evidently went into such defences (Themistius, *Oration* 10. 36–138; for his defensive posture, cf. *Or.* 16.208C, 211A). This was not in itself an absurd strategy, but it was a second best. After Hadrianople, not even the most competent of Roman military leaders, Theodosius I and Stilicho, could aspire to defeat the Goths in a definitive fashion. The coin-types of Theodosius and his son Honorius sometimes, following tradition, celebrated 'victory' [Figure 6.2], but the resources were not there for any such victory as Marius, Caesar, or Trajan might have aspired to. Occasional flashes of a more aggressive attitude (visible, for example, in *Theodosian Code* [*CTh* from here onwards] 7.17.1 of 412) were merely another belated charade.[21]

[21] Cf. Charles 2007, 169–70.

Another 'strategic' factor that might have made a serious difference was the final division of the empire into east and west, which occurred when Theodosius was succeeded in 395 by Honorius and his other son Arcadius (both of whom were still children). This division had a positive aspect to it in the sense that it limited the range of problems that a single emperor and his military commanders had to deal with, but the western emperor Honorius together with Stilicho wasted time and resources on trying to subordinate the east to the west or at least to take the diocese of Illyricum under western control.

The confused sequence of events involving Alaric and his followers between 405 and 408 shows quite vividly the impossible strategic choice that now faced the rulers of the western empire. The realistic Stilicho attempted to compromise with the Goths, had Alaric appointed to command Roman troops (Sozomen, *Ecclesiastical History* 8.25.3, 9.4.2), and later prevailed on the Senate to pay him 4,000 lbs of gold. But Stilicho himself was vulnerable, and when he was murdered some three months after this, at the instance of the courtier Olympius, the latter, it seems, attempted to take a harder line with Alaric, as the majority of the senators in Rome had desired (Zosimus 5.29.6–9). This policy had no prospect whatsoever of success: there were not enough reliable soldiers to support it (all the fewer after the events following the murder of Stilicho, to which we shall return in a moment).

Emperors and senior officers were normally faced with a narrow range of choices, and some of the evils they had to contend with accrued gradually. At one time, for example, allowing 'barbarian' populations to settle in Roman provinces had been a safe enough policy; and there were precedents stretching back to the first century. When Franks settled in northern Gaul from the 350s on, it may have been to the emperor's advantage.[22] When Theodosius made a treaty with the Goths in 382 that allowed them to live independently of Rome inside Roman provinces, including Moesia, the Dacias, and Macedonia,[23] one can hardly say that the emperor should have done otherwise – he had no better option. And they provided military manpower. But 'the peace of 382 sanctioned a major departure in imperial policy, the Goths retaining their identity as an at least semi-independent tribal group'.[24] Themistius (speaking not far way in Constantinople) expressed the hope that they would become

[22] So Stickler 2007, 500–2.
[23] Heather 1991, 157–92.
[24] Heather 1991, 166.

Romans just as the once-barbarian Galatians had (*Oration* 16.211CD), but there was little or no basis for such optimism. By the time such German 'allies' of Rome were proving over and over again in the 390s and 400s that they were not docile or amenable, it was too late to expel them.

On the tactical level, it is hard to know whether the crisis was much affected by incompetent military leadership.[25] On a contingent level, it did matter to some extent that the wretched emperor Honorius, who was ten when he succeeded his father in 395, was far from being an adequate champion even when he grew to manhood [Figure 6.3]. Thanks to Ammianus we know quite a lot about what had happened at the Battle of Hadrianople in 378, and on that occasion the Roman commanders made serious mistakes. Unfortunately we have nothing like such good information about any subsequent engagement. Certainly some high Roman officers showed themselves incompetent from time to time: if, for instance, we are to believe Zosimus (5.45.2) – as on this point we probably should – the reason why, in Italy in 409, Alaric was able to destroy a force of 6,000 men who were 'the elite of the Roman army' was that their commander failed to take sufficient precautions and found his path blocked by the massed forces of the enemy. But even in republican times generals had sometimes done foolish things and suffered severe defeats in consequence, and we may be better off looking at the military forces as a whole.

Neither the number nor the quality of the troops at the disposal of the Roman emperors who ruled from Valens and Valentinian, through the great German crisis of 406–10, to the final years of the western empire, were sufficient. Numbers first: historians still have a bad habit of inventing highly arbitrary totals for the western Roman forces of this period, about which nothing precise can be ascertained despite the document known as the *Notitia Dignitatum* (which included the names of all military units).[26] When someone writes that 'the Roman army in this period [350–425] was at least 300,000 and may have been 600,000 strong',[27] the reader needs to know that these figures are guesswork, and bad guesswork at that, quite apart from the fact that many of the soldiers in question were assigned to internal policing (though probably not as many as around AD 300 – see above, p. 202). What chiefly makes an army of 600,000 incredible is that

[25] We scarcely need Ammianus to tell us (25.8.11) that, as in earlier times, an outstanding general was likely to be suspected of aiming for the throne.

[26] We must not follow Nicasie in seeking to know 'the size of the Roman army in the fourth century' (1998, 75), for it almost certainly shrank considerably *during* that century.

[27] Elton 1996, 128. In the same general sense: Whitby 2007, 517. The larger total was unfortunately accepted by McCormick 2001, 42.

(Ed.ne Alinari) P.a I.a N.o 15313. AOSTA - *Piemonte*. Cattedrale. Dittico in avorio con l'Imperatore Onorio. (V secolo.)

Figure 6.3. Ivory diptych of the emperor Honorius and the consul Anicius Petronius Probus, AD 406. 'In nomine Christi vincas semper' – 'In the name of Christ, may you always be victorious'. Aosta, Cathedral Treasury

the much richer Roman Empire of the second century had found it a strain to support an army of more than about 350,000. Such guesses admittedly go back to Mommsen and beyond.[28] They are based on two sources. First there are propagandistic figures given by sixth-century writers for the military forces of Constantine (some 870,000 according to John the Lydian, *On Months* 1.27!); these have no value at all for the period of Honorius and Arcadius. The other source is the *Notitia Dignitatum*, which, however, does not tell us how many men were supposed to be serving in any of the units named (a point on which other sources are insufficient), still less how many were actually serving; and the *Notitia* refers to diverse dates running from the mid-fourth century to at least 421. It cannot guide us to an estimate of the number of Roman troops under arms in the first years of the fifth century.[29] Meanwhile the archaeologists are agreed that all over the empire the forts of the fourth century are much smaller than those of earlier times;[30] the 'high counters' have to argue that this change was counterbalanced by an increase in the number of forts, which as far as the west is concerned is quite unproved.

When Stilicho desperately needed to put down Gildo's rebellion in Africa in 397, in order to restore the capital's grain supply, he only managed to get together 5,000 soldiers ('as they say', Orosius 7.36.6), the equivalent of less than a single high-imperial legion.[31] When even graver trouble started, with Radagaisus' invasion of Italy in 405/6, Honorius offered freedom to slaves if they would join the army (*CTh* 7.13.16)[32] – a clear sign of a military establishment that had been kept too small, largely no doubt for fiscal reasons; in the same year Honorius made a desperate attempt to raise new taxes (*CTh* 11.20.3). The 6,000-man 'elite of the Roman army' mentioned above, which was sent by Honorius to protect the city of Rome in 409 (Zosimus 5.45.1), was less numerous than the old praetorian guard had been. At no point in the entire crisis do we hear of a Roman army even remotely on the scale of the ones often fielded in late-republican times. Trajan had invaded Dacia with roughly 100,000 troops, disciplined and well-supplied; even Julian had apparently been able to take at least 65,000 to Mesopotamia (Zosimus 3.13.1),

[28] Clemente 1968, 156.

[29] For recent work on this document, see Kulikowski 2000; Dietz 2011, 63–8. For proper scepticism about its value for army numbers, see MacMullen 2006, 476, n. 21.

[30] Fear 2007, 424–5.

[31] Claudian, *On the Consulship of Stilicho* 1.333–40, is an amusing cover-up: Stilicho did not want to frighten Gildo into retreating into the Sahara.

[32] At the same time extra financial inducements were offered to the free: 7.13.7. Slaves had already been recruited in 398 (Symmachus, *Letters* 6.64).

quite exceptionally for the fourth century (many of them were 'barbarians', however).

This was probably one of the prime causes of military weakness: the tax-base had shrunk, no regular censuses were taken,[33] the 'more powerful', even under the relatively strong Constantine, shifted much of the burden to the 'lower people' – on this point see *CTh* 13.10.1 of AD 313; naturally they could not always pay. Our notions of the government's ability to collect revenue between the 370s and the crisis of the 410s are necessarily impressionistic, but even in some areas which had not yet suffered invasions there are very negative signs. In a famous letter, Ambrose of Milan describes the decayed state of town and country from Bononia to Placentia (*Letters* 39.3).[34] The literary antecedents of this text do not seriously detract from its evidentiary value.[35] By 393 the emperors acknowledged that some provinces could contribute very little (*CTh* 7.4.19). Two years later, about 40 per cent of the land of formerly wealthy Campania had to have its tax arrears forgiven.[36] The decline of the western Roman city, while not uniform, is well established and highly indicative.[37] It is drastically misleading to say that 'the empire's resources [were] undiminished'.[38]

Whether the government was able to tax the population effectively is partly a question for the next chapter. As far as the west is concerned, no source comes anywhere near to justifying A.H.M. Jones's claim that the system 'worked only too efficiently'.[39] Responsibility for raising the taxes that paid for the army was divided between the 'counts of the sacred benefactions' (*comites sacrarum largitionum*) and the praetorian prefects, but what mattered most was probably the efficiency of the low-level tax-collectors. Graft within the taxation system seems in fact to have been fairly extensive.[40] But the evidence is hard to interpret. In 378 many Thracian miners joined the Gothic side because they felt overwhelmed by Roman taxation (Ammianus 31.6.6), but they may have been something of a special case.

33 For the somewhat random ways in which tax liabilities were adjusted after this, see A.H.M. Jones 1964, I, 455, and II, 537 and 798.

34 The *Cambridge Ancient History* prefers to believe that 'Northern Italy … experienced a period of prosperity during the late 380s and early 390s': Lee 1998, 231, misrepresenting Cracco Ruggini 1961.

35 Cracco Ruggini 1961, 61, n. 145.

36 *CTh* 11.28.2, with Bransbourg 2015, 275.

37 See Liebeschuetz 2001, 74–103, though he lumps together evidence from widely separate periods. On Gaul, for example, see 84–8. But a less impressionistic survey is needed. Garnsey and Whittaker 1998, 327, ignore most of the evidence.

38 MacMullen 2006, 471 (cf. 475 and 481 – 'rising wealth'!); the date referred to is evidently the early fifth century.

39 Jones 1964, I, 468.

40 This is emphasized, somewhat indiscriminately, by MacMullen 1988.

In 444 the emperor Valentinian III stated that 'from the revenue that is with difficulty collected from the exhausted taxpayer, provision cannot be made for feeding and clothing the old army, let alone newly levied troops' (Valentinian, *Novels* 15 pr.), but was that true forty years earlier? Valentinian was in any case seeking to excuse the imposition of new taxes.

The whole concept of 'the Roman army' is quite anachronistic in this period. After Hadrianople the soldiers who saved Constantinople were 'Saracens', that is to say Arabs (Ammianus 31.16.5–7; Sozomen 7.1.1). On the Danube and in the west, practically no campaign was fought without 'federates', mostly German. What was harmful to the Roman Empire about relying on units of German troops was not of course that they were 'barbarians', but that, being essentially mercenaries, their loyalty was inclined to slip. This might on occasion work to the government's advantage: after the defeat and capture of Radagaisus at Faesulae – which was owed in part to German federates –, Stilicho enrolled some of the enemy troops on the Roman side.[41]

But rivalry between Roman troops and unruly Gothic and other troops in Roman service was often extremely harmful to the Roman state. Theodosius cleverly sent 'barbarians' from the lower Danube to Egypt while sending Egyptian troops to the Balkans, but unfortunately the two groups crossed paths in Lydia, with bloody consequences (Zosimus 4.30–1). Having made peace with Alaric in very difficult circumstances in 408, Stilicho thought it necessary, in order to control the movements of the emperor Honorius, to stir up a mutiny of 'barbarian' soldiers in the service of Rome at Ravenna (Zosimus 5.30.3). A little later in the year, a large-scale mutiny at Ticinum resulted in the murder of many of the senior officers loyal to Stilicho (Zosimus 5.32). Many Romans regarded Stilicho himself, even though he was a Vandal on his father's side, with respect, but others perhaps inevitably came to doubt his loyalty to the Roman cause (Jerome, *Letters* 123.16, written in 409; Rutilius Namatianus 2.41–60; Orosius 7.38.1).[42] The profound distrust of the Goths who fought for the Roman side that is expressed in Synesius' *On Kingship* (sects. 19–26) was presumably felt by many Romans in the west too.[43]

[41] Zosimus 5.26.5 says there were very few of them; Olympiodorus fr.9 Blockley that there were 12,000.

[42] What is more remarkable is that men of such lineage were now appointed to such high military-political positions.

[43] Synesius' 'bland recommendation to raise a national army would have raised a smile in any Roman court: emperors had been trying *and failing* [my italics] to raise a national army for centuries', according to Cameron and Long 1993, 120. In fact earlier emperors, down to the mid-third century or even Constantine's reign, had kept the soldiers, including the *auxilia*, obedient and overwhelmingly loyal to Rome.

While Alaric hovered in Noricum, Roman hostility to the federates intensified. After the death of Stilicho in 408:

> the [Roman] soldiers stationed in the cities [of Italy]… attacked the wives and children of the barbarians [i.e. the federates] in each city, slaughtered all of them as if at an agreed signal, and plundered all their property. When the relatives of the victims heard of this and gathered in one place …, they decided unanimously to join Alaric's cause and join in his war against Rome … [there were] more than 30,000 of them (Zosimus 5.35).

Roman troops themselves could not be relied on to remain loyal to the legitimate emperor. In 409, at the new *de facto* capital of Ravenna, Roman troops mutinied, apparently out of loathing for those in command (Zosimus 5.47). After the sack of Rome, Honorius was about to sail off into exile because he thought that his Roman troops might betray him (Sozomen 9.8, Zosimus 6.8.2), though he changed his mind when reinforcements arrived from the east.

That conscription was necessary can hardly cause much remark, but there are strong hints at least that it did not work well – 'the provincials … because of the audacity of these men [those who cut off their own fingers to avoid service] often suffer a shortage of recruits whom they have to supply' (*CTh* 7.13.10 [381]).[44] Vegetius says that height requirements have had to be reduced because of the shortage of recruits (*Epitome of Military Affairs* 1.5–6) and complains about the shrinkage of legionary units (2.3).[45] Others were aware that Arcadius allowed too many exemptions from military service (Synesius, *On Kingship* 19). The fact that the western government permitted commutation of such service for money during the depths of the crisis period (*CTh* 7.13.18 [407] and 20 [410], 11.18.1 [412]) may conceivably have had a net positive effect on the quality of recruits,[46] but it is certainly evidence that the population's will to resist was inadequate. The unpopularity of military service in the post-Diocletianic empire is in any case amply attested.[47]

The army that Ammianus knew, like the older Roman army, still based its discipline in part on harsh punishments, including summary execution (Ammianus 24.3.2, 29.5.31 [burning deserters alive], etc.),[48] which

[44] Ammianus 15.12.3 singles out the Italians as those who cut off their thumbs to avoid military service; the Gauls, he says, do not.

[45] In 3.1, as if facing the inevitable, he sets out the arguments in favour of small armies, with a good deal of historical distortion.

[46] Ammianus was very much of the contrary opinion, 19.11.7

[47] Fear 2007, 428–33.

[48] Cf. Rance 2007, 374 (but only for this detail).

makes it hard for a modern researcher to understand. And it is difficult to evaluate the morale of Roman soldiers even in periods when we have better sources.[49] Contemporary authors had a low opinion of the late fourth- and early fifth-century soldier,[50] but we need to privilege authors who really knew the army and concentrate on aspects of its behaviour that really counted (if soldiers got drunk from time to time, it probably did not matter). Thus the largely negative judgement of Ammianus on their psychological state tells heavily: the soldiers in the east were 'passive and enervated' (18.6.2); the army in Africa was 'slack and greedy for seizing the property of others' (27.9.1); the troops in southern Asia Minor were 'spoiled and feeble' (27.9.6); and so on, repeatedly.[51] This was not merely the resentment of a civilian in a time of danger. And what civilians say, if read critically, is sometimes informative. Libanius, for example, helps to explain how things were, notwithstanding his rhetorical flourishes:

> the soldiers starve and shiver, and haven't a penny to their name – all through the probity of their generals and colonels who feather their own nests... [they neglect their training...]. As a result, all the enemy needs to do in action is to set up a yell, and they are off and away ... their souls are fearful, their bodies little better than shadows... (*Oration* 2.37–9, trans. Norman).

And this was before the severest troubles began.

The most promising source of all should be Vegetius' *Epitome*, even though we cannot date it with certainty (a date in the period 383–95 is rightly popular, but some think that it was written as late as the period 425–50[52]). Modern claims to know the fourth-century army better than Vegetius did[53] are highly suspect if not absurd. His critique is wide ranging but what he most emphasizes is lack of training. He also complains (1.20) that since the reign of Gratian (375–83) Roman infantry no longer use the traditional heavy breastplate and helmet:[54] 'thus our soldiers ... have often been destroyed by the masses of Gothic archers'. The habit of building elaborate camps, a traditional strength of the Roman army, had died out (1.21). The effects of these factors on morale are frequently to the fore.

[49] See Harris 2006.
[50] MacMullen 1988, 175.
[51] Lee 2007a, 414–5, attempts to minimize Ammianus' complaints.
[52] Charles 2007. But no one in that period can have written of a recently ended long peace (1.7, 8, 28, 3.10).
[53] E.g. Lee 2007a, 415.
[54] Scholars have sometimes offered futile objections to this statement, but it may indeed be an exaggeration.

It is reasonable to suppose that the Roman soldiers of this period, when they were Roman at all, were irregularly paid, undertrained, insubordinate, inclined to desert,[55] and often engaged in non-military occupations.[56] But how had such conditions come about? 'Corruption', says Ramsay MacMullen, but *widespread* corruption should be seen as a symptom that in turn requires explanation. Insufficient tax revenue is part of the story and it must sometimes have put commanders such as Romanus (above, p. 226) in awkward situations.

There can scarcely be much doubt that there had been a marked decline, from the highest ranks of imperial service downwards, in people's belief in the Roman state, more specifically in the belief that it should be served even if that meant passing up financial gain, and in the belief that it would punish those who served it dishonestly. In 406 the emperors professed – unprecedentedly – to believe that the free-born provincials were motivated by patriotism (*amor patriae, amor pacis et patriae*) to undertake military service (*CTh* 7.13.16–17), but it rings somewhat false – not only because, as we have seen, the same legislation offered freedom to slaves if they would serve, but because the appeal had no detectable effect.

The inner dynamics of military morale certainly involved religion to some extent. This matter will continue to trouble us down to the end. The point here is not so much that Christian authorities professed not to care what happened to the world in which they lived (more on that below); rather, we want to know what effect religious feelings had on the men who did the fighting and on the men who might have done the fighting but did not. Traditional Roman soldiers, in all periods, seem to have been attentive towards the gods, and with some variations they agreed who the gods were and what the gods required – animal sacrifices and honour – in exchange for their favours (for the third century AD, see above, p. 177).[57] Now there was no longer much agreement, and other men in your unit might well be inviting disaster since they worshipped false gods or refused to worship the true ones, as the case might be; Mithras had been a particularly popular god among soldiers, and both texts and archaeology testify to the Christians' especial loathing for him.[58] Even when most were Christians, your fellow-soldiers

[55] Concerning desertion, see the extensive sources gathered by Fear 2007, 435–7. He considers that the western empire was 'broken down' by this problem.
[56] MacMullen 1988, chapter 4.
[57] Stoll 2007, 452–68.
[58] Winter 2000.

might profess disastrously heretical beliefs, Arian, Athanasian or (later) Monophysite.[59]

All this is wholly unmeasurable. But whereas religious diversity in the army had been more or less accepted for half a century after the death of Constantine, and religion was not a major source of trouble in the army described by Ammianus, Theodosius I brought that to an end.[60] The fierce religious and theological strife of the fourth century eventually infected military affairs too; the question is when and how deeply. Theodosius banned various traditional religious practices, including the one that was truly central, animal sacrifice (391), and it was probably he who made the soldiers swear obedience in the name of the Christian deity (cf. Vegetius 2.5). When Roman armies clashed at the Battle of the Frigidus in 394 as Theodosius struggled to suppress the usurper Eugenius, there is good reason to suppose that religious loyalties really did matter to some of the soldiery. Contemporaries saw it as in part a religious conflict, and Augustine (*City of God* 5.26) is probably to be believed when he claims that the pagan-friendly Eugenius made use of statues of Jupiter in the campaign while Theodosius emphasized his devotion to the Christian god (Eugenius was defeated and executed).[61] The victors probably exaggerated the losers' devotion to the old gods, but there was something solid there to exaggerate.

After 400, the balance of power within the army had shifted decisively to the Christians, and if 'pagan' rituals survived at all on military sites they have left few traces. There continued, however, to be soldiers who were 'pagans' or 'heretics'. When the pious young Honorius decreed that the 'enemies of the Catholic sect' could not serve as soldiers in the palace (*CTh* 16.5.42) (408), he was apparently compelled to reverse himself (Zosimus 5.46.4). For decades to come, the government employed such men as soldiers, while denying them religious and eventually civil rights as well (see *CTh* 16.5.65 of 435). Unless we suppose these soldiers were mostly irreligious – which is quite unlikely – their morale must have been hampered, and no doubt some of their Catholic fellow-soldiers would have preferred not to be serving side by side with men whose religion was so radically incorrect.

[59] Whitby 1998 attempted to show that 'the Christian church [*sic*] was able to contribute to the empire's military survival' (191), but could find no evidence to that effect from these years.

[60] Stoll 2007, 473.

[61] The efforts of Alan Cameron 2011, 93–131, to eliminate the element of religious conflict from the Battle of the Frigidus go too far for my taste. See Paschoud 2012, 364–7; Bonamente 2013; Harris forthcoming b. See further Weisweiler 2009, 387.

Thus we come to the wider and perhaps unfathomable question of civilian attitudes. Some Christians still seem to have been to a certain degree alienated from the Roman state, even though it was now on their side. Bishop Paulinus of Nola, who had grown up amid extreme privilege, his mind clouded by love of relics and miracles, attempted to persuade a military man to desert (*Letter* 25, about 400),[62] and seems to have believed that prayer could defeat the Gothic enemies of Rome (*Poems* 26.246–68; cf. 103–110).[63] Bishop Maximus of Turin voices the same thought (*Sermon* 85).[64] In 400 the emperors considered that 'many persons, either before their military service or after it has just begun ... are hiding under the pretext of religious devotion'. 'We permit no person at all to be exempted by such a pretext', they proclaimed, doubtless in vain (*CTh* 7.20.12.2). Not that pessimism was restricted to Christians: in 402 Claudian wrote (*On the Gothic War* 262–6) of a portent that some interpreted as meaning that Rome was fated not to survive beyond twelve centuries from its foundation; we should not ignore such stories.

Alan Cameron's prolonged attempt to show that the conflict between Christians and followers of other and usually older religious cults and practices did not amount to much in our period[65] has made some important points, in particular that quite a number of people did not identify unequivocally with one side or the other. But it involves too much special pleading, and loses by its lack of a comparison with the centuries when Romans were almost all at peace with each other with respect to matters of religion. It concentrates too much on the tiny fraction of the population that made up the senatorial elite in the old capital.[66] Sermons of this period 'certainly reveal Christians anxious about what they saw as the continuing threat of paganism. But how realistic was this perception?'[67] What matters here, however, is the anxiety, or rather the mutual hostility between Roman and Roman created by the religious divide, not whether Christian apprehensions were realistic. A century and a half later, 'large numbers of peasants from Spain to Syria continued to worship the old gods', and the Christian authorities were well aware of the fact.[68]

[62] The letter was probably intended for a wider audience: Trout 1999, 127.

[63] It was religious victory that Paulinus was celebrating when he wrote in 405 that 'the summit of the Capitol shakes and totters' (*Poems* 19.68), but in view of what happened five years later his lack of respect for the symbol of Rome's durable power is striking.

[64] See Cameron 2011, 97.

[65] Culminating in Cameron 2011. Fortunately, in order to dispose of the evidence, he assembles a very large amount of it: see esp. 783–801.

[66] Cecconi 2013, 153.

[67] Cameron 2011, 784.

[68] Maas 2005, 15.

Were Montesquieu, Voltaire,[69] and Gibbon then right to maintain that Christianity itself weakened the Roman Empire in these decades? 'The last remains of the military spirit were buried in the cloyster',[70] Gibbon famously claimed. Some men became deacons to avoid military service (Basil, *Letters* 54), but on the other hand many robust soldiers of these years, including Theodosius and Stilicho, were zealous Christians. Significant numbers of soldiers had been Christians ever since the time of Constantine. The victorious army at the Battle of the Frigidus must have been largely Christian. To a great extent, as has been said, 'religion achieves its effects … through the influence of ritual and symbols',[71] and the ritual and symbols that gave a meaning to many Christian lives were at odds with defending Rome's earthly power. But what probably mattered more, among psychological factors, was religious *disunity*: Christians in Italy suspected that the followers of the old gods favoured the cause of the 'pagan' invader Radagaisus (Augustine, *City of God* 5.23). Honorius' government realized, in a sense and for the wrong reasons, the desirability of religious unity: the day after Rome fell in 410, unaware of the event of course, it decreed that:

> all enemies of our holy faith are to know that if they should attempt further to convene publicly, in the accursed temerity of their crime, they will suffer the penalty both of proscription and of blood (*CTh* 16.5.51).

It was German invasions that brought the western Roman empire to an end, but it had been weakened from within. By 410 the signs of this weakness were various but obvious. No historian would now want to attribute them to a single cause. We can say that Rome had not gone far enough in converting itself from an empire into a nation, and that it was too much divided by social class and religious discord to survive (see the next chapter). Its shared rituals and myths existed, but they had never worked on the great mass of the population, and Christianity had weakened them still further. Yet economic and fiscal decline, to be associated with weaknesses in the political structure, were also important. All of these factors had been present in the mid-third century but grew more intense from the 370s onwards.

What differentiated the west from the east between the 370s and the 430s was apparently not to any great extent internal to the Roman Empire – not at first, for as we have seen, the strengths and weaknesses

[69] 'Deux fléaux détruisirent enfin ce grand colosse: les barbares, et les disputes de religion', Voltaire, *Essai sur les moeurs et l'esprit des nations*, chapter 11.

[70] Gibbon 1776–1788, chapter 38.

[71] Liebeschuetz 1990, 249.

of the two regions seem to have been much the same (though it would be hard to find an eastern bishop as subversive as Paulinus of Nola). It was the intensity of outside pressure, greatly exacerbated by the economic harm inflicted by the invasions, that made the big difference. It was the good fortune of the eastern rulers that the invasions they faced were generally much less severe (though they were dangerous enough). The difference was highly visible in 421/2: the new Rome in the east attacked the Persia of King Vararanes V (Barabanes), not without provocation, and came out of it on essentially equal terms (Socrates, *Ecclesiastical History* 7.20, etc.). Somehow or other King Attila of the Huns was prevailed upon in 450 to leave the lower Danube region in peace (Priscus of Panium, fr. 15.4–5 Blockley). After his death in 453 his kingdom disintegrated. The Persian frontier remained largely peaceful from 422 until the reign of Justin I (518–27).[72]

Two centuries later

The fall of the Byzantine Roman Empire is a quite separate story. Nothing is more deplorable in recent writing about late antiquity than the very widespread tendency to lump indiscriminately together the conditions of the fourth to seventh centuries.[73] (The great synthesis by A.H.M. Jones may be partly to blame).[74]

In AD 600 the Roman Empire was still an empire, though a fragile one. It ruled the old Roman Middle East, most of the North African littoral, parts of Italy, even some lands in Spain, and all the large Mediterranean islands; in the Balkans, however, it was weak, ruling only over the immediate hinterland of Constantinople and of the Aegean.[75] (Map 7 shows the principal locations mentioned in the sixth- and seventh-century sections of this chapter and the next).

Just as the fall of the western Roman Empire was reduced by some twentieth-century historians (of various persuasions) to a non-event, so some have argued that the fall of the Roman-Byzantine empire in the seventh century did not amount to much. But this argument rests on claims of cultural continuity that are mainly superficial and are tangential to the question of power. (Strangely the proponents of such views pay

[72] As to why, see Rubin 2000, 641–3.
[73] As even happens, for example, in such very useful works as Liebeschuetz 2001, Sabin *et al.* 2007.
[74] Jones 1964.
[75] See the map in Kaegi 2003, 20.

Map 7. The eastern Roman Empire, AD 565–641

little attention to the material lives of peasants, which may indeed not have changed much in those parts of Syria, Egypt, and North Africa that were not visited by armies between AD 600 and 700). Is it really necessary to prove the claim that 'the first wave of Arab conquests marked a great divide'?[76] Historians of Islam are clear-headed about this.[77] A new

[76] This view was 'no longer tenable' according to Averil Cameron 1998, 15, building on Fowden 1993. In truth, this tendency has a long history: Demandt 1984, 222–3; and Demandt participated in it.

[77] Cf. Donner 2008, xiii.

language (known to very few scholars of Christian late antiquity) and a new religion now dominated, taxes went to Arabia and other Muslim centres not to Constantinople, a cultural wall separated south-east and north-west.[78] The world was being re-oriented: in 644, for the first time, a fleet brought the Egyptian grain surplus not to Byzantium but to the Hijaz.[79] No greater divide occurred in the Mediterranean world between the Roman victories of the second century BC and the collapse of the Ottoman Empire in the nineteenth and early twentieth centuries AD, and in cultural terms the Muslim conquests were more potent than either of those (sets of) events. All three sets of events were, politically speaking, tsunamis.

The western parts of the restored empire of Rome had been the work of the military forces of Justinian (527–65) and to a great extent of his leading generals Belisarius and Narses, and the limitations of their success showed the maximum level that a Byzantine emperor could hope to achieve in little more than a single generation. Justinian's principal strategy was to maintain a stable frontier with Persia in order to reconquer territories in the west that had been lost to Vandals, Goths, and others. He could not foresee that the Persians would one day be strong enough to deprive the emperor Heraclius (610–41) of crucial Mediterranean provinces; even if he had, an all-out war of conquest in Persia would have been a very ambitious undertaking, even for Justinian.

In the long run, the wars in the west – in North Africa against the Vandals (533) and Moors (543–49), and more especially in Italy (535–55) and Spain (552) against the Goths and others – produced an empire that was very difficult to protect and hold together. But the modern tendency to glorify Justinian has some justification – the conquest of all Italy was especially impressive, and if his successors had held on to the new Roman Empire, taxed it, and defended it, he would no doubt be thought of as a great empire-builder. With all that that entails in the way of bloodshed and terror.

In North Africa, the victory of Justinian's forces was fairly swift, and the conquerors were to some extent able to re-integrate local economic resources into those of the Constantinople empire.[80] In Italy, the Byzantine invaders' idea was to make war against the Goths and to leave

78 With language as well as strife and religion keeping the two worlds apart; but for Muslim knowledge of Greek, see Figure 6.6.

79 Howard-Johnston 2010, 470.

80 McCormick 2001, 104.

the 'Romans' unscathed (see, for instance, Procopius, *Wars* 6.7.30, 6.17.6), but unfortunately the two populations to a considerable extent lived in the same places. Not surprisingly, most of the 'Roman' inhabitants of Italy showed little enthusiasm for the cause of Belisarius; he in turn had very little wish to enlist untrained auxiliaries. Aristocrats in the old capital had in some cases property and connections in the eastern empire,[81] but the Italians in general recognized no duty to fight for Justinian's Roman Empire.[82] Which is not to deny that there was still a sense of Roman identity (cf. Procopius, *Wars* 5.8.7, etc). Under the impact of prolonged war, in any case, the Italian rural economy largely collapsed in the period 530–50, as the archaeology shows,[83] which meant that Italian revenues would never suffice to pay for defence against the Goths, Franks, and Lombards.

By 555 the eastern Romans were able to complete their reconquest of Italy, but the price they paid in other regions was high. Even while Justinian and Belisarius were still alive in 559, Cotrigur Huns led by Zabergan,[84] having crossed the Danube, raided as far as the inner wall of Constantinople (Agathias, *Histories* 5.13.5), before being driven off, and paid off.[85] In 561/2 Justinian made peace with the Persian king Khusro [Chosroes] I, in theory for fifty years, and while the division of territories was reasonable enough, the Romans had to agree to pay an annual tribute of 30,000 gold coins, with the first seven instalments payable at once. The price was not exorbitant (it has been estimated that imperial revenue came to some five or six million *solidi* a year at this time[86]), and it was soon to be exceeded by much larger payments to other rulers, but it indicated where the balance lay on that particular frontier. The security of the eastern provinces was no worse than before, but in spite of Justinian's efforts no better; and at the time of his death in 565, the Blemmyes on the southern frontier of Egypt were once again causing serious trouble.

In the generation between the deaths of Justinian and Maurice (emperor 582–602), the Byzantine Roman Empire lost much of its Italian territory, and had the fragility of its control over the Balkans confirmed. The Lombards invaded Italy in 568, were rapidly successful in the north, and after a decade or so had reached the Bay of Naples and established a duchy

81 Averil Cameron 1985, 193–4.

82 Liebeschuetz 2001, 350. He does not, however, make good his claim (365) that significant numbers of Italians fought on the Gothic side.

83 Hodges 2010, 77–8. This can indeed be inferred from the text of Procopius.

84 *PLRE* III, 1,410.

85 It was a serious if short-lived crisis: Alan Cameron 1976, 106.

86 Hendy 1985, 172.

at Beneventum. For a time emperors were able to play them off against the other invaders, the Franks, but in the 590s Lombard power spread once again in central and southern Italy; by 602 the remaining elements of imperial control were contested almost everywhere, and Smaragdus, the Byzantine exarch (viceroy) for much of the reign of Phocas, gave up further territory. We know many details of the politics of the period in office of Pope Gregory (590–604), who cooperated with all three sides as his perceived interests dictated.[87]

Maurice evidently saw Persia and the Balkans as more pressing priorities. The main result of the attack on Persia by the emperor Justin II (565–78) in the 570s had been a destructive counter-invasion of Syria (Evagrius Scholasticus, *Ecclesiastical History* 5.10, and other sources).[88] Persian wars continued through the first years of Maurice's reign, but on February 6, 590, he experienced some good fortune in the shape of the assassination of the Persian king Hormizd [Hormisdas] IV, which led to an internal Persian power-struggle. From this, Hormizd's son and successor Khusro [Chosroes] II (590–628) was only able to emerge victoriously (591) by making concessions to Rome, or rather to Maurice personally (Theophylact Simocatta, *History* 4.11).[89] Eleven years of somewhat illusory peace followed. But even in these relatively favourable conditions the emperor was unable to defend the Balkan provinces consistently. Annual payments of 100,000 *solidi* to the Avars, enemies from across the lower Danube, were insufficient to keep them quiet. Already in the fifth century the Constantinople emperors had sometimes had to pay large sums to Attila and other enemies, and the sums paid by Maurice may have been sensible short-term investments. As Benjamin Isaac points out,[90] *not* paying could well turn out to be more expensive than paying. But paying was a clear sign of relative weakness.

The Slav allies of the Avars threatened the Long Wall of Constantinople in 584, and when they encountered resistance sowed destruction in Thrace; they also seem to have paid a lengthy and destructive visit to central Greece (reaching Argos) in the same general period.[91] After 590 the Romans sometimes did better (the sequence of events is hard to recover),

[87] For a summary account of the situation in Italy, see Jones 1964, I, 312–3. Gregory corresponded with Franks (many letters to Queen Brunhilda) as well as with Romans and Lombards.

[88] For a map of the frontier with Persia: *CAH* XIV, 93. For the archaeological evidence concerning the counter-invasion, see Foss 1997.

[89] Sources in *PLRE* III, 307.

[90] Isaac 1995, 129–32.

[91] The exact chronology is elusive: see Metcalf 1962; Whitby 1988, 88; Haldon 1997, 44.

campaigning as far north as the Danube towns of Durostorum, Novae, and even Singidunum (on the site of Belgrade).[92] But in 598 the Avars once again visited southern Thrace (Theophylact 7.14.11), which casts serious doubt on Theophylact's claim that they then recognized the Danube as the Avar-Roman frontier (7.15.14). Fighting in any case continued;[93] and when the emperor ordered Roman troops to winter north of the Danube (602) they mutinied and overthrew him.

Maurice was arguably the last ruler who might have stabilized the Roman Empire as an empire, and there will be more to say about his reign both for this reason and because he was apparently the author of a surviving military manual, the *Strategikon*. Peace with Persia in the 590s had been a largely fortuitous respite. Not that even Maurice could possibly have neutralized the forces and factors that were inexorably diminishing Roman power (this is of course hindsight, the historian's privilege).

The news of Maurice's overthrow and assassination in 602 and of the accession of Phocas brought on war with Persia once again:

> And so Chosroes exploited the tyranny [i.e. the rule of Phocas] as a pretext for war, and mobilized that world-destroying trumpet: for this became the undoing of the prosperity of Romans and Persians. For Chosroes feigned a pretence of upholding the pious memory of the emperor Maurice (Theophylact 8.15.7, trans. Whitby and Whitby).

Khusro in fact seized an opportunity.[94] The Persians had the better of it throughout the reign of Phocas (602–10), gradually taking possession of Roman Armenia, and eventually crossing the Euphrates in 610. After Heraclius' rebellion, which had started in 608, triumphed finally in 610, the Romans did even worse: the Persians defeated him near Antioch in 613, captured the quasi-capital Jerusalem in 614, and in 615 or 616 sent a raiding force all the way to the Bosporus.[95] The Constantinople Senate begged for mercy. For the time being the Persians were content to plunder and to extend their control in Syria and Palestine. Then they invaded Egypt, capturing Alexandria in 619, and by 621 they ruled the

[92] For the Singidunum campaign, facilitated by the fact that the Romans had river vessels, see Theophylact 7.11.7–9. For the topography, see Barrington maps 21 and 22.

[93] Not, however, in the plain of the Tisza, as commonly supposed: the river Theophylact refers to as the Tissus (8.3) must have been far nearer to Tomi, where the Avar prisoners were taken (more than 500 miles by river from the confluence of the Danube and the Tisza…). This gives us a more realistic view of the extent of Roman power.

[94] Howard-Johnston 2010, 436.

[95] Sources in Howard-Johnston 2010, 439. Cf. Haldon 1997, 42–3.

Figure 6.4. The battle between David and Goliath, represented here, was fairly often invoked under the emperor Heraclius, probably to symbolize the conflict between Rome and Persia (Rome as the underdog!) (cf. Kaegi 2003, 114, 198). This silver plate was made between AD 613 and 630. New York, Metropolitan Museum of Art

whole of the old Roman Middle East from the Taurus round to borders of Cyrenaica [Figure 6.4].[96]

Next it was the turn of Anatolia, which Heraclius was ill-situated to defend because he also had to face the threat of the Avars coming from the opposite direction. The latter were temporarily bought off in 623 at the considerable price of 200,000 gold *solidi* (Nicephorus, *Breviarium* 20),

[96] For maps illustrating the Roman Empire's conflicts with the Sasanids and the Muslims in the seventh century, see Wittke *et al.* 2007, 240–3.

but in 626 they and the Persians, quite possibly by design, both converged on the Bosporus and laid siege to the capital. In the end, unsuccessfully:[97] Constantinople survived – though without the use of its great and vital aqueduct.[98] This was also the year when the Romans lost the remaining territory that Justinian's soldiers had won in Spain.

Heraclius' behaviour during the siege was rather surprising. He was far away to the east, usually nearer to the Caspian than to the Black Sea,[99] and made no attempt to return, evidently believing that his best strategy was to threaten the Persians from the north, even while there were Persian armies on the loose in Asia Minor.[100] Up to a point it worked: when he invaded the Persian heartland in 627 – 'a daring counter-offensive'[101] –, he defeated the enemy in a major battle near Nineveh, and precipitated a successful conspiracy that overthrew the long-time king Khusro II, thereby pitching Persia into a four-year dynastic crisis. The emperor's forces reoccupied Rome's lost provinces. It was a brilliant success, but it was the success of an Alaric or an Attila, in other words of a super-condottiere, not that of an emperor who guarantees a measure of order in the whole core area of an empire.[102] More and more, this had been the story since late in the reign of Justinian, in spite of his efforts: the emperor could on occasion inflict severe defeats on Rome's enemies, but that did not mean that he could defend the integrity of the provinces, and his failure to do that diminished imperial revenues – with inevitable consequences.

A new and even more dangerous assault was soon coming. The first battle between the Romans and the followers of Muhammad took place at Mu'ta, south-east of the Dead Sea, in 629,[103] but much graver incursions began once Muhammad's successor Abu Bakr had consolidated his control of Arabia (the Prophet having died in 632). The first major loss of territory then came quickly.[104] In 634–5 the Muslims, in a series of engagements, drove Rome's forces out of Palestine. The sources and the scholars disagree about the relative importance and the topography of the

97 For a basic narrative, see Kaegi 2003, 132–41, who should hardly, however, have called the lifting of the siege 'a great triumph' (138).

98 Broken in 626: Crow *et al.* 2008, 19. Not that it had always worked perfectly before, if we are to believe Procopius, *Secret History* 26.23.

99 For a map showing his movements in 624–8, see Kaegi 2003, 123.

100 Sources: Howard-Johnston 2010, 443. The most important are translated in Greatrex and Lieu 2002, II, 209–27.

101 Rubin 2000, 644. Another analysis: Isaac 1995, 133.

102 For a different assessment, see Haldon 1997, 52.

103 See the map in Kaegi 2003, 232.

104 The sources for these events are poor, but not as poor as is sometimes supposed: see Howard-Johnston 2010.

subsequent battles for Syria, but the battle by the River Yarmuk (east and south of Lake Tiberias, now the frontier line between Syria and Jordan), in which the Muslims routed an army as sizeable as the Romans could now put together, is usually considered to have been decisive (August 636). Another clash further north, between Damascus and Emesa, was also a Roman disaster. (A major historian of this period has recently contested this 'violent conquest' model of this phase of Muslim expansion,[105] but he seems only to have established that the opponents of the Muslims sometimes exaggerated the extent of the resulting destruction).

Fortunately for the Romans, the invaders now turned most of their attention to the Sasanian empire (the best date for the important Muslim victory at the Battle of Qadisiyya, 500 miles to the east of the Yarmuk and near to the Euphrates, seems to be in January 638),[106] and they conclusively destroyed it in the course of sixteen years. Meanwhile Heraclius failed in 637/8 to regain Syria, and then at the end of 639 the Arab general 'Amr bin al-'As invaded Egypt, where he conducted a masterly campaign – relatively well known to us thanks to the narrative of John of Nikiu –, eventually occupying Alexandria (641) and bringing to an end some 670 years of Roman rule. 'Amr's next thought was for Cyrenaica and Libya; and in 645/6 he foiled a last desperate Byzantine attempt to retake Alexandria. Meanwhile he had restored to working order Trajan's canal from the Nile to the Red Sea.[107]

These losses so reduced the Byzantine Roman state that it was no longer a pan-Mediterranean empire of the kind that the Romans had held together for more than eight centuries. Losing Syria and Egypt meant the loss of perhaps as much as 75 per cent of the state's Balkan and eastern revenues.[108] Egypt's grain surplus now went to Arabia, as already mentioned. And Muslim successes continued, leading in 652 to the final destruction of the Sasanian state. In 654 they attacked Constantinople itself.

The government of Constans II (641–68; he was only ten at the time of his accession) fruitlessly attempted to roll back Lombard power in Italy. In mid-century, Byzantium controlled, more or less, a large part of Asia Minor, a small European hinterland near the capital, some of the Greek mainland (but there were already Slavs settled in the Peloponnese), most

105 Donner 2010, 106–18, diverging from his own earlier accounts.
106 Howard-Johnston 2010, 329; for the site, see his map 11.
107 Cf. Aubert 2004, 230.
108 See Hendy 1985, 620.

of the major islands of the Mediterranean and Aegean, plus an area corresponding approximately to Tunisia and eastern Algeria (but less and less of it), some tracts of territory in Italy, and very little else. Much now depended, as it had eight centuries earlier, on naval power.[109] In 649 and 650 the Muslims invaded Cyprus; the Roman Empire had neither the funds nor perhaps the expertise to mobilize an adequate response. Constans himself ended ignominiously some years later, being assassinated in a bathhouse in Syracuse.

Starting in 643, the Muslims rode relentlessly westwards along the north African litoral, reaching what is now Tunisia in 647/8 and imposing taxes there, arriving in Morocco in the 680s.[110] After the Battle of the Yarmuk, in short, the power of Rome was greatly reduced, and over the next two generations it steadily declined still further.

The unsustainability of Justinian's empire

Explaining these events is a problem parallel to explaining the fall of the western empire two centuries earlier. Outside invaders who should not perhaps have been invincible caused irreversible harm to the existing state, permanently changing the geopolitical landscape. But both the invaders' advantages and the disadvantages of the defenders are open to endless dispute.

In view of the importance that people have attributed to the fall of the Roman Empire, it is surprising how little effort has gone into explaining the Roman failure in the first half of the seventh century. It seems symptomatic that the last chapter of Jones's great history of the later Roman Empire has virtually nothing to say on the subject, concentrating on the earlier fall of the western empire, whereas much of the body of the work had concerned the east. Even careful accounts of late-antique warfare[111] largely avoid the problem. To a remarkable extent, in fact, late-antique historians seem to be in denial: 'over this period [284–641]', writes one, 'the Roman army won far more actions than it lost, and the worst casualties of most of its defeats were trained personnel and Roman prestige rather than territory and cities'.[112] So much for the fall of the western empire, so much for the Byzantine Roman government's inability to defend the

[109] See Howard-Johnston 2010, 476–8, 489–95.
[110] On the conquest of North Africa, see Kaegi 2010.
[111] Such as Sabin *et al.* 2007, chapters 7 to 12.
[112] Rance 2007, 378.

Balkans and later on Anatolia, so much for the disasters under Maurice and Heraclius. Once again, we recognize sleight-of-hand. Such writers are evidently scared of breathing the word 'decline', not noticing that the consequence is that the history of warfare is reduced to a series of accidents, an absurd and anti-historical position (though no one will deny that war always breeds accidents great and small). There is an almost pathological reluctance to deal with the crucial decades and in particular with Roman defeats: in a weighty recent volume devoted to 'The Late Roman Army in the East … to the Arab Conquest' only three out of thirty-two articles – astonishingly – paid attention to what happened to Rome's military forces in or after the reign of Justinian.[113] Another still more recent book, *War and Warfare in Late Antiquity: Current Perspectives*, avoids all discussion of the failure to resist the Muslims adequately.[114]

Yet many consider that the Persian wars had left the Roman Empire 'easy prey' for the Muslim attackers.[115] That judgement in turn confronts us with the problem of deciding on the basis of very poor source material whether the Muslims of the 630s and 640s were merely ferocious marauders or also a sizeable, disciplined, and well-organized invasion force (the latter view seems more persuasive). In any case the proximate cause of both Roman and Sasanian weakness in the 630s was that the two empires had been engaged in a virtually continuous military struggle for an entire generation (602–30).

We should in theory consider both sides in the conflicts that have just been alluded to. Rome's principal enemies of the late sixth and seventh centuries need to be understood, the Lombards, Avars, Persians and others, and above all the Muslim Arabs, if we are to work out how effective they were as Rome's opponents – but the sources, even in the case of the Lombards, are far too poor to provide more than general impressions. Were the invaders too numerous? Were they driven by stronger motives than the defenders? Did the societies in which the invaders lived form a stronger base, economic or psychological, than that of the Romans? These are clearly crucial questions.

What then made the Byzantine Romans relatively 'easy prey', if they really were? In so far as informed contemporaries sought to explain the Roman Empire's seventh-century defeats in human terms, some pointed to internal

113 Lewin and Pellegrini 2007. This is all the more astonishing given the existence of Maurice's *Strategikon*.
114 Sarantis and Christie 2013, 1,084 pages.
115 Humphries 2007, 238.

strife (George of Pisidia, *On the Invasion of the Barbarians* 58–62, referring to the Avars and the first years of the reign of Heraclius). The contemporary historian Theophylact Simocatta probably implies that Rome and Persia would be well-advised to practise détente (4.13).[116] Some were well aware that the Roman Empire in its Justinianic form simply had too many hostile neighbours (cf. Menander Protector, fr. 26.1, Blockley, written in the 580s; also fr. 24, 25.2).[117] Unfortunately we have no similar witnesses for the 630s or 640s. By the 610s, however, many knew that there was a deep crisis – that indeed is likely to have been the reason why Heraclius often led his armies in person, unlike his sixth-century predecessors.

Justinian's empire was in fact unsustainable. His successors needed to defend the core area of the empire, which for fiscal reasons had to include Anatolia, Syria, and Egypt. But over and over again they found themselves expending scarce men and money to hold on to their possessions in Africa and (less rationally) Italy. And the weaker the defences of the provinces nearer to the capital became, in Greece and Syria for instance, the less tax-revenue those regions can have produced. Part of the problem was no doubt a nostalgic desire for what had been lost: thus Maurice's will, made in 596/7, appointed one of his sons 'emperor of old Rome' (Theophylact 8.11.9), old Rome, which was actually ruled by a wily and energetic pope. And Maurice had no resources to spare for reimposing Roman control of the Italian peninsula or anywhere else in western Europe.

This Byzantine Roman unsustainability has three main, closely related, aspects to it, the quantity and quality of the available manpower, and money. The financial problem is the easiest to outline, though even here our information is extremely limited. Even under Justinian, expeditionary forces 'were consistently starved of money'.[118] Even during the short war against the Vandals, the pay of the soldiers was in arrears (Procopius, *Wars* 4.26.12), and while this might occasionally happen in any ancient army, it happened too often during the war in Italy to be discounted as a rare misfortune (see Procopius, *Wars* 7.11.13–15, 7.12.2–3 and 6–8, etc.).[119] No doubt the comments of Justin II, the year after Justinian's death, were exaggerated, but his lament certainly had some factual basis to it: 'we found the fiscus burdened with many debts and reduced to utter poverty'. The army, he asserted,

[116] Cf. Howard-Johnston 2010, 146.

[117] See further Agathias 5.13.8.

[118] Jones 1964, 1, 298. For the extraordinary measures he took to supply the Lower Danube army, see Lee 2007a, 408.

[119] On Justinian's difficulty in putting together a large enough army for the war in Italy, see Schmitt 2007, 413–14.

had been 'ruined by lack of supplies', resulting in perennial incursions of the barbarians (Justinian, *Novels* 148 pr.; Justin naturally claimed to have solved all these problems). Justinian was largely able to get away with this deficiency because his armies were frequently victorious; his successors were less skilled and less fortunate.

It was in good part lack of funds with which to organize the defence of both the Balkans and the Persian frontier, not to mention Italy and North Africa, that prevented Maurice from holding on to the whole of Justinian's domain. In 588 and again in 594 he attempted to reduce the pay of troops stationed on the frontiers, even though he must have realized that they would strongly object (see respectively Theophylact 3.1, a reduction by one-quarter, and 7.1); what ultimately happened on these two occasions is unclear.

Financial problems intensified further under Phocas and Heraclius, as their reduced-weight coinage reveals: the government was desperately short of the necessary metals.[120] There were moments of black humour, as when, the emperor Phocas' end being near, he and his treasurer Leontius threw the contents of the imperial treasury into the sea (so at least it is claimed by John of Nikiu, *Chronicle* 110;[121] but the story may have been invented to explain a shortage of funds). Cities were generally in economic decline, at different speeds in different places, and for reasons that are debated.[122] When Heraclius lost control of many of his prime tax-paying provinces for a decade, in the case of Syria for nearly two decades, his ability to defend the rest declined precipitously. The capital's bread dole was terminated in 618. Syria, Palestine, and Egypt must have produced less tax-revenue after they had been occupied by the Persians and re-occupied by the Byzantines.[123] Needing to finance a campaign against Persia in 622, the emperor borrowed on a large scale from 'pious houses', that is to say monasteries, 'which', as has rightly been remarked, 'would have been quite unthinkable earlier'.[124] Then he melted down the gold and silver plate of Constantinople's churches (all this: Theophanes Confessor, *Chronography* pp. 302–3 De Boor). But the most significant aspect of the matter is probably that the monasteries possessed such a conspicuous proportion of the empire's wealth. Some time in his last years Heraclius, belatedly, instructed his treasurer Philagrius to register all the land in the Roman Empire for

120 Harl 1996, 201.
121 Also Fredegarius, *Chronicle* 4.63.
122 Potter 2011, 257–8, using the archaeological evidence.
123 Howard-Johnston 2010, 521–2, seems unrealistic on this point (a north-south difference is also involved). The violence of Shahrbaraz's conquests of Judaea and Egypt should not be minimized.
124 Brandes and Haldon 2000, 161, q.v. for other signs of Heraclius' dire fiscal problems.

tax purposes,[125] which had certainly not been done for many generations; what if anything he achieved we do not know.[126] In 640 Heraclius' viceroy ('exarch') in Italy, Isaac, confiscated the ecclesiastical treasures of the Lateran Palace, and sent a portion of them to the emperor.[127]

With improved military fortunes, the monetary system had briefly recovered, but then they severely deteriorated again (with economic effects that go beyond the scope of this study), once the Muslim attack intensified.[128]

'The relationship between state, fiscal instruments, and economy was a brutal zero-sum game'.[129] Year by year, the emperor's tax agents, including those who were the local landowners, had to collect and hand over the coin and the material goods with which to pay and supply the army. What we ideally need to know, therefore, is how gross domestic product fluctuated during the last century of the Roman Empire, and whether the government's ability to extract a sufficient proportion of it improved or deteriorated. At best we have proxy indicators, like those just mentioned.

To take a number of important areas one by one: Dacia, Moesia, and Thrace, which had been tax-paying regions under Justinian, can have produced very little Roman revenue in the seventh century.[130] Under Heraclius many people from the Greek mainland fled to Sicily and southern Italy, and the rural population declined (there is survey evidence).[131] Lycia, reasonably prosperous, it seems under Justinian, was 'first ravaged by the Persians ... the Arabs, though, inflicted far more widespread devastation [from 655 onwards]';[132] this too is an archaeological judgement. The Persians did a great deal of damage in inland Anatolia.[133] Syria seems to have been in a reasonable economic state in the sixth century, to judge from the amount of building,[134] but in the early seventh the evidence seems to show that the connectivity of earlier times had largely given way to urban decay and a more narrowly agricultural economy.[135] Much of the damage had in this case been done by the Persians.

125 Brandes and Haldon 2000, 162, Brandes 2002, 459–60.
126 There had been piecemeal efforts at census-taking in various places: Jones 1964, I, 454–5.
127 See *PLRE* III Isaacius 8.
128 Harl 1996, 202–3.
129 Shaw 1999, 140.
130 Cf. Liebeschuetz 2001, 284–5.
131 Liebeschuetz 2001, 285–7.
132 Foss 1994, 2–3.
133 See the cautious archaeologically based account of Brandes 1989, 50–1
134 Brandes and Haldon 2000, 146–7.
135 There is a large bibliography: for a useful survey, see Foss 1997, who is, however, too liable to deduce economic health from church construction. See further Conrad 2000, 693.

In Egypt, the Delta area had suffered from a rebellion under Maurice, and in 609–10 the usurpation of Heraclius brought on civil war.[136] The claim that the economy of Roman North Africa in this period was 'basically healthy'[137] makes no sense at all; the archaeology shows that both urban and rural areas were in decay after 600.[138] De-urbanization (ugly but necessary word) must have had negative effects on the ability of armies to supply themselves (cf. George of Pisidia, *On the Emperor Heraclius and the Persian Wars* 3.300–1). Thus economic conditions varied a lot about 600, but many of the areas that were still undamaged suffered gravely in the first decades of the following century.

It may be worth saying that, while much more has been learned recently about climate change in late antiquity, there is no reason to think that the Roman Empire experienced any climate-based improvement or worsening of its economic conditions that was not also experienced by its neighbours.[139] The best place to look is the Arabian peninsula: if it could be shown that the seventh-century climate there was relatively benign to human beings, to the point of permitting significant demographic growth, then we would know something historically valuable.

We cannot know how many soldiers the seventh-century emperors could put into the field, and there is the added difficulty of knowing how much the so-called *limitanei*, the old frontier troops, were still trained soldiers.[140] 'Optimistic' and 'pessimistic' historians alike depend on guesswork, but the pessimists have the independent evidence of the coins on their side.[141] Maurice's *Strategikon* disparages the importance of numbers, saying that generalship and morale are what count:

> For it is not true, as some inexperienced people believe, that wars are decided by courage and numbers of troops, but, along with God's favour, by tactics and generalship, and our concern should be with these rather than wasting our time in mobilizing large numbers of men (Book 7, preface, trans. G.T. Dennis).

But there is something definitely defensive about this; and the author seems to reveal that the reason why Byzantium cannot put trained troops on the ground is lack of money. The army also had to compete with the church for manpower (see Gregory, *Letters* 3.61, AD 593).

136 Liebeschuetz 2001, 269–72, 274–6.
137 Kaegi 2010, 64.
138 Liebeschuetz 2001, 101–2.
139 Cf. Harris 2013c.
140 Cf. Whitby 1995, 68–75.
141 Above, p. 252.

In 555 Narses, probably the best Roman general of the age and at the height of his prestige after the Battle of Busta Gallorum (in Umbria) three years earlier, assembled an army of 'scarcely' 18,000 men to oppose the Franks in southern Italy (Agathias 2.4.10). Agathias claims that late in Justinian's reign there were 'scarcely' 150,000 Roman soldiers (5.13.7) spread out from Spain to Georgia.[142] Heraclius cannot have afforded nearly as many soldiers as Justinian. Never again, as it happens, do we hear of a Byzantine force that reached the modest dimensions of 555. On the other hand a number of communities probably now had militias substantially independent of the imperial government.[143]

At one time the Roman Empire had enjoyed a demographic advantage over its foreign enemies. Had this come to an end by the seventh century? The question partly depends on long-term economic trends and partly on the long-term effects of the outbreak of bubonic plague that reached the Roman Empire in 541 ('Justinian's Plague'). It may have some significance that we sometimes hear hints in the sources that the Romans suffered more than their opponents from the plague's effect on manpower (Paul the Deacon, *History of the Lombards* 2.4, 5.26). The plague was still making itself felt in the eastern Mediterranean under Heraclius,[144] and it has been argued that the Arabs were less affected because their population was not as settled as the Romans were;[145] their armies were affected to some extent, however,[146] and the victorious Muslim commander at the Yarmuk, Abu 'Ubayda ibn al-Jarrah, died of the plague three years later. Heraclius could not in practice draw troops away from the lands reconquered by Justinian, and the population of his core territories was probably smaller than it had been when Justinian came to power in 527. On the other side, it would be wrong to see the Muslim conquests of this period as the triumph of huge hosts of soldiers: 'Amr bin al-'As seems to have conquered Egypt with fewer than 15,500 soldiers.[147] When a Muslim army, which cannot have been very numerous, arrived in Roman-ruled Tripolitania, the place was insufficiently garrisoned.[148] But the small size of Heraclius' military forces was probably more the result of financial and political-social problems than of demographic ones.

142 Scholars sometimes fantasize that Agathias was not counting everyone.

143 As at Asemus (in Moesia) in 594, Theophylact 7.3, and at Jericho in the 610s (Howard-Johnston 2010, 168).

144 Stathakopoulos 2004, 119.

145 Horden 2005, 138.

146 Little 2007, 28.

147 Morimoto 1994. 354, accepted by Kennedy 2001, 4.

148 Kaegi 2010, 106.

If in fact the Byzantines outnumbered the Muslims at the Battle of the Yarmuk, as scholars usually suppose,[149] that shifts the blame on to their performance. The defenders had some advantages, such as a relatively centralized state at their shoulders, and (potentially at least) better knowledge of the terrain.

In the longer term, it was probably a disadvantage that hardly any of the Roman emperors of this period were soldiers: they were usually courtiers. Maurice had been a partial exception, but even he had had little if any military experience before he was appointed to a senior generalship at the age of thirty-eight. Heraclius is not known to have held any command before he became emperor at about thirty-five, though he may have learned a good deal about soldiering from his homonymous father, who was a competent general. The Theodorus who commanded the Roman forces disastrously at the Yarmuk, and died there, seems to have been a financial official by training,[150] and certainly was not very good at his job. Roman generals periodically panicked and ran away, leaving their troops behind: Philippicus and Comentiolus under Maurice; Domnitziolus the brother of Phocas and Phocas' general Bonosus (both of these in civil war, however); Theodorus the brother of Heraclius in 634; and Domentianus in Egypt in 640/1 (twice!).[151] The contrast between these men and their counterparts in republican times could not be more extreme. Few generals in these years can have inspired their men as great leaders.

The styles of warfare practised in the Roman wars of the seventh century are difficult to analyse, as are the systems of logistic support on which the various sides depended. Roman willingness to borrow military technology from other peoples, especially the Avars,[152] might suggest that they will seldom have been at a technical disadvantage. On the other hand, current research suggests that if the Romans had adopted the Avar stirrup – an exceedingly useful device – in the period under discussion here, it was only on an insignificantly small scale.[153] But it is even hard to say whether under Heraclius the Romans relied more on infantry and less on cavalry than before (Maurice's *Strategikon* had essentially been a cavalry manual) and whether the state arms factories (the *fabricae*) were still functioning properly.[154]

[149] Cf. Kennedy 2001, 3–4.
[150] *PLRE* III, no. 164.
[151] Sources in *PLRE* III s.vv. The Theodorus in question is no. 163.
[152] Rance 2007, 357–8; Trombley 2007, 347–8. Much remains unclear about the nature and significance of these changes.
[153] Curta 2013, 813–22.
[154] James 1988, 286, points to the mention of some *fabrikesioi* in the *Life of Theodore of Sykeon* (159). But arms-production was partly at least in private hands under Justinian: *Code* 12.35.

The Muslims may have presented an unfamiliar challenge: some have suggested that they had superior mobility,[155] and one of the very few contemporary narratives of these wars, that of John of Nikiu, seems to show that during the invasion of Egypt the Muslims relied on cavalry (113, 114, 118), while the Romans, though not without cavalry, depended more on infantry (111, 112). But a determined attempt to work out what technical factors may have caused the Roman military failure in the 630s ended inconclusively;[156] there is simply not enough evidence.

The sixth- and seventh-century Roman soldier was lightly armed and armoured by the standards of the high empire,[157] and that may have been due to shortages of funds as well as to the changes in the type of fighting he had to undertake.

But the biggest military conundrum is perhaps the morale of the rank-and-file on both sides. Some will have it that the Roman soldiers at the Yarmuk were not ineffective.[158] One possible source of weakness was ethnic diversity: substantial Armenian and Arab contingents were included on the Byzantine side. There was admittedly nothing new about this: Belisarius' army in Italy in the 530s was polyglot, as Justinian's armies usually were, and his troops are likely to have had only a limited sense of Roman identity, or in the case of the Huns and Sclaveni (Slavs) none at all.[159] The Romans had of course always employed foreign soldiers, but under the high Empire the foreigners' subordinate position had usually been clear. And it seems likely that the negative effects of a multi-ethnic army intensify greatly if circumstances constantly put it on the defensive. Heraclius was no Justinian, and everyone knew it.

As to military discipline, it had often been poor in the time of the emperor Maurice,[160] and more generally it is hard to imagine a Roman general of much earlier ages writing, as Maurice did (*Strategikon* 2.6), that 'few outstanding soldiers [capable of fighting in the front rank] are found in any unit'.[161] After some successes the army, or at least its officers, could still in 586 show some spirit by rejecting a reasonable Persian peace offer

155 Kennedy 2001, 6.
156 Trombley 2002.
157 Rance 2007, 351.
158 E.g. Whitby 1995, 121, who considers that Roman tactics and logistics were deficient.
159 See the nuanced discussion of Greatrex 2000: 'no soldier and few generals appear to have harboured an unwavering loyalty to Justinian or the Roman state' (274).
160 Theophylact 2.12.1–2, 2.13.1, 2.15.8–9, 2.18.26, 3.1.9–3.3.11, etc.
161 And Maurice wrote pessimistically in *Strategikon* 1.6, for example, that 'a large army should not be assembled in one place when there is no hostile activity, for with time on their hands the soldiers may give themselves to sedition and improper plans'.

Figure 6.5. The 'Trier Ivory'. The Christians of the very late Roman Empire set immense store by 'relics'. This panel from a reliquary made in Constantinople, probably in the sixth century, represents the arrival of a relic in a procession led by the (unidentified) emperor (H.A. Klein in Bagnoli *et al.* 2010, 38). Trier, Cathedral Treasury

(Theophylact 1.15.1–11). But there seems to have been a gradual deterioration: Maurice did not recognize the limitations of his own troops, and when ordered to spend the winter north of the Danube (for good reasons) in 593/4, they refused (Theophylact 6.10.1–3). The *Strategikon* is an impressive document, but in practice the Roman army increasingly resembled a large band of brigands. Maurice fell in 602 because of a mutiny occasioned once again by the soldiers' unwillingness to winter north of the river, and Roman troops overthrew Phocas. For the reign of Heraclius we seem to lack explicit evidence.

The significance of civilian morale is even harder to assess than the strictly military factors. That there was a substantial cleavage between imperial authority and the populations it claimed to rule is, however, clear enough. It is reasonable to suppose that sharp social-economic divisions made the poor, urban and rural alike, quite indifferent to the fate of the regime.[162] The Egyptian John of Nikiu tells us that people in Egypt 'began to help the Moslem' soon after the invasion began (113; see further 114, 118–19).

The effects of Christian devotion to such defence policies as acquiring relics of the saints must remain uncertain [Figure 6.5]. When Maurice sent to Thessalonica for a relic to serve as his 'ally' in the war against the

[162] Cf. Sarris 2006, 228–34.

Avars (John of Thessalonica, *Miracles of St Demetrius*, sect. 51 Lemerle), we may think that he was wasting his time, but if he had succeeded he might have been able to improve Roman morale.

The attempted enforcement of orthodox Christian doctrines, mainly orthodox 'Chalcedonians' persecuting Monophysites over theological trivialities that were perceived as matters of life and death, certainly helped to alienate many people from the central power, and make them quite content to be ruled by Persians or Muslims instead. Most of the inhabitants of Syria were Monophysites in Heraclius' time,[163] as were the great majority of Egyptians. It was religious persecution that made the Egyptians hate Heraclius, says John of Nikiu (115), who, however, was himself a Monophysite bishop and may therefore have exaggerated this factor. Persecution of the Jews, which had intensified under Justinian and was far worse now than it had been even in the fourth century, had similar effects: some naturally collaborated with the invading Persians.[164] How much any of this affected military performance can only be guessed, but the contrast with the religious unity of the first-generation Muslims is obvious. Imperial armies operating in Syria and Egypt were surrounded by civilians whom Heraclius had seriously alienated. Tiberius II (578–82) had been quite explicit in resisting the request of the patriarch Eutychius for new persecutions: 'we have enough wars against the barbarians…' (Michael the Syrian, *Chronicle* 10.8).[165] But the persecutors often had their way, as we shall see in the next chapter.

So there was some psychological similarity with the failure of the Roman Empire in the west two centuries before: religious dissension interfered with the defenders' cohesion. Poor Heraclius undoubtedly wanted religious conformity and attempted to achieve it in 638 by an imperial decree propounding 'monotheletism', but it was far beyond his grasp.

The holy man Theodore of Sykeon (d. 613) is said to have foreseen the end of the imperial state, the *basileia*, and the coming of the 'Adversary' (*Life* 134), though all this may be an invention by his disciple and biographer. Heraclius' last years seem in any case to have produced several eschatological texts, Jewish as well as Christian.[166] The deep pessimism of the emperor himself after the Yarmuk is clearly indicated by his use of a destructive scorched-earth policy in Cilicia.[167] Of course we could say

163 Foss 1997, 262.
164 Haldon 1997, 345–8. For persecution under Heraclius, see Kaegi 2010, 84–6.
165 Quoted by Greatrex 2007, 291, with parallels.
166 Howard-Johnston 2010, 156.
167 Liebeschuetz 2001, 290.

that his attitude was merely realistic; and the Muslims too are said to have believed that the world was coming to an end.

Experts on the earliest Islamic expansion are divided over a number of issues, such as the extent to which it was a centrally organized enterprise. For one such scholar, there is no proof that a unified Islamic state existed by 632.[168] Another concludes, however, that the early conquests 'displayed both conceptual and strategic-operational organization or unity';[169] yet another scholar goes further – there is 'clear evidence of strategic direction on a grand scale' in the whole phase from 632 to 652.[170] We need not decide these issues, but we should without doubt banish all thoughts of tribesmen spreading haphazard mayhem.

It remains difficult if not impossible to judge what gave Muslim troops their superiority, a superiority that is all the more striking because it was not spoiled by success – or by the Muslim civil war of 656–61. Religious conviction and cohesion must certainly have been a powerful force, though we cannot know how deeply religion affected the ordinary warrior in the 630s or 640s. It is in any case reasonably evident that Islamic society in the seventh century was more wholeheartedly devoted to success in warfare than its Roman opponents, and consequently used more of its economic resources for that end. Raiding and fighting were a way of life,[171] all the more attractive, we must suppose, when it became clear in the 630s that neither of the major Middle-eastern powers was anything like invincible. Most of the adult male population was actively involved; 'men fought for their religion, the prospect of booty, and because their friends and fellow tribesman were also doing it'.[172] An expert on the Arabic sources writes of 'traditional Arab values: personal honour and glory, the vaunts of one's own tribe, and competition for distinction among the various provincial centres where the Arab conquerors were based'.[173] They did not hesitate to slaughter civilian women and children when it suited them to do so (in Egypt, for example: John of Nikiu 111–12, 118).

The faith of Muslim troops 'endowed [them] … with extraordinary élan … The armies which invaded the Roman and Persian empires were in essence ordered arrays of suicide fighters, endowed with extraordinary

168 Décobert 1991, 64, cited from 2008, 97.
169 Donner 1995, 359.
170 Howard-Johnston 2010, 471.
171 Kennedy 2001, 1.
172 Kennedy 2001, 6.
173 Conrad 2002, 135.

courage and daring', says another historian,[174] surrendering to a stereotype. The same scholar argues that Islam's dynamic expansion 'defies explanation in ordinary human terms',[175] by which he means that it resulted from the Muslims' uncompromising religious commitment. But religious commitment is an ordinary human phenomenon and its depth and nature always need to be explained (admittedly neither psychologists nor historians are very good at this yet). The Byzantines of this time were devout – and in some ways weakened militarily by their religion, as we have seen. Explanations of Muslim success should return to earth, and here we shall find a cohesive group of warriors who after the Yarmuk, if not before, must usually have believed, as no Roman soldier could in the seventh century, that their side was invincible.

Both the republican Romans and the seventh-century Muslims were exceptionally good at holding on to what they had conquered. What 'organizational techniques' (Michael Mann) enabled the Muslims to do that? The Caliph at the time of the Battle of the Yarmuk, 'Umar ibn al-Khattab, favoured a policy of settling the conquering Muslims in garrison towns, but there were strikingly few of these.[176] The conquerors' religious policy, unburdened by the numerous and officious men of religion who plagued the Roman-Byzantine state, was to a significant degree more intelligent – theirs was a policy of, in Michael Gaddis' phrase, 'repressive pluralism'.[177] It is in Egypt, as before, that we can see government administration at work [Figure 6.6], and what happened there was that the *amir*, while he continued to rely on district administrators drawn from the local landowning class, strengthened central control and the monitoring of local officials.[178] The Muslims knew in short how to maintain an empire as well as how to acquire one.

Conclusion

Looking forward to the next chapter, we can here ask once again how the internal power structures of the Roman Empire hindered its ability to resist outside threats. Prior to 602, the eastern empire had long been exempt from successful military insurrections, and even the distractions

[174] Howard-Johnston 2010, 451. The majority of scholars now apparently hold that the religious convictions of the Muslims added to their military effectiveness.
[175] Howard-Johnston 2010, 463.
[176] Howard-Johnston 2010, 502. See further Donner 2010, 136–41.
[177] Gaddis 2005, 332.
[178] Howard-Johnston 2010, 504.

Figure 6.6. One of the reasons why the Muslim conquests endured was that the conquerors rapidly learned how to manage their new territories. This letter, written not in Arabic but in Greek, the primary language of Roman administration in Egypt, was composed by Subeeit (Zubayd), the commander of the Thebaid district in upper Egypt, to a local official, with orders about the affairs of a fisherman. Probably AD 667. *PSI* 15.1570

caused by the overthrow of Maurice and the overthrow of Phocas, by the big conspiracy against Heraclius in 637 (which led to the emperor's mutilating members of his own family),[179] and by the power-struggle that followed his death in 641, would not have mattered in an empire with reasonably secure frontiers. Similarly the power of the clergy and of monasteries to acquire resources and use them on causes that were largely irrelevant, if not harmful, to the interests of the state was a factor that the empire of Justinian could arguably tolerate but the seventh-century emperors could not. (Under 'resources' we should include psychological commitment).

It is commonly supposed that the emperors of this age were exceptionally powerful within their own borders (see the next chapter). The financial difficulties they encountered may make one doubt it. And in the last phase of Heraclius' reign he was even losing his authority over his own high officials. His general Peter in Numidia refused to send troops to reinforce Egypt in 633.[180] In 640 the Patriarch of Alexandria, and *de facto* ruler of Egypt, Cyrus[181] negotiated a peace-settlement with the Muslims that was unacceptable to the emperor, and when he was summoned to Constantinople he argued publicly with Heraclius about it (all of which led to his being dismissed and exiled) (Nicephorus, *Breviarium* 28–30).

To summarize: a number of factors prevented the Roman Empire from resisting the Muslim invasion successfully, and it is difficult to hierarchize them. To some extent there was another vicious circle: foreign invasions made gathering sufficient taxes more difficult, which weakened the army, and so on. Justinian had taken an enormous gamble that ended very badly. Other factors which might not have damaged a more robust empire, in particular the various distractions of rampant Christianity, took their toll. Other questions remain unavoidably unanswerable: would matters have turned out differently if the inhabitants of the state ruled by the emperors from, say, Maurice to Constans II had been more wholeheartedly devoted to the Roman Empire or its rulers?

179 Kaegi 2003, 260–3.

180 *PLRE* III, Petrus 70; see *Scripta Saeculi* VII *Vitam Maximi Confessoris Illustrantia*, ed. Allen and Neil, p. 15.

181 *PLRE* III, Cyrus 17.

CHAPTER 7

The Romans against each other in two long crises

Sixty crucial years of imperial power

Constantine died an uncontested ruler on 22 May AD 337. Before the summer was out, no fewer than nine of his relatives had been murdered – largely at the instigation of Constantius (aged 19), the second of his three surviving sons.[1] No one was harmed, however, apart from the immediate victims, for the empire could not be ruled by a committee of miscellaneous family-members. It needed a strong, effective government at the centre, and intra-dynastic bloodshed does not in any case rank high among the causes of the late-antique decline in Rome's power.

But how in fact was power divided and exercised in the later Roman Empire? And can we relate late-antique developments to the unravelling of Rome's external power we have just been considering? As in the previous chapter, I will concentrate on, and sharply distinguish, the periods from the 370s to the 430s and from the death of Justinian to Constans II, though explaining what had changed will sometimes take us outside these limits.

The western Roman Empire fell to German invaders. It could have defended itself from them if it had possessed a reasonably stable and vigorous central government, an upper social elite that felt a sense of responsibility for the state's ability to defend itself against outside enemies, an efficient system of gathering enough taxes to pay for large and properly trained military forces, and, finally, military forces that were both reliably loyal and strong in morale. In the crucial decades, all these assets were lacking.

In some important respects the Roman world changed quite little in the years between Constantine's death and reign of Honorius. The role and the nature of slavery, for instance, changed little: slaves continued to do the bulk of the work on large estates, the 'middle class' – notably smaller, however, by the end of this period, in the western European

[1] On all this see Julian, *Epistle to the Athenians* 270cd, Ammianus Marcellinus 21.16.8.

provinces and in Italy – continued to be slave-owners, and the lives of most slaves were harsh.[2] Even when Roman slaves joined the forces of Alaric outside Rome in 410 (Zosimus 5.42.3),[3] they were only doing what many Roman slaves would have done before if they had had the opportunity. Manumission had already declined, in my view,[4] but freedmen and slaves still did managerial work.[5] Slavery – that is to say, the number of slaves – did decline to some extent in the fifth-century west, because of 'the collapse of the material and institutional structures that drove the use of slave labor',[6] but the institution still survived and on quite a large scale.

Similarly with respect to national identity and language use, we can detect certain changes during the fourth century, but no radical difference, with the highly important exception that far fewer people came to identify their own interests – so I shall maintain – with those of the Roman state.

In fact the Roman state weakened considerably in the century after the death of Constantine. Scholars have sometimes claimed the opposite, beguiled in part by the elaborate ceremonial of the court. But if we consider instead the degree of power that emperors ceded to ecclesiastics, and in particular to bishops, the weakening of civil peace in many areas, and the declining effectiveness of the tax-gathering system – not to mention the military deficiencies outlined in the previous chapter – such a view is impossible to accept.

Some eleven men exercised power as Augusti during the years from 375 to the 430s, if we include the principal 'usurpers' and exclude some minor ones. Of these eleven, no fewer than six (Gratian, Valentinian II and III, Arcadius, Honorius, and Theodosius II) were children when they nominally took office. This might not have mattered much if the frontiers had been largely untroubled. And even now, there were effective stand-ins available. In the west, military commanders often became the dominant figures. Thus Arbogast effectively ruled from 388 until 394 (he committed suicide after the Battle of the Frigidus), then Stilicho (395–408),[7] and a

2 See the wide-ranging discussion of Harper 2011, going down to 425.

3 Zosimus' evidence about this event is far from clear.

4 Harper 2011, 243–6, is ambivalent on this issue, underestimating in my opinion the evidence for the huge role played by freedmen in the high empire.

5 Harper 2011, 121–2.

6 Harper 2011, 30.

7 Should we attribute any importance to the fact that Arbogast, like Bauto (Master of the Soldiers *c.* 380–5), was a Frank, and that Stilicho's father was a Vandal? They provide evidence that Roman ethnic prejudices were weaker than we might have expected.

little later Constantius,[8] who was the most powerful man in the western empire from 411 to 421. Later figures of this kind included Aetius (dominant from 435 until the emperor Valentinian III personally murdered him in 454), and Odoacer, who deposed the last western Roman emperor, Romulus Augustulus, in 476.

The only power that could set one emperor up in place of another remained that of army units. As in earlier ages, the soldiers' preferences mostly depended on a mixture of money, dynastic loyalty, and personal repute. All three factors joined together to get Julian's army to proclaim him Augustus in 360, and it was military units, or rather their officers, that brought Valentinian to power after the mysterious murder of Jovian. This is a fascinating case, where military repute played a part, but additional factors apparently came into it too: other key players were Pannonian officers like Valentinian himself (Ammianus Marcellinus 26.1.6); Valentinian's somewhat ostentatious Christianity may have helped him, and one of his chief rivals was rejected because he was 'harsh and fairly uncouth (*subagrestis*)' (26.1.4).[9] Civilians did not come into the matter, naturally. On Valentinian's death in 375, the dynastic principle prevailed, even though it meant that two of the three Augusti were children or scarcely more (Gratian was sixteen). After the disaster at Hadrianople in 378, Gratian turned to a soldier in his early thirties who was in virtual exile in his native Spain, Theodosius, and made him co-emperor. What commended Theodosius was undoubtedly his outstanding reputation as an army officer (Zosimus, *New History* 4.24, etc.). When the succession next had to be decided, during the declining years of Theodosius' son Honorius (d. 423), family ties were once again in play: Constantius was a successful commander who became co-emperor after being taken into the imperial family as the husband of Galla Placidia, the emperor's half-sister. The Theodosian dynasty continued, in the person of Theodosius II in the east (b. 401; Augustus from 402 to 450), and Galla Placidia herself (b. about 388; Augusta 421–50) together with her son Valentinian III (b. 419; Augustus 425–55) in what remained of the western empire.

What sort of monarchy was this now? In formal terms, it was absolute,[10] and it both threatened and carried out dire punishments if its orders were

[8] *PLRE* II, Constantius 17.

[9] Zosimus, *New History* 3.36, has a different account, but agrees that it was the army and its 'leaders' who decided. Valentinian too turned out to be remarkably cruel (Ammianus 29.3), but as emperor he practised religious tolerance (Ammianus 30.9.5).

[10] See A.H.M. Jones 1964, I, 321–9. But see Eich and Eich 2004, esp. 101, for the interesting claim that emperors were now less not more absolute than in the high empire.

not obeyed. A word from Valentinian I and off with a former provincial governor's head.[11] As before, the emperor's willingness to control his own anger was often crucial.[12] Another mark of absolutism was the intermittent power of female members of the imperial family, most notably Galla Placidia in the west, and Pulcheria and Eudocia, sister and wife respectively of Theodosius II, in the east [Figure 7.1].[13] It was also in a sense a government of laws, but when the emperor desired to change the law he did so, within the limits of his prudence.

The highest council of the state was a body of uncertain but restricted size, the emperor's Consistory (all except the emperor normally remained standing, hence its name); how much it produced useful discussion we cannot tell. According to Jones, 'it debated matters of moment and advised the emperor upon them',[14] but this probably gives an exaggerated idea of its independence.

It was those who had strong personal relations with the emperor who counted most, obviously; the correct model is always an imperial court,[15] often in this period an itinerant court (but that had almost always been true). The power of a strong praetorian prefect such as Rufinus (in office 392–5 under Theodosius I)[16] depended partly on ruthlessness but fundamentally on his personal relationship with his superior (Zosimus 4.51.1). Even more obviously, the powerful court eunuchs of this period – Eusebius under Constantius II, Eutropius under Arcadius, Chrysaphius under the second Theodosius – derived their sometimes very great power (and wealth) from their closeness to the ruler. The court was thronged with lesser persons, however, and was widely seen, plainly with some justification, as an institution that cut the emperor off from reality:[17]

> Diocletian [before he became emperor] declared that ... four or five men gather and form a plan to deceive the emperor, then tell him what he must approve. The emperor, who is shut up in his palace, cannot know the truth ... (*Augustan History*, *Aurelian* 43; the whole passage deserves attention: it is fictional but a reflection of fairly informed opinion in the last quarter of the fourth century).

[11] Ammianus 29.3.6. But one may wonder whether Honorius, later, could have done this.
[12] Harris 2002, 259–62.
[13] See Holum 1982.
[14] Jones 1964, I, 334.
[15] For the fullest discussion, see R. Smith 2007, who, however, is not much focused on power.
[16] *PLRE*, I, Rufinus 18.
[17] R. Smith 2007, 161–3, appositely citing Ammianus 18.4.3–4, Synesius, *On Kingship* 14, and Procopius, *Wars* 3.2.39 (a bizarre anecdote about Honorius), as well as the passage quoted in the text.

Figure 7.1. A recently discovered portrait of the empress Eudocia, wife of Theodosius II, Augusta 423–60. A beautiful and educated Athenian, she attracted the attention of the court in Constantinople and was baptized so that she could be married to the emperor, with whom she had three children. Some of her numerous writings are extant. Athens, New Acropolis Museum

Meanwhile the Senates of both Rome and Constantinople, or rather their leaders, could from time to time formulate opinions that might differ from the preferences of the emperor,[18] but their power in really important matters was nil; the fact that nominal membership of the senatorial order had been extended to large numbers of secondary officials is a symptom of this.

It is possible that emperors could be at least as well informed about what was happening in the army and the provinces as earlier emperors had once been through their procurators and others. They had potential sources, including confidential agents, the *agentes in rebus* (who fulfilled other functions too: above, p. 189) and *curiosi*, and inspectors sent out by the central state offices. But the number of such officials may have been inadequate,[19] and absolute rulers are not necessarily receptive to bad news. The difficulties that emperors experienced in trying to find out which of their subordinates were failing in their duties – such as the apparently highly corrupt Romanus who commanded the army in Africa under Valentinian I (see Ammianus 28.6)[20] – may have been no worse than in any earlier period. But the costs were now higher – in the case of Romanus, the repeated devastation by invaders of parts of the quite prosperous tax-paying province of Tripolitana. And if Honorius really believed in 423 that there were no more 'pagans' (*CTh* 16.10.22), his information about his subjects was woefully poor (but it may have been an ideological falsehood like President Ahmadinejad's claim that there were no gays in Iran).

Three themes, however, dominate conventional accounts of imperial power in these years: increased centralization; the further growth of what has been called 'a sophisticated and well-organized bureaucracy'; and official corruption.[21] All three notions need contextualizing and defining.

The ceremonial grandeur of the court was impressive. It can be seen indirectly on the famous silver-and-gold plate known as the *missorium* of Theodosius I, manufactured in 388 [Figure 7.2]. The emperor and his two younger colleagues are represented sitting on their thrones and gazing rigidly forwards, while Theodosius bestows office on a figure kneeling before him, and armed barbarian guards stand in the wings; in the exergue

[18] Heather 1998, 199–204.
[19] *CTh* 6.29.2.1 of 356 or 357 stated that two *agentes in rebus* per province were sufficient. How they mainly spent their time remains mysterious. Schuller 1975, 3–8, is still a useful account.
[20] *PLRE* I, 768.
[21] Cf. C. Kelly 1998, 138.

Figure 7.2. The *missorium* of Theodosius I (AD 388), presumably made in Constantinople. The emperor is flanked by his co-rulers Arcadius (his son) and Valentinian II. See the text. Madrid, Real Academia de Historia

below, the reclining figure of Earth tells us that the emperors ruled the whole prosperous planet.[22] Meanwhile courtiers and flatterers constantly called the emperors gods, and even when the emperor was not listening it could be said, at least by a non-Christian, that he was 'in the first ranks of the gods' (Firmicus Maternus, *Astrological Learning* 2.30.6, late in Constantine's reign; he incidentally makes it clear that it was appallingly dangerous to cast the emperor's horoscope).

[22] MacCormack 1981, 214–20.

The Christians, though some of them found the adulatory terms Eusebius had applied to Constantine inappropriate, joined in enthusiastically, while giving a Christian cast to what happened to the emperor after his death (this can be seen in Ambrose's oration *On the Death of Theodosius*).[23] There was, however, an element of tension here, one that reflected the largely successful struggle on the part of the bishops and other Christians to establish themselves as a set of powers independent of the authority of the state. A loyal churchman could depict the emperor as god's representative – but it was a question, in his eyes, whether the emperor was worthy: 'dear to the great king [i.e. god] is the one here who bears the same name [i.e. the emperor]', wrote Synesius (*On Kingship* 8), 'provided that he is not false to that name'; and Synesius went on to claim that the emperor Arcadius was living the life of a jelly-fish (*ibid.* 14).[24]

The fantastically exaggerated distinction between the emperor and other humans, which had already gathered strength with Diocletian and Constantine,[25] probably made the emperor a degree more secure, and, as suggested in Chapter 5, earlier emperors would have been well advised to imitate the Chinese model of celestial superiority. The imperial status of Gratian did not prevent his being killed by the usurper Magnus Maximus (383), but then there was a relatively long interval by Roman standards until another Roman emperor met a violent end – Valentinian III, assassinated in 455. (The execution of the short-lived claimant Ioannes in 425 scarcely counts).[26]

But how much Honorius and Arcadius were able to impress their ordinary subjects – as distinct from their courtiers – with their grandeur is an open question. The main means of communication with the masses remained coin-types. Allusions to contemporary events and current imperial policies had already decreased on coins after the mid-third century, but in the late fourth century they became quite rare;[27] the population was sometimes told that the emperor had 'triumphed over barbarian races' (though never again after 407).[28] As in earlier times, a good deal of effort went into distributing the emperor's portrait, which might commonly, in the fourth century, claim that he was a military victor (Gregory

[23] For the continuation of the imperial cult down to Theodosius, see Trombley 2011.

[24] Much ink has been employed over the question whether this essay was written in 397 or 400, but its frankness would be quite remarkable if it was published before Arcadius' death in 408.

[25] Cf. MacCormack 1981, 106–15.

[26] *PLRE* II, Ioannes 6.

[27] Carson 1990, 191.

[28] J.P.C. Kent 1994.

of Nazianzus, *Oration* 4.80; Eunapius fr. 68 Blockley). Few city-dwellers can have missed such images, but how much awe, loyalty, or respect they produced it is hard to gauge. With respect to imperial portraits, emperors seem to have been concerned that they should be displayed in an appropriately dignified fashion (cf. *CTh* 15.7.12 of 394) – that is to say that such portraits mattered.

Roman emperors continued to be absolute monarchs whose desire to control what went on in the army and the provinces was limited by practical and other constraints. Since at least the time of Tiberius, they had attempted to be all-controlling, and since at least Trajan they had intervened in many minor issues of provincial governance. The tetrarchic growth in the civil service naturally created problems about who could give orders to whom, which emperors sometimes attempted to resolve (for example, in *CTh* 6.30.4 of 384), a sign that the men at the top would have liked to have clear chains of command.

The survival of the approximately 2,500 laws contained in the *Theodosian Code*, which are of course restricted – according to the instructions that Theodosius II gave his legal experts – to those issued by the previous *Christian* emperors (plus Julian), seems to have given some scholars the false impression that these emperors had legislated on a wider variety of subjects than their predecessors. There has been much discussion of Theodosius' intentions in commissioning his code: he claimed to have dispelled legal darkness and to have given the laws 'the light of brevity' (Theodosius, *Novels* 1.1.1). He clearly meant to diminish 'pagan' law-givers and their laws, and at the same time he reasserted his claim to authority in the west (on this see 1.1.6). The point here, however, is that there was already plenty of minute imperial legislation, and 'legal darkness', under the pre-Christian emperors too. And while the emperor was an autocrat, no emperor of the period that concerns us here is known to have reduced the power of officials, still less that of bishops, in any significant way whatsoever. Indeed it could be argued that in the age of Stilicho and Fl. Constantius (later Constantius III), the Roman Empire was *less* not more centralized than it had usually been under earlier emperors.[29]

It partly depends how we see late-fourth and early-fifth-century officialdom (from now on, I avoid the prejudicial term 'bureaucracy'). There are two tricky problems here: one is to know how many extra officials there were; the other is to know what effects it had that so many men

[29] Jones 1964, II, 1056, takes centralization for granted (without dating it) and assumes that it was 'excessive'.

got themselves on to the public payroll. By pre-modern standards the lower officials may have been numerous (though that is difficult to establish): Jones calculated, mainly on the basis of the *Notitia Dignitatum* and fourth-century provisions in the *Theodosian Code*, that 'the grand total of regular officials was ... not much in excess of 30,000', which he judged to be a 'not vast' total in relation to the size of the whole empire, and a relatively small expense given the low level of official salaries.[30] Kelly, more recently, is unclear, but puts forward a figure of the same order of magnitude.[31] As far as the fourth century is concerned, we have decrees that specify some exact numbers: 224 salaried officials in the 'palatine' offices (the emperor's own civilian staff) (*CTh* 6.30.15 of 399), and 546 on the staff of the chief financial official, the Count of the Sacred Largesses (*ibid.* section 16, same date); and we know that (some) provincial governors were supposed to be limited to staffs of 100 (Justinian, *Code* 12.57.9, of 396). With a large amount of extrapolation these figures have allowed scholars to build up broadly agreed totals.

An intriguing aspect of these officials is that, probably starting early in the reign of Constantine, they presented themselves as quasi-soldiers, drawing 'rations' and wearing uniforms; their service and their offices were called *militia.*[32] It has been suggested that this came about because 'casual speech' recognized that more jobs that were essentially civilian were being assigned to soldiers.[33] A more probable explanation is that the emperor and the senior officials wanted their subordinates to be as disciplined as the ideal soldier.

The corruption question occasions dispute, partly because it is hard to define what was regarded in those times as excessive in the way of gift-giving and gift-receiving,[34] partly because it is hard to estimate how extensive certain practices were in an age when some were inevitably more unscrupulous than others. Yet bribery and corruption exist in almost every age – which leads to the hard question of whether the sale of offices and of government services in the western Roman Empire in this period did serious harm to the state. Economists seem not to be much interested

[30] Jones 1964, 1057.

[31] C. Kelly 2004, 115, gives 30,000 to 35,000 for the undivided empire, but seems to be taking this from the total he has conjectured for the sixth century (111). Of course it is not impossible that the number is roughly right for both dates.

[32] For the date, see MacMullen 1963, 49. References to civilian office-holding as *militia* in legal writers of the second and third centuries (*TLL* s.v., cols. 963–4) are likely to result from later editing.

[33] MacMullen 1963, 50; but the probably earliest such language is official (*CJ* 12.29.1 of 314).

[34] As Heather has pointed out (2010b, 249, n. 9), no scholar has yet provided a full account of what was acceptable and what was unacceptable corruption in late antiquity.

in bribery, for they consider it to be simply a form of queuing.[35] Britain acquired much of its empire at a time when parliamentary seats and military commissions and promotions were commonly purchased – usually by men who were more or less competent. Comparisons with modern Mediterranean countries would be superfluous. It is more relevant to record that by the mid-second century BC Roman senators were sometimes willing to sell out the interests of the state (Diodorus the Sicilian 31.27a, etc.), without catastrophic effects.

There has in any case been much dispute about the significance of venality in this era.[36] In my view, both the maximizers (those who see it as a huge, even fatal, defect in the system of government) and the minimizers are in error. Both sides commonly confuse several different issues: whether men were promoted for reasons other than merit in a modern sense (very frequently, as they had always been);[37] whether important positions were often purchased and if so from whom; whether such trafficking did much genuine harm; whether bribery subverted the implementation of important imperial policies; and whether these difficulties, if they existed, increased markedly in the decades of crisis.

What was actually harmful? When Libanius complains that his rights as a landowner have been diminished by the local army commander, the system was taking no harm, even if his allegations of bribery (*Oration* 47.4–34) are true, – quite the contrary perhaps. When Basil, bishop of Caesarea, plotted to use bribery to obtain an exemption from civic duties (*Letters* 190.2), the public interest was being harmed, but in a secondary fashion, and even if we multiply this incident many times the tax exemption of now wealthy bishops did considerably more harm.

Even when 'Saint' Cyril of Alexandria (one of the least saintly persons of the age) defied Theodosius II, a relatively weak emperor, in 431 and successfully did down his doctrinal rival Nestorius by massively bribing members of the eastern imperial court (he spent about half a ton of gold for this purpose), the event has to be given its proper dimensions. The Patriarch of Alexandria prevailed over the emperor, but it is absurd to call it a '*coup d'état*':[38] what was at issue was ecclesiastical office and an abstruse matter of theology, not continuing command of the state. The case is

[35] Lui 1985, etc.

[36] MacMullen 1988; C. Kelly 2004; Cecconi 2005; MacMullen 2006, 478–81.

[37] That friendship, seniority, and 'good' birth entered in was not of course anything new; see above, p. 199.

[38] MacMullen 2006, 480.

thus crucially different from what happened some 200 years later when the Patriarch of Alexandria Cyrus disobeyed the emperor Heraclius and ultimately got away with it. What is most interesting about Cyril's case (apart from the fact that life-and-death matters of Christian orthodoxy ultimately depended on money) is the enormous untaxed wealth of the Alexandrian patriarchate. It is also intriguing to see which courtiers cost Cyril most; the praetorian prefect was evidently considered unreachable, so his wife was bribed instead.[39]

The implication of a law of the reformist Julian (*CTh* 2.29.1) is that buying office was quite common. And this practice may have been penetrating to higher levels than before. Eutropius, the young emperor Arcadius' head chamberlain from 395 till his death in 399, was charged by the court poet Claudian with having sold numerous provincial governorships (*Against Eutropius* 1.196–209). Claudian was attacking his master Stilicho's opponent, and was presumably at the very least exaggerating, but what matters is, first, that such a charge was credible,[40] and second that Eutropius' appointees may not in any case have been much less competent than those who would otherwise have been promoted. Historians are often censorious about the numerous letters of recommendation written by Symmachus and Libanius, even though they write a great many themselves.

The big question here, going beyond the matter of bribery, is whether emperors possessed the means to get their orders obeyed, and whether there were effective chains of command. The *Theodosian Code* shows them constantly trying. Certainly the emperor, at least if he was an adult, was relatively free, within the bounds of social and religious prejudice, to choose the people he would work with, taking account of their competence and likely loyalty.[41] But that left a heavy burden on his intelligence and strength of character.

It was clearly a serious obstacle to effective government that the turnover in high office was fairly rapid.[42] That allowed emperors to satisfy more of their high-ranking subjects, and in 396, with the imperial power fragile after the death of Theodosius I, the emperors reduced from three years to two the period of office of the chiefs of the palatine offices and

[39] Details: Jones 1964, 1, 346.
[40] And Theodosius may well have shown the way (Zosimus 4.28.3–4, no doubt exaggerating too).
[41] As to how much fourth-century emperors considered ability, prior friendship, and other factors in making senior appointments, see Cecconi 2005, 284–7.
[42] C. Kelly 1998, 153.

imperial bureaux (*CTh* 6.30.14). Important officials frequently held office for still shorter periods: between 407 and the second sack of Rome in 455, for example, some 32 men are known to have held the vital office of praetorian prefect for Italy and Africa, and the list we have is by no means complete.[43] Many of the men who held such positions were genuine professionals, but in the Roman conditions of these years it was practically impossible for short-term office-holders to do their jobs well.

When it comes to serious tests of internal power, such as whether the emperor could suppress rebellions, get people to pay taxes, and serve in the army, the results are mixed. Sheer survival was not now as difficult for the emperor as it had been before: Theodosius I died of natural causes, Honorius survived various usurpations and died in his bed after nominally ruling for twenty-eight years.

But as for getting taxes paid, the government was no longer very good at it (above, p. 232), quite apart from the fact that large areas of the western provinces were sometimes not in any sense under its control[44] There were arrears and defaulters and inefficiencies in all periods, but by the late fourth century there had been a real deterioration. Diocletian's census-taking system fairly quickly turned out to be unworkable: instead, 'piecemeal [i.e. local] assessments were made from time to time on demand',[45] and the central government never knew with any accuracy what there was to tax. It also bestowed inopportune exemptions: in 412, with the western empire in deep crisis, Honorius confirmed or granted tax privileges to a wide swathe of officials (*CTh* 6.26.14).

Duncan-Jones calculated that tax-yields on agricultural land in Egypt, the only province where we have any chance of calculating such things, declined between the early empire and the first half of the fourth century (and declined further by the sixth century);[46] he suggested that the reason was overtaxation, but that does not seem to explain why large blocks of land that were being farmed should have paid less – it seems more likely that the government now had weaker powers of extraction (less force and less fear at its disposal). There is ample evidence that fourth-century

[43] Two men, Palladius (*PLRE* II, Palladius 19) and Albinus (Albinus 10), held this office for five or six years each. Was that because of superior competence? See further C. Kelly 2004, 194.

[44] The exact extent of Roman control can be debated: in 410, according to Bransbourg 2015, 277, it was 'effectively limited to Italy, north Africa, and a very few areas in Iberia and Gaul'. The map in P. Brown 2012, 386, grossly overstates in any case the power of the western Roman government in AD 450.

[45] Jones 1964, I, 454.

[46] Duncan-Jones 1994, 56–9.

tax-payers were often in arrears,[47] and the government often attempted to prevent tax-flight (*CTh* 11.24.1–5).

As to finding military recruits, it seems to have become increasingly difficult, and whatever the population of the Roman Empire was in, say, 400 (few scholars have been rash enough to mention a figure), this was in all likelihood for reasons of indiscipline and disinterest not demography.

Bishops, priests, and the state

Bishops and priests were the new privileged order. Already under Constantine, bishops had privileges that no other category of person had ever enjoyed. All clerics, including 'sub-deacons, exorcists, lectors and doorkeepers', were free from taxation and compulsory public services (*CTh* 16.2). Some of them at least were on public payrolls (cf. Sozomen, *Ecclesiastical History* 5.5.2). Clerics charged with crimes had the right to be tried by bishops (*Sirmondian Constitutions* 15, AD 411; and if the accused were acquitted, the accuser was to be punished), and in law-courts the unsupported testimony of a bishop had to be accepted as true (*Sirmondian Constitutions* 1).

Meanwhile the whole nature of episcopal office had changed. In the course of the fourth century, major bishoprics became extremely wealthy, and became important sources of welfare. The lavish lifestyle now available to the bishop of Rome was, according to Ammianus (27.3.12–15), what caused so much strife when Damasus was elected to the post in 366; the strife was so intense that 137 bodies were found in the church which later probably became Santa Maria Maggiore. (However it was only later, in the fifth century, that the Roman see established its ascendancy over the other western churches.[48]) The role of bishop was now attractive to an ambitious administrator such as Ambrose of Milan, the son of a praetorian prefect who himself achieved high political office at about the age of 34 (in 374), before becoming bishop of Milan without any clerical preparation. The wealth of the churches was not uniform, but by the early fifth century it was immense.[49]

Tax exemptions, the right to trial in ecclesiastical courts, and privileged testimony were derogations of state power, and the concerns of bishops with matters of doctrinal orthodoxy and church property soon led them

[47] MacMullen 1988, 232. n. 147.
[48] Jones 1964, I, 210.
[49] For a brief account, see Hunt 1998, 257–62.

to invoke the military power of the state (see below). But in the fourth century they seldom exercised direct political power. When a gang of Christians led by the local bishop destroyed the synagogue at Callinicum on the Euphrates in 388, and Theodosius wanted to punish him, Ambrose claimed that the Jews were fair game and was able to get the bishop off.[50] Theodosius' retreat represented a significant weakening of the Roman state's always limited monopoly of force.

But it was Christianity, to which the emperor was deeply committed, not episcopal power as such, that was in the process of marginalizing the empire's Jewish citizens, so that, starting in 404 – simply to mention one aspect of the matter – a series of laws prohibited Jews from holding positions in the imperial service.[51]

On another famous occasion, after a crowd at Thessalonica had murdered the commanding officer of the entire region and Theodosius had ordered large-scale reprisals, the emperor did penance in Ambrose's church, but this, though remarkable enough, was not an epoch-making new submission of the state to the Italian church. A hundred years earlier, naturally, no Roman emperor would have listened to what the priest of an eschatological cult had to say about such a matter. But on this occasion, according to a reasonable view, Ambrose merely 'turned the catastrophe into a public relations triumph for the emperor'.[52] John Chrysostom exercised power within the eastern church, but the emperor Arcadius twice sent him into exile for ecclesiastical offences.[53]

By the 390s, bishops and other Christian leaders could command gangs of religious enforcers, often monks, in more and more places, and their actions were authorized by the emperors.[54] Bishops could increasingly impinge on state interests, or at least on public affairs, and they were protected by their unquestioned exemption from the grave punishments to which secular officials were exposed. It was hardly surprising, for example, that a provincial bishop could obtain a pardon for men who 'had betrayed to the barbarians the art of building ships' (*CTh* 9.40.24

50 McLynn 1994, 298–309 (who judges that 'the loser in this unhappy affair was Ambrose', 308; for a different view, see Gotter 2011).

51 Schwartz 2001, 195.

52 McLynn 1994, 323.

53 J.N.D. Kelly 1995, chapters 16–18.

54 Eunapius says of the Egyptian monks in the 390s that 'every man who wore a black robe and consented to behave disgracefully in public had the power of a tyrant' (*Lives of the Philosophers* 472). Official approval is to be inferred from the reference to *ecclesiastica manus* in *CTh* 16.10.19 = *Sirmondian Constitutions* 12, of 407. For the growing power of the Gallic bishops from about 400, see Beaujard 1996, 129–35.

[419 AD]). Bishops also lasted longer, on average, than high state officials. As they came to be recruited increasingly from the upper class,[55] they naturally exerted greater and greater influence. And they were of course the prime agents of the religious intolerance which, so I argued in the last chapter, was more harmful to the state than is usually acknowledged (see further below, p. 291).

One myth – the invincibility of Rome – was massively, though gradually and not completely, replaced by another – the central importance of Christian beliefs, and indeed of conforming, orthodox, Christian beliefs. It is worth quoting the somewhat clumsy law of the emperors of 380 at length:

> We wish all peoples subject to the rule of our clemency to live in the religion (*in tali … religione versari*) that religion … tells us that the divine Peter the apostle transmitted to the Romans. And this is the religion, it is clear, that is followed by the *pontifex* Damasus [Bishop of Rome] and by Peter, Bishop of Alexandria, a man of apostolic sanctity. That is to say that according to apostolic discipline [teaching?] and the doctrine of the gospel we should believe that the Father, Son and Holy Spirit constitute a single deity, with equal majesty and in a holy trinity. We order all those who follow this law to embrace the name of Catholic Christians, and, judging everyone else to be demented and insane, we order that they shall bear the disgrace of heretical belief, and that having first been punished by divine vengeance they are also afterwards to be subjected to the revenge of our resentment, which we have engaged with in accordance with the judgement of heaven (*CTh* 16.1.2).

(This text was substantially repeated later by Justinian at the beginning of his law code.) The new law did not of course mean that the government set out to put 'pagans', Jews, 'heretics', and others to death *en masse*, and the emperors knew that they could do nothing of the sort. It was simply another step in the marginalization of the very large segment of the population that did not conform. We have already mentioned how 'pagans' and Jews were affected. As to what should and could be done about Arians, who held slightly different views about God's nature from those endorsed by Theodosius, that was a serious problem. A generation later, in 407, the government attempted to confiscate the property of the Donatists and several other kinds of 'heretics', and to prevent them carrying on virtually any economic activity (*CTh* 16.5.40). At the same time it even used the apparatus of the state to prevent non-Christian funeral rites.[56] In 425

[55] Though this trend is not to be exaggerated: Bowes 2008, 219.
[56] See the law referred to in the previous note.

it aspired to expel all who held non-Catholic beliefs from 'diverse cities' (*Sirmondian Constitutions* 6).

Now, religious identity and its implications were complex in this age, with opportunism, accommodation, and divided loyalties taking up as much space as fanaticism. It is not in any case my concern here to analyse the origins of Christian intolerance. Alan Cameron has divided the Roman population of this era into five religious categories: committed Christians; committed traditionalists ('pagans') – both of these, he claims, 'a relatively small proportion of the entire population' –; 'center-Christians'; 'center-pagans'; and finally those who are hard to classify.[57] Much depends here on what is meant by a committed Christian or a 'center-Christian', where what matters in practical terms is not for example theological expertise but vigorous self-identification of the kind that became stronger and stronger under Theodosius (see the law of 380 quoted above), Honorius, and Arcadius. And religious developments seem to have weakened Roman power in two ways, apart from the perhaps not very important Christian contempt for this-worldly affairs.

In the previous chapter, I discussed the likely effects of divided religious feelings on military morale. In addition, troops were quite often employed in religious conflicts among Roman subjects: 'religion occasioned the most frequent [internal] disruptions to require military intervention'.[58] Eastern and western soldiers apparently differed, with 'paganism' surviving longer among the latter. Constantine must have used soldiers when he destroyed a number of temples and statues of the gods in the eastern provinces (for details of this campaign the best source, though it is extremely partisan, is Eusebius' *Life of Constantine* 3.54–8),[59] and under Constantius II eastern Christians could apparently rely on the forces of the state to support them as they set about destroying temples (cf. Libanius, *Oration* 30.38). Libanius' essay *To the Emperor Theodosius for the Temples* is a desperate defence, more or less politely alluding to the fact that, in the countryside even more than the cities (his focus is naturally eastern), bands of Christian enthusiasts were busy destroying the shrines of the gods (*Oration* 30.8–9, 21–7), with the support of the imperial power (ibid. 12–13, 43). We mostly hear details when important cities are involved, Apamea, Edessa, Alexandria, or Gaza. Cynegius,

57 Cameron 2011, 176–7. This analysis is unduly weighted towards men of letters.

58 Whitby 2007, II, 319.

59 The attempt of Fowden 1998, 540–1, and others to eliminate this evidence are also partisan. According to Sozomen, *Ecclesiastical History* 2.5, it was not soldiers but 'Christians in the palace' who carried out Constantine's instructions.

trusted servant of Theodosius and praetorian prefect in the east 384–8, was especially active,[60] and his victims are not likely to have been much consoled by the fact that his successor was a 'pagan',[61] for he did not undo Cynegius' handiwork. Meanwhile the use of the surviving temples was progressively restricted until it was completely forbidden in 391 (*CTh* 16.10.11). Similar events happened in the west, perhaps with a slight delay. But when Honorius sent senior officials to close the temples of Carthage and other places in North Africa in 399, they certainly took soldiers with them.[62] They needed to, for the locals sometimes fought back – causing sixty Christian deaths in one town according to Augustine (*Letters* 50).[63]

This evidence about the violent suppression of religious practice, and by extension of religious belief, points in a fairly clear direction. Christian readers will not want to hear this, and the predominantly Christian historiography of modern times has often obscured the fact, but in the late-fourth and early-fifth centuries the Roman Empire experienced an important degree of social disintegration; further evidence will shortly emerge. This is not to claim that Christianity was the sole cause of the phenomenon or to deny that Christianity also had some positive social effects. But the breaking down of bonds within the population and the spread of internal hatreds are historical facts.

Social disintegration

Those outside the formal apparatus of the state who exercised great power, in addition to the bishops, were of course the landowners. We know of a number of very wealthy families in Italy and the western provinces, while both the cities there and what we have called the middle classes (landholders farming a few dozen hectares, the more prosperous townsmen) were fewer and certainly poorer than they had been in high imperial times. The power of wealthy landowners over their tenants and smaller neighbours may well have grown stronger since that era, though this impression might largely be due to the changed nature of the sources. We have

60 Zosimus 4.37.3, with Paschoud's note. McLynn 2005, 112–17, attempts to whitewash Cynegius.

61 As pointed out by Cameron 2011, 57.

62 For the sources, see *PLRE* II, Gaudentius 5. In all this I implicitly reject the account of the role of Christianity in the history of this period offered by Heather 2005, 119–28, according to whom '[the] religious revolution was achieved more by trickle-down effect than by outright confrontation' (127), not that I doubt that many became Christians, as indeed Eusebius complained, for worldly reasons.

63 On this incident, see Shaw 2011, 249–51.

more sermons, such as the one that included the following words by John Chrysostom concerning the region of Antioch:

> Who could be more oppressive than landowners? If you look at the way in which they treat their miserable tenants, you will find them more savage than barbarians. They lay intolerable and continual imposts on men who are weakened with hunger and toil throughout their lives ... They use their bodies like asses and mules ... Moreover the tortures and beatings, the exactions and ruthless demands for services which such men suffer from the agents are worse than hunger ... (*Sermons on Matthew* 61.3, *PG* 58.591).

Was there anything new about this ill treatment? The question is intimately bound up with the controversial problem of the *coloni*, the tenants, already mentioned in Chapter 5.[64] On a reasonable view, their legal condition deteriorated markedly between the 360s and the 390s, and while the main conscious aim of the legislators was fiscal, landowners, including the emperor himself, also benefited. 'The tied colonate suited the richer landowners well'.[65] Among other things the *coloni* may not move away from the land to which they belong; 'they appear to be free, but they are to be considered slaves of the land where they were born' (*CJ* 11.52.1, AD 393). It seems to have been taken for granted, incidentally, that a landowner should be able to determine his dependants' religious practices.[66]

Another difficult problem concerns the 'curials' or 'decurions', the members of town councils. They were a vital part of the machinery of government, and it is generally thought that this part of the mechanism was in crisis in the fourth century.[67] No source gives us an overview, and once again we are dangerously dependent on the *Theodosian Code*, where the curials form the subject of what is easily the longest single chapter (12.1). Under increasing pressure to produce tax revenue as well as looking after their own communities, they became harder to replace. But the dimensions and chronology of the crisis, not to mention its local variations, are impossible to establish. Local amenities such as aqueducts and roads tended to deteriorate, but whether there was a large shift of power may be doubted.

64 Garnsey and Whittaker 1998, 288–94, provide a good summary of the problem as far as this period is concerned.

65 Garnsey and Whittaker 1998, 291.

66 Augustine, *Letters* 57.2, 112.3, 139.2. What the dependants thought about this can only be imagined. The contrary interpretation of Dossey 2010, 188, is the merest special pleading.

67 For a good account, see Ward-Perkins 1998, 373–88, with some reservations, especially concerning his use of the term 'aristocrats' to refer to local councillors: many were quite small landholders (*CTh* 12.1.33, 342).

The question of civil peace in this era will serve as a transition away from those who exercised much power to those who exercised petty power or none at all. It is a historian's perpetual problem to discern whether legislation aimed at suppressing a certain phenomenon, brigandage in this instance, should be taken as a sign that the phenomenon had intensified or as a sign that the rulers were growing more attentive or ambitious. In 364 Valentinian and Valens, focusing on Italy, decreed that 'no person, without our knowledge and advice, shall be granted the right to employ any weapons whatsoever' (*CTh* 15.15.1), and in order to reduce brigandage they severely restricted the right to ride a horse (ibid. 9.30), measures that are not likely to have been very effective. They seem so desperate that we should probably suppose that in rural Italy at least public order was thought to have deteriorated. Some twenty years later, in 383, Symmachus, a wealthy senator, did not dare to go to stay even in the *suburbanitas* of Rome itself because of bandits (*Letters* 2.22 – though he generally seems to have travelled about Italy without anxiety). Gaul, Syria, Isauria, and Egypt were other areas seriously troubled by the same problem, but none was exempt.[68] The emperors noted despairingly that the *latrones* had sometimes acquired powerful patrons (*CTh* 1.29.8, 392). There had always been brigands,[69] but a great deal of evidence suggests that the cities of the empire had lost much of the rural control which they had once possessed. As for the cities and towns themselves, it seems characteristic of this period – though that is impossible to prove – both that the police force at Oxyrhynchus had been reduced by 392, presumably to save money,[70] and that in 409 the city prefect of Rome, Pompeianus, was killed in the very forum by a crowd angry about bread.[71]

Meanwhile the boundary between legitimate forces and violent marauders had grown thinner: the Goth Tribigild, for example, an imperial count in command of barbarian troops at Nacoleia in Phrygia, passed easily from one category to the other when he decided to plunder the provinces of Asia Minor in 399 and caused a fair amount of misery in Lydia, Pisidia, and Pamphylia as well as Phrygia.[72] Tribigild's relative Gainas, also an imperial count, was equally unreliable and destructive.[73] It

[68] For Gaul, see Rubin 1995, 148–9.

[69] For a collection of evidence, see MacMullen 1966, 255–68.

[70] *P.Oxy.* VII.1033 = *Select Papyri* no. 296. And it is possible that this petition resulted in reinforcements.

[71] *PLRE* II, Pompeianus 2.

[72] Sources in *PLRE* II, Tribigildus.

[73] For an outline of his career, see *PLRE* I, Gainas.

is not surprising that Synesius regarded the Gothic troops in the emperor's service as wolves (*On Kingship* 19).

Religious violence of one kind or another is attested in every region. In Egypt, Abbot Shenoute [Figure 7.3], having ransacked the house of an old-religionist, defended himself by proclaiming that 'there is no such thing as robbery for those who truly possess Christ'.[74] Alexandria was a scene of frequent religious violence, between Christians and Christians as well as between Christians and 'pagans' – the hacking-to-death of the scholarly Hypatia at the instigation of 'Saint' Cyril [415] is simply the most famous incident –, but no province was exempt. The violent conflict between the Catholics and the so-called Circumcellions is well known from the partisan pages of Augustine.[75] Religious violence intensified under Theodosius I, and continued even after the traditionalists had been marginalized, because 'heretics' were always numerous.[76]

As the population apparently grew more violent, so did the government. Punishments, always gruesome at Rome, became more so: Constantine's reign had marked a new phase, the reigns of the brothers Valentinian (364–75) and Valens (364–78), respectively in the west and east, yet another.[77] More and more offences were punishable with death, dozens of them. This soon included various 'heresies' (*CTh* 16.5.9.1 of 382), and starting with Priscillian and some of his followers (385) we know of individual heretics who were put to death. The practices of the old religion, still dear to great numbers of people, had already rendered one liable to capital punishment in the time of Constantius:

> It is also our will that all shall abstain from sacrifices. But if anyone should perpetrate anything of this kind let them be struck down by the avenging sword… The governors of the provinces shall be punished similarly if they should neglect to avenge such crimes (*CTh* 16.10.4 of the year 356).[78]

Theodosius intensified this persecution.

The causes of this draconian trend are of course debatable. One answer attributes it to the increased distance between the ruling elite and the rest,[79] but that is not enough, because the victims of the new savagery

74 Barns 1964, 156. See further Gaddis 2005, 1 and chapter 5.
75 See Rubin 1995, 156–79; we need not decide how much the Circumcellions were a movement of social protest. Augustine, *Letters* 93.1–14, justifies the persecution of non-Catholic Christians at length.
76 For religious violence between the 380s and 420s, see especially MacMullen 1984, 88–101.
77 MacMullen 1986a.
78 Sacrifice had already been prohibited in 341: *CTh* 16.10.2.
79 N. 77.

Figure 7.3 The violent Egyptian abbot Shenoute, as represented in the seventh century, some two centuries after his death. Red Monastery Church, near Sohag, Egypt

included members of the elite itself. In the background lay the decline, now far in the past, of the humanistic education of the upper orders. The role of Christianity remains to be defined. It is in any case the effects that matter here, and it may be supposed that one of them was a kind of social disintegration, exacerbated by religious differences. Any Roman might turn out to be a heretic, or one who honoured the old gods. One wonders too whether the Romans' diminished ability to behave odiously towards other peoples turned them more and more against each other.

'Social relations in the country indubitably deteriorated at the expense of the lower classes', one historian concludes.[80] That is a very sweeping statement. And it should be allowed that there was a good deal of local variation: in some provinces, for example, soldiers were mostly recruited in the same provinces, and they can be presumed to have had at least some ties with the local population, while in other places they were outsiders.[81] But mistreatment of civilians by soldiers – not by any means a new phenomenon – is commonly thought to have increased in diverse areas of the Roman Empire in the late fourth century.[82] A chapter of the *Theodosian Code* (11.24, 'On the Patronage of Villages'; see also Libanius, *Oration* 47) shows that army officers and other men with clout sometimes provided 'protection' against tax-collectors, acquired more land for themselves, and exercised local power to the exclusion of the government, which repeatedly, from 360 onwards, tried to prevent the practice.

It was true, however, everywhere that the citizens' most basic freedoms had been further eroded by Constantine and his successors, and this sharpened the division between mass and elite in country and town alike. In 382 the emperors moved to limit access to themselves still further ('the oppressed provincials … must convey to our sacred imperial ears <only> those matters which may reasonably be alleged before the Emperor…', *CTh* 12.12.9.1; in a similar vein: 12.1.9 [AD 324], 12.12.3 [AD 364]). In the same period, more importantly, the government set about making it prohibitively expensive for ordinary people to seek remedies at law.[83]

Whatever the exact contours of the endlessly debated 'colonate', it meant that in many parts of the empire free farmers – in this overwhelmingly rural

80 Marcone 1998, 358.
81 Bagnall 1993, 177, contrasting Egypt (local recruitment) with Numidia and Palestine.
82 Lee 1998, 230–1.
83 C. Kelly 2004, 139–45. But some rulers professed to regret this: so Valentinian III in 451 (Valentinian, *Novels* 32.8).

society – were progressively reduced to a state not much different from slavery.[84] Constantine's law of 332, quoted previously, reads like a sick joke:

> *coloni* [tenant farmers] who plan flight are to be bound with chains and reduced to a servile condition, so that by virtue of their condemnation to slavery, they may be compelled to fulfil the duties that befit free men (*CTh* 5.17.1).[85]

Theoretically this applied at once to all the provinces, but in practice the oppression of the *coloni* spread gradually, in both geographical and legal terms, over the next two or three generations. From the 360s onwards we can see the colonate becoming hereditary (*CJ* 11.68.3). Peasant proprietors continued to exist, but a large part of the rural population was, bit by bit, reduced to serfdom. We have already seen how John Chrysostom portrayed some of the consequences (p. 282). The agents of oppression were soldiers, local police of various kinds, and the servants of the landowners.

Did women too have a decline and fall? Kate Cooper has posed the question and answered it in the affirmative.[86] The lives of women were affected by most of the changes that affected men. For every Melania (the name of a grandmother and granddaughter of extreme wealth whose lives covered the period *c.* 340 to 439),[87] there were millions of peasant mothers and daughters. Christian writers sometimes claim that the old pattern of women's subordination changed,[88] but the supposition is entirely false. The most important novelty was that wealthy women such as the two Melanias in the west and Olympias (361–408)[89] in the east founded monasteries, for both men and women. In the churches, meanwhile, virtually all power belonged to men – whereas this was not always so in the imperial court. A detailed investigation has shown that in the social stratum we know most about, the aristocracy, women 'did not convert [to Christianity] any earlier than men in the years after Constantine',[90] as we might have expected if it had somehow offered them a higher degree of respect.

A careful study of Roman law as it affected the lives of late-antique women concludes that the period that concerns us here saw no major

84 See among recent writers, Banaji 2011, 119–24.
85 For sensible commentary on this passage, see Rosafio 2002, 167–9.
86 Cooper 2009, 195–8.
87 *PLRE* 1, Melania 1 and 2.
88 Marcone 1998, 344–8, for example.
89 *PLRE* 1, Olympias 2.
90 Salzman 2002, 176.

changes.[91] But Constantine had almost entirely eliminated a woman's right to initiate a divorce (*CTh* 3.16.1), a valuable prerogative. There are reasons to doubt that this ruling was very effective in the provinces,[92] but it certainly did have some effect, and it was substantially confirmed in 421 (*CTh* 3.16.2).[93]

It is a modern assumption that no society can function well unless it enjoys a reasonable degree of social mobility, and even a pre-modern society doubtless needed to allow a certain amount of social promotion. We are in fact in no position to say whether Roman society, in the decades in question here, became more or less fluid. Some will have it that social mobility actually increased.[94] Very few of the men of great power in these years came from powerful old lineages, and there were new careers in the churches – although as soon as bishops acquired worldly power, they began to be recruited much more from among men of property. Libanius parades some leading figures of the 350s and 360s who had working-class fathers, or so he claims (*Oration* 42.23–5),[95] and in the course of the fourth century the growth of the Constantinople Senate resulted in higher rank for many men from the cities of the eastern provinces.[96] But what matters vastly more is upwards mobility from one social class to another, and that it is scarcely possible to measure. East and west may have differed significantly by the early fifth century. There were now fewer ways, especially in the western European provinces, of notably improving your lot, and unless the epigraphic record is severely misleading, a slave's chances of manumission grew much more remote than they had once been. Meanwhile the position of the free citizens who were classified as *coloni* more and more resembled that of the slaves (hence, downwards social mobility of a whole category).

This social disintegration I have referred to was all relative and not by any means all-pervasive. The history of a large empire cannot be so simple. It may surprise a historian to encounter humanitarian measures taken by Roman governments in this era, but there were some: the chapter of the *Theodosian Code* on imprisonment (9.3), for example, contains a variety of

91 Arjava 1996.
92 On what happened in Egypt, see Bagnall 1993, 193–5.
93 See further G. Clark 1993, 21–7.
94 Hopkins 1961; MacMullen 1964; cf. Banaji 2011, 113.
95 Even if Libanius was telling the truth, it may be doubted whether this could have happened a generation later: R. Smith 2007, 185–6.
96 Cf. Heather 1994, 12–21. In the late 350s Constantius II moved the eastern senators to Constantinople.

provisions dating from 320 to 409 that attempt to ensure prompt criminal trials and relatively decent conditions for those awaiting trial. No one will want to idealize the results (see above, p. 201, on prisons), but the government seems to have been trying to help some of those who were in a highly vulnerable condition.

However, the substantial argument likely to be advanced against the social-disintegration thesis is the growth of Christian charitable works. Newly wealthy Christian churches allowed bishops to live well and engaged in extensive building, but they also upended the system of Roman philanthropy by concentrating on the needy rather than on citizens as such. It is from Augustine (*Letters* 20.2 ed. Divjak) that we first hear of a *matricula pauperum*, a formal local list of poor people. Social solidarity! – and furthermore of a type unprecedented in mainstream Graeco-Roman society. But it was not solidarity of society as a whole, rather of the Christians who happened to be in power in a particular place (Arians or Nicenes), with heretics and non-Christians left to their own devices.[97] In the throngs who received food from the wealthy Pammachius on the death of his wife in 396 (Paulinus of Nola, *Letters* 13.11–14) there were no doubt some intruders, but it was not simply symbolic that the event took place in St. Peter's: admission could be controlled. Julian as a worshipper of the old gods commented contemptuously that such charity made the needy profess devout 'atheism', that is to say Christianity (*Misopogon* 363a).

Ideas

We are moving once again towards the power of ideas. At the beginning of this chapter, I suggested that the Roman Empire needed 'an upper social elite that felt a sense of responsibility for the state's ability to defend itself against outside enemies', and it is time to enquire further about love of country. The wealthy magnates flourished, and when Roman power in the west had declined they often, like the Gallo-Roman magnate and man of letters (and bishop) Sidonius Apollinaris (*c.* 430–80s), accommodated themselves to the new political order.[98] Meanwhile the upper order of society was widely infected with an other-worldly outlook, which though it did not amount to defeatism came perilously close to resignation. We

[97] The division is emphasized when Augustine says that it is all right to rob a 'pagan' if you give the proceeds to a Christian (*Sermon* 178, *PL* 38.963).

[98] For a summary of his career, see *PLRE* II, Apollinaris 6.

cannot of course read off the attitudes of such people from the writings of ecclesiastics such as Paulinus of Nola or Augustine, but many of them were on more or less close terms with these two and with Jerome (vast numbers of letters survive). The well-to-do might indeed be intensely patriotic, like the Spanish Christian poet Prudentius (though his concern for Rome's future was for its complete Christianization),[99] and Rome never had more rapturous patriots than the poets Claudian (from Alexandria) and Rutilius Namatianus (from Gaul),[100] both members of the upper social elite who did not subscribe to the new official religion. But this social elite was excluded from military leadership, and there is no sign that they wished it otherwise; the contrast with the Roman Republic could not be more complete.

As for the *amor patriae* of the rest of the free population (see above, p. 236), we have no direct access. The best proxy evidence, wholly unsurprising in view of the social disintegration we have been describing, is the evidence about resistance to conscription that we encountered in the previous chapter. Oppression does not entail the military defeat of the society that practises it, but it would be absurd to ignore the condition of the civilian population, its psychological as well as its economic condition, in any attempt to conjecture the state of military morale.

What were the most powerful ideas characteristic of the decades we are considering? Even when we make all proper allowances for the possibility that surviving works of art and literature do not accurately reflect the preoccupations of the time, it is plain that these ideas were religious. The central ideas of fourth-century Christianity – sin, redemption, rewards and punishments in a life after death, the praiseworthiness of a life devoted to the Christian religion, the ready availability of miracles, the vital importance of exactly correct religious belief – are too familiar to need description. As in the comparable section of Chapter 5, what concerns me here is the power of these and other ideas 'to reinforce, modify or subvert political and social-power relationships'.

The effects of these ideas on the main political actors of the period varied from slight at the beginning of the list (sin) to considerable at the end of it (correct religious belief). Men and women of power, including the last 'pagan' emperor Julian, believed much more in the miraculous than their first-century counterparts had done, and the age is awash in healing

[99] See Prudentius, *On the Crowns of the Martyrs* [*Peristephanon*] 2.1–16, *Against Symmachus, passim.*

[100] See respectively Claudian, *On the Consulship of Stilicho* 3.130–73, and Rutilius, *On his Return* 1.47–66.

miracles. Pious Christians greatly valued 'relics'. On the other hand, the powerful are not known to have attributed military or other successes to miraculous interventions.

How much did they care about religious orthodoxy, when it came to matters of practical policy? Theodosius and his sons recklessly imperilled social harmony by persecuting the great mass of those who disagreed with them about religion, but Theodosius made senior appointments without much apparent regard for orthodoxy: Eutolmius Tatianus, his praetorian prefect in the east in the years 388–92, was a 'pagan', as was the latter's counterpart in the west Nicomachus Flavianus, who sided with the usurper Eugenius and committed suicide after the Battle of the Frigidus in 394.[101] The sons of Theodosius I, on the other hand, and Theodosius II only appointed 'pagans' to the highest civilian and military offices in exceptional circumstances, as when Honorius decided that he could not do without the 'barbarian' general Generidus in 408/9 (Zosimus 5.46.4).[102]

As for the effects of Christian ideas, and the laws that attempted to impose Christian orthodoxy, on social-power relationships, different views are possible. Peter Brown has described this era as a transition from an 'open society' to a closed one,[103] and there is clearly much truth in that judgement. The newly dominant ideology was profoundly repressive in many areas, intellectual, sexual, and religious. The instruments of this change were new authority figures, miracle-workers and ascetics (both categories had their classical predecessors, who, however, had commanded much less respect), as well as bishops and other clergy.

Rome's military failures in these decades simply shattered the power of the Roman state in the west, though the outer forms persisted. The internal changes in the structures of power which we have noted had, for the most part, internal causes.

How did these changes affect Rome's ability to defend itself? Some claim that the emperors' inability to control official corruption made an important difference. I have argued in effect that religious dissension – between Christians as well as between Christians and 'pagans' – was a

[101] See respectively *PLRE* I, Tatianus 5 and Flavianus 15.

[102] See von Haehling 1978; Cameron 2011, 187–98. The only praetorian prefect after 395 who was definitely 'pagan' was Rufius Antonius Agrypnius Volusianus (*PLRE* II, Volusianus 6), in Italy in 428–9. Herculius in Illyricum in 408–10 (*PLRE* II, Herculius 2) is another possible case. The Gothic general Fravitta, having performed vital service for Arcadius in 400, obtained the special favour of being allowed to practise his ancestral religion. The office of Prefect of the City of Rome seems to have been exceptional in that it was held by at least five 'pagans' between 402 and 414 (*pace* Cameron), no doubt because of the residual strength of the traditionalists there.

[103] Brown 1964, 111.

more important factor. The only solution to the problem of religious dissension that the emperors of this period offered – that the whole population should be Catholic – was to say the least unrealistic. Other factors, political, economic, and psychological, certainly made military success more elusive. Of those mentioned at the beginning of this chapter, what probably mattered most, beside the problem of military morale, was simply the state's failure to collect enough taxes to finance a sufficiently large and effective army.

From Justinian to Heraclius and beyond

Justinian's empire was in the long term impossible to defend: it too was incapable of raising enough taxes to provide itself with armed forces adequate to its needs. But why not? The economic difficulties of the reigns of Maurice, Phocas, and Heraclius (that is, of the period 582–641), which we considered in Chapter 6, are a large part of the explanation, but there were other factors too, and the evidence will never, I think, allow us to hierarchize these factors in a definitive way.

No existing scholarly history attempts to compare the era of Augustus and Trajan with that of Heraclius and Constans II. That is probably one reason why much of the scholarly literature exaggerates the power of the successors of Justinian. A common view states that the 'late Roman emperor dominated his society as few rulers before or since'.[104] That is to mistake trappings and ceremony for effectiveness as far as the crucial period from 565 to 636 is concerned (a common enough error in contemporary scholarship), and to ignore the sources. To start with, the emperors in question were no more safe in their own persons than earlier emperors: Maurice, Phocas, and probably Tiberius II (574–82) were murdered, notwithstanding the fact that they maintained ample numbers of domestic spies, as may be inferred from Procopius (*Secret History* 1.2).

No one is denying of course that the emperor's rule was in principle absolute: when angered he could order 'confiscations and banishments' (John the Lydian, *On the Magistracies of the Roman People* 3.17) and execute his enemies.[105] Seven years before the Battle of the Yarmuk, so it seems, the Roman emperor finally took the official title *basileus* (king).[106] Like

[104] McCormick 2000, 135. The reference is to the period 425 to 600.

[105] Cf. Procopius, *Gothic War* 1.6. John has much to say about the theory of monarchy: *On the Magistracies* 1.3–4.

[106] Exactly what this signified is uncertain: see Chrysos 1978. Emperors of much earlier date had come close to using it: cf. Millar 1977, 613–14.

the Augustae of two centuries earlier, the emperors' wives, if they were determined, could acquire serious political power: the two great examples from this period are Sophia, the wife of Justin II, and Martina, the wife of Heraclius. But the emperors of this era – Justin II, Tiberius, Maurice, Phocas, and then Heraclius, and Constans II – had to tolerate other internal forces, in particular circus factions, prelates and their followers, local men of power, and of course the soldiers. All of these except the soldiers were more powerful than they had been two centuries earlier.

It is a vivid symptom of the diminished power of the emperor that Justin II deferred the power of nominating provincial governors to 'the most holy bishops and principal inhabitants of each province' (Justinian, *Novels* 149), evidently believing that this would improve the flow of taxes.[107] We noted in the previous chapter (p. 263) some of the difficulties Heraclius encountered during the last decade of his rule in controlling his own officials. The official class, throughout this period, worked to a great extent for its members' own benefit.

The formal structure of civil government seems to have been little changed under Maurice and his successors.[108] We meet the senior civilian officials – the praetorian prefects, the Counts of the Sacred Largesses, the Quaestors of the Sacred Palace, and the Master of the Offices – less often, but that is probably a consequence of the poor state of our sources for the reigns of Phocas and Heraclius, except that under Heraclius the office of *sacellarius* (the emperor's treasurer) seems to have gained importance at the expense of the Count of the Sacred Largesses[109] – it is unclear why. How well this administration functioned we shall consider later.

Internal rivals

The loyalty of the soldiers was as always crucial. The emperors Maurice and Phocas were both overthrown by military force, their successors having suborned the soldiers with relative ease. Phocas was able to do this in spite of having previously been no more than a centurion. The most powerful military man in the empire under the emperor was normally the Count of the Excubitors, that is to say the palace guard – namely Philippicus under Maurice, Priscus under Phocas and Heraclius, then Nicetas under Heraclius, and Valentinus under his successor Constantine.[110] Of these

[107] Jones 1964, I, 395.
[108] See the lucid summary of Barnish, Lee, and Whitby 2000.
[109] For the individuals in question, see *PLRE* III, pp. 1483, 1486.
[110] *PLRE* III Philippicus 3, Priscus 6, Nicetas 7, Valentinus 5. The full succession is not known.

guard commanders, Priscus, Nicetas, and quite possibly Valentinus betrayed ruling emperors, Priscus in particular demonstrating remarkable skill as a turncoat. Maurice had been more or less able to rely on Philippicus since the latter was married to his sister.

As for military discipline among the ordinary troops, shortages of resources, combined with the very mixed record of the imperial armies in post-Justinianic times, subjected it to severe strain (above, p. 257). There is in fact no reason to think that the soldiers were any less loyal to the throne than in previous ages; their performance in battle is another matter.[111]

The circus factions, the famous Blues and Greens – the organized supporters of the charioteers who raced in these colours –, though a very old phenomenon, had grown much more powerful in the course of the early sixth century,[112] and spread to many cities.[113] The great Nika riot of 532, in which the city population of Constantinople came near to destroying Justinian, only ended when the emperor's supporters prevailed on the Blues – his own faction – to desist. The factions could bring about the dismissal of high officials such as the Count of the East.[114] When Maurice was faced with a disobedient military in 602,

> he was distraught by anxieties and engulfed in great helplessness … on the fourth day the emperor summoned to the palace the leaders of the circus factions … [and] enquired the precise number of the faction-members … the Roman masses had sunk into passions for the two colours, and thereby extreme troubles came upon our world, since as this raging madness gradually increased the Roman fortunes perished (Theophylact 8.7.8–11, trans. Whitby and Whitby, adjusted).

The factions too deserted him, and a few days later he was killed. The Greens prevented the leading senator Germanus from succeeding him, with the result that Phocas became emperor (Theophylact 8.9.14–16).

So what in the end did the factions' power amount to, and who led and belonged to them? The emperor needed the committed support of at least one of the two main factions, and they were allowed to get away with a great deal of violence; on the other hand they were sometimes severely punished for rioting, punishment that did not, however, seem to change their behaviour very much.[115] Some authors profess to see the factions as

[111] For a good survey of the imperial army in Italy in this period, see T.S. Brown 1984, chapter 5.
[112] Cf. Roueché 1993, 143.
[113] Alan Cameron 1976, 314–17.
[114] Liebeschuetz 2001, 217.
[115] Liebeschuetz 2001, 213.

being, in the main, instruments in the hands of the emperor, others see them as instruments of local bigwigs – who provided at least some of their funds.[116] (Others misguidedly compare them with soccer hooligans). There were also elements of popular protest and popular disorder involved, and these sometimes went far beyond anything that can have been acceptable to the possessing classes. The faction members occasionally performed military duties in emergencies,[117] but at times they were very much out of imperial control; Liebeschuetz has argued quite cogently that their disturbances under Maurice and Phocas, in Egypt for instance, indicate the military weakness of the imperial power.[118] It remains unclear why we hear less of Blue and Green trouble under Heraclius after the 610s: George of Pisidia claims that Heraclius persuaded them to behave themselves (*On the Emperor Heraclius and the Persian Wars* 2.34–70), those in the capital anyway; if so, he must have used some highly convincing threats.[119]

Ecclesiastical power raises questions that are still more complex (and here we shall necessarily be looking forward to the power of religious ideas). Senior churchmen could sometimes take on political and diplomatic missions: Gregory, patriarch of Antioch 570–93, helped overcome a major mutiny on the Persian frontier in 589, and performed other political services for the emperor Maurice.[120] Pope Gregory exercised very great political power in Byzantine Italy. In Constantinople the patriarch Sergios (610–38) seems to have had a measure of political influence with Heraclius.[121] The latter even entrusted the government of Egypt to an ecclesiastic: the Cyrus who later surrendered Egypt to the Muslims was both patriarch of Alexandria and governor of the country from 631 to 640.[122] Throughout the empire, since the times of the emperor Anastasius (491–518), local bishops, lifelong office-holders locally chosen, had gradually assumed more powers in the secular and practical affairs of their communities, though there was little that was systematic about this.[123] Justin II (565–74), as we have seen, allowed bishops a shared role with powerful laymen in the nomination of provincial governors.

[116] Liebeschuetz 2001, 206.

[117] Alan Cameron 1976 attempted to minimize the evidence, but admitted that the factions were 'regularly' among those called on to defend the walls of the capital (109).

[118] Liebeschuetz 2001, 278–9.

[119] It may be that in the capital, the place of most interest to the relevant sources, the Greens were now dominant.

[120] Lee 2007b.

[121] Kaegi 2003, 60, 84, 105–6.

[122] *PLRE* III Cyrus 17 (his exact political office is not clear).

[123] Liebeschuetz 2000, 217–22.

Two distinct though related religious questions arise: (1) whether the conflicts between religious groups within the empire were seriously debilitating; and (2) whether religious concerns in any way hindered emperors or high officials from exercising their power effectively.

As already suggested, the answer to the first of these questions has to be 'yes'. Justinian and his successors put much effort into stamping out Montanists, Monophysites, and others, on occasion using armed force,[124] but as far as the Monophysites were concerned they did not succeed – far from it, and this conflict continued to be a major distraction under Phocas and Heraclius.[125] The population of the capital would not let the emperor Tiberius make a church available to his Gothic soldiers on the grounds that they were Arian heretics (John of Ephesus, *Ecclesiastical History* 3.26). The Ghassan, sometimes called Ghassanids, Christian Arabs who since the time of Justinian had been crucial Roman allies in southern Syria, were supposedly 'a loyal component of the Roman army at the battle of the Yarmuk',[126] but they were Monophysites and one wonders how devoted they were to Heraclius; after the battle many of them, including their leader Jabalah ibn al-Ayham,[127] deserted to the Muslims (only to desert back again two years later). A scholar has recently tried to show that the Egyptian Monophysites – the great majority of the population – did not in fact welcome the Muslim invaders, but he could only do that by putting the question in crude terms and playing down significant evidence:[128] the question is not whether the Egyptians 'reason<ed>, "Since we are Monophysite Egyptians, we no longer want to be Roman" ', but whether they made much effort to resist the attackers – and it is entirely evident that they did not, and that after the conquest, in consequence, the Muslims treated the Christians relatively well.[129] The mutual hatred of Monophysites and Chalcedonians was a serious factor. It was quite unsurprising that the army commander Gregorius, whom Heraclius sent to guard the Cilician Gates against the Muslims, took time out to execute a bishop for being a Monophysite.[130] According to one recent writer, the strong tendency towards religious partisanship was a 'fatal blow' to imperial defence (that is a little exaggerated perhaps).[131] Not surprisingly,

[124] MacCoull 1995; MacMullen 2008, 247–9.
[125] On the latter, see Kaegi 2003, 214.
[126] Howard-Johnston 2010, 472.
[127] *PLRE* III Gabala.
[128] Palme 2012. A classic case of an article that proves the opposite of what the author intended.
[129] Palme 2012, 84, etc.
[130] *PLRE* III Gregorius 17.
[131] Greatrex 2007, 291.

however, some well-to-do Christians in both Egypt and coastal Syria found the prospect of living under Islamic rulers unacceptable, and migrated westwards.[132]

We might compare Heraclius' position in the 630s with that of Queen Elizabeth I's position in the face of Catholic attacks; if the English Catholics had been more numerous and there had been a land frontier with a Catholic power, the result might have been different. But the comparison brings out other features of the empire of Heraclius, in particular the shortage of reliable military commanders (see below).

To return in any case to the effects of religion in the late-sixth and early-seventh centuries, did it hinder high officials? It was hardly of great consequence for the power of the emperor Maurice that the Constantinopolitan patriarch John Nesteutes had a 'magician' of quite high social rank put to death against the emperor's wishes (Theophylact 1.11.16).[133] And the emperor's attention to religious ceremonies no doubt strengthened his prestige with a substantial segment of the population. If Maurice's general Philippicus had actually been able to obtain the head of Symeon the Stylite, a powerful 'relic' with which he wished to protect his army (Evagrius, *Ecclesiastical History* 1.13), he might in fact have improved military morale by this bizarre procedure. Although a modern biographer of Heraclius asserts that he showed 'a strong interest in religious affairs from the beginning' [Figure 7.4],[134] we cannot be sure that he spent much more energy on such pursuits than many other Roman emperors.

Did it then matter much that the churches were now even stronger in relation to the state? It certainly mattered that their officials did not pay taxes and were not subject to criminal law,[135] and that they could use state power against 'heretics' and non-Christians (not to mention lesser privileges). The fiscal effects of monasticism also need to be considered. A cadastral document of the period 525–40 shows that at Aphrodito in upper Egypt monasteries already owned approximately one-third of the land;[136] the proportion will have continued to increase thereafter.[137] Such

[132] Banaji 2011, 136. This is not to say that the Islamic conquest resulted in a large-scale migration westwards, as is sometimes suggested.
[133] *PLRE* III Paulinus 3.
[134] Kaegi 2003, 59.
[135] Heraclius confirmed their privileges in 629: Kaegi 2003, 186.
[136] Gascou and MacCoull 1987, 118. They note that we cannot say whether this was so elsewhere, but no one doubts that monasteries were ubiquitous in all provinces.
[137] Cf. Keenan 2000, 620.

Figure 7.4. Gold solidus of Heraclius, 639–41. Note the ubiquitous crosses, the civilian dress of the emperor and his sons (a), and on the reverse (b) the Latin invocation of victory (the empire's lingua franca was now Greek). Part of the same series as Grierson no. 43 (Grierson 1968, 262)

lands were taxable, but on occasion – how often? – monasteries succeeded in getting their taxes forgiven.[138]

How does the much-talked-of 'holy man' enter into this picture? He could occasionally play a part in discrediting or alternatively legitimating a ruler, as Symeon Stylites (the Younger) and Theodore of Sykeon did when Tiberius was replaced by Maurice, and as Theodore did again when Phocas was replaced by Heraclius.[139] It is hard to say who was impressed and how much. Hagiographers such as Cyril of Scythopolis, a contemporary of Justinian, liked to emphasize the deferential attitude of emperors towards such personages, and the latter could sometimes obtain favours for their

[138] Rousseau 2000, 760.
[139] Whitby 1988, 22; Kaegi 2003, 53, 73.

communities. Beyond that, their main effect was probably to heighten the illusion that divine aid might help the empire or its inhabitants.

If there is any consensus as to what, in addition to external and fiscal factors, weakened emperors in these years, it concerns local men of power, largely landowners. But how much they were a cause of the empire's most serious troubles and not merely a symptom can be disputed. The case always cited is that of the enormously rich and very well-connected Apiones in sixth-century Egypt: they seem, for example, to have made use of imperial soldiers for their own purposes (which was illegal), and they had a private prison on their estates.[140] They were loyal to the throne, as far as is known. (They finally disappear from the documents during the Persian occupation of Egypt in 617–29).[141] More typical perhaps was the family of one 'Abaskiron' (the name comes to us via Ethiopic and is not accurate), whose rebellious violence in the Egyptian delta and elsewhere, during the reign of Maurice, is known from John of Nikiu's *Chronicle* (97): he was a man of wealth who nonetheless initiated extensive mayhem.[142] Yet such disturbances may be mainly a sign of a shortage of military manpower.

Much depends on the Romans' ideas about themselves. But before we can even face that issue we have to look more closely at those who helped the emperor rule the Roman state, not forgetting that even in much earlier times it had sometimes depended on outside helpers. Changes in the nature of Roman identity were not necessarily harmful: the disappearance of Latin from imperial administration, for example, was merely a belated recognition of reality.[143] But patriotism, as Wolf Liebeschuetz has noted, is a real issue here.[144] Did the Armenians so prominent in imperial service identify with the Romans in any sense (Justinian thought that they were barbarians, *Novels* 21)? In what way might it have mattered if they did not? Some of them were certainly, as far as is known, loyal and efficient servants of the emperor, such as the Armenian Isaac who was the exarch in Italy in the 630s.[145] Other Armenians preferred the Persians, as the Armenian history of Pseudo-Sebeos shows for the reigns of Maurice, Phocas, and Heraclius alike.[146]

[140] On the use of soldiers – who may well have been raised and supplied by the rich proprietors – Sarris 2006, 22, 162–75. On the prison: Keenan 2000, 631, referring to *P.Oxy* I.135 = *Select Papyri* no. 26 (AD 579). The extent of the Apiones' wealth has been exaggerated according to Hickey 2012.
[141] *PLRE* III Apion 4.
[142] See *PLRE* III s.v., with Liebeschuetz 2001, 279–82.
[143] See Croke 2005, 73–6.
[144] Liebeschuetz 2001, 347–50.
[145] *PLRE* III Isaacius 8.
[146] See chapters 20–1, 28, and 38 respectively.

The high ranks of Rome's armed forces were sometimes occupied by non-Romans. Fully half of the Roman commanders in Italy between 578 and 604 had been Germans.[147] Of the four Roman commanders at the Battle of the Yarmuk, one was Armenian, the formerly successful general Baanes (Vahan). Another, Nicetas, was Persian,[148] and a third was the Ghassanid Arab previously mentioned, Jabalah ibn al-Ayham. Baanes, whose complete loyalty is highly doubtful,[149] was killed in the battle, and afterwards both Nicetas, the son of one of Rome's fiercest Persian enemies, and Jabalah went over to the Muslims. The Caliph did not trust Nicetas and executed him, but the most extraordinary aspect of the matter is that when Jabalah and his men re-deserted to the emperor two years later they were accepted – a sure sign of the weakness of the Constantinopolitan state. At least we can say that the behaviour of Nicetas and Gabala made it significantly more difficult for Rome to recover from the Yarmuk disaster. In all these tergiversations the commanders in question seem to have been able to carry their soldiers with them.

Most of the inhabitants of the Roman Empire apparently continued to think of themselves as Romans, but what effect did that identity have on them? It is true that in the very long term there had taken place 'the transformation of a state which was the property of all the citizens (*res publica*) into one which belonged to an all-powerful monarch',[150] except that in the seventh century the monarch was (as we have seen) anything but 'all-powerful' – and the transition had taken place long before the crisis we are now examining. The specific internal weaknesses of the seventh-century Roman Empire *as a nation* lie elsewhere: the institutions that had once held the empire together, in particular the imperial cult and the military forces, had been transformed beyond recognition, and religious hostilities continued to eat away at internal unity, perhaps even more insistently than they had in the era of the first Theodosius.

Internal power, external power

It was 'the combination of unlimited economic power and political power in the hands of the propertied class, their emperor and his administration which ultimately brought about the disintegration of the Roman empire', according to a well-informed Marxist historian.[151] (He was referring to

[147] 14 out of 26 to be exact: T.S. Brown 1984, 73. What happened in the next generation is unclear.
[148] *PLRE* III Nicetas 9.
[149] See the sources referred to in *PLRE* III s.v.
[150] Liebeschuetz 2001, 348.
[151] De Ste Croix 1981, 497.

both the periods of failure that have been discussed in this chapter.) One element in this analysis does not stand up, for the emperor's power was far from unlimited during the seventh-century crisis we have been examining. But the propertied class, in this view, persistently placed the main burden of taxation on the shoulders of the poor. Such a theory can maintain that the poor were too poor to provide enough revenue, and too alienated by the oppression that they suffered to care whether the Roman Empire lived or died. The oppression of poor tax-payers was not new in late antiquity, and in order to understand its ill effects we have to attach them to the cumulative, spasmodic, and uneven decline of the Roman economy – a phenomenon which some recent scholarship has done it best to obscure. The historian's real difficulty here is that in the, say, fifty years prior to the Battle of the Yarmuk, we are further than ever from being to able to measure the condition of the Roman economy or the fiscal problems of the Roman state.

That in turn makes it more difficult to estimate the relative importance of the religious differences and preoccupations that diminished the unity and cohesion of the Roman Empire's population, detaching it from its self-confident past and creating intense internal hatreds and fears.

There are almost too many explanations for the failure of the seventh-century Roman Empire, just as there are almost too many explanations of the failure of the western empire two centuries earlier. Justinian's military over-reach (with its fiscal consequences), internal religious conflicts, the vigour and suddenness of the Islamic attack, the weak national consciousness of the provincial elites, were all important factors. Contrary to a common opinion, the emperor's position was also relatively weak, especially perhaps under Maurice and Phocas. How much economic and demographic weakness made a difference it is hard to tell, but the coinage confirms what is in any case obvious that, for a variety of reasons, in particular ruinous wars within what should have been prosperous tax-paying provinces, the economy could no longer support military forces of the size and quality that Rome had often fielded from the third century BC to the fourth century AD. As to whether the empire of Heraclius was actually worth saving is a thought-provoking question, but not a historical one.

We have seen at length in the second half of this chapter how the weakened internal power structures of the surviving Roman Empire made effective defence very difficult indeed, if not impossible. But how, to raise this kind of question for the last time, did the contraction of Rome's external power between 582 and the 640s affect the structures of power within the empire? In general, it weakened the ruling emperor. In periods of foreign incursions, Roman governments and their representatives were radically less able to maintain internal order. Military discipline was poor – though possibly better under Heraclius than under Maurice. At a time when the emperor needed more tax revenues, he probably tended to receive less, especially after the Persian occupation of many Roman provinces under Heraclius. At a time when emperors needed to arouse more support from all social classes, they may well have received less: once again, the irresponsibility of the social elite and the alienation of many of the poor are both visible. There may also have been some connection between, on the one hand, the decline in the myth of Rome's and the emperor's invincibility and on the other the growth in the prestige and power of men of religion. But this needs careful analysis because emperors continued right down to the end to claim military glory – the contemporary poet George of Pisidia compared Heraclius favourably with Alexander the Great. Foreign incursions are in any case likely to have encouraged both attempts to impose religious orthodoxy (in order to please the deity) and a tendency to seek a life outside the political-military world (especially via monasticism, constantly proliferating).

At the end of the previous chapter, I pointed out the main internal factors that seem to have prevented the Roman Empire from resisting the Muslim invasion successfully, emphasizing the vicious circle of foreign invasions and fiscal penury. In this chapter, I have attempted to fill out this picture by considering the failings of the Roman elite and the fissures created by fervent Christianity. It would in any case have been difficult for the Roman state to defeat the Muslims decisively in the 630s or 640s after the destructive and exhausting though ultimately triumphant war against the Persians that had lasted in effect from 602 to 628.

CHAPTER 8

Retrospect and some reflections

Since this book is already to a considerable extent a summary, it could not be summarized without some loss of essential qualifications and nuances. But history books ought to sum up their conclusions, and so this chapter aims to bring out the main themes of the previous seven chapters and to develop them a little further.

It should be plain, first of all, that we can gain a great deal from comparing the Romans of widely diverse periods. Strange to say, the Romans who constructed an empire and the Romans who lost one have very seldom met each other in the pages of a scholarly history. The contrast between these two populations is extremely illuminating. While it is in any case reasonably obvious that the Romans of the third and second centuries BC were warlike and very often aggressive, no one who compares their behaviour with the behaviour of the markedly different Romans of late antiquity could possibly doubt it. Conversely, no one who has studied the mid-republican Romans could possibly write very favourably about the military capacities of the Roman state in either of the two late-antique periods described in Chapters 6 and 7.

More contestably, if we contemplate the cohesive and disciplined Roman state of the middle Republic, the fragmented and distracted world of the Roman state in the age of Theodosius I and his sons becomes even more obviously dysfunctional. This applies still more to the empire of Phocas and Heraclius and to the fragments of it that passed to their successors.

Throughout this book I have attempted to correlate the workings of external power and the workings of internal power. Thus we have been concerned with military, political, social, and economic power all at the same time, but also with gender power and the power of ideas, and with all the channels, especially ideological ones, through which power was exercised. And it has constantly been necessary to ask how much these historical processes disclose the dominance of a single social class.

I asked at the outset why Roman power spread so widely and lasted so long. Many factors worked together in the middle Republic to produce an extraordinary though not uninterrupted train of military victories: these factors included geographical location and demographic success, which was greatly assisted by the enslavement of defeated enemies and by the incorporation of manumitted slaves. And the Romans' exceptional devotion to war becomes visible from virtually the beginning of their well-recorded history.

By the last decade of the fourth century BC, if not earlier, Rome's resources overshadowed those of most of its chosen enemies. With exceptional skill, Rome managed to exploit the manpower resources of other communities, at first the Latins, then, by the 270s at the latest, other Italians. Another feature that emerges clearly by the time of the first war with Carthage is Rome's capacity for absorbing military technology from other nations.

Social discipline, however, was crucial, including the discipline that sustained aristocratic competition while never letting it get out of hand. There is no sign at all in this period that ordinary Romans were reluctant to serve in the army, but an aristocracy, very powerful though not all-powerful, guided the state's external policy and did so in a consistent fashion. Much in all this remains uncertain of course – there are hardly any contemporary texts, and we do not know for instance whether the pathological and intimidating violence that Polybius and his informants saw in Roman soldiers already differentiated them from other Italian peoples around, say, 300 BC.

We are better informed about the 'organizational techniques' (to repeat Michael Mann's phrase) that enabled Rome to hold on to what it had won in peninsular Italy, and they have been studied extensively: colonization, land-confiscations, road-building, the spread of Roman citizenship and Italian identity, together with a limited degree of cultural and religious interference. Rome always tended to favour the local men of wealth and power if they were willing to cooperate, as many of them were.

It only just worked: Hannibal came fairly close to destroying Rome's control over peninsular Italy, and the anger of the Italians themselves boiled over in the widespread revolt of 91–90 BC. On both occasions, however, there were so many Italian 'allies' who were either favourable to Rome or at any rate disinclined to take up arms in rebellion that Rome prevailed.

Explaining Rome's military success in its conflicts with the other great Mediterranean powers, down to the destruction of Carthage in 146, is another challenging task. Carthage and Macedon disappeared as independent states, and the empire of the Seleucids, much reduced, had to recognize its subordinate role after the Battle of Pydna in 168. Naval power was crucial: between 260 (the Battle of Mylae) and 190 (the Battle of Myonnesus) Rome appropriated the Mediterranean, aided once again by several advantages – in particular, the economic resources necessary for the construction and renewal of large fleets, and the more or less voluntary cooperation of Greek cities possessed of naval expertise. But the majority of Rome's fighting over this 120-year period was on land, against many different opponents. It was often an unequal contest, but that was not at first the case with the great Mediterranean powers, and indeed it was not a foregone conclusion either that Rome would conquer a large part of Iberia. Roman armies always prevailed in the end, for reasons that are to a considerable degree unfathomable. Discipline, both social and military, had much to do with it once again, and discipline was at the centre of Polybius' explanation. He also told how the ferocity of Roman soldiers intimidated their Macedonian counterparts, who at the time were probably as tough as any others in the Mediterranean world.

As in Italy, so in the territories that Rome came to control down to 146, the victors devised organizational techniques that were fully sufficient to sustain long-term control: on the one hand, provinces and new magistracies, diplomacy of a much more ambitious kind, accompanied by appropriate slogans, together with, once again, support for cooperative local men of property; on the other hand, brutal displacement when it was considered necessary, culminating in the destruction of the historic cities of Carthage and Corinth and the distribution of their land to Roman and Italian settlers.

Rome suffered some spectacular military defeats during the remaining 130 years of unrelenting imperial expansion – in particular at Arausio (105), Carrhae (53), and the Teutoburg Forest (AD 9) – the inevitable consequences, we may say, of a highly aggressive, sometimes over-confident, manner of dealing with the outside world. But the overall record was still triumphant, for Rome's resources and commitment were enough to deal with any remaining enemy anywhere in the Mediterranean area or in northern Europe – with one exception, the empire of the Parthians. In the north, however, Roman determination flagged at a crucial time (from AD 9 onwards) – for good rational reasons – and so the lands to the east of the Rhine and north of the Danube remained free.

Through all this era of republican and Augustan expansion, we can relate Rome's external and internal power relations. The broad outlines are clear: competition between aristocrats in a warrior society, a society furthermore in which citizen power did not produce detectable democratic aspirations of a serious kind until the age of the Gracchi, demanded constant warfare. Military prestige remained indispensable to anyone who claimed to rule, at least down to the time of Tiberius. In the end imperial expansion became less attractive in large part because it did not suit the monarchical ruler to entrust large army commands to potential rivals, or to raise added revenue for this purpose.

The growth of Rome's external power, meanwhile, revolutionized Roman society, above all by filling it with slaves and by separating the wealthy more and more from the ordinary people. Never a democracy, mid-republican Rome nonetheless left important powers to the citizens. It was the aristocracy that dominated, however – an aristocracy fortified by assorted social and religious practices that cut across class lines, but always an aristocracy. The Roman family contributed to an exceptional degree of civic discipline. Prevailing values such as *fides* and *virtus* tended to strengthen this discipline; the ideal of *libertas*, on the other hand, had more complex effects. In any case the Senate, which was quite large in relation to the size of the citizen population, dominated the body politic. There were some warning signs in the mid-second century, but until about 140 the senatorial order and its allies seemed to be in very firm control. They had enriched themselves and judiciously shared the benefits of successful imperialism. But they had left many of the needs and aspirations of ordinary Romans unsatisfied; and meanwhile their own culture was changing, away from militarism (though this trend must not be exaggerated) and towards competition and enjoyment in many other areas of life (Greek influence making itself felt here).

The discontents of the late Republic were of at least four different kinds. Most easily accommodated were the aspirations of the emerging class of moderately well-off citizens who inspired the ballot laws of the 130s. Much more problematic and never to be accommodated in any way was the rebelliousness of the slaves, at its height between 140 and 71. Extreme trouble came from the non-citizen Italians, who, however, were eventually accommodated at the cost of the most radical policy reversal in the whole of Roman history, mainly encapsulated in the Julian law that gave most of them Roman citizenship in the year 90.

The fourth kind of conflict, no graver perhaps than slave rebelliousness or the discontent of the Italians, but not susceptible of resolution without civil war, consisted of the needs of the poorer section of the population all over the Italian peninsula. These needs could be accommodated, but only when they were channelled into the ranks of quasi-revolutionary armies and subjected to the ambitions of the aristocrats who vied for personal dominance in the two generations from Sulla to Octavian. The result was more than fifty years of turmoil and insecurity.

It is hardly surprising that the senatorial order was unable to control the rise of mighty dynasts from amidst its own ranks. It made many questionable moves, and in the end lost its political supremacy, though not decisively so until the reign of Tiberius; and even then the social class of rentiers, having survived the proscriptions and other dangers of the late Republic and triumviral periods – when many aristocratic families died out or declined – lived on, substantially invulnerable to popular discontent.

Octavian/Augustus, having shed great quantities of Roman and other blood to establish himself as sole ruler, restored a degree of stability that had been unknown since at least the start of the Social War, sixty years before the Battle of Actium. With extraordinary astuteness and a whole panoply of institutional and ideological weapons he rendered himself invulnerable, and eventually handed on power to his chosen successor.

That successor, Tiberius, put into effect a change in Rome's behaviour in the outside world that turned out to be long lasting. Whereas Augustus had challenged the Germanic peoples but not the Parthians, Tiberius largely left both to their own devices. Over the next 200 years Roman expansion sharply decelerated, for several different reasons. These varied in their relative importance: the single most significant factor was probably the need that the emperor inevitably felt to protect himself from usurpers, for it was obvious that a spectacularly successful army-commander threatened the man at the top, while very few emperors desired, as Trajan did, the real task of personally leading arduous conquests. An empire with a long frontier and many restless subjects was inevitably engaged very frequently in secondary conflicts. Rome's military forces were quite a heavy financial burden, especially after the Great Pestilence – beginning under Marcus Aurelius – reduced the tax base, and after Septimius Severus increased the number of legions, and this too was a major restraining influence. It also mattered that many Romans could convince themselves that there was nothing outside the empire that was worth conquering, and that in an absolute monarchy the emperor could claim to be a conqueror without actually conquering anything. It is evident furthermore that virtually the whole governing class had lost its republican passion for military glory.

Thus Rome came in practice to settle down behind a largely unchanging frontier, which it defended in part by periodically terrorizing its neighbours. The empire of Constantine was larger than that of Tiberius, and its frontiers seemed fairly secure, but it had its military weaknesses as well as its potentially severe internal problems. That it had spent too much – in both men and money – during the civil wars after the end of the tetrarchy might not have mattered if it had not been for the certainty that civil war would soon return once Constantine disappeared. It is very tempting to see in the tetrarchic-Constantinian army the seeds of future troubles – huge expense, plus the imperfect identification of 'barbarian' troops with Rome.

Under the middle Republic, a very large percentage of the healthy male citizens did at least some military service: we might guesstimate that in the mid-second century BC at least 50 per cent of them saw service at some time or other. Once the veterans of the Actium campaign had died out, in Tiberius' reign, the proportion of the male population that knew military service at first hand declined: we can estimate that by the mid-second century AD something like 4 per cent of living citizen males were serving in the military or had done so, and an even smaller percentage of the total male population. Of those who did serve at that time, fewer experienced real fighting against formidable enemies. Hence there will have been far fewer citizens with old wounds, far fewer young widows – and far fewer citizens hardened by warfare. The Roman state was less belligerent, and it was less ready for major conflicts.

The durability of the Roman Empire obviously depended a great deal on its internal structures of power, and thanks to an extensive documentary as well as literary record these structures can be better known in the first to fourth centuries than earlier or later. There always remains the secrecy of the imperial court, but the main systems are quite visible.

Roman emperors from Tiberius onwards were absolute and to some extent sacralized rulers, operating within a court setting and within often uneasy relationships with both the senatorial order and the military. They never succeeded either in making themselves personally secure, let alone invulnerable, or in devising an effective system of succession, but the central political structure all the same survived. One reason was that emperors *did* succeed in co-opting a large proportion of the provincial elite, and enough of those more modest provincials who were willing to serve in the army. It is not surprising that they were able to do so, since the Roman Empire now served the economic interests of great numbers of its inhabitants, as long as it kept the peace.

There was something more, however, a widely diffused loyalty to the idea of Rome, ranging from a sentiment that was little more than acceptance of Rome's power to a more articulate belief in the eternity and virtual universality of Roman rule. The latter set of beliefs must have been strongest among those – a minority of the population, but a large and steadily growing minority – who were honoured with Roman citizenship. These factors even carried the Roman Empire through the third-century crisis, though not without major difficulties. This is not to deny that many other of Rome's subjects were alienated and inclined to rebellion.

How was power distributed within the Roman imperial world? Down to the reign of Marcus Aurelius, or perhaps even the Severan emperors, the long-term trend was probably for the central government to take a more active role, but power was inevitably diffused across the military, the landowners, and officials at all levels. There was no bureaucracy in a modern sense, but there was a large network of men ready to carry out the regularized procedures of administration. As far as efficiency was concerned (a largely modern criterion), the results were mixed, better in some provinces than others. Civil order depended to a great extent on self-help, and to a considerable degree penal procedures were determined by social class.

Fitting the various kinds of social power together is only possible up to a point. A reasonably clear model of the Roman Empire's social structure is indispensable. The continuing dominance of the landowning class is in any case clear. But while the chief victims of social power were of course the slaves (we need scarcely repeat the usual qualifications to the effect that slavery was the name of a legal not an economic status), many of the most oppressed were simply the indigent. A woman's power or subjection corresponded, personal factors aside, to her social class, with the main added complication that local traditions had great influence. (It is tempting to suppose that other things being equal it was better for a woman to be as far away from Greek traditions as possible, but semi-Greek Alexandria was very different from semi-Greek Tarsus). The educational practices of the high Roman Empire, which served mainly to convey language skills of various kinds, created an exquisite and secluded world for the social elite in which allusions to the literary classics were essential, while the great mass of the population remained outside, beyond the pale of schooling of any kind. But this system only worked because there were intermediate conditions, and because you could acquire, at one level, literacy, at another level a polished education, *if* you had the money and the will to do so. Once again, much also depended on location, town versus country, the more Hellenized and Romanized places versus the rest (the

Greeks before the Romans in this case, because they continued to favour education more).

The most severe challenge is perhaps to assess the political and social power of ideas. My account tends to play down the reinforcing effect of some prevalent Roman ideas, and it is undoubtedly the case that doctrines about ethics and the organization of society tend to lose their purity in real life. But the idea of Rome itself is not, I think, an idea that has an exact parallel in any modern national idea, exercising a strong appeal to people of heterogeneous origin without much pretence at being democratic (cf., however, above, p. 9). Incorporation was most definitely a limited phenomenon, but at least from Flavian times onwards a very large number of people, not only the upper elite but local elites, as well as most of the military, took it for granted that Rome was worthy of their devotion.

Subversive ideas are easier to isolate and assess, largely because of the victory of Christianity. The rejection of the Roman state by many Christians and by some other cultists was arguably a minor phenomenon as far as power was concerned, but all that began to change when Constantine started giving the Christians privileges. The major effects of Christian ideas came later.

The late-antique contraction of the Roman Empire took place in two entirely separate phases, in the west in the decades on either side of the year 410, in the east in the half-century 600–50. I have to reiterate that these were separate chains of events: they had their similarities, but they will never be understood unless they are analysed separately.

The nature of the contraction that took place in the earlier of these two periods has been contested, but it is plain that the area in the western empire within which the Roman state exercised power was sharply reduced. By 476 there was no western Roman Empire. Our question here is whether the invaders' successes and Rome's military and political failure were due to some new or at least relatively new factors on one side or the other or both. Perhaps because they sensed weaknesses in the empire's defences, the invaders were relatively numerous. The military forces at Rome's disposal were neither large enough, notwithstanding some assertions to the contrary, nor of sufficient quality. They were less well armed and less well trained than their high-imperial counterparts (Vegetius is in the end an incriminating witness). In material terms, the Roman Empire was still rich enough to attract predators but could not apparently afford to defend itself adequately – and it became less able to do so with every new campaign. With respect to morale, these military forces that fought for Rome were too much in conflict among themselves, ethnically and religiously – and this latter conflict mattered.

The spread of Christianity might not have made more than a marginal difference to the empire's ability to defend itself, if it had not brought with it Christian intolerance, intolerance that often took the form of loathing for both pagans and Jews and for those Christians who had different opinions about the supernatural. As for the civilian population, it was unequal to the crisis. While the upper social elite of republican and high-imperial times was driven by personal ambitions and interests, like most human beings, it also demonstrated a patriotic sense of responsibility that was now hard to find. The mass of the population was largely uninterested in defending the status quo, if not alienated from it; our sources only hint at the reasons, but they can probably be summed up as social oppression.

Until the turn of the fifth century, the eastern empire was probably in as much danger from foreign invasions as the western part, but it was the weight of these invasions that collapsed the western regime. Both halves had already been weakened from within (and we can break with the order of the exposition in Chapters 6 and 7 to pursue that story here), but it was the west that was tested.

The central government by this time delivered very little to its subjects, even by ancient standards. Its power has sometimes been misunderstood, in part because it was strong within a narrow range (hence no emperor was murdered between 383 and 455, which was quite unusual for Rome) but weak beyond that range, so that it could not consistently maintain even the modest level of civil order of earlier centuries any more than it could keep the barbarians out.

Emperors attempted to be imposing figures but how much they succeeded is endlessly debatable. The formal structures of officialdom gave them the potential for detailed control, but there were two obstacles in the way in addition to the increasingly frequent loss of local military control and the failures of civil order. Bishops were one, corruption the other. Bishops and other Christian authority figures had already established by the 370s a semi-independent zone of power within the Roman community, but although this zone included more and more people and possessed greater and greater wealth, its effects on the state were still largely indirect. Financial corruption, meanwhile, though not the central problem of Roman government, as has sometimes been claimed, was also a hindrance. Very rapid turnover in high office may in fact have been as great an obstacle to government effectiveness. In these circumstances neither the gathering of taxes nor the raising of army recruits kept pace with the empire's needs.

Nothing could be less surprising than the lack of enthusiasm for the Roman state on the part of the mass of the population in the crucial decades. Between, on the one hand, the delegitimization of cherished religious practices and beliefs and, on the other hand, the oppression of the *coloni* and others, many had reasons to feel alienated. The whole population now experienced a degree of social disintegration. Christian churches offered solidarity to their members, but engaged in sharp and sometimes violent conflicts with their rivals.

Far from being a strong centralized state, the Roman Empire of these years, while still an immense structure that stood up well against its chief eastern rival – Sasanian Persia –, was incapable of mobilizing enough of its resources to resist the Germanic invasions.

There are parallels between the western military crisis and the later one in the east – we could say that the eastern Roman Empire was still, in the early seventh century, rich enough to attract predators but could not afford to defend its full over-extended territorial claims (Justinian's Folly). As in Italy in 410, it could not even defend its physical kernel in a reliable fashion, let alone its main sources of tax revenue, still less its outer periphery. But which other factors mattered most is even harder to discover, the evidence being quite deficient. Poor generalship and poorly disciplined troops undoubtedly contributed. But there were profound differences too: Justinian's empire was in the long run unsustainable as Constantine's was probably not (except that every empire is unsustainable in the very long run).

Other factors that contributed to the Muslims' fatal impact on the empire of Heraclius and his successors are even harder to define, but they include a degree of militarization on the Muslim side that recalls the militarized Roman society of the middle Republic. The Roman Empire's deep division between Chalcedonian and Monophysite Christians was also very damaging. There may have been as much religiosity on the Muslim as on the Christian side, and it can be no more than a question whether the Roman state of these years suffered from devoting so much of its manpower and its economic resources to religion.

The successors of Justinian were absolute monarchs, but their internal power was in practice limited or at least fragile. One striking symptom of this was Justin II's surrender of the power to appoint provincial governors, another was the independent power of the circus factions. But there are other signs too, in particular the power of ecclesiastics and the power of the big landowners. Heraclius could not find within his own realm dependable high-quality military men to take command of his armed forces, and could not harness enough of the energy of his subjects to sustain more than a fragment of what had for long ages been a great and intimidating empire.

Throughout this book there is a tension between material and psychological factors. On the one side I have insisted on the importance for Rome's external power of its manpower resources and its financial resources, which made the construction of a durable empire possible, and I have insisted on the damaging shortage of such resources in crucial periods of late antiquity – shortages that are often, it has to be said, more presumable than proven. In between came long centuries in which occasional imperial misadventures on the battlefield, while they may have helped to define the limits of Roman expansion, made no significant difference to the stability of the state. If one were to speculate, as a historian should from time to time, about other important material factors, there are a number that could quite plausibly be imagined: establishing Mediterranean naval domination, for instance, essentially in the years 260 to 190 BC, may have been made possible by Rome's having better access to ship-building timber than the Hellenistic states (and Carthage?) did.[1] We may also wonder whether the German neighbours of Rome had in the late fourth century AD acquired better weapons or learned better ways of organizing their fighting forces than had been the case in earlier centuries.

Material factors were also of course fundamentally important in the structuring of internal power. One could write a history of the ancient Mediterranean starting from the physical environment and the institution of slavery, which presumably antedated by millennia any attempt to codify it.[2] Add in property rights, and the scene is set for competition for land and for every other economic resource. The permanent victory of large landowners has been a leitmotif of this study, a dominance that was most complete under the middle Republic, then slightly, but only slightly, imperilled in the age of agrarian laws (133 to 59 BC). In the high Empire the emperors protected property rights, though as we saw earlier

[1] Of course there had been a great deal of naval warfare in the Mediterranean from the sixth through to the fourth centuries. Syracuse and Carthage possessed some of the largest navies, and Sicily was no doubt largely deforested of tall trees by the time the Romans first arrived.

[2] Cf. Broodbank 2013, 549.

the price could be high. In late antiquity the large proprietors were largely unchallenged.

Psychological factors have also made frequent and important appearances. The psychological peculiarities of the Roman soldiers of mid-republican times – disciplined obedience, a deep proclivity to bloodthirsty violence, and, more arguably, a strong sense of honour – were some of the main foundations of the mid-republican empire. The ruthlessness, ambition, and courage of many members of the senatorial order were very much in evidence. The professionalism of the high-imperial soldiers, both legionaries and 'auxiliaries', was a psychological fact as well as a tradition instilled in them by generations of officers. In this age, let us say from Tiberius to Gordian III (14 to 244), the psychological characteristics of the leaders of the state – the emperors and the leading officials both military and civilian – were more variable, but we can observe, among such characteristics, that a good proportion of them were markedly, if understandably, complacent with respect to the outside world.

That religious intolerance was a feature of both of the late-antique crisis periods we have examined needs no further arguing. I have suggested that both periods were also marked by a relatively weak national consciousness among the population at large, and that too is a psychological characteristic. It also seems likely, for example, that the increased ferocity of late-antique punishments, had a social-psychological basis. All this too is an essential part of a history of power.

This is not a book about American power, but no historian long resident in the United States can write about Roman power without reflecting about the ways in which, ever since the onset of the Cold War, western writers and film-makers, mainly but not only Americans, have made use of Roman history to justify this or that political line or course of action.[3] In recent years a huge more or less popular literature has grown up around the question whether the USA *is* in some sense Rome, to which the answer is obviously 'No', unless that is you want to treat the Roman Empire as an archetype of empires (and there is of course the intriguing parallel that what passes for the American Empire, like the Roman Empire, came into being in a period of ostensibly and partially democratic government – unlike most other empires). This literature tends to arouse the scorn of scholarly historians,[4] not surprisingly, yet it has a great deal to contribute

[3] See Malamud 2009.

[4] As observed by Vasunia 2011, 232.

to the understanding of the history of empires. When, for example, a historian – prostituting historical facts – claims that the Romans were reluctant imperialists, just like us, we can see the neo-imperialist propagandist at work.[5] The study of modern empires is indeed indispensable to a historian of power.

I was once accused by a right-wing reviewer of suffering from 'the Vietnam syndrome of the American intellectual'. Leaving aside the fact that I was not an American, I consider that living through the Vietnam War as a politically involved person was very valuable to me as a historian. It taught above all how little the words of an imperialistic government may correspond to its actions, and what a great range of perceptions, motives, and attitudes may, sometimes at least, be found in an imperial nation. It taught yet again how the inhabitants of warring states dehumanize one another.[6] And the learning continued long afterwards: an American officer who was deeply implicated in a war crime in Vietnam and was subsequently elected to the United States Senate said to me in 2001, on learning that I had taken part in peace marches during the war, that it didn't matter because we were 'both young and foolish'. Only one of us, Senator!

The clear reason why there is such a large American literature about empires in these times has little to do with historical investigation. It stems partly from the anxiety-producing but unanswerable question how long American military dominance will last. More interestingly, it also stems from the political and moral questions that confront the thinking citizens of an imperial republic. By what right, with what justification, can the United States or its surrogates kill Afghans, Iraqis, Somalis, Syrians, or anyone else?[7] But is it not safer, is it not better in at least some important sense, to live in a world in which an imperial power and its allies make sure that wars are always peripheral? Unless, that is to say, you happen to live in the 'periphery'. A historian may have many things to say about such questions – including the observation that current conditions are radically unprecedented –, but these questions are not historical, they are practical and moral.

[5] Madden 2008.

[6] The classic study of this theme is perhaps John W. Dower's *War without Mercy: Race and Power in the Pacific War* (New York, 1986).

[7] Some of course would be content to rely on a modern equivalent of Belloc's saying: 'Whatever happens, we have got/The Maxim gun, and they have not'.

References

Adams, J.N. (2003). *Bilingualism and the Latin Language*, Cambridge.
Alföldy, G. (1985). *The Social History of Rome* (trans. D. Braund and F. Pollock), London (original edn: *Römische Sozialgeschichte*, Wiesbaden 1979).
Alram, M. (2008). Early Sasanian Coinage. In V. Sarkhosh Curtis and S. Stewart, eds., *The Sasanian Era*, London, 17–30.
Alston, R. (1994). Roman Military Pay from Caesar to Diocletian. *JRS* 84, 113–23.
(1995). *Soldier and Society in Roman Egypt: a Social History*, London.
(2007). The Military and Politics [in the late Republic and the Principate]. In Sabin, Van Wees, and Whitby, II, 176–97.
Ando, C. (2000). *Imperial Ideology and Provincial Loyalty in the Roman Empire*, Berkeley.
(2008). Decline, Fall, and Transformation. *Journal of Late Antiquity* 1, 31–60.
(2011). Law and the Landscape of Empire. In S. Benoist, A. Daguet-Gagey and C. Hoët-van Cauwenberghe, eds., *Figures d'empire, fragments de mémoire: pouvoirs et identités dans le monde romain imperial*, Villeneuve-d'Ascq, 25–47.
Anievas, A. (2010). *Marxism and World Politics: Contesting Global Capitalism*, London.
Arena, V. (2013). *Libertas and the Practice of Politics in the Late Roman Republic*, Cambridge.
Arendt, H. (1969). *On Violence*, San Diego.
Arjava, A. (1996). *Women and Law in Late Antiquity*, Oxford.
Arnason, J.P. and K.A. Raaflaub, eds. (2011). *The Roman Empire in Context: Historical and Comparative Perspectives*, Chichester.
Astin, A.E. (1988). Regimen morum. *JRS* 78, 14–34.
Aubert, J.-J. (1995). Policing the Countryside: Soldiers and Civilians in Egyptian Villages in the Third and Fourth Centuries AD. In Y. Le Bohec, ed., *La Hiérarchie (Rangordnung) de l'armée romaine sous le haut-empire,* Paris, 257–65.
(2004). Aux origines du canal de Suez? Le canal du Nil à la mer Rouge revisité. In M. Clavel-Lévêque and E. Hermon, eds., *Espaces intégrés et ressources naturelles dans l'Empire romain*, Besançon, 219–52.
Ausbüttel, F.M. (2011). Die Gründung und Teilung der Provinz Germania. *Klio* 93, 392–410.

Austin, N.J.E. and N.B. Rankov (1995). *Exploratio: Military and Political Intelligence in the Roman World from the Second Punic War to the Battle of Adrianople,* London.

Averdung, D. and R.K. Pedersen (2012). The Marsala Punic Warships. *Skyllis* 12, 125–31.

Badian, E. (1968). *Roman Imperialism in the Late Republic*, 2nd edn, Oxford.

(1983). *Publicans and Sinners: Private Enterprise in the Service of the Roman Republic*, new edn, Ithaca, NY.

(1984). Hegemony and Independence. Prolegomena to a Study of the Relations of Rome and the Hellenistic States in the Second Century BC. In J. Harmatta, ed., *Actes du VIIe Congrès de la Fédération Internationale des Associations d'Études classiques*, Budapest, 397–414.

(1990). The Consuls, 179–49 BC. *Chiron* 20, 371–413.

Bagnall, R.S. (1993). *Egypt in Late Antiquity*, Princeton.

(1995). *Reading Papyri, Writing Ancient History*, London.

(2011). *Everyday Writing in the Graeco-Roman East*, Berkeley.

Bagnall, R.S. and B.W. Frier (1994). *The Demography of Roman Egypt*, Cambridge.

Bagnoli, M., H.A. Klein, C.G. Mann, and J. Robinson (2010). *Treasures of Heaven: Saints, Relics, and Devotion in Medieval Europe,* Cleveland.

Ball, W. (2000). *Rome in the East: the Transformation of an Empire*, London.

Banaji, J. (2011). Late Antiquity to the Early Middle Ages: What Kind of Transition?. *Historical Materialism* 19, 109–44.

Bang, P.F. (2012). Predation. In W. Scheidel, ed., *The Cambridge Companion to the Roman Economy*, Cambridge, 197–217.

Barnes, T.D. (1996). Emperors, Panegyrics, Prefects, Provinces and Palaces (284–317). *Journal of Roman Archaeology* 9, 532–52.

Barnish, S., A.D. Lee, and M. Whitby (2000). Government and Administration. In *CAH* XIV, 164–206.

Barns, J. (1964). Shenute as a Historical Source. In J. Wolski, ed., *Actes du Xe Congrès international de papyrologues,* Wroclaw, 151–9.

Baronowski, D.W. (2011). *Polybius and Roman Imperialism*, London.

Barrett, A.A. (2002). *Livia: First Lady of Imperial Rome*, New Haven.

Bartman, E. (1999). *Portraits of Livia: Imaging the Imperial Woman in Augustan Rome*, Cambridge.

Bauman, R.A. (1992). *Women and Politics in Ancient Rome*, London.

(1996). *Crime and Punishment in Ancient Rome,* London and New York.

Beard, M. (1990). Priesthood in the Roman Republic. In Beard and North, 17–48.

(2007). *The Roman Triumph*, Cambridge, MA.

Beard, M. and J. North, eds. (1990). *Pagan Priests*, London.

Beard, M., J. North, and S. Price (1998). *Religions of Rome*, 2 vols., Cambridge.

Beaujard, B. (1996). L'évêque dans la cité en Gaule aux Ve et VIe siècles. In C. Lepelley, ed., *La fin de la cité antique et le début de la cité médiévale de la fin du IIIe siècle à l'avènement de Charlemagne*, Bari 127–45.

Bell, H.I., V. Martin, E.G. Turner, and D. van Berchem, eds., (1962). *The Abinnaeus Archive. Papers of a Roman Officer in the Reign of Constantius II*, Oxford.

Bennett, J. (1997). *Trajan, optimus princeps: a Life and Times*, London.
Béranger, J. (1953). *Recherches sur l'aspect idéologique du principat*, Basle.
Bergk, A. (2011). The Development of the Praetorship in the Third Century BC. In H. Beck, A. Duplá, M. Jehne, and F. Pina Polo, eds., *Consuls and res publica,* Cambridge, 61–74.
Bergmann, M. (1998). *Die Strahlen der Herrscher. Theomorphes Herrscherbild und politische Symbolik im Hellenismus und in der römischen Kaiserzeit*, Mainz.
Beschaouch, A. (1966). La mosaïque de chasse à l'amphithéâtre découverte à Smirat en Tunisie. *Comptes-Rendus de l'Académie des Inscriptions et Belles-Lettres*, 134–57.
Birley, A. (1988). *The African Emperor: Septimius Severus*, revised edn, London.
(2000). Hadrian to the Antonines. In *CAH* XI, 2nd edn, 132–94.
(2007a). The Frontier Zone in Britain: Hadrian to Caracalla. In De Blois and Lo Cascio, 355–70.
(2007b). Two Types of Administration Attested by the Vindolanda Tablets. In Haensch and Heinrichs, 306–24.
Bishop, M.C. and J.C.N. Coulston (1993). *Roman Military Equipment: from the Punic Wars to the Fall of Rome*, London.
Bispham, E. (2006). *Coloniam deducere:* how Roman was Roman Colonization during the Middle Republic? In Bradley and Wilson, 73–160.
Bleicken, J. (1982). *Zum Regierungsstil des römischen Kaisers*, Wiesbaden.
Blockley, R.C., ed. (1981). *The Fragmentary Classicising Historians of the Later Roman Empire*, Liverpool.
Bomgardner, D. (2009). The Magerius Mosaic Revisited. In T. Wilmott, ed., *Roman Amphitheatres and Spectacula: a 21st-Century Perspective*, Oxford, 165–177.
Bonamente, G. (2013). Chapter 3: the Frigidus. In Lizzi Testa, 53–70.
Bonamente, G. and R. Lizzi Testa, eds. (2010). *Istituzioni, carismi ed esercizio del potere (IV–VI secolo d.C.)*, Bari.
Boulvert, G. (1974). *Domestique et fonctionnaire sous le haut empire romain. La condition de l'affranchi et de l'esclave du prince*, Paris.
Bowersock, G.W. (1973). Greek Intellectuals and the Imperial Cult in the Second Century AD. *EFH* 19, 177–212.
(1983). *Roman Arabia*, Cambridge, MA.
(1987). The Mechanics of Subversion in the Roman Provinces. *EFH* 33, 291–317.
Bowes, K.D. (2008). *Private Worship, Public Values, and Religious Change in Late Antiquity*, Cambridge.
Bowman, A.K. (1970). A Letter of Avidius Cassius? *JRS* 60, 20–6.
(1986). *Egypt after the Pharaohs, 332 BC–AD 642*, London.
(2005). Diocletian and the First Tetrarchy, AD 284–305. In *CAH* XII, 2nd edn, 67–89.
Bowman, A.K. and G. Woolf, eds. (1994). *Literacy and Power*, Cambridge.
Bowman, A.K. P. Garnsey, and D. Rathbone, eds. (2000). *CAH* XI, 2nd edn.
Bradley, G. and J.-P. Wilson, eds. (2006). *Greek and Roman Colonization: Origins, Ideologies and Interactions*, Swansea.

Bradley, K.R. (1994). *Slavery and Society at Rome*, Cambridge.
Brandes, W. (1989). *Die Städte Kleinasiens im 7. und 8. Jahrhundert*, Amsterdam.
(2002). *Finanzverwaltung in Krisenzeiten: Untersuchungen zur byzantinischen Adminstration im 6.-8. Jahrhundert*, Frankfurt am Main.
Brandes, W. and J. Haldon (2000). Towns, Tax and Transformation: State, Cities and their Hinterlands in the East Roman World, c. 500–800. In G.P. Brogiolo, N. Gauthier, and N. Christie, eds., *Towns and their Territories between Late Antiquity and the Early Middle Ages*, Leiden, 141–72.
Bransbourg, G. (2015). The Later Roman Empire. In Monson and Scheidel, 258–81.
Bratož, R. (2011). Die Auswanderung der Bevölkerung aus den pannonischen Provinzen während des 5. und 6. Jahrhunderts. In Konrad and Witschel, 589–614.
Braund, D.C. (1985). *A Sourcebook on Roman History, 31 BC–AD 68*, London.
(1989). Function and Dysfunction: Personal Patronage in Roman Imperialism. In Wallace-Hadrill, 137–52.
Brélaz, C. (2005). *La sécurité publique en Asie Mineure sous le Principat (Ier–IIIe s. ap. J.-C.)*, Basle.
(2011). Aelius Aristide (Or., 50.72–93) et le choix des irénarques par le gouverneur: à propos d'une inscription d'Acmonia. In *Philologos Dionysios: mélanges offerts au professeur Denis Knoepfler*, Neuchâtel, 603–37.
Brennan, P. (2007). Zosimus II.34.1 and 'The Constantinian Reform': Using Johannes Lydos to Expose an Invidious Fabrication. In Lewin and Pellegrini, 211–18.
Brennan, T.C. (2000). *The Praetorship in the Roman Republic*, 2 vols., Oxford.
Broodbank, C. (2013). *The Making of the Middle Sea: a History of the Mediterranean from the Beginning to the Emergence of the Classical World*, Oxford.
Broughton, T.R.S. (1951–2). *The Magistrates of the Roman Republic*, 2 vols., New York.
(1986). *The Magistrates of the Roman Republic*, III: Supplement, Atlanta.
Brown, P. (1964). St. Augustine's Attitude to Religious Coercion. *JRS* 54, 107–16, repr. in *Religion and Society in the Age of Saint Augustine*, London, 1972 260–78.
(2012). *Through the Eye of a Needle: Wealth, the Fall of Rome, and the Making of Christianity in the West, 350–550 AD*, Princeton.
Brown, T.S. (1984). *Gentlemen and Officers: Imperial Administration and Aristocratic Power in Byzantine Italy, AD 554–800*, London.
Bru, H. (2011). *Le pouvoir impérial dans les provinces syriennes: représentations et célébrations d'Auguste à Constantin (31 av. J.-C.–337 ap. J.-C.)*, Leiden.
Brunt, P.A. (1971). *Italian Manpower, 225 BC–14 AD*, Oxford.
(1975a). Two Great Roman Landowners. *Latomus* 34, 619–35.
(1975b). Did Imperial Rome Disarm her Subject? *Phoenix* 29, 260–70, repr. in Brunt 1990, 255–66.
(1975c). Stoicism and the Principate. *Papers of the British School at Rome* 43: 6–35, repr. in *Studies in Stoicism*, Oxford, 2013, 275–309.
(1988). *The Fall of the Roman Republic and Related Essays*, Oxford.

(1990). *Roman Imperial Themes*, Oxford.
Brunt, P.A. and J.M. Moore, eds. (1967). *Res gestae Divi Augusti*, Oxford.
Bryen, A.Z. (2013). *Violence in Roman Egypt: a Study in Legal Interpretation*, Philadelphia.
Burton, G.P. (1995). The Inheritance of the Consulate in the Antonine Period: a Problem Revisited. *Phoenix* 49, 218–31.
(2002). The Roman Imperial State (AD 14–235): Evidence and Reality. *Chiron*, 249–80.
Busch, A.W. (2007). Militia in urbe. The Military Presence in Rome. In De Blois and Lo Cascio, 315–41.
Caballos, A. (1996). Testimonios recientes con referencía a municipios. In E. Ortiz de Urbina and J. Santos, eds., *Teoría y práctica del ordenamiento municipal en Hispania,* Vitoria, 175–210.
Cain, P.J. and A.G. Hopkins (2001). *British Imperialism, 1688–2000,* London.
Callinicos, A. (2011). *The Revolutionary Ideas of Karl Marx*, Chicago.
Cameron, Alan (1976). *Circus Factions*, Oxford.
(2011). *The Last Pagans of Rome,* Oxford.
Cameron, Alan and J. Long (1993). *Barbarians and Politics at the Court of Arcadius*, Berkeley.
Cameron, Averil (1985). *Procopius and the Sixth Century*, London.
ed. (1995). *The Byzantine and Early Islamic Near East, III: States, Resources and Armies*, Princeton.
(1998). The Perception of Crisis. In *Morfologie sociali e culturali in Europa fra tarda antichità e alto medioevo, 3–9 aprile 1997* (Settimane di Studio del Centro Italiano di Studi sull'Alto Medioevo 45), Spoleto, 9–34.
Camia, F. (2008). Imperial Priests in Second Century Greece: a Socio-political Analysis. In A.D. Rizakis and F. Camia, eds., *Pathways to Power: Civic Elites in the Eastern Part of the Roman Empire*, Athens, 23–41.
Campana, A. (1987). *La monetazione degli insorti italici durante le Guerre Sociale (91–87 a.C.)*, Soliera, Modena.
Campbell, J.B. (1984). *The Emperor and the Roman Army, 31 BC–AD 235*, Oxford.
(1994). *The Roman Army, 31 BC–AD 337: a Sourcebook*, London.
(2002). Power without Limit: 'the Romans Always Win'. In A. Chaniotis and P. Ducrey, eds., *Army and Power in the Ancient World*, Stuttgart, 167–80.
(2005). The Military Reforms of Diocletian and Constantine. In *CAH* XII, 2nd edn, 120–30.
Carrié, J.-M. (2005). Developments in Provincial and Local Administration. In *CAH* XII, 2nd edn, 269–312.
Carson, R.A.G. (1990). *Coins of the Roman Empire*, London.
Cecconi, G.A. (2005). Conscience de la crise, groupements de pression, idéologie du ‹beneficium›: l'État impérial tardif pouvait-il se réformer?. *Antiquité Tardive* 13, 281–304.
(2013). Alan Cameron's Virius Nicomachus Flavianus. In Lizzi Testa, 151–64.

Chalon, G. (1964). *L'édit de Tiberius Iulius Alexander. Étude historique et exégétique,* Lausanne.
Champlin, E. (1980). *Fronto and Antonine Rome*, Cambridge, MA.
Charles. M.B. (2007). *Vegetius in Context: Establishing the Date of the Epitoma rei militaris*, Stuttgart.
Chaussende, D. (2009). Review of Y. Pines, *Envisioning Eternal Empire: Chinese Political Thought of the Warring States Era. Études chinoises* 28, 267–76.
Cherry, D. (1998). *Frontier and Society in Roman North Africa*, Oxford.
Chrissanthos, S.G. (2001). Caesar and the Mutiny of 47 BC. *JRS* 91, 62–75.
Chrysos, E.K. (1978). The Title *Basileus* in Early Byzantine International Relations. *DOP* 32, 29–75.
(1996). The Roman Political Identity in Late Antiquity and Early Byzantium. In K. Fledelius, ed., *Byzantium: Identity, Image, Influence*. Copenhagen, 7–16.
Clark, A.J. (2007). *Divine Qualities: Cult and Community in Republican Rome*, Oxford.
Clark, G. (1993). *Women in Late Antiquity: Pagan and Christian Life-styles*, Oxford.
Clemente, G. (1968). *La Notitia Dignitatum*, Cagliari.
Cloud, D. (1998). The Origin of *provocatio. Revue de Philologie* 72, 25–48.
Coarelli, F. (1984). Comment in W.V. Harris, ed., *The Imperialism of Mid-Republican Rome*, Rome, 85–6.
(1996). Isis Capitolina. In Steinby III, 112–13.
(1999). *La colonna traiana*, Rome.
(2005). Un santuario medio-repubblicano a Posta di Mesa. In W.V. Harris and E. Lo Cascio, eds., *Noctes Campanae. Studi di storia antica ed archeologia dell'Italia preromana e romana in memoria di Martin W. Frederiksen*, Naples, 181–9.
(2008). *La colonna di Marco Aurelio*, Rome.
(2013). *Argentum signatum: le origini della moneta d'argento a Roma*, Rome.
Connolly, S. (2010). *Lives behind the Laws: The World of the Codex Hermogenianus*, Bloomington, IN.
Conrad, L.I. (2000). The Arabs. In *CAH* XIV. Cambridge, 678–700.
(2002). Heraclius in Early Islamic Kerygma. In Reinink and Stolte, 113–56.
Cooley, A.E. (2009). *Res gestae divi Augusti: Text, Translation, and Commentary*, Cambridge.
Cooley, A.E. and B. Salway (2012). Roman Inscriptions, 2006–2010. *JRS* 102, 172–286.
Cooper, K. (2009). Gender and the Fall of Rome. In P. Rousseau, ed., *A Companion to Late Antiquity*, Oxford, 187–200.
Corbier, M. (2005). Coinage and Taxation: the State's Point of View, AD 193–337. In *CAH* XII, 2nd edn, 327–92.
(2006). *Donner à voir, donner à lire: mémoire et communication dans la Rome ancienne*, Paris.
Cornell, T.J. (1989). The Conquest of Italy. In *CAH* VII, 2, 2nd edn, Cambridge, 351–419.
(1993). The End of Roman Imperial Expansion. In J. Rich and G. Shipley, eds., *War and Society in the Roman World*, London, 139–70.

(1995). *The Beginnings of Rome: Italy and Rome from the Bronze Age to the Punic Wars*, London.
Coulston, J.C.N. (2003). Overcoming the Barbarian. Depiction of Rome's Enemies in Trajanic Monumental Art. In De Blois, 389–424.
[Cracco] Ruggini, L. (1961). *Economia e società nell'Italia annonaria. Rapporti fra agricoltura e commercio dal IV al VI sec. d. C.*, Milan.
Cracco Ruggini, L. (2004). The Italian City from Third to Sixth Centuries: 'Broken History' or Ever-Changing Kaleidoscope?. In C. Straw and R. Lim, eds., *The Past before Us: the Challenge of Historiographies of Late Antiquity*, Turnhout, 33–48.
Crawford [Thompson], D. J. (1976). Imperial Estates. In M. I. Finley, ed., *Studies in Roman Property*, Cambridge, 35–70.
Crawford, M.H. (1974). *Roman Republican Coinage*, 2 vols., Cambridge.
(2006). From Poseidonia to Paestum via the Lucanians. In Bradley and Wilson, 59–72.
et al., eds. (1996). *Roman Statutes*, 2 vols., London.
Croke, B. (2005). Justinian's Constantinople. In Maas, 60–86.
Crook, J.A. (1996). Augustus: Power, Authority, Achievement. In *CAH* x, 2nd edn, Cambridge, 113–46.
Crow, J., J. Bardill, and R. Bayliss (2008). *The Water Supply of Byzantine Constantinople*, London.
Curta, F. (2013). Horsemen in Forts or Peasants in Villages? Remarks on the Archaeology of Warfare in the 6th to 7th c. Balkans. In Sarantis and Christie, 809–50.
Daly, L.W., ed. and trans. (1961). *Aesop without Morals: the Famous Fables, and a Life of Aesop*, New York.
D'Arms, J.H. (1990). The Roman *convivium* and the Idea of Equality. In O. Murray, ed., *Sympotica: a Symposium on the Symposion*, Oxford, 308–20.
Daube, D. (1969). *Roman Law: Linguistic, Social and Philosophical Aspects*, Edinburgh.
David, J.-M. (2007). Aux sources de la sanction pénale: les conditions procédurales de la définition du crime, à Rome, sous la République. In J.-P. Genet, ed., *Rome et l'État moderne européen*, Rome, 287–311.
De Blois, L., P. Erdkamp, O. Hekster, G. de Kleijn, and S. Mols, eds. (2003). *The Representation and Perception of Roman Imperial Power*, Amsterdam.
De Blois, L. and E. Lo Cascio, eds. (2007). *Impact of the Roman Army (200 BC–AD 476): Economic, Social, Political, Religious, and Cultural Aspects*, Leiden.
Décobert, C. (1991). *Le mendicant et le combatant*, Paris.
de Kleijn, G. and S. Benoist, eds. (2014). *Integration in Rome and in the Roman World*, Leiden.
Delfino, A. (2009). L'incendio gallico: tra mito storiografico e realtà storica. *Mediterraneo Antico* 12, 339–60.
Demandt, A. (1984). *Der Fall Roms. Die Auflösung des römischen Reiches im Urteil der Nachwelt*, Munich.
De Martino, F. (1973). *Storia della costituzione romana* II, 2nd edn, Naples.

(1975). *Storia della costituzione romana* IV, 2nd edn, Naples.
Dench, E. (2005). *Romulus' Asylum: Roman Identities from the Age of Alexander to the Age of Hadrian*, Oxford.
De Souza, P. (1999). *Piracy in the Graeco-Roman World*, Cambridge.
De Ste Croix, G.E.M. (1954). *Suffragium*: from Vote to Patronage. *British Journal of Sociology* 5, 33–48.
(1981). *The Class Struggle in the Ancient Greek World*, London.
Dettenhoffer, M.H. (2009). Eunuchs, Women, and Imperial Courts. In Scheidel, 83–99.
Diederich, S. (2007). Sklaverei bei den römischen Agrarschriftstellern. In M.E. Kabadayi and T. Reichardt, eds., *Unfreie Arbeit: ökonomische und kulturgeschichtliche Perspektiven*, Hildesheim, 149–65.
Dietz, K. (2011). Zur Verteidigung der Nordgrenze des römischen Reiches in der Spätantike aus althistorischer Sicht. In Konrad and Witschel, 63–77.
Diller, H. (1936). Thessalos 6. In Pauly-Wissowa, *Realencyclopädie der classischen Altertumswissenschaft* VIA, 1, cols. 168–82.
Dixon, S. (2001).*Reading Roman Women: Sources, Genres, and Real Life*, London.
Dmitriev, S. (2009). The Rise and Quick Fall of the Theory of Ancient Economic Imperialism. *Economic History Review* 62, 785–801.
Donner, F.M. (1995). Centralized Authority and Military Autonomy in the Early Islamic Conquests. In Averil Cameron, 337–60, repr. in Donner 2008, 263–86.
ed. (2008). *The Expansion of the Early Islamic State*, Aldershot.
(2010). *Muhammad and the Believers: at the Origins of Islam*, Cambridge, MA.
Dossey, L. (2010). *Peasant and Empire in Christian North Africa*, Berkeley.
Dower, J.W. (1986). *War without Mercy: Race and Power in the Pacific War*, New York.
Downey, G. (1961). *A History of Antioch in Syria: from Seleucus to the Arab Conquest*, Princeton.
Drew-Bear, T., W. Eck, and P. Herrmann (1977). Sacrae litterae. *Chiron* 7, 355–83.
Duncan-Jones, R.P. (1990). *Structure and Scale in the Roman Economy*, Cambridge.
(1994). *Money and Government in the Roman Empire*, Cambridge.
(2006). Who were the ‹equites›? In C. Deroux, ed., *Studies in Latin Literature and Roman History*, 13, Brussels, 183–223.
Eck, W. (1995). Die Umgestaltung der politischen Führungschicht – Senatorenstand und Ritterstand. In *Der Verwaltung des römischen Reiches in der hohen Kaiserzeit: ausgewählte und erweiterte Beiträge* I, Basle, 103–58.
(2000). Government and Civil Administration. In *CAH* XI, 2nd edn, Cambridge, 195–292.
(2012). Die Seuche unter Mark Aurel: ihre Auswirkungen auf das Heer. In E. Lo Cascio, ed., *L'impatto della 'peste antonina'*, Bari, 63–77.
Eckstein, A.M. (2008). *Rome Enters the Greek East: from Anarchy to Hierarchy in the Hellenistic Mediterranean, 230–170 BC*, Oxford.
Eich, A. and P. Eich (2004). Thesen zur Genese des Verlautbarungsstils der spätantiken kaiserlichen Zentrale. *Tyche* 19, 75–104.

(2005). War and State-Building in Roman Republican Times. *Scripta Classica Israelica* 24, 1–33.
Eich, P. (2005). *Zur Metamorphose des politischen Systems in der römischen Kaiserzeit: die Entstehung einer 'personalen Bürokratie' im langen dritten Jahrhundert*, Berlin.
Elton, H. (1996). *Warfare in Roman Europe: AD 350–425*, Oxford.
(2012). Warfare and the Military. In Lenski, 325–46.
Erdkamp, P. (2007a). Polybius and Livy on the Allies in the Roman Army. In De Blois and Lo Cascio, 47–74.
ed. (2007b). *A Companion to the Roman Army*, Oxford.
Fagan, G.G. (2011). *The Lure of the Arena: Social Psychology and the Crowd at the Roman Games*, Cambridge.
Fear, A. (2007). War and Society [in the Later Roman Empire]. In Sabin, Van Wees, and Whitby, II, 424–58.
Feig Vishnia, R. (2008). Written Ballot, Secret Ballot and the *iudicia publica*: a Note on the *leges tabellariae. Klio* 90, 334–46.
Fernoux, H.-L. (2011). *Le Demos et la cité: communautés et assemblées populaires en Asie mineure à l'époque imperial*, Rennes.
Ferns, H.S. (1953). Britain's Informal Empire in Argentina, 1806–1914. *Past and Present* 4, 60–75.
Ferrary, J.-L. (1988). *Philhellénisme et impérialisme: aspects idéologiques de la conquête romaine du monde hellénistique*, Rome.
Findlay, R. (1975). Slavery, Incentives, and Manumission: a Theoretical Model. *Journal of Political Economy* 83, 923–34.
Fink, R.O. (1971). *Roman Military Records on Papyrus*, Cleveland.
Finley, M.I. (1980). *Ancient Slavery and Modern Ideology*, London.
(1983). *Politics in the Ancient World*, Cambridge.
Fishwick, D. (2002). *The Imperial Cult in the Latin West: Studies in the Ruler Cult of the Western Provinces of the Roman Empire* (Leiden, 1987–2005), 8 vols., III.1: *Institutions and Evolution*, Leiden.
Flaig, E. (2011). The Transition from Republic to Principate: Loss of Legitimacy, Revolution, and Acceptance. In Arnason and Raaflaub, 67–84.
Flemming, R. (2007). Women, Writing and Medicine in the Classical World. *CQ* 57, 257–79.
Flower, H.I. (1996). *Ancestor Masks and Aristocratic Power in Roman Culture*, Oxford.
Forni, G. (1953). *Il reclutamento delle legioni da Augusto a Diocleziano*, Milan.
(1992). *Esercito e marina di Roma antica: raccolta di contributi*, Stuttgart.
Foss, C. (1994). The Lycian Coast in the Byzantine Age. *DOP* 48, 1–52, repr. in *Cities, Fortresses, and Villages of Byzantine Asia Minor*, Aldershot.
(1997). Syria in Transition, AD 550–750: An Archaeological Approach. *DOP* 51, 189–269.
Foucault, M. (1980). Truth and Power. In *Power/Knowledge: Selected Interviews and Other Writings 1972–1977*, ed., C. Gordon, New York, 109–33 (the original appeared in Foucault's *Microfisica del potere*, Turin, 1977).

Fournier, J. (2010). *Entre tutelle romaine et autonomie civique. L'administration judiciaire dans les provinces hellénophones de l'Empire romain (129 av. J.-C. – 235 apr. J.-C.)*, Athens.

Fowden, G. (1993). *Empire to Commonwealth: Consequences of Monotheism in Late Antiquity*, Princeton.

(1998). Polytheist Religion and Philosophy. In *CAH* XIII, 538–60.

Frost, H. (1981). *Lilybaeum (Marsala). The Punic Ship. Final Excavation Report*, Rome.

Frye, R.N. (1983). The Political History of Iran under the Sasanians. In *Cambridge History of Iran* 3, 1, 116–80.

Fuhrmann, C.J. (2012). *Policing the Roman Empire: Soldiers, Administration, and Public Order*, New York.

Gaddis, M. (2005). *There Is No Crime for those who Have Christ: Religious Violence in the Christian Roman Empire*, Berkeley.

Galbraith, J.K. (1983). *The Anatomy of Power*, Boston.

Gardner, J.F. (1986). *Women in Roman Law and Society*, London.

Garnsey, P.D.A. (2010). Roman Patronage. In S. McGill, C. Sogno, and E. Watts, eds., *From the Tetrarchs to the Theodosians: Essays on Later Roman History and Culture, 284–450 CE*, Cambridge, 33–54.

Garnsey, P.D.A. and C.R. Whittaker (1998). Trade, Industry and the Urban Economy. In *CAH* XIII, 312–37.

Gascou, J. and L. MacCoull (1987). Le cadastre d'Aphroditô. *Travaux et Mémoires du Centre de Recherche d'Histoire et Civilisation Byzantines* 10, 103–58.

Gaughan, J.E. (2010). *Murder Was Not a Crime: Homicide and Power in the Roman Republic*, Austin, TX.

Gebhardt, A. (2002). *Imperiale Politik und provinziale Entwicklung: Untersuchungen zum Verhältnis von Kaiser, Heer und Städten im Syrien der vorseverischen Zeit*, Berlin.

Gelzer, M. (1962–4). *Kleine Schriften*, 3 vols., Wiesbaden.

(1968). *Caesar: Politician and Statesman* (trans. P. Needham), Oxford, (original edn: *Caesar, der Politiker und Staatsmann*, 6th edn, Wiesbaden, 1960).

Giardina, A. (1977). *Aspetti della burocrazia nel basso impero*, Rome.

Gibbon, E. (1776–1788). *The History of the Decline and Fall of the Roman Empire*, London.

Gilliver, C.M. (1996). Mons Graupius and the Role of Auxiliaries in Battle. *Greece and Rome* 43, 54–67.

Giuliani, L. (2008). *Imagines maiorum*: öffentliche Bildnisstatuen und die Extensivierung der *res publica*'. In M. Bernett, W. Nippel, and A. Winterling, eds., *Christian Meier zur Diskussion*, Stuttgart, 143–59.

Glas, T. (2014). *Valerian. Kaisertum und Reformansätze in der Krisenphase des Römischen Reiches*, Paderborn.

Goldsworthy, A. (2007). War [in the Later Republic and the Principate]. In Sabin, Van Wees, and Whitby, II, 76–121.

Gordon, R. (1990). The Veil of Power: Emperors, Sacrificers and Benefactors. In Beard and North, 201–31.

Gotter, U. (2008). Cultural Differences and Cross-cultural Contact: Greek and Roman Concepts of Power. *Harvard Studies in Classical Philology* 104, 179–230.

(2011). Zwischen Christentum und Staatsraison. Römisches Imperium und religiöse Gewalt. In Hahn, 133–53.

Goukowsky, P., ed. (2001). *Appien, Histoire Romaine, VII: La guerre de Mithridate*, Paris.

Gradel, I. (2002). *Emperor Worship and Roman Religion*, Oxford.

Greatrex, G. (2000). Roman Identity in the Sixth Century. In Mitchell and Greatrex, 267–92.

(2007). Moines, militaires et défense de la frontière orientale au VIe s. In Lewin and Pellegrini, 285–97.

Greatrex, G. and S.N.C. Lieu (2002). *The Roman Eastern Frontier and the Eastern Wars,* II, London.

Green, L. (1999). Power. In E. Craig, ed., *Routledge Encyclopedia of Philosophy*, www.rep.routledge.com/article/5046/

Grierson, P. (1968). *Catalogue of the Byzantine Coins in the Dumbarton Oaks Collection* II.1, Phocas and Heraclius (602–41), Washington, DC.

Griffin, M. (2000). The Flavians *and* Nerva to Hadrian. In *CAH* XI, 2nd edn, 1–83, 84–131.

Grodzynski, D. (1984). Tortures mortelles et catégories sociales. Les *summa supplicia* dans le droit romain aux IIIe et IVe siècles. In *Du châtiment dans la cité. Supplices corporels et peine de mort dans le monde antique*, Paris, 361–403.

Gros, P. (2009). Les limites d'un compromis: de la *domus* vitruvienne à la maison augustéenne du Palatin. In F. Hurlet and B. Mineo, eds., *Le principat d'Auguste: réalités et représentations du pouvoir. Autour de la Res publica restituta,* Rennes, 169–85.

Gruen, E.S. (1991). The Exercise of Power in the Roman Republic. In Molho, Raaflaub, and Emlen, 251–67.

(2013). Did Ancient Identity Depend on Ethnicity? A Preliminary Probe. *Phoenix* 67, 1–22.

Guyot, P. (1980). *Eunuchen als Sklaven und Freigelassene in der griechisch-römischen Antike*, Stuttgart.

von Haehling, R. (1978). *Die Religionszugehörigkeit der hohen Amtsträger des Römischen Reiches seit Constantins,* I, Bonn.

Haensch, R. and J. Heinrichs, eds. (2007). *Herrschen und Verwalten: der Alltag der römischen Administration in der hohen Kaiserzeit*, Cologne and Vienna.

Haeussler, R. (2013). *Becoming Roman? Diverging Identities and Experiences in Ancient Northwest Italy*, Walnut Creek, CA.

Hahn, J., ed. (2011). *Spätantiker Staat und religiöser Konflikt*, Berlin.

Hahn, J. and P.M.M. Leunissen (1990). Statistical Method and Inheritance of the Consulate under the Early Roman Empire. *Phoenix* 44, 60–81.

Haldon, J.F. (1997). *Byzantium in the Seventh Century*, revised edn, Cambridge.

Hall, J.A. and R. Schroeder, eds. (2006). *An Anatomy of Power: the Social Theory of Michael Mann*, Cambridge.

Hall, U. (1998). *Species libertatis*: Voting Procedure in the Late Roman Republic. In *Modus Operandi: Essays in Honour of Geoffrey Rickman*, London, 15–30.
Hammond, M. (1957). Composition of the Senate AD 68–235. *JRS* 47, 74–81.
Handler, S.P., ed. (2013). *International Politics: Classic and Contemporary Reading, Washington,* DC.
Hantos, T. (1988). *Res publica constituta: die Verfassung des Diktators Sulla*, Stuttgart.
Harker, A. (2008). *Loyalty and Dissidence in Roman Egypt*, Cambridge.
Harl, K.W. (1996). *Coinage in the Roman Economy, 300 BC to AD 700*, Baltimore.
Harnack, A. von (1908). *The Mission and Expansion of Christianity in the First Three Centuries* (trans. J. Moffatt, 2nd edn), London (original edn: *Mission und Ausbreitung des Christentums in den ersten drei Jahrhunderten*, Leipzig, 1902).
Harper, K. (2011). *Slavery in the Late Roman World, AD 275–425*, Cambridge.
(2013). *From Shame to Sin: The Christian Transformation of Sexual Morality in Late Antiquity*, Cambridge.
Harris, W.V. (1971). *Rome in Etruria and Umbria*, Oxford.
(1979). *War and Imperialism in Republican Rome, 327–70 BC*, Oxford,
(1984). The Italians and the Empire. In Harris, ed., *The Imperialism of Mid-Republican Rome*, Rome, 89–109.
(1985). *War and Imperialism in Republican Rome, 327–70 BC*, revised edn, Oxford.
(1986). The Roman Father's Power of Life and Death. In *Studies in Roman Law in Memory of A. Arthur Schiller*, Leiden, 81–95.
(1989a). *Ancient Literacy*, Cambridge, MA.
(1989b). The Expansion of the Roman Empire in the West. In *CAH* VIII, 2nd edn, Cambridge, 107–62.
(1990). Roman Warfare in the Social and Economic Context of the Fourth Century BC. In W. Eder, ed., *Staat und Staatlichkeit in der frühen römischen Republik*, Stuttgart, 494–510.
(1992). An Inscription Recording a Proconsul's Visit to Samothrace in 165 AD. *American Journal of Philology* 113, 81–9.
(1994). Child Exposure in the Roman Empire. *JRS* 84, 1–22.
(2002). *Restraining Rage: the Ideology of Anger-Control in Classical Antiquity*, Cambridge, MA.
(2005). The Mediterranean and Ancient History. In W.V. Harris, ed., *Rethinking the Mediterranean*, Oxford, 1–42.
(2006). Readings in the Narrative Literature of Roman Courage. In S. Dillon and K. Welch, eds., *Representations of War in Ancient Rome*, Cambridge, 300–20.
(2007). Quando e come l'Italia divenne per la prima volta Italia? Un saggio sulla politica dell'identità. *Studi Storici* 48, 301–22.
(2011a). Bois et déboisement dans la Méditerranée antique. *Annales. Histoire, Sciences Sociales* 66, 105–140.
(2011b). *Rome's Imperial Economy*, Oxford.

(2012). The Great Pestilence and the Complexities of the Antonine-Severan Economy. In E. Lo Cascio, ed., *L'impatto della 'peste antonina'*, Bari, 331–8.
(2013a). *Politics in the Ancient World* and Politics. In Harris, ed., *Moses Finley and Politics*, Leiden, 107–22.
(2013b). Thinking about Mental Disorders in Classical Antiquity. In Harris (ed.), *Mental Disorders in the Classical World*, Leiden, 1–23.
ed. (2013c). *The Ancient Mediterranean Environment between Science and History*, Leiden.
(2014). Literacy and Epigraphy II. In C. Apicella, M.-L. Haack, and F. Lerouxel, eds., *Les Affaires de Monsieur Andreau: économie et société du monde romain*, Bordeaux, 289–99.
(forthcoming 2016a). Italy and Italies. In F. De Angelis and M. Maiuro, eds., *Oxford Handbook of Ancient Italy.*
(forthcoming 2016b). Religion on the Battlefield: From the Saxa Rubra to the Frigidus. In V. Gasparini, ed., *Miscellanea di storico-religiosi in onore* dell'80° anniversario di Filippo Coarelli, Stuttgart, 437–50.
Hassner, P. (1997). Rousseau and the Theory and Practice of International Relations. In C. Orwin and N. Tarcov, eds., *The Legacy of Rousseau*, Chicago, 200–19.
Hauken, T. (1998). *Petition and Response. An Epigraphic Study of Petitions to Roman Emperors 181–249*, Bergen.
Haynes, I. (2013). *Blood of the Provinces: The Roman Auxilia and the Making of Provincial Society from Augustus to the Severans*, Oxford.
Heather, P.J. (1991). *Goths and Romans 332–489*, Oxford.
(1994). New Men for New Constantines? Creating an Imperial Elite in the Eastern Mediterranean. In P. Magdalino, ed., *New Constantines: the Rhythm of Imperial Renewal in Byzantium, 4th–13th Centuries*, Aldershot, 11–33.
(1998). Senators and Senates. In *CAH* XIII, 184–210.
(2005). *The Fall of the Roman Empire*, London.
(2010a). *Empires and Barbarians: the Fall of Rome and the Birth of Europe*, Oxford.
(2010b). Elite Militarization and the Post-Roman West. In Bonamente and Lizzi Testa, 245–65.
Heinen, H. (2005). Die Anfänge der Beziehungen Roms zum nördlichen Schwarzmeerraum. In A. Coskun, ed., *Roms auswärtige Freunde in der späten Republik und im frühen Prinzipat*, Göttingen, 31–54.
Hemelrijk, E.A. (2014). Roman Citizenship and the Integration of Women into the Local Towns of the Latin West. In de Kleijn and Benoist, 247–60.
Hendy, M.F. (1985). *Studies in the Byzantine Monetary Economy, c. 300–1450*, Cambridge.
Herklotz, F. (2007). *Prinzeps und Pharao. Der Kult des Augustus in Ägypten*, Frankfurt am Main.
Hickey, T. (2012). *Wine, Wealth, and the State in Late-Antique Egypt: the House of Apion at Oxyrhynchus*, Ann Arbor.
Hin, S. (2013). *The Demography of Roman Italy: Population Dynamics in an Ancient Conquest Society 201 BCE-14 CE*, Cambridge.
Hind, J.G.F. (1994). Mithridates. In *CAH* IX, 2nd edn, 129–64.

Hobson, J.M. (2006). Mann, the State and War. In Hall and Schroeder, 150–66.
Hodges, R. (2010). AD 536: the Year Merlin (Supposedly) Died. In A.B. Mainwaring, R. Giegengack, and C. Vita-Finzi, eds., *Climate Crises in Human History*, Philadelphia, 73–84.
Hölkeskamp, K.-J. (2009). Review of Eckstein. *Mediterranean Anarchy, Interstate War, and the Rise of Rome. Classical Review* 59, 211–14.
(2010). *Reconstructing the Roman Republic: an Ancient Political Culture and Modern Research*, revised edn, trans. H. Heitmann-Gordon, Princeton.
Hoffmann, D. (1969–1970). *Das spätrömische Bewegungsheer und die Notitia dignitatum*, 2 vols., Düsseldorf.
Hoffmann-Salz, J. (2014). Von Räuberhauptmännern zu guten Römern: Die lokalen Eliten des Hauran in der Kaiserzeit. *Zeitschrift für Papyrologie und Epigraphik* 189, 293–304.
Holum, K.G. (1982). *Theodosian Empresses: Women and Imperial Dominion in Late Antiquity*, Berkeley.
Hopkins, K. (1961). Social Mobility in the Later Roman Empire: the Evidence of Ausonius. *CQ* 11, 239–49.
(1978). *Conquerors and Slaves*, Cambridge.
(1991). From Violence to Blessing: Symbols and Rituals in Ancient Rome. In Molho, Raaflaub, and Emlen, 479–98.
(1998). Christian Number and its Implications. *Journal of Early Christian Studies* 6, 185–226.
(2009). The Political Economy of the Roman Empire. In Morris and Scheidel, 178–204.
Hopkins, K. and G. Burton (1983). Ambition and Withdrawal: the Senatorial Aristocracy under the Emperors. In Hopkins, *Death and Renewal*, Cambridge, 120–200.
Hopwood, K. (2002). Aspects of Violent Crime in the Roman Empire. In *Thinking Like a Lawyer: Essays on Legal History and General History for John Crook on his Eightieth Birthday*, Leiden, 63–80.
Horden, P. (2005). Mediterranean Plague in the Age of Justinian. In Maas, 134–60.
Hornblower, S. (2007). Warfare in Ancient Literature: the Paradox of War. In Sabin, Van Wees, and Whitby, I, 22–53.
Howard-Johnston, J. (2010). *Witnesses to a World Crisis: Historians and Histories of the Middle East in the Seventh Century*, Oxford.
Humfress, C. (2010). Episcopal Power in Forensic Contexts: the Evidence from the Theodosian Code. In Bonamente and Lizzi Testa, 267–72.
(2012). Civil Law and Social Life. In Lenski, 205–25.
Humm, M. (2005). *Appius Claudius Caecus: la République accomplie*, Rome.
Humphries, M. (2007). International Relations [in the Later Roman Empire]. In Sabin, Van Wees, and Whitby, II, 235–69.
Hunt, D. (1998). The Church as a Public Institution [sic]. In *CAH* XIII, 238–76.
Huyse, P., ed. (1999). *Die dreisprachige Inschrift Šbuhrs I. an der Ka'ba-i Zardušt (ŠKZ)* (*Corpus Inscriptionum Iranicarum* III, 1, 1), London.

Inglebert, H. (2002). Citoyenneté romaine, romanités et identités romaines sous l'Empire. In H. Inglebert, ed., *Idéologies et valeurs civiques dans le monde romain: hommage à Claude Lepelley*, Paris, 241–60.
Isaac, B. (1992). *The Limits of Empire*, 2nd edn, Oxford.
(1995). The Army in the Late Roman East: the Persian Wars and the Defence of the Byzantine Provinces. In Averil Cameron 1995, 125–55, repr. with postscript in *The Near East under Roman Rule: Selected Papers*, Leiden, 437–69.
(2004). *The Invention of Racism in Classical Antiquity*, Princeton.
James, S. (1988). The *fabricae*: State Arms Factories of the Later Roman Empire. In J.C. Coulston, ed., *Military Equipment and the Identity of Roman Soldiers*, Oxford, 257–331.
Jones, A.H.M. (1949). The Roman Civil Service (Clerical and Sub-clerical Grades). *JRS* 39, 38–55, cited from *Studies in Roman Government and Law*, Oxford, 1960, 151–75.
(1964). *The Later Roman Empire, 284–602 AD*. 3 vols., Oxford.
Jones, C.P. (1978). *The Roman World of Dio Chrysostom*, Cambridge, MA.
(2004). The Revolt of Aristonicus and the New Metropolis Inscriptions. *Journal of Roman Archaeology* 17, 469–85.
Kaegi, W.E. (2003). *Heraclius, Emperor of Byzantium*, Cambridge.
(2010). *Muslim Expansion and Byzantine Collapse in North Africa*, Cambridge.
Kaizer, T. and M. Facella, eds. (2010). *Kingdoms and Principalities in the Roman Near East*, Stuttgart.
Kautsky, J.H. (1982). *The Politics of Aristocratic Empires*, Chapel Hill, NC.
Kay, P. (2014). *Rome's Economic Revolution*, Oxford.
Keenan, J.G. (2000). Egypt. In *CAH* XIV, 612–37.
Kehoe, D.P. (2007). *Law and the Rural Economy in the Roman Empire*, Ann Arbor.
Kelly, C. (1998). Empires, Government and Bureaucracy. In *CAH* XIII, 138–83.
(2004). *Ruling the Later Roman Empire*, Cambridge, MA.
(2012). Bureaucracy and Government. In Lenski, 183–204.
Kelly, J.M. (1966). *Roman Litigation*, Oxford.
Kelly, J.N.D. (1995). *Golden Mouth. The Story of John Chrysostom – Ascetic, Preacher, Bishop*, Ithaca, NY.
Kennedy, H. (2001). *The Armies of the Caliphs: Military and Society in the Early Islamic State*, London.
Kent, J.P.C. (1994). *The Roman Imperial Coinage. 10, The Divided Empire and the Fall of the Western Parts, A. D. 395–491*, London.
Kent, P. (2012). Reconsidering socii in Roman Armies before the Punic Wars. In Roselaar, 71–83.
Klein, C.F. (2001). Impersonation of Deities. In D. Carrasco, ed., *The Oxford Encyclopedia of Mesoamerican Cultures*, Oxford, II, 33–7.
Kloft, H. (1970). *Liberalitas Principis. Herkunft und Bedeutung. Studien zur Prinzipatsideologie*, Cologne.
Kneissl, P. (1969). *Die Siegestitulatur der römischen Kaiser. Untersuchungen zu den Siegerbeinamen des ersten und zweiten Jahrhunderts*, Göttingen.
Knight, A. (2002). *Mexico, from the Beginning to the Spanish Conquest*, Cambridge.

Kolb, A. (2000). *Transport und Nachrichtentransfer im Römischen Reich*, Berlin.
(2003). Wege der Übermittlung politischer Inhalte im Alltag Roms. In G. Weber and M. Zimmermann, eds., *Propaganda – Selbstdarstellung – Repräsentation im römischen Kaiserreich des 1. Jhs. n. Chr*, Stuttgart, 127–43.
Konrad, M. and C. Witschel, eds., (2011). *Römische Legionslager in den Rhein- und Donauprovinzen – Nuclei spätantik-frühmittelalterlichen Lebens?* Munich.
Kovács, P. (2009). *Marcus Aurelius' Rain Miracle and the Marcomannic Wars*, Leiden.
Krieckhaus, A. (2006). *Senatorische Familien und ihre patriae (1./2. Jahrhundert n. Chr.)*, Hamburg.
Kroll, J. (2012). Review of Gaughan, *Murder Was not a Crime*. *JRS* 102, 355–6.
Kulikowski, M.E. (2000). The *Notitia Dignitatum* as a Historical Source. *Historia* 49, 358–377
(2012). Constantine and the Northern Barbarians. In Lenski, 347–76.
Kunkel, W. and R. Wittmann (1995). *Staatsordnung und Staatspraxis der römischen Republik II. Die Magistratur*, Munich.
Lane Fox, R. (1986). *Pagans and Christians*, London.
(1994). Literacy and Power in Early Christianity. In A.K. Bowman and G. Woolf, eds., *Literacy and Power in the Ancient World.*, Cambridge, 126–48.
La Rocca, E. (1994). Arcus et arae Claudii. In V.M. Strocka, ed., *Die Regierungszeit des Kaiser Claudius (41–54 n.Chr.): Umbruch oder Episode?* Mainz, 267–93.
La Rocca, E. and S. Tortorella, eds. (2008). *Trionfi romani*, Milan.
Lavan, M. (2013). *Slaves to Rome: Paradigms of Empire in Roman Culture*, Cambridge.
(forthcoming). *Making Citizens: Quantifying the Spread of Citizenship from Augustus to Caracalla.*
Le Bohec, Y. (2010). Préface. In M. Vannesse, *La défense de l'Occident romain pendant l'Antiquité tardive: recherches géostratégiques sur l'Italie de 284 à 410 ap. J.-C.*, Brussels, 6–7.
Lee, A.D. (1998). The Army. In *CAH* XIII, 211–37.
(2007a). Warfare and the State [in the Later Roman Empire]. In Sabin, Van Wees, and Whitby, II, 379–423.
(2007b). Episcopal Power and Perils in the Late-Sixth Century: the Case of Gregory of Antioch. In *Wolf Liebeschuetz Reflected: Essays Presented by Colleagues, Friends, and Pupils*, London, 99–106.
Le Gall, J. (1990). Le serment à l'empereur: une base méconnue de la tyrannie impériale sous le Haut-Empire?. In Nicolet, 165–80.
Lendon, J.E. (1997). *Empire of Honour: the Art of Government in the Roman Empire*, Oxford.
(2006). The Legitimacy of the Roman Emperor: against Weberian Legitimacy and Imperial 'Strategies of Legitimation'. In A. Kolb, ed., *Herrschaftsstrukturen und Herrschaftspraxis*, Berlin, 53–63.
Lenski, N., ed. (2012). *The Cambridge Companion to the Age of Constantine*, revised edn, Cambridge.

Leunissen, P.M.M. (1989). *Konsuln und Konsulare in der Zeit von Commodus bis Severus Alexander (180–235 n. Chr.). Prosopographische Untersuchungen zur senatorischen Elite im römischen Kaiserreich*, Amsterdam.

Levick, B. (1982). Propaganda and the Imperial Coinage. *Antichthon* 16, 104–16.

(1990). *Claudius*, New Haven.

ed. (2000). *The Government of the Roman Empire: a Sourcebook*, 2nd edn, London.

Lewin, A. (2002). Politics and *Limites* in the East. In P. Freeman, J. Bennett, Z.T. Fiema, and B. Hoffmann, eds., *Limes XVIII: Proceedings of the XVIIIth International Congress of Roman Frontier Studies*, Oxford, 1, 91–101.

Lewin, A. and P. Pellegrini, eds. (2007). *The Late Roman Army in the Near East from Diocletian to the Arab Conquest*, Oxford.

Lewis, N. and M. Reinhold (1990). *Roman Civilization: Selected Readings*, 3rd edn, New York.

Leyerle, B. (2009). Mobility and the Traces of Empire. In P. Rousseau, *A Companion to Late Antiquity*, Chichester, 110–23.

Liebeschuetz, J.H.W.G. (1990). *Barbarians and Bishops: Army, Church, and State in the Age of Arcadius and Chrysostom*, Oxford.

(2000). Administration and Politics in the Cities of the Fifth to the Mid Seventh Century: 425–640. In *CAH* XIV, 207–37.

(2001). *Decline and Fall of the Roman City*, Oxford.

Linderski, J. (1986). Watching the Birds: Cicero the Augur and the Augural templa. *Classical Philology* 81, 330–40, repr. in *Roman Questions*, Stuttgart, 1995, 485–95.

Linke, B. (2006). Bürger ohne Staat? Die Integration der Landbevölkerung in der römischen Republik. In M. Jehne and R. Pfeilschifter, eds., *Herrschaft ohne Integration? Rom und Italien in republikanischer Zeit*, Frankfurt am Main, 65–94.

Lintott, A.W. (1993). *Imperium Romanum: Politics and Administration*, London.

(1999). *The Constitution of the Roman Republic*, Oxford.

Little, L.K. (2007). Life and Afterlife of the First Plague Pandemic. In Little, ed., *Plague and the End of Antiquity: the Pandemic of 541–750*. Cambridge, 3–32.

Lizzi Testa, R., ed. (2013). *The Strange Death of Pagan Rome*, Turnhout.

Lo Cascio, E. (1988). Ancora sui censi minimi delle cinque classi ‹serviane›. *Athenaeum* 66, 273–302.

(2007). Il ruolo dei ‹vici› e delle ‹regiones› nel controllo della popolazione e nell'amministrazione di Roma. In Haensch and Heinrichs, 145–59.

Low, P. (2007). *Interstate Relations in Classical Greece: Morality and Power*, Cambridge.

Lui, J.T. (1985). An Equilibrium Queuing Model of Bribery. *Journal of Political Economy* 93, 760–81.

Lukes, S., ed. (1986). *Power*, Oxford.

Maas, M., ed. (2005). *The Cambridge Companion to the Age of Justinian,* Cambridge.

(2005). Roman Questions, Byzantine Answers. In Maas, 3–27.

MacBain, B. (1982). *Prodigy and Expiation: a Study in Religion and Politics in Republican Rome*, Brussels.
MacCormack, S. (1981). *Art and Ceremony in Late Antiquity*, Berkeley.
MacCoull, L. (1995). 'When Justinian Was Upsetting the World': a Note on Soldiers and Religious Coercion in Sixth-century Egypt. In *Peace and War in Byzantium: Essays in Honor of George T. Dennis*, Washington, DC, 106–13.
Mackie, N. (1992). Popularis Ideology and Popular Politics at Rome in the First Century BC. *Rheinisches Museum für Philologie* 135, 49–73.
MacMullen, R. (1963). *Soldier and Civilian in the Later Roman Empire*, Cambridge, MA.
(1964). Social Mobility and the Theodosian Code. *JRS* 54, 49–53.
(1966). *Enemies of the Roman Order*, Cambridge, MA.
(1974). *Roman Social Relations, 50 BC to AD 284*, New Haven.
(1984). *Christianizing the Roman Empire (AD 100–400)*, New Haven.
(1985). How to Revolt in the Roman Empire. *Rivista storica dell'antichità* 15, 67–76, repr. in MacMullen 1990, 198–203.
(1986a). Judicial Savagery in the Roman Empire. *Chiron* 16, 147–66, repr. in MacMullen 1990, 204–17.
(1986b). Personal Power in the Roman Empire. *American Journal of Philology* 107, 512–24, repr. in MacMullen 1990, 190–7.
(1988). *Corruption and the Decline of Rome*, New Haven.
(1990). *Changes in the Roman Empire: Essays in the Ordinary*, Princeton.
(2006). The Power of the Roman Empire. *Historia* 55, 471–81.
(2008). The Problem of Fanaticism. *EFH* 54, 227–51.
Madden, T.F. (2008). *Empires of Trust: How Rome Built – and America is Building – a New World*, New York.
Madsen, J.M. (2009). The Ambitions of Mithridates VI: Hellenistic Kingship and Modern Interpretations. In J.M. Højte, ed., *Mithridates VI and the Pontic Kingdom*, Aarhus, 191–201.
Maier, C.S. (2006). *Among Empires: American Ascendancy and its Predecessors*, Cambridge, MA.
Maiuro, M. (2012). *Res Caesaris: ricerche sulla proprietà imperiale nel principato*, Bari.
Malamud, M. (2009). *Ancient Rome and Modern America*, Chichester.
Mann, M. (1986). *The Sources of Social Power*, 1, Cambridge.
(2006). The Sources of Social Power Revisited: a Response to Criticism. In Hall and Schroeder, 343–96.
Manning, S. (2013). The Roman World and Climate: Context, Relevance of Climate Change, and Some Issues. In W.V. Harris, ed., *The Ancient Mediterranean Environment between Science and History*, Leiden, 103–70.
Marcone, A. (1998). Late Roman Social Relations. In *CAH* XIII, 338–70.
Marichal, R. (1988). *Les graffites de La Graufesenque*, Paris.
Marsden, A.B. (1997). Between Principate and Dominate: Imperial Styles under the Severan Dynasty and the Divine Iconography of the Imperial House on Coins, Medallions, and Engraved Gemstones AD 193 to 235. *Journal of the British Archaeological Association* 150, 1–16.

Marzano, A. (2007). *Roman Villas in Central Italy: a Social and Economic History*, Leiden.
Mattern, S.P. (1999). *Rome and the Enemy: Imperial Strategy in the Principate*, Berkeley and Los Angeles.
Mattingly, D.J. (2011). *Imperialism, Power, and Identity: Experiencing the Roman Empire*, Princeton.
Mattingly, H. (1940). *Coins of the Roman Empire in the British Museum IV: From Antoninus Pius to Commodus*, London.
(1966). *Coins of the Roman Empire in the British Museum III: Nerva to Hadrian*, revised edn, London.
(1976). *Coins of the Roman Empire in the British Museum I: Augustus to Vitellius*, corrected edn, London.
McCormick, M. (2000). Emperor and Court. In *CAH* XIV, 135–63.
(2001). *Origins of the European Economy: Communications and Commerce, AD 300–900*, Cambridge.
McDonnell, M. (2006). *Roman Manliness:* virtus *and the Roman Republic*, Cambridge.
McGushin, P. (1992). *Sallust: the Histories*, vol. 1. Oxford.
McLynn, N.B. (1994). *Ambrose of Milan: Church and Court in a Christian Capital.* Berkeley.
(2005). 'Genere Hispanus': Theodosius, Spain and Nicene Orthodoxy. In K. Bowes and M. Kulikowski, eds., *Hispania in Late Antiquity: Current Perspectives*, Boston, 77–120.
Mennen, I. (2011). *Power and Status in the Roman Empire, AD 193–284*, Leiden.
Metcalf, D.M. (1962). The Slavonic Threat to Greece circa 580. Some Evidence from Athens. *Hesperia* 31, 134–57.
Michels, A.K. (1967). *The Calendar of the Roman Republic*, Princeton.
Miles, G.B. (1990). Roman and Modern Imperialism: a Reassessment. *Comparative Studies in Society and History* 32, 629–59.
Millar, F. (1977). *The Emperor in the Roman World*, London.
(1984). The Political Character of the Classical Roman Republic, 200–151 BC. *JRS* 74, 1–19.
(1990). L'empereur romain comme décideur. In Nicolet, 207–20.
(1993). *The Roman Near East: 31 BC-AD 337*, Cambridge, MA.
(1998). *The Crowd in Rome in the Late Republic*, Ann Arbor.
(2002). *The Roman Republic in Political Thought*, Hanover, NH.
Mitchell, S. (1993). *Anatolia: Land, Men, and Gods in Asia Minor*, 2 vols., Oxford.
Mitchell, S. and G. Greatrex, eds. (2000). *Ethnicity and Culture in Late Antiquity*, London.
Modrzejewski, J. (1974). À propos de la tutelle dative des femmes en Égypte romaine. In E. Kiessling and H.A. Rupprecht, eds., *Akten des XIII. Internationalen Papyrologenkongresses*, Munich, 264–92.
Molho, A., K.A. Raaflaub, and J. Emlen, eds. (1991). *City States in Classical Antiquity and Medieval Italy: Athens and Rome, Florence and Venice*, Stuttgart.

Monson, A. and W. Scheidel, eds. (2015). *Fiscal Regimes and the Political Economy of Premodern States*, Cambridge.

de Montesquieu, Charles de Secondat, Baron (1965). *Considerations on the Causes of the Greatness of the Romans and their Decline* (trans. D. Lowenthal), Indianapolis (original edn: *Considérations sur les causes de la grandeur des Romains et de leur décadence*, 1734).

Morales, H. (2008). The History of Sexuality. In T. Whitmarsh, ed., *The Cambridge Companion to the Greek and Roman Novel*, Cambridge, 39–55.

Morimoto, N. (1994). The *diwans* as Registers of the Arab Stipendiaries in Early Islamic Egypt. In *Itinéraires d'Orient: hommages à Claude Cahe*, Bures-sur-Yvette, 351–65.

Morley, N. (2011). Slavery under the Principate. In K. Bradley and P. Cartledge, eds., *The Cambridge World History of Slavery I: The Ancient Mediterranean World*, Cambridge, 265–86.

Morris, I. and W. Scheidel, eds. (2009). *The Dynamics of Ancient Empires: State Power from Assyria to Byzantium*, Oxford.

Motyl, A.J. (2001). *Imperial Ends: the Decay, Collapse, and Revival of Empires*, New York.

Mouritsen, H. (1998). *Italian Unification: a Study in Ancient and Modern Historiography*, London.

(2001). *Plebs and Politics in the Late Roman Republic*, Cambridge.

(2011). *The Freedman in the Roman World*, Cambridge.

Nedergaard, E. (1993). Arcus Augusti (a. 19 a.C.). In Steinby, I, 81–5.

Nicasie, M.J. (1998). *Twilight of Empire: the Roman Army from the Reign of Diocletian until the Battle of Adrianople*, Amsterdam.

Nicolet, C., (1966). *L'ordre équestre à l'époque républicaine*, 2 vols., Paris.

(1976). *Le métier de citoyen dans la Rome républicaine*, Paris.

(1988). *Rendre à César: économie et société dans la Rome antique*, Paris.

ed. (1990). *Du pouvoir dans l'antiquité: mots et réalités*, Geneva.

Nisbet, R.G.M. and M. Hubbard (1970). *A Commentary on Horace: Odes Book I*, Oxford.

Nock, A.D. (1947). The Emperor's Divine *comes*. *JRS* 37, 102–16, repr. in his *Essays on Religion in the Ancient World* (Oxford, 1972), II, 653–75.

Noreña, C. (2009). The Ethics of Autocracy in the Roman World. In R.K. Balot, ed., *A Companion to Greek and Roman Political Thought*, Chichester, 266–79.

North, J.A. (1981). The Development of Roman Imperialism. *JRS* 71, 1–9.

(1986). Review of P. Moreau, *Clodiana Religio*, and other books. *JRS* 76, 251–8.

(1989). Review of Brunt, *The Fall of the Roman Republic and Related Essays*. *JRS* 79, 151–6.

(2011). *Lex Domitia* Revisited. In J.H. Richardson and F. Santangelo, eds., *Priests and State in the Roman World*, Stuttgart, 39–61.

Oakley, S.P. (1985). Single Combat in the Roman Republic. *CQ* 35, 392–410.

(1997–2005). *A Commentary on Livy, Books VI-X*, 4 vols., Oxford.

Östenberg, I. (2011). *Staging the World: Spoils, Captives and Representations in the Roman Triumphal Procession*, Oxford.

Oliver, J.H., ed. (1989). *Greek Constitutions of Early Roman Emperors from Inscriptions and Papyri*, Philadelphia.

Palme, B. (2012). Political Identity versus Religious Distinction? The Case of Egypt in the Later Roman Empire. In W. Pohl, C. Gantner, and R. Payne, eds., *Visions of Community in the Post-Roman World: the West, Byzantium and the Islamic World, 300–1100*, Farnham, Surrey, 81–98.

(2014). Roman Litigation: Reports of Court Proceedings. In J.G. Keenan, J.G. Manning, and U. Yiftach-Firanko, eds., *Law and Legal Practice in Egypt from Alexander to the Arab Conquest*, Cambridge, 482–502.

Palombi, D. (1996). N[umen] Augusti, Ara. In Steinby III, 349.

Pani Ermini, L. (1999). Roma da Alarico a Teoderico. In W.V. Harris, ed., *The Transformations of Urbs Roma in Late Antiquity*, Portsmouth, RI, 35–52.

Parchami, A. (2009). *Hegemonic Peace and Empire: the Pax Romana, Britannica and Americana*, London.

Paschoud, F. (2012). On a Recent Book by Alan Cameron: *The Last Pagans of Rome*. *Antiquité Tardive* 20, 359–92.

Paterson, J. (2007). Friends in High Places: the Creation of the Court of the Roman Emperor. In Spawforth, 121–56.

Patterson, J.R. (2006). Colonization and Historiography: the Roman Republic. In Bradley and Wilson, 189–218.

(2012). Contact, Co-operation, and Conflict in Pre-Social War Italy. In Roselaar, 215–26.

Pekáry, T. (1987). *Seditio.* Unruhen und Revolten im römischen Reich von Augustus bis Commodus. *Ancient Society* 18, 133–50.

Perdue, P.C. (2005). *China Marches West: the Qing Conquest of Central Eurasia*, Cambridge, MA.

Pernot, L. (2009). Aelius Aristides and Rome. In W.V. Harris and B. Holmes, eds., *Aelius Aristides between Greece, Rome and the Gods*, Leiden, 175–201.

Pfeilschifter, R. (2007). The Allies in the Republican Army and the Romanisation of Italy. In R. Roth and J. Keller, eds., *Roman by Integration: Dimensions of Group Identity in Material Culture and Text*, Portsmouth, RI, 27–42.

Phang, S.E. (2008). *Roman Military Service: Ideologies of Discipline in the Late Republic and Early Empire*, Cambridge.

Pina Polo, F. (2006). The Tyrant Must Die: Preventive Tyrannicide in Roman Political Thought. In F. Marco Simón, F. Pina Polo, and J. Remesal Rodríguez, eds., *Repúblicas y ciudadanos: modelos de participación cívica en el mundo antiguo*, Barcelona, 71–101.

Pölönen. J. (2004). Plebeians and Repression of Crime in the Roman Empire: From Torture of Convicts to Torture of Suspects. *Revue Internationale des Droits de l'Antiquité* 51, 217–57.

Pomeroy, S.B. (2007). *The Murder of Regilla: a Case of Domestic Violence in Antiquity*, Cambridge, MA.

Pontrandolfo, A., A. Rouveret, and M. Cipriani (1998). *Le tombe dipinte di Paestum*, Paestum.

Potter, D.S. (1994). *Prophets & Emperors: Human and Divine Authority from Augustus to Theodosius*, Cambridge, MA.

(2004). *The Roman Empire at Bay, AD 180–395*, London.

(2009). *Ancient Rome: a New History*, New York.

(2011). Cities in the Eastern Roman Empire from Constantine to Heraclius. In O. Dally and C. Ratté, eds., *Archaeology and the Cities of Asia Minor in Late Antiquity*, Ann Arbor, 247–60.

Price, S.R.F. (1984). *Rituals and Power: the Roman Imperial Cult in Asia Minor*, Cambridge.

Purcell, N. (2001). The *ordo scribarum*: a Study in the Loss of Memory. *Mélanges de l'École Française de Rome: Antiquité* 113, 633–74.

Raaflaub, K.A. (1986a). From Protection and Defense to Offense and Participation. Stages in the Conflict of the Orders. In Raaflaub (1986b), 198–243.

ed. (1986b). *Social Struggles in Archaic Rome. New Perspectives on the Conflict of the Orders*, Berkeley.

(1996). Born to be Wolves? Origins of Roman Imperialism. In *Transitions to Empire: Essays in Greco-Roman History, 360–146 BC in Honor of E. Badian*, Norman, OK, 273–314.

Ramsey, J.T. (1999). Mithridates, the Banner of Ch'ih-yu, and the Comet Coin. *Harvard Studies in Classical Philology* 99, 197–253.

Rance, P. (2007). Battle [in the Later Roman Empire]. In Sabin, Van Wees, and Whitby, II, 342–78.

Rathbone, D. (1993). The Census Qualifications of the *assidui* and the *prima classis*. In *De agricultura. In memoriam Pieter Willem De Neeve (1945–1990)*, Amsterdam, 121–52.

(1996). The Imperial Finances. In *CAH* X, 2nd edn, 309–23.

(2007). Military Finance and Supply [in the Late Republic and the Principate]. In Sabin, Van Wees, and Whitby, II, 158–76.

Rawlings, L. (2007). Army and Battle during the Conquest of Italy (350–264 BC). In Erdkamp, 45–62.

Rawson, E. (1989). Roman Rulers and the Philosophic Advisor. In M. Griffin and J. Barnes, eds., *Philosophia togata: Essays on Philosophy and Roman Society*, Oxford, 233–57.

Rei, A. (1998). Villains, Wives, and Slaves in the Comedies of Plautus. In S.R. Joshel and S. Murnaghan, eds., *Women and Slaves in Greco-Roman Culture: Differential Equations*, London, 92–108.

Reinink, G.J. and B.H. Stolte, eds. (2002). *The Reign of Heraclius (610–641): Crisis and Confrontation*, Leuven.

Reynolds, J.M., ed. (1982). *Aphrodisias and Rome. Documents from the Excavation of the Theatre at Aphrodisias*, London.

Reynolds, S. (2006). Empires: a Problem of Comparative History. *Historical Research* 79, 151–65.

Rich, J.W. (1976). *Declaring War in the Roman Republic in the Period of Transmarine Expansion*, Brussels.

(1989). Patronage and International Relations in the Roman Republic. In Wallace-Hadrill, 117–35.

(2003). Augustus, War and Peace. In De Blois, 329–57.

Rich, J.W. and G. Shipley, eds. (1993). *War and Society in the Roman World*, London.

Richardson, J.S. (1983). The *Tabula Contrebiensis*: Roman Law in Spain in the Early First Century BC. *JRS* 73, 33–41.

(1987). The Purpose of the *lex Calpurnia de repetundis*. *JRS* 77, 1–12.

(1991). *Imperium Romanum*: Empire and the Language of Power. *JRS* 81, 1–9.

(2003). Imperium Romanum between Republic and Empire. In De Blois, 137–47.

(2008). *The Language of Empire: Rome and the Idea of Empire from the Third Century BC to the Second Century AD*, Cambridge.

Rives, J.B. (1999). The Decree of Decius and the Religion of Empire. *JRS* 89, 135–54.

Robert, L. (1940). *Les Gladiateurs dans l'Orient grec*, Limoges.

Robinson, O.F. (2007). *Penal Practice and Penal Policy in Ancient Rome*, London.

Robinson, R. and J. Gallagher (1961). *Africa and the Victorians: the Climax of Imperialism in the Dark Continent*, London.

Rosafio, P. (2002). *Studi sul colonato*, Bari.

Rose, C.B. (2005). The Parthians in Augustan Rome. *American Journal of Archaeology* 109, 21–75.

Roselaar, S.T. (2010). *Public Land in the Roman Republic: a Social and Economic History of ager publicus in Italy, 396–89 BC*, Oxford.

ed. (2012). *Processes of Integration and Identity Formation in the Roman Republic*, Leiden.

Rosenstein, N. (1990). *Imperatores Victi: Military Defeat and Aristocratic Competition in the Middle and Late Republic*, Berkeley.

(2012). Integration and Armies in the Middle Republic. In Roselaar, 85–103.

Rossignol, B. (2012). Le climat, les famines et la guerre: éléments du contexte de la peste antonine. In Lo Cascio, 87–122.

Rothe, U. (2009). *Dress and Cultural Identity in the Rhine-Moselle Region of the Roman Empire*, Oxford.

Roueché, C. (1993). *Performers and Partisans at Aphrodisias, in the Roman and Late Roman Periods*, London.

Rousseau, P. (2000). Monasticism. In *CAH* XIV, 745–80.

Rowan, C. (2012). *Under Divine Auspices. Divine Ideology and the Visualisation of Imperial Power in the Severan Period*, Cambridge.

Rowe, G. (2013). Reconsidering the 'auctoritas' of Augustus. *JRS* 103, 1–15.

Rowlandson, J. (1998). *Women and Society in Greek and Roman Egypt: a Sourcebook*, Cambridge.

Rubin, Z. (1995). Mass Movements in Late Antiquity – Appearances and Realities. In *Leaders and Masses in the Roman World. Studies in Honor of Zvi Yavetz*, Leiden, 129–87.

(2000). The Sasanid Monarchy. In *CAH* XIV, 638–61.

Russo, F. (2012). The Beginning of the First Punic War and the Concept of Italia. In Roselaar, 35–50.

Sabin, P., H. Van Wees, and M. Whitby, eds. (2007). *The Cambridge History of Greek and Roman Warfare*, 2 vols., Cambridge.

Saller, R.P. (1982). *Personal Patronage under the Early Empire*, Cambridge.

(2000). Status and Patronage, in *CAH* XI, 2nd edn, 817–54.

Salmon, E.T. (1982). *The Making of Roman Italy*, London.

Salzman, M.R. (2002). *The Making of a Christian Aristocracy: Social and Religious Change in the Western Roman Empire*, Cambridge, MA.

Santangelo, P. (2014). *L'impero del Mandato Celeste. La Cina nei secoli XIV–XIX*, Rome and Bari.

Sarantis, A. and N. Christie, eds. (2013). *War and Warfare in Late Antiquity: Current Perspectives*, 2 vols., Leiden.

Sarris, P. (2006). *Economy and Society in the Age of Justinian*, Cambridge.

Scheid, J. (2007a). Le sens des rites: l'exemple romain. *EFH* 53, 39–63.

ed. (2007b). *Res gestae diui Augusti*, Paris.

Scheidel, W. (2007). Roman Funerary Commemoration and the Age at First Marriage. *Classical Philology* 102, 389–402.

(2008). Roman Population Size: the Logic of the Debate. In L. de Ligt and S. J. Northwood, eds., *People, Land, and Politics: Demographic Developments and the Transformation of Roman Italy, 300 BC-AD 14*, Leiden, 17–70.

ed. (2009a). *Rome and China: Comparative Perspectives on Ancient World Empires*, Oxford.

(2009b). Sex and Empire: a Darwinian Perspective. In Morris and Scheidel, 255–324.

(forthcoming). The Roman Emperor in the Wider World (available as an audio recording at http://sms.cam.ac.uk/collection/1173950)

Schmitt, O. (2007). From the Late Roman to the Early Byzantine Army: Two Aspects of Change. In Lewin and Pellegrini, 411–19.

Schuller, W. (1975). Grenzen des spätrömischen Staates. Staatspolizei und Korruption. *Zeitschrift für Papyrologie und Epigraphik* 16, 1–21.

Schulz, R. (1997). *Herrschaft und Regierung. Roms Regiment in den Provinzen in der Zeit der Republik*, Paderborn.

Schwartz, S. (2001). *Imperialism and Jewish Society, 200 BCE to 640 CE*, Princeton.

Sedley, D. (2009). Epicureanism in the Roman Republic. In J. Warren, ed., *The Cambridge Companion to Epicureanism*, Cambridge, 29–45.

Shapiro, I. (2003). *The State of Democratic Theory*, Princeton.

Shaw, B.D. (1985). The Divine Economy: Stoicism as Ideology. *Latomus* 44, 14–54.

(1986). Autonomy and Tribute: Mountain and Plain in Mauretania Tingitana. In P. Baduel, ed., *Desert et montagne: Hommage à Jean Dresch*, Aix-en-Provence, 66–89, repr. in Shaw, *Rulers, Nomads, and Christians in Roman North Africa* (Aldershot, 1995).

(1999). War and Violence. In G.W. Bowersock, P. Brown, and O. Grabar (eds.), *Late Antiquity: a Guide to the Postclassical World*. Cambridge, MA, 130–169.

(2000). Rebels and Outsiders. In *CAH* XI, 2nd edn, 361–403.

(2011). *Sacred Violence: African Christians and Sectarian Hatred in the Age of Augustine*, Cambridge.
Sherk, R.K., ed., (1969). *Roman Documents from the Greek East. Senatus consulta and epistulae, to the Age of Augustus*, Baltimore.
(1984). *Translated Documents of Greece and Rome, IV: Rome and the Greek East to the Death of Augustus*, Cambridge.
Sherwin-White, A.N., ed. (1966). *The Letters of Pliny. A Historical and Social Commentary*, Oxford.
(1973). *The Roman Citizenship*, 2nd edn, Oxford.
Sidebottom, H. (2007). International Relations [in the Late Republic and the Principate]. In Sabin, Van Wees, and Whitby, II, 1–29.
Smith, R. (2007). The Imperial Court of the Late Roman Empire, c. AD 300–c. AD 450. In Spawforth, 157–232.
Smith, R.R.R. (1988). *Simulacra Gentium*: the *Ethne* from the Sebasteion at Aphrodisias. *JRS* 78, 50–77.
(1997). The Public Image of Licinius I: Portrait Sculpture and Imperial Ideology in the Early Fourth Century. *JRS* 87, 170–202.
(2012). Monuments for New Citizens in Rome and Aphrodisias. In F. de Angelis, J.-A. Dickmann, F. Pirson, and R. von den Hoff, eds., *Kunst von Unten? Stil und Gesellschaft in der antiken Welt von der 'arte plebea' bis heute*, Wiesbaden, 171–84.
(2013). *The Marble Reliefs from the Julio-Claudian Sebasteion*. Aphrodisias, 6. Mainz.
Sommer, M. (2009). Imperiale Macht und lokale Identität: universalhistorische Variationen zu einem regionalhistorischen Thema. In M. Blömer, M. Facella, and E. Winter, eds., *Lokale Identität im Römischen Nahen Osten*, Stuttgart, 235–48.
(2010). Le ragioni della guerra: Roma, i parti e l'ultimo imperativo di Cesare. In G. Urso, ed., *Cesare: precursore o visionario?* Pisa, 123–40.
(2013). In the Twilight: Hatra between Rome and Iran. In L. Dirven, ed., *Hatra: Politics, Culture and Religion between Parthia and Rome.*, Stuttgart, 33–44.
Spawforth. A.J.S., ed. (2007). *The Court and Court Society in Ancient Monarchies*, Cambridge.
Speidel, M.A. (1992). Roman Army Pay Scales. *JRS* 82, 87–106.
(2007). Einheit und Vielfalt in der römischen Heeresverwaltung. In Haensch and Heinrichs, 173–94.
Stahl, M. (1989). Zwischen Abgrenzung und Integration. Die Verträge der Kaiser Mark Aurel und Commodus mit den Völkern jenseits der Donau. *Chiron* 19, 289–317.
Stathakopoulos, D. (2004). *Famine and Pestilence in the Late Roman and Early Byzantine Empire: a Systematic Survey of Subsistence Crises and Epidemics*, Aldershot.
Stein, E. (1949). *Histoire du Bas-Empire, II: De la disparition de l'Empire d'Occident à la mort de Justinien (476–565 n.Chr.)*, Bruges.

Steinby, M., ed. (1993 and 1996). *Lexicon Topographicum Urbis Romae I* and III, Rome.
Stewart, P. (2008). *The Social History of Roman Art*, Cambridge.
Stickler, T. (2007). The Foederati. In Erdkamp, 494–514.
Stoll, O. (2007). The Religions of the Armies. In Erdkamp, 451–76.
Stolte, B.H. (2003). Jurisdiction and Representation of Power, or The emperor on Circuit. In De Blois *et al.*, 261–8.
Straw, C. and R. Lim, eds., (2004). *The Past before Us: the Challenge of Historiographies of Late Antiquity*, Turnhout.
Strobel, K. (2007). Strategy and Army Structure between Septimius Severus and Constantine the Great [sic]. In Erdkamp, 267–85.
Syme, R. (1939). *The Roman Revolution*, Oxford.
(1958a). *Tacitus*, 2 vols., Oxford.
(1958b). *Colonial Elites. Rome, Spain and the Americas*, Oxford.
(1971). *Emperors and Biography. Studies in the Historia Augusta*, Oxford.
(1988). Military Geography at Rome. *Classical Antiquity* 7, 227–51, repr. in *Roman Papers* VI (Oxford, 1991), 372–97.
Talbert, R.J.A. (1984). *The Senate of Imperial Rome*, Princeton.
Tan, J. (2008). 'Contiones' in the Age of Cicero. *Classical Antiquity* 27, 163–201.
(2011). *Competition between Public and Private Revenues in Roman Social and Political History (200–49 BC)*. Unpublished Ph.D. dissertation, Columbia University.
(2015). The Roman Republic. In Monson and Scheidel, 208–28.
Tanner, J. (2000). Portraits, Power, and Patronage in the Late Roman Republic. *JRS* 90, 18–50.
Thonemann, P. (2007). Estates and the Land in Late Roman Asia Minor. *Chiron* 37, 435–78.
Thorne, J. (2007). Battle, Tactics, and the Emergence of the Limites in the West. In Erdkamp, 218–34.
Thurman, W.S. (1970). The Application of *subiecti* to Roman Citizens in the Imperial Laws of the Later Roman Empire. *Klio* 52, 453–63.
Todd, M. (2005). The Germanic Peoples and Germanic Society. In *CAH* XII, 2nd edn, 440–60.
Traina, G. (2007). Introduzione. Imperi, città e spazio mediterraneo dal 343 al 27 a.C. In A. Barbero, ed., *Storia d'Europa e del Mediterraneo,* V, Rome, 17–48.
(2010). *La resa di Roma: 9 giugno 53 a.C., battaglia a Carre*, Rome and Bari.
Tröster, M. (2009). Review of A.M. Eckstein, *Mediterranean Anarchy, Interstate War, and the Rise of Rome*. *Gnomon* 81, 42–5.
Trombley, F.R. (2002). Military Cadres and Battle during the Reign of Heraclius. In Reinink and Stolte, 241–59.
(2007). The Operational Methods of the Late Roman Army. In Lewin and Pellegrini, 321–56.
(2011). The Imperial Cult in Late Roman Religion (ca. AD 244–395): Observations on the Epigraphy. In Hahn, 19–54.
Trout, D.E. (1999). *Paulinus of Nola: Life, Letters, and Poems*, Berkeley.

Turchin, P. (2005). *War and Peace and War: the Life Cycles of Imperial Nations*, New York.
(2009). A Theory for the Formation of Large Empires. *Journal of Global History* 4, 191–207.
Turchin, P., T.E. Currie, E.A.L Turner, and S. Gavrilets (2013). War, Space, and the Evolution of Old World Complex Societies. *Proceedings of the National Academy of Sciences* 110, 16,384–9.
Ungern-Sternberg, J. von (1982). Weltreich und Krise: äussere Bedingungen für den Niedergang der römischen Republik. *Museum Helveticum* 39, 254–71 (repr. in Ungern-Sternberg 2006, 372–89).
(1986). The End of the Conflict of the Orders. In Raaflaub (1986b), 353–77.
(2001). M. Furius Camillus – ein zweiter Romulus?. In M. Coudry and T. Späth, eds., *L'invention des grands hommes de la Rome antique*, Paris, 289–97 (repr. in Ungern-Sternberg 2006, 51–9).
(2006). *Römische Studien: Geschichtsbewusstsein – Zeitalter der Gracchen – Krise der Republik*, Munich.
Vanacker, W. (2014). Differentiated Integration Trajectories of the Nomadic Population in Roman North Africa (1st–3rd Cent. AD). In de Kleijn and Benoist, 197–216.
Vasunia, P. (2011). The Comparative Study of Empires [review article]. *JRS* 101, 222–37.
Veyne, P. (2002). L'empereur, ses concitoyens et ses sujets. In H. Inglebert, ed., *Idéologies et valeurs civiques dans le monde romain: hommage à Claude Lepelley*, Paris, 49–74.
Vujcic, N. (2009). Greek Popular Assemblies in the Imperial Period and the Discourses of Dio of Prusa. *Epigraphica Anatolica* 42, 157–69.
Walbank, F.W. (1957). *A Historical Commentary on Polybius*, 1, Oxford.
Wallace, C. (2014). *Ager publicus* in the Greek East. *Historia* 63, 38–73.
Wallace-Hadrill, A. (1981). The Emperor and His Virtues. *Historia* 30, 298–323.
ed. (1989). *Patronage in Roman Society*, London.
(1996). The Imperial Court. In *CAH* x, 2nd edn, 283–308.
(2008). *Rome's Cultural Revolution*, Cambridge.
Walsh, J.J. (1996). Flamininus and the Propaganda of Liberation. *Historia* 45, 344–63.
Ward-Perkins, B. (1984). *From Classical Antiquity to the Middle Ages: Urban Public Building in Northern and Central Italy, AD 300–850*, Oxford.
(1998). The Cities. In *CAH* XIII, 371–410.
(2005). *The Fall of Rome, and the End of Civilization*, Oxford.
(2007). The Making of Late Antiquity. In *Wolf Liebeschuetz Reflected: Essays Presented by Colleagues, Friends, & Pupils*, London, 9–16.
Warmington, E.H. (1935–1940). *Remains of Old Latin*, 4 vols., London.
Watson, A. (1987). *Roman Slave Law*, Baltimore.
Weaver, P.R.C. (1972). *Familia Caesaris: a Social Study of the Emperor's Freedmen and Slave*, Cambridge.

Weber, M. (1968). *Economy and Society: an Outline of Interpretative Sociology* (trans. E. Fischoff *et al.*), Berkeley (original [4th] edn: *Wirtschaft und Gesellschaft*, 1921–1922), 2 vols.

Webster, J. (2010). Routes to Slavery in the Roman World: a Comparative Perspective on the Archaeology of Forced Migration. In H. Eckardt, ed., *Roman Diasporas: Archaeological Approaches to Mobility and Diversity in the Roman Empire*, Portsmouth, RI, 45–65.

Weisweiler, J. (2009). Christianity in War: Ammianus on Power and Religion in Constantius' Persian War. In A.J. Cain and N.E. Lenski, eds., *The Power of Religion in Late Antiquity*, Aldershot, 383–96.

Welch, K. (2012). *Magnus Pius: Sextus Pompeius and the Transformation of the Roman Republic*, Cardiff.

Wheeler, E.L. (2007). The Army and the Limes in the East. In Erdkamp, 235–66.

Whitby, M. (1988). *The Emperor Maurice and his Historian. Theophylact Simocatta on Persian and Balkan Warfare*, Oxford.

(1995). Recruitment in Roman Armies from Justinian to Heraclius (ca. 565–615). In Averil Cameron, 61–124.

(1998). 'Deus nobiscum': Christianity, Warfare, and Morale in Late Antiquity. In *Modus operandi: Essays in Honour of Geoffrey Rickman*, London, 191–208.

(2007). Army and Society in the Late Roman World: a Context for Decline? In Erdkamp, 515–31.

Whitehorne, J. (2004). Petitions to the Centurion: a Question of Locality? *Bulletin of the American Society of Papyrologists* 41, 155–69.

Whittaker, C.R. (2004). *Rome and its Frontiers: the Dynamics of Empire*, London.

Wiersma, S. (1990). The Ancient Greek Novel and its Heroines: A Female Paradox. *Mnemosyne* 43, 109–23.

Wilbur, C.M. (1943). *Slavery in China during the Former Han Dynasty, 206 BC–AD 25*, Chicago.

Wilkes, J.J. (1996). The Danubian and Balkan Provinces. In *CAH* x, 2nd edn, 545–85.

(2005). Provinces and Frontiers. In *CAH* xii, 2nd edn, 212–68.

Will, E. (1966–1967). *Histoire politique du monde hellénistique (323–30 av. J. C.)*, 2 vols., Nancy.

Williamson, C. (2005). *The Laws of the Roman People: Public Law in the Expansion and Decline of the Roman Republic*, Ann Arbor.

Winter, E. (2000). Mithraism and Christianity in Late Antiquity. In Mitchell and Greatrex, 172–82.

Winterling, A. (1999). *Aula Caesaris: Studien zur Institutionalisierung des römischen Kaiserhofes in der Zeit von Augustus bis Commodus (31 v. Chr.-192 n. Chr.)*, Munich.

Wirszubski, C. (1950). *Libertas as a Political Idea at Rome during the Late Republic and Early Principate*, Cambridge.

Wiseman, T.P. (1971). *New Men in the Roman Senate, 139 BC–AD 14*, Oxford.

(2002). Roman History and the Ideological Vacuum. In Wiseman, ed., *Classics in Progress: Essays on Ancient Greece and Rome*, Oxford, 287–310, repr. in *Remembering the Roman People: Essays on Late-Republican Politics and Literature* (Oxford, 2009), 5–32.
Wittke, A.-M., E. Olshausen, and R. Szydlak, eds. (2007). *Historical Atlas of the Ancient World*, Leiden.
Woolf, G. (1998). *Becoming Roman: the Origins of Provincial Civilization in Gaul*, Cambridge.
(2000). Literacy. In *CAH* XI, 2nd edn, 875–97.
Yates, R.D.S. (2001). Slavery in Early China: a Socio-cultural Approach. *Journal of East Asian Archaeology* 3, 283–331.
Yavetz, Z. (1996). Caligula, Imperial Madness and Modern Historiography. *Klio* 78, 105–29.
Zanker, P. (1988). *The Power of Images in the Age of Augustus*. Trans. A. Shapiro, Ann Arbor.
Ziółkowski, A. (1992). *The Temples of Mid-Republican Rome and their Historical and Topographical Context*, Rome.
(2011). The Background to the Third-century Crisis of the Roman Empire. In Arnason and Raaflaub, 113–33.
Zuiderhoek, A. (2009). *The Politics of Munificence in the Roman Empire: Citizens, Elites and Benefactors in Asia Minor*, Cambridge.

Index

Dates are BC except as specified.